RELIVING THE PAST

RELIVING THE PAST

THE WORLDS OF SOCIAL HISTORY

EDITED BY OLIVIER ZUNZ

CONTRIBUTORS

DAVID WILLIAM COHEN CHARLES TILLY

WILLIAM T. ROWE OLIVIER ZUNZ

WILLIAM B. TAYLOR

The University of North Carolina Press

Chapel Hill and London

© 1985 The University of North Carolina Press

Manufactured in the United States of America

Library of Congress Cataloging in Publication Data
Main entry under title:

Reliving the past.

  Bibliography: p.
  Includes index.
    1. Social history—Addresses, essays, lectures.
  2. Social history—Historiography—Case studies.
  3. Social history—Cross-cultural studies.   I. Zunz,
  Olivier.   II. Cohen, David William.
  HN8.R45 1985   907'.2   85-1065
  ISBN 0-8078-1658-2
  ISBN 0-8078-4137-4 (pbk.)

For François Furet and

Emmanuel Le Roy Ladurie,

who paved the way

CONTENTS

ACKNOWLEDGMENTS

It is a pleasure to thank Lewis Bateman of the University of North Carolina Press for first suggesting and then encouraging the writing of this volume. I would also like to thank Richard L. Kagan, Stephen Innes, and Lucette Valensi, who helped define its direction. Charles Feigenoff contributed his outstanding editorial skills, and Lottie McCauley saw the manuscript through several stages of production.

The Corcoran Department of History of the University of Virginia and the Department of History of the Johns Hopkins University provided the support for us to exchange ideas during the preparation of these chapters. Charles Tilly, David William Cohen, and William T. Rowe visited Charlottesville and presented drafts of their essays to a graduate seminar in social history that William B. Taylor and I conducted at the University of Virginia in the Fall of 1983. Many ideas formulated in our weekly meetings with the students found their way into this book, and I thank all who participated in the seminar. A few months later, the contributors met as a group in Baltimore to review their drafts again and to continue the collective reexamination of the questions and methods of social history that stimulated the writing of this volume.

Olivier Zunz
Charlottesville, Virginia
Spring 1985

RELIVING THE PAST

INTRODUCTION

BY OLIVIER ZUNZ

The emergence of social history in the 1960s and 1970s as an innovative intellectual movement profoundly affected historical consciousness by broadening both the subject matter and methods of history. The new praxis had a liberating quality. Pointing to the records of ordinary lives as a source of evidence, social historians called into question the merit of using the acts of elites as a measure of the past and challenged historians in general to reexamine their assumptions, regardless of their ideological commitments. This infusion of new evidence and technique inspired reappraisal of theory as well as detailed evocation of a new past. But social historians have embraced so many problems and have engaged in so many inquiries that the field now needs reordering. The reflections by five historians offered in the following chapters are meant as part of this reassessment. Our interest is in the future of social history and in the integration of varied studies in large syntheses. We are not concerned specifically with the history of ordinary people—inasmuch as significant proportions of this history have now been written—but with the ways specialists of different regions of the world choose to see the connections between major transformations—ideological, political, economic, and social—and the form and character of lives shaped in different environments.

The factors that contributed to the pivotal role of social history during the last thirty years are well known. First, its growth paralleled the demographic surge of historians. The new field benefited from an unprecedented number of able young intellectuals who shared in the excitement of enlarging the vision of history. Second, the methods of social history were enriched by the post–World War II discourse between scientists and humanists at universities and research institutes. In particular, social historians drew methods from all of the expanding social sciences, principally from anthropology and sociology but also from such fields as linguistics and psychoanalysis, and added significantly to the list of accepted auxiliary sciences. This methodological exploration was also advanced by the timely appearance of computers, which allowed social historians to redefine the concept of an archive and to make sophisticated connections between sources not achievable by traditional methods. Third, and in retrospect most important, social historians actively participated in the new pluralist vision of the 1960s. At stake was more than a simple enlargement of history's vision. By devising methods which allowed them to build judgments from thousands of observations of ordinary people, they could investigate groups heretofore ignored or at best misunderstood. For the first time, historians could divide the social structure into an infinite number of segments and explain the positive role of diverse communities within the society at large. They could, for example, envision the "proletariat" as a group of heterogeneous and often conflicting human beings, not simply as the idealization projected by the international labor movement. Historical discourse gained strength and credibility from concrete and manifold details of people's existence. No longer an abstraction, "the people" began to reassume the garb of life.

But in the excitement of innovation, social historians neglected some essential concerns. For one, social history was never fully explicated. Admittedly a multifaceted venture, it soon became whatever social historians chose to write. While it is true that strict definitions tend to reduce the scope of investigation or prevent the uncovering of important evidence, in this case the absence of a clear program, except that of enlarging the scope of history, led to fragmentation and a diminished focus. Furthermore, the search for ad hoc methodologies has often superseded the search for answers to large historical questions. In the process, social historians' use of theories from the social sciences became increasingly uncritical. In 1974, when Jacques Le Goff and Pierre Nora edited Faire de l'histoire, a collection on the newest of the "new" history written in France up to that time, they realized that they could not impose a framework on the varied research then underway and grouped the contributions under the rubric of "new problems," "new approaches," and "new objects." They particularly warned, however, against the submission of history to the social sciences. As they put it, "the new history, besides its important critique of historical events and facts, has developed a tendency to conceptualize which risks it becoming something else, be it Marxist determinism, Weberian abstraction, or structural atemporality."[1] A decade later, the same criticism was even heard from anthropologist Claude Lévi-Strauss, whose seminal work on structuralism pulled some historians of society toward the atemporal. Pointing to similarities between the genealogy of the few and the collective biography of the many, Lévi-Strauss concluded that "between narrative history and the new history—one recording the daily activities of dignitaries, the other attentive to the slow demographic, economic and ideological changes that have their origins in the very foundation of society—the distance does not appear to be so great any longer."[2]

Mapping a new course for social history, however, is no obvious or simple task. Indeed, a vocal minority in the history profession has recently advocated a disengagement from the distracting apparatus and theory of the social sciences and a return to rejuvenated forms of traditional narrative. Critics point out that social history, instead of enlarging history, has instead fragmented it. As a consequence of opening fresh areas of knowledge and adopting new methods, historians have lost their ability to recapture the totality of the past through evocative and richly textured narrative. If the trend is not reversed, these critics fear, history—traditionally the broad domain of the generalist—will remain divided into separate specialized fiefdoms. Lawrence Stone believes the new integrative narrative should concentrate on the unified theme of mentalité, the complex reconstruction of vanished mind sets.[3] Others propose a less psychological but more intellectualized history. Thus François Furet advocates "a problem-oriented history that assembles its elements on the basis of questions that arise from an explicit conceptual framework."[4] This variant distances itself from both narrative history and empirical ventures and especially from the massing of large numbers of individual observations which enable the social historian to discriminate between the particular and the common. To the five historians who wrote this book, these prescriptions for historical study do not concern themselves enough with issues of fundamental causation and change. We think that a rejuvenated social history has a major role to play in resolving these issues, and we are concerned that the gains made in the last thirty years not be lost.

How, then, do we conceive of social history? Our collective definition, which we owe to Charles Tilly, could be more properly called a "theory" of social history. The role of social history is to connect everyday experience to the large structures of historical analyses and major changes of the past. We believe that history should illuminate the complex interplay between large structural changes and alterations in the character of the dynamics of populations, social hierarchies, and routine social life. Such a simple formulation provides the elusive link between individuals' experience and the large changes of the past. Asking how "people lived the big changes," we stress the need to uncover the processes of social change over long periods of time and seek to discover patterns of social relations that are truly contextual, not simply deduced from social theory and "verified" in the records. In doing so, we go beyond conflicting perspectives on major developments, not to mediate between them but instead to locate the simultaneity of significant meanings which interpretative oppositions too often mask.

If we conceived of this book as embracing nonwestern as well as western societies, it is in part because discussions of the historical methods have been so far too narrowly focused on western history, as if historians of nonwestern societies were bound to apply the concepts and techniques developed in a western context despite an insufficient documentary base (as in Africa) or insurmountable problems of access (as in China). It is also because heretofore unheard voices of the past, in regions of the world traditionally dominated by western powers, are now being recorded by social historians. Widespread knowledge of these freshly unearthed human experiences might well reinvigorate the whole field of social history by unveiling processes of social construction which have been ignored.

Although we are indebted to world historians such as William H. McNeill, Immanuel Wallerstein, Fernand Braudel, and Eric R. Wolf who remind us of the vital connections between parts of the world, our purpose is not to define a new theory of macro-history. For that matter, those chapters devoted to regions at the "periphery" of the world system are explicitly critical of the study of large world processes which, by their scale and emphasis on domination and coercion, risk masking the richness of the history of the "people without history"[5] and misconstruing historical processes in local settings. Despite our canvass of regional analyses and interest in large population movements (like those provoked by the slave trade), this book is neither comparative history nor world history. We do not propose to be exhaustive or encyclopedic. Our intent is not to compare population, structures, and processes in different parts of the world but rather to give place its due in the development of a more integrated historical discourse and to counterpoise place and our respective units of analyses in these discussions of social history. Thus, William B. Taylor and David William Cohen remind us that the ideas embodied in the concept of "society," ideas which European and American historians take for granted, are not self-evident to the student of Latin America or Africa. In the last analysis, it is historical realities that shape questions and methods. In China, as William T. Rowe points out, social history can illuminate diversity and spatial variation within a history that has traditionally lent itself to depiction as a single homogeneous process.

Each of us speaks with his own voice and from his separate experience in different parts of the world and in periods which have produced their own distinctive historiographies. Tilly demonstrates the incremental growth of European social history by contrasting our current state of knowledge to that in 1950, while I see the development of American social history affected by a series of turning points. In turn, Rowe, Taylor, and Cohen observe the tensions between topics highlighted by western historiography and issues prompted by the political and ideological debates on and within their regions of study.

Some fruitful tension within the book helps broaden the debate in which we have engaged. For Cohen, the program proposed by Tilly to connect "large processes, big social structures, and whole populations," while basically sound, can be applied only with caution to Africa; it could lead the historian to miss the very particulars of African society that were heretofore left aside precisely because the big changes in Africa seemed for so long to be only the result of outside intervention. Cohen, therefore, advocates the need to move away from "notional boundaries" and "era-bound" processes as bases for research in African history and advises African historians to concentrate on "the intimate areas of social life where real contradictions are managed and actual structures are enraveled," to look there for the locations of large structural changes. Only such a contextual approach, Cohen argues, will free African history from treating "external causes" as prime explanation or falling back on "custom" as a last resort. Taylor places more weight on the impact of world processes of domination, but the same caution about the importance attributed to outside intervention leads him to develop a forceful critique of "dependency" theory, which has shaped much of the recent discourse on Latin America, and to search for a more realistic link between social structure, *mentalité*, and social theory.

These suggestive differences in perspective do not hide, however, the striking similarity of our preoccupations. All the authors felt the need to move away from the study of individual segments and advance toward a greater fusion between the parts and whole. The five of us emphasize the critical connection between state and society. For Europe, Tilly tells us, state formation—"the exceptional power of the distinctive organizations we call national states"—and the development of capitalism—especially "the prevalence of work for wages under conditions of expropriation"—are the two large-scale phenomena which most affected the lives of ordinary people and are, therefore, the master problems of European social history since the sixteenth century. He argues that practically every other change in modern European history is secondary to these two broad processes, because only they made a difference in the life of every inhabitant in the land. His claim should stir controversy; yet the ties between people's daily routines and the all-encompassing framework of their lives cannot be made more clearly. The other contributors emphasize problems of domination in history as well as the questions of linkages between parts of societies. Taylor suggests that the expansion of the Spanish State affected the core areas of early Latin American society more profoundly than the change in mode of production, which remained "basically tributary both before and after the conquest." Having made this point, Taylor sees social history as moving the history of Latin America beyond the assumption of internal consent and the ideas of coercion and manipulation that have characterized dependency theories. He concentrates instead on linkages among members of society, and he searches for the activities of the many "power brokers" who served simultaneously as embodiments of obedience to domination and of choice. In his Latin America, "most people are in some sense both rulers and ruled," and "power relationships . . . involve many conflicting obligations and loyalties." In his turn, Cohen explains how "the varied and multiple efforts to comprehend the [African] region—using the evaluations of shared or continuous culture, market networks, cult distributions, arenas of social movements, growth processes, migration tracks . . . have taken us far from the view of state and society as congruent." Tilly has criticized the old notion of "societies" as "things apart." This old notion collapses as Cohen reviews Africa's past.

Rowe, too, shows how the social history of China, although still in its infancy, is struggling to free itself from broad systems of explanation borrowed largely from western social thought (such as the old concept of the Asiatic mode of production). In his essay, the views of the relationship between state and society which inform the work of the other contributors take on their full significance. Rowe reviews the gamut of politically and culturally based theories of what Wittfogel called "oriental despotism." He then points both to spatial analyses of marketing areas and to studies of social intermediaries as a means of understanding the reordering of traditional authority structures. In the American case, I do not address the relationship between a bureaucratic state and society as much as I examine the relationship between the perception of national character and the realities of social relations in the United States. I contrast the ideological permanence embedded in the notion of "American exceptionalism" to the visions of change and conflicts. The social history of America, like that of the other regions in this volume, shows how patterns of conflict and systems of mediation evolve and produce society.

The following chapters seek to reflect the richness of sources, methods, and themes of social history. Perhaps social historians are not fully prepared to dismantle their bulwarks which allow them to operate within the limits of an agreed-upon ideology, a commitment to a technique, or a well-circumscribed period and specialty. But the need to move out of intellectually confining camps and to establish broader connections is felt everywhere, and the growing recognition that traditions stretching across what were once considered impermeable national boundaries make such an expansion imperative. History is changing, and so is the place of social history within it. The essays in this volume focus on ties between ideology and social change, the links between culture and behavior, and the connections between political and social processes. What this book calls for is a creative use of social history to join large structural processes of change to life at the local level. Each author draws from his own work to suggest directions that promise eventually to establish this connection. Although social historians have heretofore produced an impressive vein of new knowledge, they must now integrate it within history, or, as Taylor phrases it, put more history into it. It is our hope that, by strengthening the analytical tools of social history, by continuously enlarging its field of vision, and by pursuing the search for causes and connections, a new creative synthesis will be written.

NOTES

1. Jacques Le Goff and Pierre Nora, eds. *Faire de l'histoire*, 3 vols. (Paris: Gallimard, 1974), 1:xi.

2. Claude Lévi-Strauss, "Histoire et ethnologie," *Annales: Economies, sociétés, civilisations* 38 (Novembre–Décembre 1983): 1231; initially delivered at the fifth Conférence Marc Bloch of the Ecole des Hautes Etudes en Sciences Sociales.

3. Lawrence Stone, "The Revival of Narrative: Reflexions on a New Old History," *Past and Present*, no. 85 (November 1979): 3–24.

4. François Furet, *L'atelier de l'histoire* (Paris: Flammarion, 1982), 29; trans. as *In the Workshop of History* (Chicago: University of Chicago Press, 1984).

5. Eric R. Wolf, *Europe and the People without History* (Berkeley: University of California Press, 1982).

CHAPTER 1

RETRIEVING

EUROPEAN LIVES

BY CHARLES TILLY

Why Go Back?

How did Europeans live the big changes? In different European regions and eras, what were the connections—cause, effect, or correlation—between very large structural changes such as the growth of
national states and the development of capitalism, on the one hand,
and the changing experiences of ordinary people, on the other? The
complex second question merely amplifies the first. In its muted or
its amplified form, this question defines the central mission of European social history.

Many experts think otherwise. Despite appearances, in the first
place, my definition is rather modest. For social historians incline to
imperial definitions of their field. In the preface to his enormously
popular *English Social History*, G. M. Trevelyan offered one of the best-
remembered definitions. "Social history," he declared, "might be defined negatively as the history of a people with the politics left out."
Trevelyan argued for a three-layered analysis: Economic conditions
underlie the social scene, which in turn provides the foundation for
political events. "Without social history," he continued, "economic
history is barren and political history is unintelligible."[1]

Perhaps because Trevelyan defined his social history negatively,
latter-day practitioners of the art have commonly announced more

I am grateful to audiences at Keene State College and at the University of Virginia
for raising questions concerning oral presentations of parts of this text and to the
contributors to this volume for their vigorous criticism.

positive programs. But those programs have been equally massive. Social history "might be defined," comments Peter Burke, "as the history of social relationships; the history of the social structure; the history of everyday life; the history of private life; the history of social solidarities and social conflicts; the history of social classes; the history of social groups 'seen both as separate and as mutually dependent units.' These definitions are very far from being synonymous; each corresponds to a different approach, with its advantages and disadvantages."[2] Some group of scholars has opted for each of these approaches, and others still.

Yet most of these definitions of social history make hopelessly ambitious claims. The "history of social relationships," for example, encompasses almost any subject any ordinary historian might claim to study, plus a great deal more. After all, politics, diplomacy, war, economics, and important parts of cultural production consist of social relationships. What is more, social relationships extend throughout the domains of the social sciences and into the study of other animals than *homo sapiens*.

To the extent that people who define social history as the history of social relationships mean what they say, they are claiming an empire. In the Netherlands today, a number of social historians attach themselves to a discipline called *Maatschappijgeschiedenis*: the history of society. Dutch imperialism is apparently alive after all; the very name declares an exceedingly ambitious program. (Dutch historians have not gone to sea alone, however; some German historians similarly aim to build a *Gesellschaftsgeschichte*, while their French neighbors escalate with a claim to *histoire totale*.) Taken seriously, an effort to construct a full history of "society" will surely destroy itself.

To be sure, two competing meanings of the word "history" confuse the issue. On the one hand, we have history as the connection of experiences in time; on the other, history as the analysis of that connection. In the first sense, social relationships certainly have a history; they have connections over time. In the second sense, however, it is not humanly possible to construct a coherent analysis of the history of all social relationships; the object of study is simply too complex, diverse, and big.

Social history has other less ambitious versions as well. Some social historians try to supply deeper explanations of major political events, institutions, movements, or changes than straightforward political history ordinarily provides. They want to place politics in its social context. Others hope to recapture an ethos, an outlook, a rhythm of everyday life in much the manner that a professional traveler portrays exotic climes and peoples. They give us sketches of an age, of a city, of a social class. Still others rake the coals of the past for evidence bearing on present-oriented theories: theories of fertility decline, of capital accumulation, of authoritarianism. They then produce studies that differ little in texture from contemporary analyses of the same phenomena.

All of these efforts qualify as social history. All of them, at times, produce outstanding work: Richard Trexler's fresh interpretation of public life in Renaissance Florence uses social history deftly to give meaning to well-known political events.[3] Our understanding of European social life would be the poorer without Emmanuel Le Roy Ladurie's *Montaillou*, an essentially ethnographic account of a fourteenth-century Pyrenean village.[4] Ron J. Lesthaeghe's analysis of fertility decline in nineteenth-century Belgium provides a telling empirical critique of standard notions about the transition from high to low fertility.[5] Social historians can claim these accomplishments proudly. Nevertheless, a social history composed entirely of studies like those of Trexler, Le Roy Ladurie, and Lesthaeghe, for all its scintillation, would lack a common core. What makes social history a coherent field of inquiry?

As a distinct enterprise, social history grew up in opposition to political history, defined in terms of statecraft and national politics. In France, for example, the *Annales* of Marc Bloch and Lucien Febvre (inspired to some extent by Emile Durkheim's program for a regal sociology and François Simiand's search for suprahistorical rhythms to account for the ebb and flow of historical experience) called for a global history that would surpass and explain mere events.[6]

In England, likewise, Marxists and other materialists sought to construct histories resting firmly on changing modes of production and corresponding shifts in popular life; well before World War II, the works of Sidney and Beatrice Webb, of J. L. and Barbara Hammond, and of R. H. Tawney exemplified the contributions of English radicals to social history.[7] In Germany, Max Weber and his followers typified the effort to place the history of European states in a broad context of social experience.[8]

Although all these enterprises (not to mention their counterparts elsewhere in Europe) formed in opposition to narrow political history, each of them implies a somewhat different alternative: global history, the history of material life, the comparative study of societies, and so on. What is more, social history branches into a set of specialties, each typically concerned with a particular social structure or process: family history, urban history, agricultural history, demographic history, the history of crime and punishment, the history of social movements, and many more. The field as a whole also overlaps with other long-established specialties, such as labor history and economic history.

Finally, the negation of existing political histories frequently engages social historians of a given country in the acceptance of the prevailing questions concerning that country, and in battling on behalf of a competitor to the prevailing answers. Thus, as Jürgen Kocka points out, German social historians find it difficult to escape a compelling pair of questions: Why did the Social Democrats fail? Why did the Nazis come to power?[9] Similarly, social historians of Russia, both inside and outside the Soviet Union, have invested a large share of their effort in studying the background of 1917's revolution. Ronald Suny reported that at a meeting of American specialists in Russian labor history:

> Some dissatisfaction was expressed by those who remained convinced that "real" social history was not well served by the concern with politics and consciousness. Indeed Russian labor history has not had many practitioners interested exclusively in issues such as family patterns, fertility, and daily life; rather the brevity of the period 1870–1917 in which the Russian working class emerged and the volatility of its engagement in political life have encouraged its historians to deal with the points of contact between workers, intellectuals, managers, capitalists, and state officials.[10]

In Germany, Russia, and other countries the hope of explaining major political events, movements, or transformations animates a significant part of social historians' work. As a result, to some extent each country has its own branch and brand of social history.

A Program for European Social History

As actually practiced, then, European social history includes a wide range of enterprises, not all of them consistent with each other. Its boundaries are unclear. European social history resembles a strong-poled magnetic field: Most of the work that has a clear rationale pivots around a single core. European social history's central activity, as I see it, concerns reconstructing ordinary people's experience of large structural changes.

The statement has a descriptive side and a normative side. As a matter of description, the search for links between small-scale experience and large-scale processes informs a large share of all the work European social historians actually do. As a matter of prescription, that linkage identifies the one enterprise to which all the others connect, the one enterprise to which social historians have the greatest opportunity to enrich our understanding of social life. Neither the effort to construct "social" explanations of major political events, the attempt to portray a full round of life, nor the search for past evidence bearing on present-day social-scientific theories—for all their obvious value—motivate the sustained, cumulative, and partly autonomous inquiry entailed by asking how people lived the big changes. That inquiry, the central quest of European social history, will occupy most of this essay.

Need I say that this program is controversial? Readers of David Cohen's splendid chapter on African social history, elsewhere in this very book, will find him skeptical of proposals to organize studies of that continent's past around large structural changes, for fear of imposing simple, alien categories on a complex experience. Among European historians, a vocal minority reject the entire program as not merely useless, but dangerous. The English historian of France, Tony Judt, for example, has called the sort of social history I am advocating a repellent imposter, a "clown in regal purple."[11] Others tolerate the clown's existence, but prefer more modest attempts to reconstruct one corner or another of social life. The proposal to organize social history around big changes and their correlates in routine social life (even if it does, as I claim, describe what the majority of European social historians are already doing) will certainly stir up dissent among the professionals.

Which big changes deserve attention? Taken back to the ages we can reach only through archeology and extended to the continent's outermost limits, European social history's "big changes" include the rise and fall of the Roman Empire, the creation of a vast Christian church, the growth of Islamic empires around the Mediterranean, the seafaring of the Normans, the repeated armed invasions from Central Asia, the shift of trade and civilization from the Mediterranean toward the Atlantic, and much more. These changes will figure little, or not at all, in my survey, and I will concentrate on Western, Central, and Northern Europe since about 1500.

Two great circumstances distinguish that block of European life from life anywhere at any other time: (1) the exceptional power of the distinctive organizations we call national states and (2) the prevalence of work for wages under conditions of expropriation. Throughout the world, principalities and empires have risen and fallen throughout the world for seven millennia. But national states— large, specialized, centralized organizations exercising monopolistic control over the principal concentrated means of coercion within sharply bounded territories—only became the dominant European structures after 1500. Again, many forms of forced labor on means of production not belonging to workers have arisen through the same seven millennia, but the combination of formally free wage labor and concentrated, expropriated means of production marks off from all others the capitalist era since 1500 or so.

To be sure, a number of other characteristics also distinguish our era from all others: the complexity of technology, the wide use of inanimate sources of energy, the threat of nuclear war, the proliferation and power of huge organizations, the speed of communication, the prevalence of high life expectancy and still other markers of modern times. Statemaking and the development of capitalism count as more profound changes than the emergence of these other conditions on two grounds:

1. To the extent that we can distinguish them, the formation of national states and the development of capitalism touched the lives of ordinary people more directly and deeply than the other changes on the list. In terms of the allocation of activities among hours in the day, for example, the expansion of salaried, scheduled work in factories and offices far from home—a direct consequence of the development of capitalism—made more difference than any other change. Via conscription, taxation, registration, surveillance, the institution of elections, and the organization of social services, similarly, national states reached directly into the daily lives of ordinary people.

2. Broadly speaking, the development of capitalism and the formation of national states underlay all the other changes. The mak-

ers of states, for example, created the largest, most powerful organizations of all, and determinedly pushed toward more and more deadly means of destruction. Although all such influences are mutual, the development of capitalism likewise promoted high-energy production and large organizations rather more strongly and directly than those two phenomena promoted capitalism.

Modern European social history has no reason to neglect complex technologies, the shift to inanimate sources of energy, and other great changes. But capitalism and statemaking provide its largest frame. The unifying, motivating task of European social history since about 1500 is this: connecting the changing experiences of ordinary people to the development of capitalism and the formation of national states.

Bad Ideas

In order to discover the connections between the experiences of ordinary Europeans and the big changes—especially the formation of national states and the development of capitalism—social historians have to fight their way past plausible but bad ideas about social change. The strongest of these bad ideas originated in the very encounters of nineteenth-century European observers with the big changes. As European burghers, aristocrats, and intellectuals faced the facts of a growing proletariat, of vast, unhealthy industrial cities, of concentrating capital, labor, and population, of militant popular movements, they fashioned for themselves a set of mistaken analyses of what they saw.

The central arguments run roughly as follows: Under normal circumstances the world divides up into distinct, coherent societies each having its own unifying beliefs and institutions. Those societies remain coherent through a balance between the extent of their differentiation and the strength of their integrating beliefs and institutions. Social change generally proceeds through increasing differentiation. When differentiation occurs slowly and evenly, it leads to social advancement. But when it becomes rapid and irregular, change exceeds the integrative capacity of existing beliefs and institutions.

That gap, according to the standard argument, causes trouble. As a result of declining integration—detachment of people from unifying beliefs, weakened ability of institutions to control their members, and so on—disorder spreads. Disorder ranges from individual pathology and crime to collective conflict. In the face of rapid differentiation, at the extreme, drastically declining integration produces revolution. But normally a society faced with social change develops new beliefs and reformed integrating institutions; after a period of disorder associated with excessively rapid social change, a new equilibrium between differentiation and integration comes into being.

In commonsense forms, these ideas became the bases of standard nineteenth-century bourgeois discussions of the problems of cities, of crime, of the poor, of popular rebellion. Refined, abstracted, and attached to regularized observations, they formed the backbones of multiple sociologies and programs of social reform. They also provided a major basis for social historians' interpretations of nineteenth- and twentieth-century social change.

These ideas are seductive. They are widely held. Yet they are wrong. They are bad ideas, both because they rest on a series of unfortunate fictions and because they contain empirical propositions that fail to fit reality. The fictions include the notion of distinct, coherent, integrated societies, the supposition of integrating institutions and ideas, the postulation of a general process of change through differentiation. These fictions are unfortunate because they encourage explanations of social phenomena in terms of the functioning—or malfunctioning—of the fictitious systems, which are no explanations at all.

The empirically incorrect propositions include the assertion that a rapid pace of social change promotes more disorder than a slow pace of change, the thought that collective conflict and individual pathology spring from similar causes, the expectation that drastically declining commitment to existing beliefs and institutions causes revolutions. By now, we have strong evidence that these propositions are simply wrong.[12]

Although some social historians still hold bad nineteenth-century ideas, cumulative empirical critique via the actual practice of social history has little by little destroyed their credibility. No single alternative has supplanted them. Yet on the whole today's European social historians lean toward organizational realism: toward the idea that states, corporations, families, associations, parties, plus a great many other groups exist and act, but that "societies" are at best convenient fictions.

Organizational realism sometimes aligns social historians with Karl Marx's historical materialism, sometimes with Max Weber's structural idealism, sometimes with John Stuart Mill's rationalistic individualism, sometimes with other major traditions of social thought, and sometimes with a sort of eclectic pragmatism. In the last case, the social historians involved usually lack a coherent scheme, and content themselves with partial theories about particular kinds of organizations or with agnostic descriptions of social situations. Despite the loss of a certain unity, however, European social historians are better off for having abandoned the basic nineteenth-century scheme.

Social History Forms and Reforms

Although the distinctive enterprise of European social history reaches back into the nineteenth century, it began flourishing as never before following World War II. One sign is the set of historical publications featuring social history. While such journals as *Past and Present*, *Quaderni Storici*, *Annales: Economies, sociétés, civilisations*, and *Comparative Studies in Society and History* frequently printed social history, others made it their main business: *Social History*, the *Journal of Social History*, *History Workshop*, the *Journal of Interdisciplinary History*, *Passato e Presente*, *Società e Storia*, *Geschichte und Gesellschaft* stood beside more specialized journals such as *Annales de Démographie Historique*, the *Journal of Family History*, or the *Journal of Urban History*. Learned societies, conferences, courses, collective volumes, handbooks, and critical essays likewise proliferated. More important, European historians trained their sights on a wide range of social experience, especially concerning the period since 1700.

The flourishing of social history did not merely add another specialty to the European historian's division of labor. It also expanded the range of an attitude that had been rare in previous histories: a belief that within limits ordinary people make their own history. Of course, as a preface to more serious matters the chapter or book concerning popular customs and daily life dates back to the Greeks. To be sure, romantics such as Jules Michelet had long since written history as the work of an abstract People, and Marxist historians such as Jean Jaurès had portrayed the working class as a major historical actor. Nevertheless the effort to retrieve past experience by reconstructing the lives of ordinary people and connecting them to great structures, crises, and changes came into its own with European social history following World War II.

One name for the program was "history from below." As practiced by E. J. Hobsbawm, George Rudé, and many others, history from below took up crucial historical events by building up portraits—individual and collective—of their rank-and-file participants.[13] It argued the meaning of those events, at least in part, as a function of the characteristics of their participants. George Rudé's Crowd in the French Revolution, for example, examined a series of Parisian events before and during the Revolution of 1789–1799: the struggles over food in 1775, the popular opposition to the government in the fall of 1788, the attacks on manufacturers Reveillon and Henriot in April 1789, the search for arms that preceded the invasion of the Bastille in July 1789, and so on.

In each case, Rudé assembled such biographical material as he could from arrest records and similar documents; he then used detailed accounts of the action to establish its sequence, direction, geography, and rationale. Rudé sought to make revolutionary crowds coherent, meaningful historical actors by actual reconstruction of their membership and action rather than by assigning them a priori some grand (or diabolical) historical role.

In one version or another, that sort of populism inspired a whole generation of European social historians. Temma Kaplan, for example, treats the politics of Andalusia's little people seriously. She roots Andalusian anarchism in the nineteenth-century experience of artisans and proletarian winegrowers who faced an alliance of large landowners and merchants with a corrupt state.[14] For Kaplan, the moves of rural people elsewhere in Europe toward collectivist and capitalist solutions serve as implicit markers of alternative roads from the nineteenth century.

Rainer Wirtz's treatment of nineteenth-century German conflicts likewise illustrates the populism of social historians.[15] Attempting to construct a contemporaneous analysis of "violent social protest" in Baden from 1815 to 1848, Wirtz seizes on E. P. Thompson's metaphor of a field of force defining the relations among classes. Describing 101 incidents over those years, Wirtz works out from the events to questions about their social setting. He makes a plausible case that

1848 marked the disintegration of a whole system of rights, under-standings, and class relations, a "moral economy" giving poor people claims on the powerful.

By no means all populist social historians share the broadly Marxist interpretations of Rudé, Kaplan, and Wirtz. John Brewer, for exam-ple, vividly portrays the eighteenth-century mock election at Garrat, a village south of London. "The mock elections," he reports, "were boisterous and exuberant, like a carnival. Drink flowed freely, there was dancing and music in the streets, men and women accompanied the ludicrous candidates dressed as zanies or merry andrews . . . or in their best holiday finery."[16]

During the 1760s, Brewer notes, the long-established mock elec-tion became the object of struggle, in the press and on the stage as well as in Garrat's streets, between radicals and their opponents. A London theatrical presentation of the ceremony attracted national attention, and drew thousands to the village each year. But its follow-ing declined radically in the 1790s.

Brewer uses his well-told tale to make three points: (1) that eigh-teenth-century popular politics did not merely have a theatrical side; to an important degree it *was* theater; its dramatic discourse united plebeians and powers; (2) that nevertheless the attempt of radicals to appropriate political theater to a national cause exposed them to their opponents, who could easily evoke the elite contempt and fear stirred by the identification of the cause with riotous popular festivals; (3) that in the age of the French Revolution, the sober radi-cal search for respectability encouraged activists to turn away from suggestions of irresponsible spontaneity and debauch; political the-ater therefore declined. Brewer makes these points persuasively. He makes them by appealing implicitly to his readers' understanding of what came before and after: "The Garrat election therefore represents both a particular moment in the history of English radicalism, and a particular phase in the development of class relations in eighteenth-century England."[17]

Social historians in Brewer's vein reject Rudé's framework of class conflict. But they tend to agree with Rudé in (1) resisting the reduc-tion of popular collective action to a faceless, irrational crowd and (2) seeking the secret of that action by means of close study of real participants and their actual behavior. Essentially similar attitudes—rejection of condescending attributions of irrationality, insistence on the direct study of everyday participants—characterize a wide range of social history: Family history, demographic history, urban history, and many other histories have taken on a populist cast.

Collective Biography and Systematic Comparison

One general procedure became the emblem of all these social histories: collective biography. Collective biography consists of the assembly of comparable files concerning the lives of many individuals, followed by the regrouping of those files into a collective portrait of the population involved. Rudé's tallying of arrest lists for distributions of ages, occupations, and geographic origins illustrates collective biography at its simplest. The obvious next step is to search out further information concerning the individuals identified by the arrest list in other sources: censuses, parish registers, and so on. Full-fledged collective biography usually involves compiling biographical information on many individuals systematically from more than one source.[18]

The most comprehensive and successful uses of collective biography have appeared in historical demography. There, historians have painstakingly abstracted individual parish registrations of births, deaths, and marriages (more exactly, of baptisms, burials, and weddings) into skeletal family histories, and thence into estimates of fertility, mortality, and nuptiality for whole populations—local, regional, or even national.[19]

Historical demographers have moved from individual vital events to aggregate population dynamics over two different paths: via *families* and via *localities*. On one side, they have grouped observations by family, concentrated their attention on those families that lived out their lives (and therefore their demographic histories) within the locality under study, and aggregated information on the women who had completed their childbearing into estimates for the population as a whole. This is the painstaking method of "family reconstitution."

Family reconstitution has disadvantages: It excludes mobile families and is enormously time-consuming. Its advantages, however, are to be extremely precise within the population it covers and to permit close comparisons among different types of individuals. Thus, examining the population of Caen from 1740 to 1789, Jean-Claude Perrot establishes that (despite very low illegitimacy and infrequent prenuptial conception) Protestants averaged higher fertility than Catholics. That was due, he goes on to show, not to the large size of Protestant families, but mainly to the fact that the married Catholics of Caen went completely childless more often than their Protestant neighbors.[20] Reconstituting families of nearby Rouen from 1670 to 1789, Jean-Pierre Bardet shows that completed family size declined in all social classes, but that notables led the way with a drop from 7.2 live births per married woman from 1670 to 1699 to 4.1 live births from 1760 to 1789.[21] The findings on Rouen and Caen help us understand how their province of Normandy became one of Europe's earliest regions of long-term definitive fertility decline. Painstaking family reconstitution made such findings possible.

On the other side, demographic historians sometimes bypass the family to accumulate observations of births, deaths, and marriages for whole communities. Then typically the series yield annual rates, while characteristics of communities—rich or poor, agricultural or industrial, and so on—substitute for variation in household characteristics. The most salient disadvantages of this aggregative method stem from the uncertain relationship between the vital events and the population at risk; with no change in behavior patterns, for example, the selective out-migration of young people tends by itself to depress the birth rate.

The advantages of aggregative methods are their relative efficiency and their sensitivity to year-to-year changes. Thus in their massive analysis of England's population history from 1541 to 1871, E. A. Wrigley and R. S. Schofield aggregate births, deaths, and marriages from 404 Anglican parish registers, then correct and augment those series for internal bias, various forms of under-registration, and the absence of non-Anglicans.[22] (They also check some of their estimates against results of a dozen English family reconstitutions.) They are then able to show, among a great many other things, that English marital fertility actually rose during the eighteenth century, that fluctuations in marriage played a very important part in annual fertility fluctuations, and that marriage rates themselves responded strongly to changes in wage levels; rising wage levels encouraged more people to marry young. Malthus's Positive Check—the rise in death rates when population overran subsistences—had much less effect than most people have believed. Collective biography took Wrigley and Schofield through dry-as-dust technical procedures to the dynamics of marriage and birth.

Essentially the same procedures yield estimates of occupational mobility, of the social composition of political movements, or of the distribution of wealth. In studying the laboring classes of Renaissance Florence, for example, Samuel Kline Cohn, Jr., reconstructed workers' and patricians' networks of personal association from baptismal registers and marriage contracts, then integrated the results with evidence from criminal prosecutions to reveal the activation of citywide coalitions of workers in the time of the Ciompi insurrections (1342–1383).[23] In quite a different vein, Kristian Hvidt transcribed from police registers the characteristics of 172,000 Danes who emigrated from 1868 to 1900; his analysis demonstrated, among other things, the intimate interdependence of rural-urban migration within Denmark and the great flight to America. In essence, regional and transatlantic migration formed a single system.[24]

Although in these cases the units observed are most often single individuals, collective biography sometimes deals with households, firms, properties, even events. John Bohstedt, for example, based his study of community politics in England and Wales from 1790 to 1810 on a catalog of 617 events found according to a standard definition in the *Annual Register*, two newspapers, and the general domestic correspondence of the Home Office.[25] The logic is the same as in collective biography of individuals: comparable observations on multiple units compounded into systematic collective accounts of unity and variation.

How systematic, however, is a question that has divided European social historians. The beauty of collective biography, in principle, is that it permits its practitioners to retain all the idiosyncrasy of personal experience while identifying uniformities and variations across many personal experiences. In practice, the beauty fades somewhat; the simplification required to identify uniformities and variations—for example, Rudé's reduction of the many occupations of arrested persons to a limited number of categories, or Wirtz's grouping of Baden's manifold violent incidents into a handful of types—often suppresses particularity. If the historian has many instances to examine, he or she is likely to adopt a crude simplification: hand tallying into two or three categories at the extreme, punches in cards representing choices among nine or ten mutually exclusive categories as a slightly more refined version of the tallying procedure.

At the other extreme, some European social historians have abandoned the search for common properties and systematic variations in favor of the loving reconstruction of exemplary individual lives.

An outstanding example is the English historian of France, Richard Cobb.[26] Cobb's early work fell into the sort of collective biography inspired by the great French revolutionary historian Georges Lefebvre; while George Rudé examined revolutionary crowds, while Albert Soboul and others did collective biographies of *sans-culottes*, Cobb studied the volunteer revolutionary armies that played such an important part in mobilizing young men to the revolutionary cause and in enforcing the decisions of revolutionary activists. As compared with Soboul, Rudé, and many other students of revolutionary activists, Cobb never showed much enthusiasm for taxonomies or statistics. Nevertheless, his studies of army units did catalog the officers and describe the men in great detail, characterizing both their origins and their behavior.

Then Cobb moved increasingly toward the portrayal of single individuals who illustrated some principle of revolutionary action, or who simply lived interesting lives. He came to disapprove of the approaches of Soboul and Rudé. Speaking of Colin Lucas's remarkable work, Cobb commented that Lucas "has proposed collective definitions and groupings that are far more sophisticated than the crude jumble sale of Soboul's *mouvement de masse* or Rudé's wearisomely repetitive *Crowd* (always 'tending' to do something or other, spending all its time 'tending,' whether to riot on a Monday, or to get drunk in a wine-shop, or to destroy a threshing machine if it did not like a threshing machine, or to riot on or near a market, if there were a market day, or on or near a grain port, if there were a lot of grain coming through.)"[27] Instead, Cobb took up portrayals of individuals suffering or profiting at the Revolution's margins. Cobb's scintillating portraits led the way out of collective biography.

In principle, with great effort, a social historian can both retain individuality and deal with uniformity or systematic variation; all it takes is a refined recording system and a way of relating well-described individuals to the distribution of all individuals. Few have had the patience, the expertise, or the resources to build such a system. In practice, European social historians have commonly stationed themselves somewhere along this continuum:

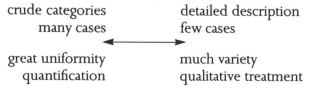

crude categories	detailed description
many cases	few cases
←	→
great uniformity	much variety
quantification	qualitative treatment

Having chosen a position on the continuum for a particular analysis, they have stuck to it. As compared to George Rudé's, John Brewer's studies of popular politics generally take up the detailed qualitative description of a few cases varying considerably from each other.

An unnecessary but understandable division arose among people who had chosen different positions on the continuum—broadly, a division between "collectivists" and "individualists." Collectivists tended to group many cases into crude categories, attempting to examine uniformities among their cases by quantitative means. Individualists tended to provide detailed descriptions of a few cases, stressing their variety via qualitative comparison. With the incessant creation of new specialties, whole subjects clustered near a single point on the continuum. The study of the adoption of new technologies, for example, came to concentrate near the "collectivist" end of the range, while the attempt to do psychohistory, to use contemporary psychological categories to label and explain historical actions, settled near the "individualist" end of the range.

The German program of studying *Alltagsleben*, everyday life, illustrates the division. Criticizing Hans-Ulrich Wehler, Alf Lüdtke complains of the view that "everyday life is almost necessarily marked by its distance from the forces and battlefields of the historical process; everyday life comes to signify merely the 'private' sphere."[28] Lüdtke sees that segregation and relegation of everyday life as a correlate of overzealous quantification. "Rigorous statistics of production, consumption, and life chances," he counters, "only become meaningful together with a qualitative account of the various modes of production and of the nature of the social relations of production."[29] The special feature of the analysis of everyday life, as he sees it, is "its attempt to expose the contradictions and discontinuities of both the modes and relations of production, in the context of the life-style of those affected; to make these evident and to explain them."[30]

Lüdtke illustrates the counterprogram with his study of work breaks in German factories at the end of the nineteenth century. The analysis itself falls clearly at the "individualist" end of the continuum. Lüdtke distinguishes between the breaks built into the schedule as a consequence of worker/boss struggles, and those breaks workers took illegally, at their own initiative:

> The permitted breaks served mainly the function of physical reproduction and so were directly related to the business of

physical survival. Even here, though, there were moments of 'mere' togetherness, the beginnings of personal and collective identity. In the illegal breaks such moments were predominant: the capacity for action and the possibilities of expression could be tested and developed; there were further opportunities to be alone and to be with others—to push back the forces of the factory, even while not directly fighting them.[31]

Lüdtke regards the mere counting of breaks, or the study of strikes in which the issue of breaks came up, as at best secondary and at worst misleading. That is because the meaning and use of work breaks, or of any other feature of daily work life, loom much larger for him than do the brute facts of their distribution in time and space.

That the choice is false, however, appears from a good look at another outstanding work in labor history, Michelle Perrot's Les ouvriers en grève.[32] Perrot painstakingly assembled information concerning every strike she could find anywhere in France from 1870 to 1890. She found about 3,000 strikes. She prepared a crude machine-readable description of each one, and tabulated the incidence of strikes by industry, region, year, issue, outcome, and a number of other characteristics. Perrot thereby constructed a comprehensive descriptive grid for strike activity fom 1870 to 1890. She built the means of identifying uniformity and variation by means of a special sort of collective biography.

If Perrot had stopped there, she would have provided a useful body of evidence for other historians of the period, but would have left herself vulnerable to the accusation of ignoring the strikes' meaning and use. But Perrot used her quantification largely to specify what must be explained: Why, for example, did sudden strikes without prior warning occur more often in industries with large worksites, yet decline in importance as big industry grew? Her discussion of that subject begins with the statistics, but soon leaves them behind; it ends with the conclusion that the unionization of big industry reduced the scope for workers' spontaneity. It moves from statistics to conclusion via numerous individual examples displaying the variety of mechanisms by which strikes actually began, as well as the different ways in which union leaders sought to contain them. Perrot put the bulk of her effort into the close examination of cases falling into different positions within her descriptive grid: the actual content of grievances concerning hours of work, the conditions for workers' victory, loss, or compromise in strikes, and so on.

Michelle Perrot did not simply find a happy midpoint on the continuum from quantitative/many cases, and so on to qualitative/few cases, and so on, or spring gracefully between two happy positions, one at each end. Nor do other first-rate social historians. Keith Wrightson and David Levine, for example, use a combination of demographic analysis and local history to reconstruct the experience of a single Essex village from 1500 to 1725.[33] During the sixteenth century, they detect rapid population growth due to relatively early marriage and resulting high fertility. After 1625, they discover a slowing of population growth as fertility declined and "extra" children had fewer chances to stay in the village. The demographic findings hereby raise precise questions about social change in the village.

Searching out that change, Wrightson and Levine show the creation of a sharp division between a small, dominant property-holding class and a large, subordinate class of land-poor and landless workers, with a religious ideology, a complex of social definitions, and a set of legal controls that reinforced the division. Reading Wrightson and Levine, we watch the local version of capitalism emerge as a contingent product of struggle between the few and the many.

Such work demonstrates that the continuum from "individualist" to "collectivist" is itself an illusion, an unfortunate simplification. The illusion results from placing oneself along the diagonal of the space shown in Figure 1.

Work is easier along the diagonal than above it. Most results below the diagonal are not very useful. The utility of results rises more rapidly with a move toward refined variety than with a move toward many cases. Yet, in principle, the most useful results come from stationing oneself not at the upper right-hand corner (few cases, refined variety) but near the upper left corner (many cases, refined variety). Michelle Perrot's work pushes above the diagonal toward that corner. With an effort, we can go even farther in that direction.

The program of "social science history" seeks to push social history above the diagonal. The term itself covers a variety of efforts; they run from the incorporation of sound historical evidence into contemporary social-scientific investigations to the use of social-scientific concepts as interpretive devices in standard historical investigations. The core of social science history, however, has three distinguishing features: (1) the explicit statement of falsifiable arguments; (2) the

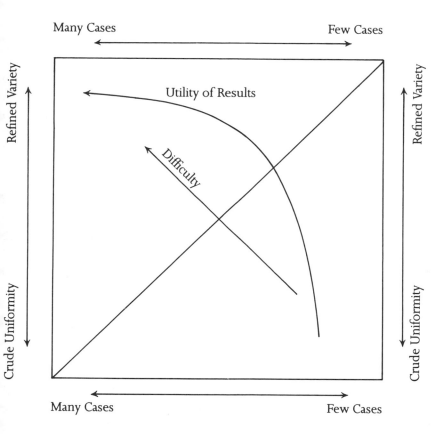

Figure 1. *Difficulty and Utility of Variety and Multiplicity in Social History*

generation of evidence bearing on the validity of those arguments by means of rigorous measurement; (3) the use of systematic comparisons among cases to verify or falsify the arguments in question. These features establish two different sorts of ties between contemporary social science and social history: First, they point to the distinctive features of social science in general. Second, the "falsifiable arguments" in play are quite likely to come from those disciplines that specialize in the contemporary equivalents of pressing social-historical questions, the social sciences.

Thus we find social science historians:

* Asking how and why various European populations proletarianized, using ideas about the logic of capitalistic production;[34]

* Seeking to explain regional and temporal variations in fertility, using ideas about the demographic transition;[35]

* Examining the correlates and effects of women's employment in different European cities, using ideas about household economic strategies;[36]

* Studying the spread of literacy among classes and communities, combatting standard ideas about modernization;[37]

* Reviewing historical patterns of rural-urban migration in Europe, drawing on ideas developed in the analysis of contemporary Third World migration.[38]

All these adventures, and more, profit from their casting in a social-scientific mold.

A case in point comes from the study of literacy. On the one hand, abilities to read and write vary enormously in contemporary Europe; not only the technical skills but also the meanings and consequences of the activity differ from one person to the next. No simple standard—so many years of school, ability to sign one's name, or perhaps purchase of printed matter—captures the variations in skill, meanings, and consequences of literacy. Yet Europeans on the whole clearly have become much more literate during the last century or two. It is hard to escape the feeling that the ability to read and write (and the increasing demand that citizens, employers, soldiers, drivers, and other whole categories of people be literate) altered people's daily experience. But how to translate that feeling into historical research?

For the period since national churches and state bureaucracies began intervening actively in the daily lives of ordinary people, European social historians have drawn their evidence about popular literacy mainly from the by-products of those interventions. Signing of documents, enrollment in school, and screening for admission to military service, prison, or some other bureaucratized institution provide the most abundant evidence. Using such sources for different regions of France, then delving into memoirs and inspection reports, François Furet and Jacques Ozouf show that the skills of reading and writing spread somewhat separately from each other; French Protestants, for example, commonly learned enough reading to decipher verses from the Bible, but did not necessarily learn to write. Writing skills connected closely with commercial activity.[39]

In Sweden, a national Lutheran church, strongly backed by the state, monitored the ability to read closely; pastors regularly tested (and recorded) the skills of their parishioners at reading and interpreting scripture. From the eighteenth century onward, many unschooled Swedes learned to read at home. According to studies of church examination registers, military recruitment records, school statistics, and other sources by Egil Johansson and his collaborators, elementary reading ability became quite general in Sweden before the end of the eighteenth century, but the ability to write only generalized with the extension of formal schooling after 1800.[40]

In the French and Swedish investigations of literacy, the conclusions resulted from close examination of thousands of instances. The sheer scale of the inquiries pushed the researchers toward the methods of the social sciences.

The risks of a relationship between history and contemporary social science are obvious: wholesale exportation from contemporary frames of models, concepts, arguments, and methods that fit historical experience badly; subordination of fundamental historical questions to the agenda of contemporary social science; building of false analogies between contemporary and historical experience or evidence. Yet these risks are avoidable. And the potential benefits are great.

Tasks of Social History

Whether practiced in a social-scientific mode or otherwise, the fundamental work of European social historians remains the same. It consists of (1) documenting large structural changes, (2) reconstructing the experiences of ordinary people in the course of those changes, and (3) connecting the two.

Documenting large structural changes involves a miscellany of activities, from the compilation of government statistics to the collation of observers' opinions. The available documentation itself reflects the course of European history: produced mainly by the agents of states and secondarily by the agents of churches; consisting largely of residues from taxation, conscription, civil registration, policing, and other efforts at controlling subject populations; increasing enormously in volume over time as a result both of expanding bureaucracy and of sheer survival of more recent records; crystallizing into regularly reported series monitored by specialists chiefly in the nineteenth century. An important part of social-historical expertise has gone into using the disparate evidence available from the period before censuses, surveys, and statistical services to extend the standard recent series back into the eighteenth, seventeenth, or earlier centuries. Myron Gutmann, for example, studied the impact of war on the population of the Basse-Meuse, a region straddling today's Dutch and Belgian borders, between 1620 and 1750. In that prosperous area, he found that war perturbed the population and the economy in characteristic but surprisingly moderate ways. In order to arrive at detailed analyses of war's consequences, however, he had first to construct long series of observations concerning "normal" fluctuations of taxes, agricultural production, food prices, religious practice, births, deaths, marriages, and more. In each case, furthermore, he had to construct his series by means of proxies and approximations: baptisms for birth, burials for deaths, communion-taking for religious practice, and so on. It was heroic, painstaking work.[41]

As Gutmann's research also illustrates, social historians have made their most original contributions to the second task: *reconstructing the experiences of ordinary people*. The greatest discovery was no discovery at all; it was the realization that if ordinary people left few narratives of their lives, innumerable documents of great diversity bore traces of those lives. The traces could, with care and expertise, fit together into skeletal histories of a great many lives. Religious registers, notaries' files, judicial proceedings, tax records, cadasters, censuses, voting rolls, city directories, account books, and many other routine residues of contacts between individuals and large organizations all provided voluminous information on many people outside the elite.

Long before World War II, people who were tracing their ancestors had used many of these same sources to locate individuals. Collective biography made the transition from single individuals to whole populations; one of the critical moments for social history, indeed, arrived when demographer Louis Henry realized that genealogies would, if properly analyzed, yield estimates of changes in vital rates: fertility, mortality, and nuptiality.[42] (Other demographic processes, notably migration, came later.)

Although collective biographies of Roman senators, of British parliamentarians, and of other elites long preceded the reconstitution of family demographic histories from genealogies and from parish records of births, deaths, and marriages, it was the extension of collective biography to run-of-the-mill families that released the creativity of social historians. The sources available for popular collective biography rarely made it possible to assemble richly anecdotal histories of individual lives. But they permitted a much closer approximation to a standard life history for ordinary people than ever before.

Connecting the aggregate observations of structural change with the social experiences sets the most difficult challenge. On the whole, European social historians have met the challenge with less imagination than they have brought to the first two tasks. When they have not settled for impressionistic interpretations of the social experience, they have commonly relied on crude correlations: dividing the entire population into several rough categories to establish that their social experiences differed, using local populations as proxies for distinct social groups, or pointing to a broad correspondence between the fluctuations in time of the measured social experience and of a large structural change. For example, many European urban histories divide up their cities into parishes, then use carefully assembled evidence to show that parishes containing many poor people also have relatively high mortality, more criminal offenders, more foundlings, and so on—important information, to be sure, but a far cry from an analysis of causal connections among the phenomena.[43]

Such crude methods of making the connection between big processes and small-scale social experience entail a double loss. First, they reduce the possibility of any strong statements of causal priority: What causes what? Second, they ignore the precious information contained in the variation from one experience to the next. It is hard to make mousse with a cement mixer.

Nevertheless, social historians sometimes use fine variation in time and space to their great advantage. Some do it by taking a small number of instances, and then making fully documented and precisely controlled comparisons among them. David Gaunt, for instance, looked at the varieties of family structure in central Sweden during the seventeenth and eighteenth centuries by close comparison of just five parishes. He did not choose the five places as a representative sample; he chose them because they had significantly different economic bases, and because they had rich sources, including obituaries of their parishioners. One parish included many miners and small-scale metalworkers, another consisted largely of peasants who hauled goods in the off-season, and three housed large estates which employed many day laborers. Gaunt's comparison of the parishes brought out the great population mobility of the estate-dominated parishes: Of the people over 60 who died in the parishes, only 5 to 26 percent had been born in the same parish. In the peasant and semi-industrial parishes, the percentages native were 59 and 67. The peasant and semi-industrial parishes, furthermore, had substantially larger households, more complex households (including adult offspring), and more single people. Gaunt relates the differences effectively to the household's control over its own land and livelihood.[44]

Other social historians sacrifice some of the richness, but still carry out fine comparisons over large numbers of observations. That almost always requires quantification. Sooner or later, almost all analysts of industrial conflict find that in order to keep their grip on the many factors causing strikes to occur and endure they are better off using quantitative comparisons among industries, localities, and periods. Again, the national studies of fertility decline in Europe carried on by Ansley Coale and his associates have generally followed a set of small geographic areas covering an entire country from census to census for a century or more; only quantification has made that effort feasible.[45]

Still others do some of each: They combine a moderately rich analysis of variation over many cases with a very rich analysis of variation among a small number of cases, in hopes that the two analyses will complement and confirm each other. Tracing variations in Hungarian household structure, Rudolf Andorka and Támas Faragó undertake comparisons among eleven scattered communities for which household listings are available. For different subsets of the communities, they compare overall household composition, age distributions of different kinds of household members, and kinship relations within households. Then they use censuses to compare whole counties over most of Hungary. Like David Gaunt for Sweden, they establish in Hungary a strong relationship between control of property (although in Hungary the wealthier peasants were often technically serfs) and large, complex households. Contrary to widespread opinion, they also find indications of more extensive birth control and lower fertility in large, complex households. Their large-scale and small-scale analyses combine to portray the complex household as an arrangement that stabilizes the connection between a lineage and its land by strong constraints over the marriage, migration, and work opportunities of its members.[46]

In all these cases, social historians find themselves documenting large structural changes, depicting ordinary people's experiences, and connecting the two. Result: incorporation of everyday life into the great movements of history.

Retouching the Portrait

As a result of recent decades' work in social history, our picture of general changes in European life over the last few centuries has altered greatly. Not long ago, historians thought, and taught, a Europe peopled mainly by an immobile, traditional peasant mass, dominated by church and state, which broke apart after 1750 with an industrial revolution followed by a series of democratic revolutions.

Witness the 1950 edition of Robert R. Palmer's first-rate survey, *A History of the Modern World*.[47] Palmer's presentation of modern Europe outside of Italy begins with the fifteenth-century New Monarchs (Henry VII, Louis XI, and others) who established royal power and stable government, and thus laid a political foundation for a Commercial Revolution. The Commercial Revolution includes an expansion of cottage industry, in which rural people produced at home on orders from local merchants. As a result of rising prices, peasants prospered and landlords faltered in western Europe; in eastern Europe, however, landlords themselves retained control of production, thereby taking advantage of price rises while subordinating manorial workers to their personal control.

Palmer's reconstruction continues: As monarchs fortified their states for war, conquest, and internal control, worldwide exploration and the growth of scientific thinking combined to generate prosperity and modern ways:

> ... the greatest social development of the eighteenth century, with the possible exception of the progress of knowledge, was the fact that Europe, or the Atlantic region of Europe north of Spain, became incomparably more wealthy than any other part of the world. The new wealth, in the widest sense, meaning conveniences in every form, was produced by the increasing scientific and technical knowledge, which in turn it helped to produce; and the two together, more wealth and more knowledge, helped to form one of the most far-reaching ideas of modern times, the idea of progress.[48]

Palmer points out that the new wealth did not depend on concentrated industry, but "represented the flowering of the older merchant capitalism, domestic industry and mercantilist government policies. . . ."[49] Then came the nineteenth century:

> The processes of industrialization in the long run were to revolutionize the lives of men everywhere. In the short run, in the generation following the peace of Vienna, the same processes had pronounced political effects. The Industrial Revolution, by greatly enlarging both the business and the wage-earning classes, doomed all attempts at "reaction," attempts, that is, to undo or check the consequences of the French Revolution. Industrialization made the flood of progress too powerful for conservatism to dam up. It hastened the growth of that worldwide economic system whose rise in the eighteenth century has already been observed. And since industrialization first took place in western Europe, one of its early effects was to widen the difference between eastern and western Europe, and so to weaken the efforts made, after the defeat of Napoleon, to organize a kind of international union of Europe.[50]

This "industrial revolution," in Palmer's account, centered on the shift to machine production in factories. The combination of industrialization and the French Revolution "led after 1815 to the proliferation of doctrines and movements of many sorts."[51] The "isms" began; European political history took the shapes of liberalism, radicalism, republicanism, socialism, conservatism, nationalism, and occasionally humanitarianism. In the West, the bourgeoisie triumphed, and faced a mass of estranged workers.

These changes, according to Palmer, occurred in the context of rapid population growth:

> All students agree in attributing the increase to falling death rates rather than to increasing birth rates. Populations grew because more people lived longer, not because more were born. It is probable that a better preservation of civil order reduced death rates in both Asia and Europe. In Europe the organized sovereign states, as established in the seventeenth century, put an end to a long period of civil wars, stopping the chronic violence and marauding, with the accompanying insecurity of agriculture and of family life, which were more deadly than wars

fought by armies between governments. . . . In Europe, sooner than in Asia, other causes of growth were at work beyond the maintenance of civil peace. They included the liberation from certain endemic diseases, beginning with the subsiding of bubonic plague in the seventeenth century and the conquest of smallpox in the eighteenth; the improvement of agricultural output, beginning notably in England about 1750; the improvement of transportation, which, by road, canal, and railroad, made localized famine a thing of the past since food could be moved into areas of temporary shortage; and, lastly, the development of machine industry, which allowed large populations to subsist in Europe by trading with peoples overseas.[52]

Thereafter Europeans—the French first of all—began to control births, a small-family system came to prevail, and population growth slowed. Fast urbanization and vast emigration complemented the fertility decline. The huge, impersonal, anonymous city epitomized the new society that emerged from the industrial revolution.

Palmer's deft summaries of European social history, as understood in 1950, provide us with a baseline for examining what social historians have accomplished since then. A Palmer writing in 1985 would make significant changes: He would acknowledge the contribution of fertility increases to eighteenth-century population growth, stress the proletarianization of the "peasant" population before 1800, and date a number of changes in family structure well before the industrial concentration and fertility decline of the nineteenth century. He would less confidently assert Europe's eighteenth-century economic superiority to the rest of the world. A 1985 Palmer would reduce the importance of the nineteenth century in the creation of secular proletarian life, and shift emphasis from technological toward organizational change. Social historians have offered major revisions to 1950's knowledge.

Some of the revisions are essentially technical. As a consequence of social-historical research, for example, we now know that European populations recuperated very quickly from the great shocks of mortality occasioned by famine and disease—not to mention that in the great famines after 1500 people rarely starved to death, but instead became more vulnerable to various diseases. Crises accelerated the deaths of the kinds of people who already had relatively high risks of death. In the aftermaths of crises, marriages generally accelerated and fertility rose. The most plausible explanation is that the heightened mortality opened up niches—farms, jobs, household positions—permitting marriage to people who would otherwise have married later, or not at all.

That series of discoveries does not contradict any major understanding of the modern era, but it does give the lie to two common notions: first, that before recent centuries European populations declined or grew mainly as a result of the presence or absence of wars and other demographic disasters; second, that in the absence of crisis European preindustrial populations were breeding at the limit of their capacity. Thus, a technical revision significantly affects our sense of the misery of social life and limits the explanations we may plausibly offer for popular action or inaction.

Some of the revisions are chiefly factual. Social historians have established, for example, that before 1800 many European villages had rates of population turnover well above 20 percent per year; rural areas with many wage laborers had an especially strong tendency to lose residents. The fact contradicts any depiction of "preindustrial" populations, especially of rural populations, as stodgily immobile.[53] The finding therefore raises doubts about accounts of nineteenth- and twentieth-century popular political movements as responses to rising mobility and to the breaking up of self-contained, immobile communities. Since such accounts abound, the factual revision makes a difference to historical understanding.

Some recent social history, furthermore, has directly attacked prevailing interpretations of European historical experience. A generation of "historians from below," for example, have not succeeded in creating a unified popular history. But they have effectively destroyed the old characterization of European workers and peasants as a dumb, slow-moving mass that reacted mainly to extreme hardship and only developed political awareness with the various mobilizations of the nineteenth and twentieth centuries. Social historians have replaced that characterization with a multiplicity of peasants and workers, each group following a relatively well-defined path of changing interests, each acting or failing to act as a function of those changing interests.

In the very process of arguing over the proper distinctions, over the incidence of crucial changes in production and reproduction, and over the exact conditions promoting action or inaction, social historians have generally adopted a broadly Marxist conclusion: that changing interests rooted in transformations of production account for major alterations in the collective action of Europe's subordinate classes. Here no single fact or technical discovery is at issue; social history has implanted a new interpretation of a major set of changes.

At the broadest level, European social historians have dislodged two fundamental ideas about European history since 1500: (1) the idea of a single sharp break with the traditional past, dividing history into before and after, a technologically driven industrial revolution; and (2) the idea of a general process, followed in country after country, in which an inexorable logic of differentiation, depending on the expansion of markets and the advance of technical knowledge, impels social evolution—whether "advance" or "decline"—and thus poses repeated problems of integration to rapidly changing societies. Those connected ideas, once the chief devices for ordering the recent experiences of the European populace, are the principal casualties of social history's victories.

Increasingly, then, research in social history has forced a recognition of the great mobility of European rural life before 1750; of substantial swings in the rates of birth, death, and marriage long before our own time; of extensive rural involvement in regional, national, and international markets; of widespread manufacturing and significant proletarianizaton in the countryside well before the day of factories and steam power; of struggles between expanding states and populations that fought statemakers' demands for more and more resources; of the rooting of demands for popular sovereignty in resistance to the aggrandizements of states and capitalists.

Capital and Coercion

Another shift in orientation follows from the last few decades' work in European social history: a diminution of the nineteenth century's place as the pivot of modern social change. The move toward implosion and centralization, on the one hand, and the sheer quantity of displacement, on the other, certainly marked off the nineteenth century as a critical period of change. Yet the statemaking of the sixteenth and seventeenth centuries, the proletarianization of the seventeenth and eighteenth centuries, and the organizational expansion of the twentieth century all rival the nineteenth century transformations in their impact on routine social life.

The drama of "before" and "after" serves poorly as an organizing principle for European social history, whether the pivot is the industrial revolution, the onset of modernization, or something else. The true problem falls into three parts:

(1) specifying the character, timing, and regional incidence of (a) the growth of national states, (b) the development of capitalism, (c) the interaction between them (the specification must keep sight of the fact that the phenomena called "states" and "capitalism" themselves altered radically between the sixteenth and twentieth centuries, and that therefore neither the growth of national states nor the development of capitalism constitutes a unilinear, quantitative progression over the entire period since 1500);

(2) tracing through time and space the varying experiences of small social units: individuals, kin groups, households, neighborhoods, shops, communities, and others; and

(3) establishing the cause-and-effect connections between the two sets of changes.

That is a large program.

Before reviewing the facts of nineteenth-century change, let us consider the theoretical problem. Theoretically, what does the three-point program entail? Capitalism is a system of production in which people who control capital make the basic decisions concerning the productive use of land, labor, and capital, and produce by means of labor power bought from workers whose households survive through the sale of labor power. In general terms, the development of capitalism makes three conflicts salient: (1) the opposition of capital and labor; (2) the opposition of capitalists to others who claim control over the same factors of production; and (3) market competition: buyers-buyers, buyers-sellers, sellers-sellers. All three conflicts can divide an entire population in two.

The growth of national states means the increasing control of the resources in a relatively large, contiguous territory by an organization that is formally autonomous, differentiated from other organizations, centralized, internally coordinated, and in possession of major concentrated means of coercion. Like the development of capitalism, statemaking follows a triple logic: (1) the extraction of resources from the subject population; (2) competition between agents of the state and agents of other governments inside and outside the territory; and

(3) competition among organizations that are subject to the state for resources controlled by the state. Again, all three conflicts can, in principle, produce fundamental divisions of the entire population.

If capitalism and statemaking were to proceed simultaneously, we might reasonably expect accommodation between capitalists and statemakers. Here is an idealized sequence:

> *early*: capitalist property created as statemakers struggle to extract resources and check rivals; major themes of conflict: expropriation, imposition of state control, imposition of capitalist control, and resistance to all of them;
>
> *late*: within an existing state and established capitalist property, major themes of conflicts: capital-labor opposition, market competition, attempts to control the state and its resources.

These are tendencies. Rather than a rapid transition, we might expect a gradual shift of the bulk of conflicts from type 1 to type 2. In addition, the pattern should depend on the relative rapidity of the two processes; where capitalism comes early and statemaking late, for example, we may reasonably expect to find capitalists themselves opposing relatively effective resistance to the state's expansion of its extractive and coercive power. Where statemaking leads, in contrast, we are likely to find more intense popular resistance to extraction, if only because capitalists have done less to expropriate and monetize the factors of production.

So, at least, runs the theory. These statements fall far short of a documented historical account. Indeed, they contradict accounts that many people have found plausible—notably the classic nineteenth-century accounts in which rapid social change, driven by differentiation and technical innovation, disrupts stable, immobile societies and thereby promotes disorganization, disorder, and protest. My account makes the conflicts that accompany capitalism and statemaking intrinsic to their development, consequences of opposing interests built into their very structure.

European social history here sets yet another challenge: To adjudicate between the sort of interest-oriented account of statemaking and capitalism I have sketched and classic change-disorder accounts of the same changes.

What Happened in History

Nineteenth-century observers who articulated the classic change-disorder accounts were right on one count: Great alterations in social life were occurring. Let me offer a rapid summary of the changes brought by the nineteenth century, without guaranteeing that most European social historians would agree with my account.[54]

For several centuries before the nineteenth, industrial expansion occurred mainly in small towns and rural areas. Small capitalists multiplied rapidly. They did not work chiefly as manufacturers in our sense of the word. They operated instead as merchants, giving out work to formally independent groups of workers, most of them organized in households. The social relationships between capitalists and workers ranged from various "purchase" arrangements in which producers owned the tools, premises, raw materials, and finished goods to various "putting-out" arrangements in which the merchant owned some or all of them; on the whole, the less workers owned, the greater the power of merchants. These systems accumulated capital, but set serious limits on its concentration. The multiplication of semi-independent producers in households and small shops therefore accounted for most of manufacturing's large increase.

Contrary to later prejudices, the European populations involved in these merchant-dominated forms of manufacturing and in commercial agriculture moved a great deal. They moved, however, mainly within regional labor markets or in large systems of circular migration. Both regional labor markets and long-distance circuits left some migrants in cities, but altogether migration, fertility, and mortality produced only modest rates of urban growth. Cities increased and lost population largely as a function of levels of activity in their hinterlands.

The nineteenth century changed many of these traits. Capital concentrated. Individual capitalists and organized firms began to control much greater productive means than they had previously commanded. Capitalists seized hold of productive processes. Instead of continuing to organize manufacturing around supplies of self-sustaining labor, they increasingly placed production near markets and sources of energy or raw materials. Production began to edge out exchange as the pivot of capitalist social relationships.

As a result, the active sites of proletarianization shifted from country to city. More and more production went on in large firms employing disciplined wage earners. Workers migrated from dispersed industrial hamlets, villages, and towns.

This urban implosion of capital and labor accelerated rural-urban migration, spurred urban population growth, deindustrialized large sections of the countryside, and accentuated differences between town and country; the division between industrial cities and their agricultural hinterlands reappeared with a vengeance. Mechanization of production facilitated the concentration of capital and the subordination of labor.

The coincidence of implosion and mechanization created the illusion of an "industrial revolution" driven by technological change. Although new technologies certainly contributed to the fixing, disciplining and intensification of labor, much of the nineteenth-century expansion of production preceded the spread of the factory and assembly line, occurred without substantial changes in the actual techniques of production, and depended mainly on alterations in the social relations of production. In textiles, chemicals, and metal production, technical innovations promoted dramatic increases in the scale and intensity of production. But for manufacturing in general, two essentially social innovations played a larger part in transforming production: (1) the grouping of workers in large shops under centralized time-discipline; and (2) the monopolization of means of production by capitalists.

At the start of the nineteenth century, many capitalists worked essentially as merchants, buying and selling the products of workers. No need to exaggerate: In some branches of textiles and metals, full-fledged industrial capitalists ran large mills and employed full-time wage workers. In cottage industry, merchants often owned the looms and the raw materials worked by poor cottagers. In capitalized segments of European agriculture, the daily or yearly wage already provided the principal income of millions of households. Nevertheless, relatively few capitalists knew how to produce the goods they sold, and many workers did. During the nineteenth century, in industry after industry, capitalists and workers struggled over knowledge and control of detailed production decisions. By the end of the nineteenth century, many capitalists knew how to make a whole product, and few workers did. The capitalists had won.

Workers, however, received some consolation prizes. Toward the end of the nineteenth century—with great variation by region and trade—workers' real income began to rise, and some workers even began to accumulate wealth in the form of housing and household goods. An illusory *embourgeoisement* occurred: In material possessions, leisure, and personal style the apparent differences between bourgeois and proletarians diminished, as workers' control of productive capital continued to decline. To some extent, workers' organizations gained legal standing, financial strength, and the right to bargain with capitalists. Thus workers acquired a stake in the capitalist system while losing control of the means of production.

As capitalism entered a new phase of concentration and control, European *states* were also undergoing great alterations.[55] By the later eighteenth century, zealous princes, ministers, and generals had made national states the dominant organizations in most parts of Europe. The chief exceptions were the urban-commercial band extending from Northern Italy across the Alps, down the Rhine and into the Low Countries, and the southeastern flank of the continent, along which tribute-taking empires, powerful lineages, and Islamic peoples concentrated.

Where national states held sway, preparations for war became extensive and costly; military expenditure and payment for war debts occupied the largest shares of most state budgets. The strongest states built great structures for the extraction of the means of war: supplies, food, conscripts, and money.

Paradoxically, the very construction of large military organizations reduced the autonomy of military men and created large civilian bureaucracies. The process of bargaining with ordinary people for their acquiescence and their surrender of resources engaged the civilian managers of states willy-nilly in establishing perimeters to state control, limits to state violence, and regular routines for eliciting the consent of the subject population. In sixteenth-century England, Tudor monarchs succeeded in disbanding their great lords' private armies, in snatching most fortresses from private hands, and in radically reducing the settlement of disputes among nobles by force of arms. Yet even the seizure of property from churches and rebellious lords did not free Tudor monarchs from financial dependence on Parliament. Eventually, the consent of Parliament became essential to royal warmaking, and thus to state expansion itself.

The bargaining process had a different history in each state. But overall it led to the state's civilianization, and to the establishment of regular mechanisms for consulting representatives of the governed population.

Up to the nineteenth century, European states continued to rule indirectly. For routine enforcement of their decisions, collection of revenues, and maintenance of public order, they relied chiefly on local powerholders. The powerholders did not derive their tenure or their power from the good will of superiors in a governmental hierarchy. They retained room for maneuver on behalf of their own interests. Much of the work of national authorities therefore consisted of negotiating with regional and local powerholders. Ordinary people carried on active political lives, but almost exclusively on a regional or local level. When they did involve themselves in national power struggles, they ordinarily did so through the mediation of local powerholders, or in alliance with them.

In the nineteenth century, this system disappeared from much of Europe. War kept getting more expensive and deadly, but it increasingly involved conquest outside of Europe rather than struggles among European powers. Revolutionary and reformist governments extended direct rule into local communities. The French revolutionaries of 1789 and thereafter were the first Europeans to succeed in that effort at the scale of a large state; revolutionary committees, revolutionary militias, and eventually a revolutionary bureaucracy brought individual citizens face to face with the national state. The Napoleonic Empire solidified these revolutionary practices. The French Revolution was precocious and unique. But most European states soon underwent their own transitions to direct rule—many of them, in fact, as a result of conquest by French armies.

As they bargained with local people for even greater resources, statemakers solidified representative institutions, binding national elections, and a number of other means by which local people participated regularly in national politics. Here the variation ran even wider than in the institution of direct rule. At the end of the nineteenth century, the Swiss federation, the British parliamentary system, the Italian state (formally very centralized, informally very fragmented), and the bureaucratized Russian Empire represented very different alternatives.

Under pressure from their constituents, managers of most states took on responsibilities for public services, economic infrastructure, and household welfare to degrees never previously attained. On the whole, they also moved from reactive to active repression: from violent reactions against rebellion and resistance after they occurred toward active surveillance of the population and toward vigorous efforts to forestall rebellion and resistance. These activities shoved aside autonomous local or regional powerholders, and put functionaries in their places. As a consequence, powerholders lost much of their strength and attractiveness as intermediaries in the attempts of ordinary people to realize their interests. Those were the nineteenth century's great changes.

Or so it seems to me. It is only fair to warn that my synthesis remains unproven and contestable in a number of regards. Consider, for example, the question of mobility and connectedness before and after the nineteenth century. When Eugen Weber seeks to determine how France's multiple peasantries coalesced into a common Frenchness during the nineteenth century, he fixes on awareness of nationality, involvement in national politics, and responsiveness to opportunities outside the locality as the phenomena to be explained. Weber lays out the materials of folklorists and travelers brilliantly; he shows us a nineteenth-century rural France fragmented in language and custom, then much stirred by the arrival of the railroad, of obligatory primary education, of widespread military service. "Between 1880 and 1910," concludes Weber, "fundamental changes took place on at least three fronts. Roads and railroads brought hitherto remote and inaccessible regions into early contact with the markets and lifeways of the modern world. Schooling taught hitherto indifferent millions the language of the dominant culture, and its values as well, among them patriotism. And military service drove those lessons home."[56] In Weber's view a congeries of immobile rural societies broke open, connected, and began to move.

Yet Weber's basic argument is not convincing. It is debatable how much more intensely French rural people of 1900 were involved in national affairs than were their ancestors of 1800. The vast systems of temporary migration portrayed by Alain Corbin, Abel Châtelain, and Abel Poitrineau, for example, established intense ties between Alpine villages and Marseille, between impoverished farms of the Limousin and central Paris.[57] Those systems thrived in the eighteenth century, and atrophied in the nineteenth. In certain respects, the integration between those distant rural places and the rest of France actually declined. That is one of my reasons for doubting the classic account of mobilization, even when presented with the richness and sublety of Weber's analysis. But the presence of Weber's analysis and the credence many historians have given it testify that my alternative account is not self-evident.

Or take the extent of proletarianization before the nineteenth century. The evidence on European people's—and especially whole households'—employment throughout the year is quite fragmentary. It could turn out that the majority of people who worked in cottage industry before 1800 actually spent so much of their years (or their lives) cultivating their own land that the term "proletarian" describes them badly.

A lot depends, in any case, or how stringent a definition of "proletarian" we adopt: If, for instance, we insist on full-time wage earners holding closely supervised positions within large organizations, wage earners who have no other employment, then proletarianization concentrates by definition in the nineteenth and twentieth centuries.

The effect of minimizing employment in cottage industry before 1800 and adopting a very demanding definition of "proletarian" is to maintain my statements about trends but to displace the bulk of European proletarianization into the nineteenth and twentieth centuries. (In that case, we must invent a new terminology to designate the millions of European households *before* the nineteenth century, in manufacturing and agriculture alike, that came to depend for survival on wage-labor under capitalist supervision, but did not work in large firms under time-discipline, and so on.) The same sort of debate— partly factual, partly definitional—can easily arise about other elements of my summary. The general trends, nevertheless, now seem well established.

Conclusion

Not that social history has settled everything. Far from it! In challenging old ideas of popular involvement in big structural changes, European social historians have renewed and displaced the debate, but have by no means ended it. These days social historians of Europe are disagreeing about whether a modern, affectionate, egalitarian family formed, and if so how, when, and why. They are worrying about the conditions, if any, under which social classes defined by the relations of production became significant actors. They are pitting against each other alternative explanations of the general European decline in fertility. They are considering the virtues and vices of oral history, of ethnographic approaches to historical analysis, of quantification, of narrative, of most of the procedures I have described as accomplishments of social history. In very recent years, it has become much clearer that social-scientific interventions in social history, where successful, have served mainly to specify what is to be explained and to eliminate bad explanations rather than to supply new and more convincing explanations; that realization has come as a disappointment to historians who hoped for closure. In all these regards, and more, European social history remains a rough, contested terrain.

Yet European social history has much to celebrate. First, it has shown the way to renew our understanding of collective historical experience by systematic collation of many, many individual experiences; historical demography provides a dramatic example of renewed understanding through collective biography. Second, European social history has humanized and historicized those rather abstract and timeless social sciences that have come into its scope; sociology, political science, and even economics have emerged more historical from their encounter with European social history. Third, the practitioners of European social history have radically reduced the plausibility of general histories portraying ordinary people as apathetic, irrational, or stupid masses. Finally—and most important— European social history has built new accounts of the development of capitalism and the formation of national states, accounts that treat capitalism and states as concrete daily realities rather than vast abstractions, accounts in which the experiences and actions of ordinary people stand in center stage.

NOTES

1. G. M. Trevelyan, *English Social History* (London: Longman, 1944), 1.

2. Peter Burke, *Sociology and History* (London: G. Allen & Unwin, 1980), 31.

3. Richard Trexler, *Public Life in Renaissance Florence* (New York: Academic Press, 1980).

4. Emmanuel Le Roy Ladurie, *Montaillou, village occitan de 1292 à 1324* (Paris: Gallimard, 1975).

5. Ron J. Lesthaeghe, *The Decline of Belgian Fertility, 1800–1920* (Princeton: Princeton University Press, 1977).

6. See Luciano Allegra and Angelo Torre, *La Nascità della storia sociale in Francia: Dalla Commune alle 'Annales'* (Turin: Fondazione Luigi Einaudi, 1977); Traian Stoianovitch, *French Historical Method: The "Annales" Paradigm* (Ithaca: Cornell University Press, 1976).

7. Sidney and Beatrice Webb, *English Local Government*, 7 vols. (New York: Archon Books, 1963); J. L. and Barbara Hammond, *The Village Labourer, 1760–1832. A Study in the Government of England Before the Reform Bill* (London: Longman, 1911); R. H. Tawney, *The Agrarian Problem in the Sixteenth Century* (London: Longman, 1912).

8. Max Weber, *Wirtschaft und Gesellschaft. Grundriss der verstehenden Soziologie* (Tübingen: J. C. B. Mohr, 1972; 5th ed.; first published in 1921).

9. Jürgen Kocka, "Theory and Social History. Recent Developments in West Germany," *Social Research* 47 (Autumn 1980): 426–75; see also Kocka, *Sozialgeschichte. Begriff—Entwicklung—Probleme* (Göttingen: Vandenhoeck & Ruprecht, 1977).

10. Ronald Grigor Suny, "Russian Labor and Its Historians in the West: A Report and Discussion of the Berkeley Conference on the Social History of Russian Labor," *International Labor and Working Class History* 22 (Fall 1982): 50.

11. Tony Judt, "A Clown in Regal Purple: Social History and the Historians," *History Workshop* 7 (Spring 1979): 66–94. For comments on Judt's and other critiques of social history, see *Theory and Society* 9 (September 1980), special issue on social history.

12. For a review of ideas and evidence, see Charles Tilly, *Big Structures, Large Processes, Huge Comparisons* (New York: Russell Sage Foundation, 1985).

13. E.g., E. J. Hobsbawm and George Rudé, *Captain Swing* (London: Lawrence & Wishart, 1969); George Rudé, *The Crowd in the French Revolution* (Oxford: Oxford University Press, 1959); Albert Soboul, *Les sans-culottes parisiens en l'an II. Mouvement populaire et gouvernement révolutionnaire, 2 juin 1793–9 Thermidor an II* (Paris: Clavreuil, 1958). For a sample of more recent work, see Louise A. Tilly and Charles Tilly, eds., *Class Conflict and Collective Action* (Beverly Hills: Sage, 1981).

14. Temma Kaplan, *Anarchists of Andalusia, 1868–1903* (Princeton: Princeton University Press, 1977).

15. Rainer Wirtz, *'Widersetzlichkeiten, Excesse, Crawalle, Tumulte und Skandale.' Soziale Bewegung und gewalthafter sozialer Protest in Baden, 1815–1848* (Frankfurt a/M: Ullstein, 1981).

16. John Brewer, "Theater and Counter-Theater in Georgian Politics: The Mock Elections at Garrat," *Radical History Review* 22 (Winter 1979–1980): 8.

17. Ibid., 37.

18. For reviews, see Lawrence Stone, "History and the Social Sciences in the

Twentieth Century," in *The Future of History*, ed. Charles F. Delzell (Nashville: Vanderbilt University Press, 1977), 3–42, and Charles Tilly, "The Old New Social History and the New Old Social History," *Review* 7 (Winter 1984): 363–406.

19. For reviews, see Arthur Imhof, *Die gewonnenen Jahre* (Munich: Beck, 1981); Charles Tilly, "The Historical Study of Vital Processes" in *Historical Studies of Changing Fertility*, ed. Charles Tilly (Princeton: Princeton University Press, 1978); J. Dennis Willigan and Katherine A. Lynch, *Sources and Methods of Historical Demography* (New York: Academic Press, 1982).

20. Jean-Claude Perrot, *Genèse d'une ville moderne. Caen au XVIIIe siècle*, 2 vols. (Paris: Mouton, 1974).

21. Jean-Pierre Bardet, *Rouen aux XVIIe et XVIIIe siècles. Les mutations d'un espace urbain* (Paris: SEDES, 1983), 1:279.

22. E. A. Wrigley and R. S. Schofield, *The Population History of England, 1541–1871: A Reconstruction* (London: Arnold, 1981).

23. Samuel Kline Cohn, Jr., *The Laboring Classes in Renaissance Florence* (New York: Academic Press, 1980).

24. Kristian Hvidt, *Flight to America: The Social Background of 300,000 Danish Emigrants* (New York: Academic Press, 1975).

25. John Bohstedt, *Riots and Community Politics in England and Wales, 1790–1810* (Cambridge, Mass.: Harvard University Press, 1983).

26. Richard Cobb, *Les armées révolutionnaires, instrument de la Terreur dans les départements*, 2 vols. (Paris: Mouton, 1961–1963).

27. Richard Cobb, *Reactions to the French Revolution* (London: Oxford University Press, 1972), 121.

28. Alf Lüdtke, "The Historiography of Everyday Life: The Personal and the Political," in *Culture, Ideology and Politics*, ed. Raphael Samuel and Gareth Stedman Jones (London: Routledge & Kegan Paul, 1982), 42.

29. Ibid.

30. Ibid.

31. Ibid., 47.

32. Michelle Perrot, *Les ouvriers en grève. France, 1871–1890*, 2 vols. (Paris: Mouton, 1974).

33. Keith Wrightson and David Levine, *Poverty and Piety in an English Village: Terling, 1525–1700* (New York: Academic Press, 1979).

34. For reviews and syntheses, see David Levine, ed., *Proletarianization and Family Life* (New York: Academic Press, 1984) and Charles Tilly, "Flows of Capital and Forms of Industry in Europe, 1500–1900," *Theory and Society* 12 (March 1983): 123–42.

35. E.g., O. W. A. Boonstra and A. M. van der Woude, "Demographic Transition in the Netherlands. A Statistical Analysis of Regional Differences in the Level and Development of the Birth Rate and of Fertility, 1850–1890," *A. A. G. Bijdragen* 24 (1984): 1–58; John C. Caldwell, "The Mechanisms of Demographic Change in Historical Perspective," *Population Studies* 35 (1981): 5–27; Michael W. Flinn, *The European Demographic System, 1500–1820* (Baltimore: Johns Hopkins University Press, 1981); John Knodel, "European Populations in the Past: Family-Level Relations," in *The Effects of Infant and Child Mortality on Fertility*, ed. Samuel Preston (New York: Academic Press, 1978), 21–46; Wolfgang Köllmann, "Zur Bevölkerungsentwick-

lung der Neuzeit," in *Studien zum Beginn der modernen Welt*, ed. Reinhart Koselleck (Stuttgart: Klett-Cotta, 1977), 68–77; David Levine, *Family Formation in an Age of Nascent Capitalism* (New York: Academic Press, 1977); Kenneth A. Lockridge, *The Fertility Transition in Sweden: A Preliminary Look at Smaller Geographic Units, 1855–1890* (Umeå: Demographic Data Base, Umeå University, 1983).

36. For review and synthesis, see Louise A. Tilly and Joan W. Scott, *Women, Work, and Family* (New York: Holt, Rinehart & Winston, 1978).

37. For review and synthesis, see Harvey Graff, *The Literacy Myth. Literacy and Social Structure in the Nineteenth-Century City* (New York: Academic Press, 1979).

38. For review and synthesis, see Charles Tilly, "Migration in Modern European History," in *Human Migration: Patterns and Policies*, ed. William H. McNeill and Ruth S. Adams (Bloomington: Indiana University Press, 1978), 48–72.

39. François Furet and Jacques Ozouf, *Lire et écrire: L'alphabétisation des français de Calvin à Jules Ferry*, 2 vols. (Paris: Editions de Minuit, 1977).

40. Egil Johansson, "The Postliteracy Problem—Illusion or Reality," in *Time, Space and Man. Essays in Microdemography*, ed. Jan Sundin and Eric Soderlund (Stockholm: Almqvist & Wiksell, 1979), 199–212.

41. Myron P. Gutmann, *War and Rural Life in the Early Modern Low Countries* (Princeton: Princeton University Press, 1980).

42. Louis Henry and Yves Blayo, "La population de la France de 1740 à 1860," *Population*, numéro special (Novembre 1974): 72–122.

43. E.g., Pierre Léon, *Géographie de la fortune et structures sociales à Lyon au XIXe siècle (1815–1914)* (Lyon: Centre d'Histoire Economique et Sociale de la Région Lyonnaise, 1974).

44. David Gaunt, "Pre-Industrial Economy and Population Structure: The Elements of Variance in Early Modern Sweden," *Scandinavian Journal of History* 2 (1977): 183–210.

45. Ansley Coale, Barbara Anderson, and Enna Harm, *Human Fertility in Russia since the Nineteenth Century* (Princeton: Princeton University Press, 1979).

46. Rudolf Andorka and Támas Faragó, "Pre-Industrial Household Structure in Hungary," in *Family Forms in Historic Europe*, ed. Richard Wall, Jean Robin, and Peter Laslett (Cambridge: Cambridge University Press, 1983).

47. Robert R. Palmer, *A History of the Modern World* (New York: Alfred A. Knopf, 1950).

48. Ibid., 264–65.

49. Ibid., 264.

50. Ibid., 432.

51. Ibid., 441.

52. Ibid., 569.

53. E.g., Sune Åkerman, Hans Christian Johansen, and David Gaunt, eds., *Chance and Change: Social and Economic Studies in Historical Demography in the Baltic Area* (Odense: Scandinavian University Press, 1978); Ingrid Eriksson and John Rogers, *Rural Labor and Population Change: Social and Demographic Development in East-Central Sweden during the Nineteenth Century* (Stockholm: Almqvist & Wiksell, 1978); Sture Martinius, *Befolkningsrörlighet under industrialismens inledningsskede i Sverige* (Gothenberg: Elanders, 1967); John Patten, *Rural-Urban Migration in Pre-Industrial England* (Oxford: School of Geography, 1973; Occasional Papers, no. 6).

54. In ideas, sources, and text, this section draws heavily on Charles Tilly, *Big Structures, Large Processes, Huge Comparisons*.

55. For background, see Charles Tilly, ed., *The Formation of National States in Western Europe* (Princeton: Princeton University Press, 1975).

56. Eugen Weber, *Peasants into Frenchmen. The Modernization of Rural France* (Stanford: Stanford University Press, 1976), 493–94. For a critique of Weber, see Charles Tilly, "Did the Cake of Custom Break?" in *Consciousness and Class Experience in Nineteenth-Century Europe*, ed. John M. Merriman (New York: Holmes & Meier, 1979), 17–44.

57. Alain Corbin, *Archaisme et modernité en Limousin au XIXe siècle* (Paris: Marcel Rivière, 1975); Abel Châtelain, *Les migrants temporaires en France de 1800 à 1914*, 2 vols. (Villeneuve d'Ascq: Publications de l'Université de Lille III, 1976); Abel Poitrineau, *Remues d'hommes. Les migrations montagnardes en France, XVIIe–XVIIIe siècles* (Paris: Aubier, 1983).

CHAPTER 2

THE SYNTHESIS OF

SOCIAL CHANGE

REFLECTIONS ON AMERICAN

SOCIAL HISTORY

BY OLIVIER ZUNZ

The "new" social history began to affect the course of American historiography in the 1960s. Although it emerged in the United States significantly later than it did in Europe, its rise to prominence was swift, and the changes it brought with it were pervasive. It replaced the romantic and essentially undefined vision of "the people" that had satisfied historians for so long with detailed accounts of ordinary men and women who had heretofore no voice in the historical record. It displaced the conventional divisions that political historians

I wish to thank the contributors to this volume for their insightful criticisms of earlier drafts of this essay. I am grateful for the advice I received from my colleagues at the University of Virginia, especially Lenard Berlanstein, Robert D. Cross, Charles Feigenoff, Michael F. Holt, Stephen Innes, and Joseph F. Kett. Other friends have also helped me formulate my ideas on social history. Thomas Dublin and Michel de Certeau organized a most stimulating discussion of an early version of this chapter at the University of California, San Diego. In their turn, John Bodnar and Stephan Thernstrom criticized my section on assimilation at the 1984 meeting of the Organization of American Historians and presented alternative views in a forum of the *Journal of American Ethnic History* 4 (Spring 1985). And John Higham stimulated the writing of the essay by enlisting my participation in a session on "the problem of synthesis in American history" at the centennial meeting of the American Historical Association (1984), and by giving the chapter a close and critical reading.

used to discuss the past with new divisions based on economic, social, and technological change. And it exposed large reserves of neglected evidence and developed the techniques necessary to subject them to historical analysis. It is not surprising, therefore, that the appearance of this "new" social history generated great excitement in the progressive and eclectic intellectual atmosphere of the sixties. There was not a conviction or an axiom that social historians did not propose to debunk. Old questions were discarded or treated from fresh perspectives. Instead of debating abstractions that had concerned the previous generation of scholars such as the "inevitability" of the Civil War, social historians took a closer look at the institution that had for almost 200 years conditioned the outlook of Southerners. They examined the daily reality of slavery and tested its viability as a social system in antebellum America. Instead of merely adding to the endless commentary on the American myth of opportunity, they determined which groups actually benefited from the available opportunities. In recent years, however, social history has drawn criticism from various camps: from intellectual historians for failing to develop a coherent view of historical processes, from Marxist historians for being bourgeois cant, from social scientists for being descriptive.[1] These objections require serious consideration, for taken as a group they throw into question the essential validity of social history. What follows are some reflections on social history's achievements and failures, as well as on the promise it still holds for American history.

The Ideological Nature of American History

Debates over methods and terminology have brought the widely scattered members of the international community of scholars together and have established common ground for historical discourse. For instance, American historians of slavery refer to the mentalité of planters while the recent French Dictionnaire des Sciences Historiques includes an entry on the "new economic history."[2] But despite the cross fertilization of methods and terms occurring on an international level, American historians remain set apart by their belief in the unique patterns of their history. Themes like consensus, community, exceptionalism, and the pervasiveness of abundance that are found in virtually every text have no real counterpart in other national histories. Because these ideas resonate deeply in the collective consciousness, the findings of American historians have often inadvertently objectified American myths. Social history offered those historians eager to escape the reification inherent in their position the promise of coming to grips with the actual social processes hidden behind the American ethos.

One belief that had exerted a pervasive influence on American history is the idea that America had a special destiny, an idea which implied that history had been written in advance. It has often been remarked that for Americans of the eighteenth and nineteenth centuries the future seemed only an occasion to elaborate and improve on ideas already accepted or on institutions already in existence.[3] History for Americans existed only within a preexisting pattern. This ideology has had lasting impact on Americans' interpretation of their history. The view of change central to evangelical Protestantism, for example, is that it is acceptable only as an expression of continuity with the past. Thus, the religious reforms offered by the preachers of the two Great Awakenings were means to restore a failing order and to turn Americans once again to the task of meeting the requirements of their history.[4] Later in the nineteenth century, in the midst of industrialization, the men close to the misery of immigrants in large cities of the gilded age—Henry George, Edward Bellamy, Josiah Strong, Henry Demarest Lloyd—were struck by the realization that social inequities could lead American history to deviate from its prewritten course, a movement which, in their eyes, would be apocalyptic.[5]

A more recent consequence of the same belief that national traditions are fixed is that it has encouraged the study of such generalized constructs as "the American system" and "the American character." These issues have been the territory of intellectual historians, who searched to recreate "the particular configuration of tensions within a national setting, as well as the behavioral, intellectual, and emotional consequences of that configuration."[6] After World War II, intellectual historians reacted against progressive history, which had evolved around the notion of conflict.[7] The so-called consensus historians built on a tradition going back to Governor Bradford that underscored America's "mission" and uniqueness. They echoed Daniel Webster and Henry Adams's views on the singularly free nature of American political institutions, and they rediscovered Tocqueville's great insights and searched for one American "system." Following

Louis Hartz, they embarked on a great exercise in metahistory, an exercise which sometimes produced fierce debates.[8] At the same time, social scientists also explored the nature of national character; even the specific ways in which American children were brought up became a part of the "national experience." The perspective inherent in this approach is in part the product of the world-domination and the unprecedented prosperity which the United States achieved by mid-century. The prosperity that followed World War II gave support to the theme of abundance—that great deflector of conflict and the sheer size and resources of the continent made it easy for historians and social scientists to assume that similar plentitude shaped conditions in the past.[9] In this atmosphere, teleology often preempted ideology as their ideas converged to produce a definition of American history which was both timeless and exceptional.[10]

Recent Trends in History

John Higham recently wondered why "the most literate historians" of the postwar decades failed to adjust creatively to the new history of the 1960s and 1970s and the concurrent decline of "comprehensive themes and overarching generalizations."[11] To be sure, their impact continued to be felt for a long time. Even the Marxist historiography of the 1970s, which usually showed little respect for national boundaries, was partly framed around the debate on exceptionalism and national character.[12] But on the whole, most intellectuals lost the assurance of their predecessors. While some intellectuals of the 1950s had claimed the "end of ideology,"[13] those who followed them soon discovered that moments of national consensus can be deceptively brief. In the 1960s and 1970s, the Vietnam War, the Civil Rights Movement, the women's movement, the rediscovery of ethnicity, the Watergate scandal and the ensuing crisis of the Presidency, the rediscovery of deep recession after twenty-five prosperous years interrupted only by temporary economic setbacks, all combined to undermine the prevailing atmosphere of consensus and self-righteousness. No longer able to understand historical processes through a single formula, most intellectuals of the 1960s and 1970s rejected the very notion of national character.

The rejection of consensual themes led to a diminished interest in intellectual history, and consequently few advances in intellectual history were made during this era. The notable exception was the reinterpretation of the American revolution. John G. A. Pocock, in particular, enlarged and complicated the interpretations of the consensus school. He analyzed the debate surrounding the American Constitution in light of the Florentine political tradition—as a classic case of Machiavellian moment of reaction against corruption.[14] But by and large, social history replaced intellectual history as the most promising field of investigation. Even political history was refashioned as a form of "social analysis."[15] The new economic history flourished at the same time, but because of technical biases, its influence was limited to a small group of experts. For most historians, the new agenda entailed tracing the origins of visible social conflicts, not explaining intellectual consensus.

Intellectual historians respected national boundaries and tried to encompass the special relation of the state to the populations within its control. Most social historians, in contrast, considered the state as only the creation of the dominant class and argued against the study of national character, which hitherto had been considered as an ideal, immutable type.[16] They believed that large structural changes in a nation's history make national types or ideals evanescent, and they therefore viewed the attempt to define a people's features in these terms as a stylistic exercise.[17] They proposed to integrate the experience of the individual with other units such as the family, the neighborhood, the factory, or the city. Looking back on their efforts, we can see that they too quickly bypassed ideological issues of national dimension. But in the historiographical context in which they shaped their agenda, the richness gained by exploring attitudes from different angles seemed invaluable, and the hope that it would enrich history sustained its influence through the next twenty years of scholarship.

The social history of the 1960s and 1970s capitalized on three well-known interrelated trends. First, social history integrated what seemed to be an infinite number of new topics. In this endeavor, the new social historians acted as the heirs of an older generation of social historians. Arthur Maier Schlesinger began editing the thirteen volumes of the "History of American Life" series, which includes his *Rise of the City* in 1923. He and Dixon Ryan Fox, his co-editor, saw the series as a vehicle to "free American history from its traditional servitude to party struggles, war and diplomacy" and to direct attention not only to "the highest fruits of American intellectual and spiritual attainment, but also to the interests and tastes of the common man."[18] Other precursors of the new social history such as Frank Lawrence and Harriet Owsley or Merle Eugene Curti utilized large quantities of quantifiable records as early as the 1940s and 1950s.[19] Building on the work of these forebearers, the new social historians sought to uncover the lives of inarticulate people and embarked on an unprecedented effort to rewrite history from the bottom up. A salient characteristic of their agenda was a search for structure in the multiplicity of individual experiences. In an age dominated by media and the diffusion of mass market techniques, new social historians shifted the emphasis to collective processes; they concentrated no longer on individuals but on groups; their goal was not biography, but collective biography.[20] New techniques that permitted the aggregation of data from masses of individuals were developed while new fields of inquiry into the material parameters of life were opened up. Hosts of documents were collected and methods devised to study the way workers dressed and ate, the kind of houses they lived in, and the religious beliefs they shared. Every form of record became a legitimate source of evidence if it offered the potential for a fresh vantage point on the world. This approach to history from the bottom up was motivated by a real need to uncover the concerns of everyday life that had hitherto been neglected. The interest in new sources of evidence is also a reflection of the pronounced populist bias of the new social history, the feeling that ordinary people are responsible for their own history. Men, women, and children replaced abstractions. Although machines, economies of scale, bureaucracies, capital flows and other factors were still studied, the lives of the human beings who filled the factories, used the highways, plowed the fields, and built the cities were seen as fit subjects of inquiry. While history had addressed the large question of national character on the evidence of a tiny fraction of society, the "new" history shifted the locus of this inquiry to the unknown masses and, as its preliminary task, busied itself in widening the knowledge of ordinary Americans and their daily lives.

American historians joined this trend rather late. Naturally they were in part inspired by the example of the "Annales School," which appeared to Americans as a more cohesive group than it actually was.[21] But if the French Annalistes directed their effort primarily against narrative history—"l'événementiel"—the American effort was more importantly a reaction against the perceived inadequacies of the all encompassing consensual themes. However, absorbed in the enormous task of bringing such new evidence to light, new American social historians fell in the same trap as their European predecessors. They failed to address logical historical questions of change and concentrated almost exclusively on "continuities and structures." They glanced "only briefly at the conditions of passage from one state to another, from one system to another."[22] Despite this flaw (to which I will return), the efforts of social historians have so enriched the study of history that a return to the limited enquiry of the past is, if not unthinkable, undesirable.

The second trend of the 1960s and 1970s, intimately related to, but distinct from the first, was the treatment of history as a science, a perspective achieved by integrating it in the fields of social science. The new scientific status which historians claimed was different from that inspired by nineteenth-century positivism, which applied exclusively to the development of codified rules of critical analysis.[23] Social historians turned to the techniques of quantification to give history a new scientific status, and in this, they were following the lead of economic historians and historical demographers. Social historians saw that "only repetitive facts constituted in a series could provide a rigorous basis for scientific observation,"[24] and their efforts were enhanced by the timely appearance of computers, which allowed the maintenance of large data files heretofore undigestable by individual researchers and the use of sophisticated statistical techniques. In this climate, Emmanuel Le Roy Ladurie confidently proclaimed: "Tomorrow's historian will program computers or will cease to exist."[25]

Publication of the first issue of the *Journal of Interdisciplinary History* in 1970 marked the climax of this intellectual exchange between history and the social sciences, which culminated in the formation of the Social Science History Association in 1976, and a trend that has fortunately survived the retrenchment of the late 1970s and early 1980s. As Robert William Fogel aptly points out, cliometricians "believe that historians do not really have a choice of using or not using behavioral models. . . . The real choice is whether these models will be implicit, vague, incomplete, and internally inconsistent, as cliometricians contend is frequently the case in traditional historical research, or whether the models will be explicit, with the relevant assumptions clearly stated, and formulated in such a manner as to be subject to rigorous empirical verification."[26]

The third way in which social historians have affected the course of historical research is by adopting the techniques of community study. Community studies are made possible by a single, although multifaceted and powerful technique—nominal record-linkage. This procedure allows historians to picture in great detail the lives of individuals and families, as records of their births, marriages, deaths, fortunes, occupations, housing, religious affiliations, associational commitments, and other vital pieces of information combine to produce a complete picture of life, one that certainly compares well, if not favorably, with those collected in many a contemporary social science survey.[27] This rich body of evidence, often connected with more traditional, narrative sources of history, allowed social historians to come close to Marc Bloch's great image of the true historian, who "like the giant of the fairy tale ... knows that wherever he catches the scent of human flesh, there his quarry lies."[28]

The work necessary to develop these innovations and to gain acceptance for them had its cost, however. At the time it seemed impossible to devise generalizations applicable to the overall society while producing an in-depth understanding of local actors. For this reason social history has sometimes been seen as a new form of antiquarianism.[29] Social historians must now transcend the fragmentation which has characterized a generation of monographic work and attempt a higher level of generalization.

Achievements of Social History

Before offering a critique of social history and proposing to solve some of the current difficulties, it would be useful to recount some areas of historical study which have benefited from the insights of social historians during the last twenty years. In all areas, social history has expanded our understanding of structure, of the large-scale processes which affect society.[30] Too often American historians had treated concepts like urbanization, industrialization, assimilation, associational life, bureaucratization, and communication as "buzzwords," called on when needed but not fully explored or understood. These terms are mostly from the vocabulary of the sociologist, and as such, are based on the conditions of the present. They therefore contribute little to our understanding of the impact large-scale processes have on people's lives over time and can be misleading when applied to the past. The taxonomic work of sociologists—even great scholars like Max Weber—often operated against the unraveling of these processes because they were invoked as causes of change rather than explored on their own terms.[31]

The impact of social history on our knowledge of the processes that shaped the past can be seen, to take four examples, in our present understanding of migration, industrialization, urbanization, and the changing American family. The first three are large-scale processes that are especially susceptible to the methods of social history because they are collective processes best understood through the aggregation of individual experiences. These aggregated patterns, of course, only have meaning if the individual experiences which composed them are kept in mind. The discussion of the family—a small social unit—will illustrate how social history goes beyond assigning meaning to large-scale processes. It helps us envision the interplay of these processes within the immediate context of everyday life.

Migration

Migration is a good example of one important topic known until recently only in large, unfocused, ways. The movements of individuals searching for subsistence in agricultural societies or for employment in industrial societies have involved massive relocations of human beings.[32] As Eric R. Wolf put it recently, "in the course of the nineteenth century, industrialization and the introduction of large-scale cash cropping in agriculture went on apace. As capital flowed toward new areas of opportunity and into new branches of activity, it massed machines into ever larger aggregates, and brought ever new battalions of workers into the growing industrial army. . . . Political economies were refashioned, social ties rent and rearranged, and people moved from areas of supply to areas of demand."[33] In the United States, the study of migration is intimately linked to the national legend, to the question of America as a land of opportunity. Migration is further linked to cultural history through the study of assimilation. It is therefore logical that social historians saw migration as a topic of great importance and explored it. The sheer size of population movements has led social historians to refute permanently any surviving "romantic belief" in the permanence of past societies.[34] But social historians went far beyond the destruction of old myths. They placed population movements in context and recounted the stories of migrants as they were lived.

The historian Charles Tilly has proposed a system which classifies population movements according to three categories: 1) "Circular migration" takes migrants "to a destination through a set of arrangements [and returns them] to the origin after a well defined interval."[35] Examples of this type of migration include "seasonal work on harvests, pastoral transhumance, [or] the sending of young people into domestic service before they married." Such movements have been well documented in American history. Social historians have, for example, studied black workers who spend the summer on construction jobs in the city and return to cheaper living on the farm in the winter. In the process, they have corroborated many of the astute observations W. E. B. Du Bois makes in *The Philadelphia Negro*.[36] (2) "Chain migration" involves "sets of related individuals or households [who move] from one place to another via a set of social arrangements in which people at the destination provide aid, information, and encouragement to new migrants." Again, social historians have illustrated such population movements for blacks who migrated from Virginia to Boston during Reconstruction. They took the steamer in Norfolk, and received aid in Boston from other fellow immigrant Virginians.[37] Similar accounts of chain migration exist for the Great Migration; others detail the movements of French Canadian workers in the New England textile industry, the extent of their kin networks, the degree to which they relied on them at both ends of the migrating chain for such critical matters as employment, income pooling, and education.[38] (3) "Career migration" applies to persons or households that may move "in response to opportunities to change position within or among large structures: organized trades, firms, governments, mercantile networks, armies and the like." Historians of mobility patterns have documented this relatively modern form of migration while investigating the important connection between social and geographic mobility. For instance, Stephan Thernstrom, in his work on Boston, clearly identifies the major turning point in career migration in American history: Before 1930, most people on the move were unskilled workers in search of jobs, not following career patterns but simply trying to improve their lot while professional elites were relatively stable geographically;[39] after 1930, however, with the rise of national corporations, professionals began to move, following, in Tilly's words, "a circuit . . . based not on the social bonds at the migrant's place of origin, but on the logic of the large structure itself."[40]

One of the most important insights that social historians have contributed to the study of migration is the recognition that many people take part in several types of migration. Furthermore, the conditions of migration had such an overriding influence on their lives that it set them apart from the sedentary members of their national group. A comparative study by Lynn Lees and John Modell of Irish in London and Philadelphia shows that the members of Irish communities in Philadelphia and London resembled each other more than they resembled the Irish in Ireland. Citizens of both these communities became migrants at the same age—often to find a marriage partner—and entered the urban hierarchy in reverse by migrating directly from the farm to the British or American metropolises.[41] This process affected their outlook on life as well as the internal developments of the new communities they formed.

While many American historians have focused on immigration to the United States, others have documented the deleterious effects that migration has had on the countries losing population. Examining the case of the Caribbean islands, where the society depends on migration to survive, Orlando Patterson concluded that "in economic terms, [migration] has reinforced the external orientation and chronic dependence of these societies on foreign economies, and it has stifled the emergence of alternative strategies of development. Culturally, it has sustained the uprooted quality of life that was produced by the mass migration during the period of slavery, and it has led to the emergence of a modal personality syndrome devoid of trust and seemingly incapable of compromise."[42]

In short, social history has produced a new look at this uprooted individual of legend, the migrant. This reappraisal has led us to abandon the image of migrants as passive, uprooted individuals and to see them as motivated, clever people, often migrating only to return a few years later to the homeland and buy land, generally more prosperous and energetic than those who could not afford to migrate or who could no longer muster the energy to leave their depressed region. We now understand migration as both an individual *and* a collective process.

The Dimensions of the Industrial Experience

Perhaps the most important topic that historians of American society have examined is industrialization. Early industrialization helped secure the economic independence of the new nation. It transformed the United States from a decentralized rural republic to a consolidated urban country. It was also a chief determinant of migration. Industrialization attracted a larger and larger number of workers, drawn from all parts of the world, who changed the face of America. The consequences of industrialization had been treated before the rise of social history. The creation of the factory system, the change in the pace of work, the accumulation of great fortunes, the building of an internationally powerful country during World War I, the ideological and labor conflicts that accompanied industrialization had all been studied by economic, business, and labor historians. Yet social historians have contributed more than anybody else to our understanding of the complex nature of these processes. Again, it has not merely been a matter of providing strict definitions but rather of bringing out the human activity which in aggregate constitutes the process of industrialization, of telling how men, women, and children were affected by industrialization as it evolved in different parts of the country. Instead of focusing on technological and economic processes, social historians looked at the social costs of industrialization, the processes at work in social change, the differences the new organization of work made in the life of factory operatives, and the changing scale of life.

Before social history came to the fore, the social impact of industrialization had been studied primarily by those socially concerned sociologists who had multiple contacts with social work agencies. For instance, Robert Park had been Booker T. Washington's secretary before moving to the University of Chicago, where he and his colleagues maintained strong affiliations with social workers.[43] Roderick McKenzie at the University of Michigan maintained similar ties with Urban League workers in Detroit.[44] Sociology and social work were intimately linked to pioneering surveys of American industrialization such as Graham Romeyn Taylor's Satellite Cities, his study of the new industrial suburbs that emerged at the turn of the century around Chicago, Detroit, and Birmingham.[45] The first massive social survey was conducted in Pittsburgh under the direction of Paul Underwood Kellogg with funding from the Russell Sage Foundation in 1908.[46] In addition, Bureaus of Labor Statistics compiled data on working conditions, working hours, and strikes, while the U.S. Senate directed the Immigration Commission to survey the industrial labor force.[47] These contemporaneous surveys of the late nineteenth- and early twentieth-centuries industrialization, however, were all that was available to Samuel P. Hays when he wrote *The Response to Industrialism* in 1957.[48]

Since that time, social historians have greatly enriched our understanding of industrialization. They began by moving the discussion away from the industrial belt and back in time. One reason for concentrating on the small mills of the early nineteenth century was because the task of compiling individual information on the thousands who worked at the Carnegie Steel Works or Ford's Highland Park plant seemed impossible. This emphasis on the early nineteenth century, however, also served to uncover the origins of American industrialization. Life was changing everywhere in the early nineteenth century, in villages and mill towns near sources of water power and in large towns after the introduction of the steam engines. The construction of Lowell, now the best known story in American industrialization, represented the first major investment of mercantile capital in the New England textile industry. The choice of the site, dictated by sources of water power, is illustrative of the economic and geographic processes at work in America's early industrialization along rivers such as the Merrimack, the Brandywine, or the Schuylkill. Lowell also represented a conscious effort by American industrialists to create a "different," poverty-free industrial society.[49] In the absence of a cheap labor force, the manufacturers had to hire the daughters of Yankee farmers and treat them well. Although the story of these young women working in the mills had been told several times either by observers of the time or by historians relying on literary sources, social historian Thomas Dublin brilliantly showed the ways in which their lives were profoundly altered by their factory experience. After compiling a collective biography based on company payrolls and the movements of individual operatives throughout the surrounding New England countryside, Dublin could explain the full impact of industrialization on these women. Never again, he concluded, could they return to the old regimen of rural life after enjoying independence, albeit under the chaperonage of the capitalist. They retained, however, their Yankee republicanism. When they were treated like the growing numbers of Irish immigrants who joined the mills, the same women refused to be proletarianized. In order to preserve the very independence they had learned to enjoy, they became early participants in the labor movement.[50] The changes in other industries like the shoe industry, described by Alan Dawley, reflect another series of transformations: the breakup of the family economy under the master craftsman, the loss of control of the small Lynn workshops (tenfooters) to the merchants, and the construction of large factories. If New England textile operatives were liberated by their stint in the factory, Lynn shoemakers, like "S" described in an early report of the Massachusetts Bureau of Labor Statistics, became alienated by the new working conditions. But they did not turn to the labor movement for their identity; rather they developed a double consciousness as workers and citizens. Although exploited as workers, they could—unlike their English counterparts—vote. Thus Dawley suggested, "the ballot box" might have been "the coffin to class consciousness."[51]

While Lowell and Lynn grew into large mill towns, recruiting a more diverse and cheaper labor force, the countryside was also affected by industrialization. In Rockdale, a sleepy village in Chester County, Pennsylvania, entire families were hired by mill owners, although only one payment was made to the head of the household and only one entry per family was made in the employment book.[52] A similar family work system existed in Slater's mills in rural Massachusetts.[53] Outwork, then, had a different social impact than the building of factories. Instead of concentrating workers in urban areas, outwork extended the labor market into the farm. Hatmaking in New England, for example, "reinforced a traditional family economy associated with subsistence farming in an earlier period and permitted a new growth of rural population."[54] Social historians, therefore, have enabled us to see that industrialization in some instances created new individuals and in others reinforced traditional patterns.

Industrialization soon penetrated the larger cities. There existed in Philadelphia in the 1840s and 1850s a full spectrum of work environments from outwork to the unmechanized sweatshop to the fully mechanized factory environment such as could be found in the larger mills along the Schuylkill.[55] But even the larger mills distributed some work to the houses of textile workers in the Manayunk district.[56] In New York, sweatshops grew out of the increased use of the sewing machine, which "very few women workers (and few tailors too) could afford."[57] In short, social historians have uncovered the individual paths which industrialization took in the villages, small mill towns, and larger centers of the early nineteenth century and traced the ways in which innovations introduced by industrialization were embedded in lasting ways into the preexisting social structure. The great diversity of experience in the early nineteenth century uncovered by social historians is one that no simple linear theory of industrialization can encompass.

More recently, historians have refocused the discussion of industrialization to the later, classic period, from the late nineteenth century to the Great Depression, the period of massive change in the scale of production.[58] A large shoe factory in Lynn in 1850 might employ 200 workers, a railroad shop in Cleveland in 1900 perhaps 3,000 workers, but by 1914 Ford's Highland Park factory alone employed over 14,000 workers. This different scale required a redirection of effort on the part of social historians. They relied on community studies to examine industrialization in the early industrial era. For the later period, they added the study of historical issues which embraced entire regions: the creation of the industrial belt, the growth of giant corporations, the interplay between factory organization and bureaucracies, the trials and tribulations of the labor movement, and, above all, the experiences of the millions of individuals who tried their lot in the industrial universe.

The Dimensions of the Urban Experience

The social historian's interest in urbanization is a necessary complement to this attention to both migration and industrialization. The social historian's goal was to understand a process whereby an entire nation shifted from a rural base to a complex system of hierarchically organized, interacting cities. That this growing network of cities triggered social historians' interest is not surprising considering the diversity of immigrants settling in cities and the ever growing economic role played by these populations.

Until now, however, social historians have bypassed the study of rural development in favor of the city. As Harold Barron recently noted, two factors contributed to this neglect of the countryside. The impact of Turner's work led to an almost exclusive focus on the frontier, in effect only one stage of rural development, while the influence of business and economic history called attention to the technological "revolution" in American farming, a revolution that in reality affected only a small portion of the countryside.[59] Only now are the elements of a more richly textured rural history emerging. Several historians are studying the household mode of production of old rural communities or exploring midwestern immigrant rural settlements. Others are concentrating their efforts on the industrialization of the countryside. Still others are describing the efforts of Southern planters to retain their economic hegemony during Reconstruction or conversely those of black yeomen to build their freedom in a different southern rural order.[60] A "new" rural history is slowly emerging.

If they have heretofore neglected the country side, social historians have documented in detail the different steps of urbanization, substituting an "urban" chronology based on technological, spatial, and social criteria for the traditional "political" chronology of American history.[61] They have documented the evolution of the urban environment, contrasting commercial port towns along the seaboard to the autarchic communities of the frontier in the seventeenth century and outlining the growing connections between these two types of environments in the eighteenth century as a consequence of changes in transportation and the commercialization of products.[62] They have traced the integration of industry into growing cities. They have explained why the South urbanized slowly in contrast to regions such as the industrial belt, and they have shown the importance of cities both in local history as staging points for the exploration of the frontier and in national history as centers of population and capital.

Statistically speaking, the United States urbanized late in its history. It was only in 1920 that the majority of Americans lived in cities. But the importance of cities in American history is only partly related to their size. Stuart Blumin, for example, locates the urban threshold in New York State as the middle of the nineteenth century. The introduction of factory production in the 1830s signaled the end of self-sufficiency for small communities and of many forms of economic autonomy. "By 1860 there were some three hundred 'urban places' of between 2,500 and 10,000 population, and another sixty-eight of between 10,000 and 25,000. Viewed in conjunction with the larger urban centers, these smaller cities and towns represent a filling out of the urban landscape, a more complete articulation of the urban regionalization that is the surest sign of a maturing society."[63] By the end of the nineteenth century, the American urban system had created an industrial sector so large and geographically concentrated that, as Michael Conzen put it, "the national core region was synonymous with the manufacturing belt." This area was segmented in three parts by 1900: Consumer-goods originated in Boston, New York, and Baltimore; a "producer-goods axis" connected Philadelphia to Cleveland; and a cluster of manufacturing cities mostly producing consumer goods stretched west from Cleveland.[64]

Seventy years later, in 1970, however, most Americans were suburbanites, not urbanites. This statistic reflects the fundamental ambiguity of Americans toward the city, which they view not as a homogeneous space but rather as a conglomerate of conflicting spaces. Tocqueville's fear that the urban proletariat, the "multitude of Europeans who have been driven to the shores of the New World by their misfortunes or their misconduct"[65] might undo the unity of the American people has come to be shared by urbanites. The social history of the American city shows the increasing segregation of people over space. One of the main characteristics of American cities is that it inscribes in space the hard realities of the "separated society."[66] Historians have documented the different forms of segregation, from the relatively unspecialized land use of the "walking city" to the system of distinct ghettos which mark the modern metropolis, and from the voluntary separation of nineteenth-century ethnic communities to the brutal segregation of blacks in the twentieth century. For a while, romantic notions about the past and the intensity of racial discrimination in twentieth-century America gave the nineteenth-century city an aura of integration. Social history, however, showed the simplistic nature of such formulae.[67] Historians have also moved beyond broad interpretations of urbanization to uncover the web of social relations which exist in the city. Practically every aspect of routine social life has now been explored: neighborhood institutions, career patterns, leisure, crime and violence, the housing market, poverty, education, family life, and religion.[68]

The Changing American Family

Large-scale processes of social change in America have had an impact on the private spheres of life and especially family organization. In studying the family, social historians have utilized demographic techniques to penetrate the intimate world of past populations. Demographers are interested in history primarily to discover models applicable to those nonwestern areas that are now faced with a combination of hunger, high fertility, and high mortality. Historians, however, have adopted demographic methods to penetrate more completely the social reality of the past. They rely on demography to provide clues to broad processes of population history such as migration or population replacement.[69] On the local level, they use demographic information to indicate cultural and socio-economic cleavages. Taken in isolation, statistics such as fertility rates, number of people per family, household composition, and estimated life expectancy might appear abstract, but placed in the context of religious attitudes toward birth control, of ethnic outlooks on life, of social inequality, of public health, of composition of the labor force, of attitudes toward marriage, and other questions, these "abstract" quantities take on concrete significance.[70]

Our understanding of the "family economy," a limited but telling example of the translation of abstract figures into concrete facts is a case in point. The discovery of the "family economy"—the pooling of income among household members—and the recognition of its importance are by no means recent. It was the object of several studies of domestic budgets by newly formed state Bureaus of Labor Statistics in the 1870s. Such studies became a perennial feature of the federal Bureau of Labor Statistics in the 1890s and early twentieth century and were the basis for Carroll D. Wright's pioneering work in Massachusetts and Washington.[71] The various ways in which household members combined their income was also Margaret F. Byington's major preoccupation in Homestead, Households of a Mill Town, the volume she wrote for the Pittsburgh Survey.[72]

Social historians and demographers in the last decade revived budget studies because economic decisions in the household reflect cultural and behavioral patterns. For instance, demographic analysis reveals that, although kin and nonkin co-residents had well-defined and distinct roles within the economies of almost all nineteenth-century households, households differed considerably in their treatment of offspring. In some, both sons and daughters joined the labor force early. In a few groups, girls worked to put their brothers through school, while in others they did not. Clearly, the period before unionization and the welfare state was characterized by a much closer relationship between the structure of the family and sources of income than now.[73] In fact, throughout the industrialization period, family economy was a sometimes indispensable factor in survival. Because of employers' vigorous opposition to the labor movement and the movement's concentration in skilled occupations, most workers of the open-shop era could not count on labor organizations to provide security in their lives. They relied instead on their immediate kin. Most large working-class families pooled incomes. Dependence on the family economy rather than on working-class institutions contributed to make the family a close-knit, communal unit capable of supporting members through difficult winters, providing for them through sickness and old age, and sustaining them in their efforts to make their way in the industrial market place.

In all groups the male heads of households usually worked, and the married women did not. The burden of supplementing the father's income, then, rested on the children.[74] Demographic studies show that reliance on children's contribution decreased as the socioeconomic status of the head of the household rose. Family economy, however, was practiced in the homes of skilled and white-collar workers as well as in those of the unskilled. In households headed by those in skilled or white-collar occupations, the individual incomes of family members could add up to a comfortable sum of money and facilitate the acquisition of a home and luxuries like a Model T. In both cases, family income followed the same pattern, increasing as children entered the labor force and decreasing again when they left the parental home. If only a modest amount of money was needed and if there was room in the house, boarders often provided the financial relief that spared the children from working. Most immigrant families, however, did not have the space to house a boarder and needed more additional income than one boarder alone could provide. Consequently, in the late nineteenth century, boarding in American cities was more an American phenomenon than an immigrant one.[75]

The relationship between work and the family also shaped the demography of the nineteenth-century nuclear household. In contrast to the modern nuclear family, the nuclear family of the nineteenth century was large. This was especially true of immigrant families. There, unmarried children remained under the parental roof after maturity; domestic service was one of the few channels by which unmarried daughters could leave their parents' households. One solution for the immigrant family was to expand the family still further by producing children who would be able to contribute to the domestic economy. By contrast, native white American families had a more complex and diversified household structure, which meant less reliance on the family economy and a greater variety of family situations.[76] Thus Carl N. Degler argues that among native white, mostly middle-class, urban families, nineteenth-century husbands and wives built unions on affective ties and shared feelings closer to our sensibility than to those usually assumed of the nineteenth-century patriarchal family. They also adopted liberal child-rearing practices for those children who did not have to contribute to the family budget.[77]

Employers in the preunion era also depended on the "family economy." They often relied on the family to recruit workers and encouraged family members to bring relatives to work. Often the employer used community institutions to reach families. In Detroit, for example, Henry Ford built a recruiting network in the black community through Reverend Bradby of the Second Baptist Church when he initiated a new policy in 1919 of employing blacks in all hourly-wage classifications.[78] Furthermore, life in the work place, resembled life in the home. A worker's ability to adapt to the factory depended on his ability to function within a hierarchy similar to that of the family. An Amoskeag worker described how the mill's hierarchy duplicated his family: "It's like a family, the father is the big boss . . . the mother is the second hand." Hareven emphasizes that "individual adaptation to the world of work and to survival in a factory system depended on each member's ability to function as a member of a collective family unit."[79]

Against this background, it becomes clearer how the nineteenth-century family changed under the pressures of the large environmental transformations that began in the last third of the century. As work hierarchies became increasingly dominated by institutions outside the family and outside the neighborhood, the family came to take on the configuration it has today, a small cell well adapted to the educational and career movements of its individual members. It became "a more specialized unit, one devoted primarily to the expressive and child-rearing functions."[80] The transition from the autonomous working family—a spatially based unit relying on income-pooling—to a supporting structure for the achievements of individuals, occurred roughly between 1905 and 1950. We find in Byington's Homestead a good example of the first stage in that transition. In Homestead's "courts," boarders piled up in boarding houses that, by 1906, had begun to replace the family as a base for new immigrants.[81] Hareven's Amoskeag is another case in point: In the 1920s, the union replaced the family as the bargaining agent with the employer.[82] Homestead and Amoskeag were company towns, each built for the production of a single commodity, textiles in New England, steel in Pennsylvania, but the same processes were happening within the more diversified metropolises like Philadelphia, Chicago, or Detroit. Everywhere, the "modern" family took shape; it adapted to new forms of opportunity and relinquished its bargaining and its welfare functions to unions and the state. These functions were further limited when World War II and post-World War II prosperity made the familiar one wage-earner family possible.

To sum up, social historians examining the relationship between work and family have shown the ways in which various groups adapted their family strategies to new conditions which emerged between the two world wars. They have demonstrated that for the American family, especially the immigrant family, this transition did not entail just an economic adaptation from an extended to a nuclear form; it was a sociocultural shift from a semi-autonomous, multi-functional, and often ethnic, unit to an undifferentiated and functionally limited organization.

The Whole and the Parts

Social history allows us to comprehend better the impersonal forces described in intellectualized accounts of the past by revealing seemingly monolithic forces as the product of a multitude of human actions and decisions. The initial application of this vision, however, was problematic. The first generation of American social historians was willing to accept the hegemony of the social sciences. Faced with the problem of negotiating the uncharted territories opened up by social history, they turned to the social sciences, particularly sociology for guidance. In 1968, the historian Richard Hofstadter and the political scientist Seymour Martin Lipset argued for what seemed at the time a viable method: Once the work of historical investigation was completed, the results could be interpreted through the use of sociological models.[83] Historians consequently tried their hands at social analysis and "borrowed" from the social sciences theoretical frameworks to shape their narrative. Unfortunately, social science models, although helpful, do not reflect the complexity of historical change. As Pierre Vilar simply put it, "history is more complicated than theory."[84]

The difficulties created by modernization theory illustrate this point. Modernization theory has merit as a loosely conceived approach to social change. As Raymond Grew observed, "these large-scale changes that put people in schools and change their diets, redefine work, amass new wealth and power, and alter the organization through which all this is structured while maintaining surprising continuity—this whole complex process deserves a name and modernization springs to mind."[85] Grew's position is reasonable, especially when considered in light of his disclaimer that modernization theory does not really exist in an absolute sense, "only particular theories . . . related to larger historical tendencies."[86] But the widespread notion, taken from American sociology, that we should view our contemporaries as "moderns" because they are endowed with specific qualities which make them "modern" has led historians astray. Typical of this sociological approach is the volume *Becoming Modern: Individual Change in Six Developing Countries*, published in 1974. In it Alex Inkeles and David H. Smith lay out four basic categories of modernity: "informed citizen participation," "a marked sense of personal efficacy," "a high degree of independence and autonomy," "a high level of cognitive flexibility."[87] Are these characteristics modern? It is hard to think of the Puritan community without informed citizen participation; surely the United States was not "born modern." Indeed recent work on New England in the seventeenth and eighteenth centuries suggests that the autonomous Puritan community, "sealed off from the rest of the world," was more backward than the emerging commercial nodes dominated by merchant entrepreneurs.[88] It is also hard to think of many migrants to the United States without thinking of a "high degree of independence and autonomy," "efficacy," and "flexibility."[89]

Yet despite its weaknesses, modernization has profoundly marked the interpretations offered by social historians. Social historians, for example, viewed the effect of immigration in terms of modernization. Immigrations forestalled modernization: They saw a "constant re-creation of traditionalism in American society through immigration." As Samuel P. Hays put it, "most—though by no means all—migrants to the United States from abroad prior to 1924 came from peasant backgrounds. With them they brought their traditional patterns of life, and by doing so they injected into American society a set of values more traditional than those already here."[90] Herbert G. Gutman struck the same note, although he shied away from the word traditional and instead used the even vaguer "pre-modern."[91] As many practitioners of social history have begun to realize, such implied dichotomies obscure more than they reveal. They relegate most immigrants, regardless of origin or migration pattern, to the status of "pre-modern" peasants, while conferring relative modernity on the native-born frontiersman and sod-buster. They confuse "tradition" and "modernity" with "past" and "present." They categorize as mutually exclusive forces that cannot be easily separated and that often cannot even be separated. As we now realize, traditional and modern elements found in all groups worked together to produce social change. Recently, Dino Cinel explained the movement back and forth across the Atlantic of Italians as an integral part of the immigrants' struggle toward a compromise between tradition and innovation.[92] In the labor movement, protesting workers who joined the Knights of Labor in the 1880s, labor historian Richard Oestreicher concluded, "were demanding a different version of modernity as much as they were protesting violations of customary rights. The sense of solidarity which moved them was based on recently learned ideals as well as traditional habits."[93]

Other tempting, but misleading sociological theories adhered to by the first wave of social historians are also being discarded. Built on the great dichotomies of nineteenth-century social thought, they seemed to offer a ready framework for social change. Most pervasive among them is the idea of the lost community embedded in Tönnies's metaphor of *Gemeinschaft* and *Gesellschaft*. The notion of the lost community is attractive on ideological grounds because it implies that the past was better than the present and fosters a discussion of the process that produces this deterioration. But this dichotomy obliges historians only to document the increasing complexity of the social milieu. Furthermore, it permits the entire concept of deterioration itself to go unexamined. As Thomas Bender recently asked in a perceptive analysis of a dozen contributions to different periods of American history—from Winthrop's Boston to Massachusetts's urbanization—how many times did the community disappear in America? He goes on to note that although "scholars differ in their approach to history and in their perspective on the American past, the work of all of them reveals one or another version of community breakdown. . . . If we are to get at the full complexity of the communal experience in American history, it is essential to avoid both the simple sequential model whereby gesellschaft replaces gemeinschaft and the model that associates gemeinschaft with one social group and gesellschaft with another. These two dimensions of social experience transcend social groupings."[94]

On other theoretical issues, social historians are moving away from the assumptions that marked early studies. Social historians have enabled us to recognize that societies are torn apart by people's conflicting loyalties and have exposed the conflicts hidden behind the rhetoric of harmony which marks American discourse. While not yet free of the oversimplifications inherent in the use of the dichotomy of consensus and conflict, social historians have retreated from the conception of conflict advanced by Progressive historians that they perceived to be too broad, and instead have concentrated on several measurable consequences of human activity. They thus imbued the notion of conflict with a factual basis that it did not have before. They have, for instance, revealed the religious, economic, and legal divisions that disturbed the ostensible "peaceable kingdoms" of seventeenth- and eighteenth-century New England.[95] They found that violence often appeared to be an assertion of community control over basic rights and commodities. Food riots, classic events of early modern Europe, found their way in eighteenth-century port towns where people also asserted their "right to be fed."[96] Despite the greater availability of wheat in North America, it was often in short supply because some merchants reserved large stocks of grain for sale on the international market in times of shortage. City dwellers were at times forced to compel these merchants to place these stocks in local markets like the Faneuil market in Boston.[97] Violence inspired by other instances of community identity involved resistance against impersonal forces of change embodied in big corporations, like the railroads, or against state intervention, or against both as in the case of Philadelphia weavers who prevented the laying of railroad tracks in their neighborhoods.[98] By precisely targeting conflict, social historians have been able to show how conflicts affected ethnic, racial, and social groups who were competing for jobs and space in a changing environment and to illuminate how conflict became embedded in institutions vital to the welfare of the communities, such as the voluntary fire companies.[99] Although the history of American violence is still in its infancy, historians have also explored the changing forms of violence, in particular the inverse relationship between rates of homicide and rates of suicide, and the collective efforts—as well as the biases which underlay these efforts—to create a police force to control violence.[100]

But despite the sophistication that has marked some recent studies of conflict, an analysis of the greatest conflict and major crisis of identity experienced by the United States in the nineteenth century, the Civil War, still eludes social historians. Interestingly enough, as Richard Hofstadter pointed out, consensus historians, fascinated as they were by political theory, had already lost sight of the "basic challenge" the Civil War put to the consensus idea.[101] Social historians, in turn, did not address the Civil War perhaps because of their overemphasis on structure. Many argued that the major social and economic changes underway before the Secession Crisis continued during and after Reconstruction, and consequently have downplayed the social impact of the Civil War. But clearly this crisis played its part in America's shift from sectional conflict to a new form of pluralism and in the realignment of major social, political, and bureaucratic forces that reshaped the nation.[102]

Only the social history of the conflict itself—the identification of the role social groups played in it—will permit us to balance the search for causes with the search for consequences and to assess the impact of the war on social change and on the formation of a more unified nation. Significant advances have been made on at least four fronts. First, we have a better understanding of the participants in the struggle. Fortunately, we need no longer refute the once prevalent characterization of abolitionists as mere fanatics, as Oscar Handlin had to in 1950: "Surely," Handlin wrote, "there must be a difference between being fanatics for freedom and fanatics for slavery."[103] By identifying the perpetrators of violence—sometimes "gentlemen of property and standing"[104]—as well as their motives historians have been able to delineate these groups more clearly. Further studies of abolitionists have helped explain why artisans played a major role in the political movement against slavery in the free states, despite persistent racism in their ranks. Artisanal traditions partly brought from Europe mixed with American republicanism to produce an objection to slavery based on "a man's right to the fruits of his own labor."[105] Second, political historians have given us a better understanding of the Southern struggle toward legitimacy and republicanism in the context of a collapsing second party system, without which it would be impossible to understand the Secession crisis.[106] Third, social historians have provided a rich description of social conditions in the South before and after the Civil War. Here our debt to Eugene D. Genovese is immense for having illuminated the relationship between the master and the slave, and for assessing the particular character of Southern society within the wider political economy of capitalism.[107] His work has also stimulated important discussions over the extent of Southern paternalism, and the influence of those few planters who were large slaveowners.[108] The structure of Southern society after the war is also the focus of new studies measuring the impact of emancipation on Southern economy and society at the local level.[109] Last, historians are now scrutinizing the class divisions which led to increasing desertions among poor whites and led to the Confederacy's efforts being categorized as a "rich man's war and poor man's fight."[110] Slowly, social, political, and economic historians are severing their reliance on sociological models and are looking instead at the many interrelated aspects of the crisis to demarcate these forces competing for separation and unification and to determine the true impact of the Civil War on American society.

In emerging from the overly sociological framework that marked the 1970s, social historians have also to address the issue of fragmentation. The very logic of social-historical inquiry combined with the forces which encourage academic specialization have led to overly narrow subfields. Interpretations of major events lack definitiveness because the evidence used reflects the specialized interest of the historian. For example, until a few years ago, the best study available of the Second Great Awakening was Whitney R. Cross's classic The Burned-Over District, published in 1950.[111] While it recounted in detail the new religious fervor that spread over New York state and the successful preaching of Charles Finney, the causes of the Great Awakening were not fully explained. Paul E. Johnson recently reanalyzed the problem and argued that the religious revival of the 1830s was a form of social control; religion was used by master craftsmen to maintain order and discipline among the growing number—and hence the less easily supervised mass—of unskilled workers.[112] While Johnson traced the records of masters and workers to identify those involved in the religious awakening, another social historian, Mary P. Ryan, focused her analysis on the evolving family rather than on the world of work.[113] She saw the decline of old forms of rural household economy, of its forms of promiscuous cohabitation, and argued that the new degree of independence women experienced led them to take an active role in church affairs, to convert "young" boarders, often apprentices in shops, and to contribute significantly to the upsurge of religion that enveloped New York State. Taken individually, Johnson's and Ryan's studies provide only a fragmentary explanation of the Second Great Awakening; when considered together, their disparate viewpoints are hard to reconcile. One would have wished that both historians had encompassed the whole range of possible forces in their analyses of the revival.

The overspecialization typified by many studies has been easily targeted for criticism by those historians rightly committed to a higher level of generalization. This criticism is not limited to "outsiders," intellectual or political historians. Some of the leading practitioners of social history have raised doubts about developments in their own field. The editors of the French journal *Annales*, for several generations at the forefront of social history, have recognized that many of the battles waged in the past to enlarge the field of history have been won,[114] and that it is time for a new synthesis—one, however, that they have as yet not well defined.

Further fragmentation has resulted from an unfortunate split between social and labor historians. Labor history had been very much influenced by social history. Like social history, it moved away from institutional history and biographies of labor leaders to a history of the rank and file. It expanded as social history did and indeed suffered the same problem. The current effort to reintegrate biography[115] or institutional history into labor history and to understand the complex relationship between capital, labor, and the state stems from the same recognized need to recover a degree of generalization in historical discourse.[116] Labor and social history separated, however, over the merits of quantification. Many labor historians continued to ignore quantitative innovations ranging from demographic to electoral analysis because, in their opinion, behavioral analysis is irrelevant to an analysis of class consciousness. The rejection of quantification by British historian E. P. Thompson and his American disciples like Herbert G. Gutman (the consequence of which I shall discuss later) may better be understood as a debate within Marxism rather than between Marxists and non-Marxists. Indeed, those Marxist historians influenced by quantitative thought consider statistics essential to their approach. Pierre Vilar, one of the most important theoreticians of this group, put it well: "However imperfect its interpretation may still be, it is the *objectification of the subjective through statistics* which alone makes materialist history possible—the history of *masses*, that is both of *massive, infrastructural facts*, and of those human 'masses' which theory has to 'penetrate' if it is to become an effective force."[117]

The malaise caused by fragmentation has been compounded by the tendency of some social historians, inspired by current social, political, or economic interests, to lose sight of the search for historical causes.[118] Historians, of course, are never detached from current concerns, but some social historians, identifying with the actors they chose to study—immigrants, workers, women—have been preoccupied with the problems of giving voice to these groups. Too often, they have been inspired by the desire to discover a shared experience with the past, by a need to right the social injustices of the past and to illumine the injustices of the present. In the process, however, they often forget to address major questions regarding social change and causality. These historians themselves, however, are often unclear about the ahistorical motivations which affect their work. Sam Bass Warner, for example, felt compelled in the 1970s to denounce an ever increasing racial segregation in American cities, but at the same time, seemingly without realizing the irony, he celebrated the suburban ideal as "what constitutes the good life in America."[119]

In view of this continuing fragmentation and the problems caused by the specialized application of social history, the call for unity voiced in several presidential addresses at the American Historical Association,[120] at major sessions at the Organization of American Historians,[121] and in statements made by other leading historians[122] must be taken seriously. But their call for a return to an integrative narrative should be qualified because it might force us backward rather than lead us to new explorations. Social history emerged twenty years ago with the promise of enlarging—not reducing or fragmenting—history. Major practitioners like Le Roy Ladurie talked at the time of total history (*l'histoire totale*).[123] It became quickly clear that writing a total history forced investigators to include all the dimensions of ecology, politics, and society—to redact the different levels of analysis from the material bases of life to what the French call the "troisième niveau" of the "mentalités."[124] But as historians proceeded in their investigations, they felt pressured to narrow the scope of their inquiry just as they, of necessity, borrowed theories from the social sciences. In order to reach verifiable answers to testable propositions, the questions were redefined and reduced, and many research projects indeed became specialized demographic history, or specialized electoral analysis, meeting the requirements, not of an integrated historical discourse but of the subfield's standards. The knowledge acquired in these works is nonetheless essential. It is the product of a major advance in the techniques of historical analysis. But, more importantly, abandoning this knowledge and, indeed, abandoning these specialized studies for generalization would be a serious mistake, because the accumulation of specialized knowledge is the first step in achieving an overview. The task, therefore, that faces the social historian is to operate on two levels of conceptualization, a research level that must be "operationalized" and clearly focused, no matter how broadly the research may be defined, and a synthesizing level, in which the investigator strives to arrange his findings in such a way that their theoretical import becomes apparent. Trying to adapt research activity to the requirements of creative synthesis alone, however, is simply to fail to realize that specialized inquiry—an integral part of our scientific paradigm—is here to stay.

The Synthesis of Social Change

A clear understanding of the benefits social historians gain by engaging the broader issues of social change rather than just history from the bottom up can be achieved by examining the treatment of assimilation in American history. Here it is most useful to examine the late nineteenth and early twentieth century, a period simultaneously marked by large-scale immigration that served to fill up the growing ranks of working-class America, and by the large and irreversible change imposed by a new corporate structure. The growth of corporate capitalism, with its ramifications for the growing American State, reshaped society. The ways historians have treated assimilation illustrates the tensions and debates that have marked social history in recent years and especially show how conflicting ideological viewpoints prevented social historians from fully integrating the immigrant's experience with those large-scale processes of change. The work on assimilation demonstrates the need to link immigration history to those fields of historical inquiry that concern themselves with industrialization, be it the study of mobility patterns, of class, or of business history. An examination of the study of assimilation and social change shows how some advances in our knowledge of immigrant and minority groups can be integrated into the larger pattern of historical knowledge.[125]

Assimilation and Recent Social History

The neglect of assimilation by the current generation of social historians is remarkable, because the concept was central to the school of immigration history that flourished in the 1940s and 1950s. Characteristically, Oscar Handlin subtitled his *Boston's Immigrants*, first published in 1941, *A Study in Acculturation*.[126] Finding the key to assimilation unified a generation of scholars who were intrigued that American social unity could have been achieved from such diversity and saw conflict as generated by "maladjustment." The abandonment of this position should be understood in the context, already mentioned, of the collapse of the consensus vision of American history. Those historians who came to the fore in the mid-1960s, however, found the American social system less cohesive than their predecessors. Disturbed that the general prosperity which they witnessed was not capable of extinguishing poverty, they assessed the receptivity of the social system and pointed to many obstacles to mobility that impaired people's chances in life. In the process, these social historians became concerned primarily with issues of social justice rather than with the analysis of complex processes like assimilation, which can be described as "the vision of an increasingly unified society," or like pluralism, the condition of "persistent separatedness."[127] The results of these mobility studies nonetheless led to uncertainty and dissension among historians. The belief that mobility is an illusion undermines the perception of America as a "land of opportunity," while the persistent presence of minorities is a reminder of the rigidities and inequalities of the social system. Conversely, the belief that mobility is possible, that with reasonable social and economic gains people modify their alien behavior while prejudice against them diminishes and society finds its balance, reaffirms the image of a unified America. Stephan Thernstrom, at different times, embraced both beliefs. At first, although underscoring a modest achievement and optimism among workers of Newburyport, he criticized the majority view that nineteenth-century economic, technological, and environmental change produced a wide array of opportunities which benefited the majority of individuals. He later revised his position. He concluded in *The Other Bostonians*, published in 1973, that opportunities for advancement significantly offset the disadvantages that immigrants may have suffered. The availability of these opportunities impeded "the formation of class-based protest movements that sought fundamental alterations in the economic system."[128] Michael B. Katz immediately offered the sobering, although overdrawn objection that mobility merely gave the illusion of advancement.[129] Interpretations of Horatio Alger's stories stressing not the reality of upward mobility but rather luck and the fear of downward mobility, also emphasized the instability of the nineteenth-century social system.[130] Taken as a whole, therefore, the debate over mobility has helped us reach a balanced view of social reality, free from the oversimplifications of the rags-to-riches myth.

This debate has had significant implications for the future of social history, because it provides a rationale for the study of social change. Mobility historians, perhaps unconsciously or unwittingly, reconciled the progressive and consensus schools of history. In their debates, they located the *potential* for conflict in the history of ethnic, social, and racial entities. But because minorities were continually integrated into the majority, this conflict rarely materialized. By positing an ever-present social mobility as the mechanism of social change, they suggested that the two older views of America were not contradictory. Mobility was at once an assimilation device and a safety valve. But this interpretation, although attractive, leaves basic questions unresolved. Did mobility operate effectively at all times and in all places? Is mobility a constant agent of social change? Is the dynamic of American society an endless repetition of the same unvarying transformation?

By the mid-1970s, the debate shifted but these questions were still unanswered. Hartmut Kaelble accurately remarked that mobility ceased to interest American social historians when it lost its radical appeal; that is, when studies revealed that ordinary Americans experienced periods of significant upward mobility more often than frustration in their careers.[131]

Under the impetus of the ethnic revival, social historians moved away both from assimilation and from mobility studies. Instead, they successfully demonstrated the strengths and adaptability of groups that had been traditionally considered alienated from society. They revealed that the immigrant derived dignity from his position in his own world and not through the efforts of the social worker, the friendly visitor, or the naturalizing judge. Social historians have taught us to view individuals as more than mere participants in social and cultural change. Recent interpretations have insisted that immigrants were instigators, not passive recipients, of change. Thus, all become actors, anonymous workers as well as industrial leaders. Wilson Benson, an immigrant to Hamilton, Ontario, moved back and forth from Ireland to Scotland before migrating to North America living in sixteen different places and working at thirty different occupations. As Michael Katz describes him, he does not emerge as a hero—this is too grand a word—but as someone who coped successfully with the real (and new) world.[132] Although his success was modest, his story is typical of that of thousands of other migrants. In the end, Benson surmounted his trials to gain stability and respectability. In my own work, I tried to convey a sense of the commitment and resourcefulness displayed by Polish homeowners in Detroit who mortgaged the cottages built with their own hands to finance the construction of community churches.[133] David Montgomery also demonstrated this point in his last book, which he devoted to the theme of "workers' control."[134] He views the search for autonomy on the shop floor as part of the larger effort individuals make to control their own destiny. Immigrants insisted on maintaining certain standards of respectability. As Kenneth L. Kusmer reports in his study of tramps in America, nineteenth-century tramps and bums—riding from one train yard to another—were more often native-white Americans than immigrants.[135] Seen in context of these findings, assimilation is somewhat of a misnomer, an abstraction that reflects only fitfully a pluralist and fluid reality. As a result, we are beginning to understand assimilation as a complex interactive process in which immigrants are not merely unwitting beneficiaries of a growing set of opportunities. Assimilation is not a shift from minority to majority status but a collaborative process that involves the whole population.

The debate spurred by the Moynihan report is another good example of a large consensus achieved by social historians on this issue.[136] A more thoughtful hypothesis about human nature and careful analysis of the historical record allowed social historians to argue persuasively that the black family showed more stability than Moynihan granted it, that there were more "two-parent" households than his report was willing to acknowledge, and that early death of males was as plausible an explanation as marital desertion for the large number of female heads of households. They concluded that, considering the extremely high level of often violent forms of discrimination, blacks were not trapped in a "tangle of pathology," but showed many signs of resilience and inventive adaptive strategies to a hostile environment. In these studies and others, social historians put an end to widely held assumptions about the voiceless, expressionless, non-achieving character of minorities.[137]

Building on the work of anthropologists, social historians have also shown that ethnicity may be a quality that owes as much to the circumstances of settlement in a new country as it does to the culture imported from the old country. Horace Kallen's classic observation—"an Irishman is always an Irishman, a Jew always a Jew. Irishman or Jew is born; citizen, lawyer, or church-member is made"[138]—does not apply if the culture of Jewish and Irish immigrants arose, at least in part, from distinctly American conditions. Anthropologists Sidney W. Mintz and Richard Price support this view in their discussion of slave societies. They argue, for example, that the notion of an "African heritage" is subject to qualification. They explain that "the series of institutions that emerged in any early slave population may be viewed as a sort of framework by means of which cultural materials could be employed, standardized, and transformed into new traditions. Thus whether we have in mind the way slaves fell in love and created familial groupings, or the way they gathered in regular groupings to worship, the content of such behavior can be viewed as an aspect of the social relationships." They assert that the historian's task is to delineate "the processes by which those cultural materials that were retained could contribute to the institution-building the slaves undertook to inform their condition with coherence, meaning and some measure of autonomy."[139] Building on such conceptualizations, social historians like John Bodnar, Josef J. Barton, and Tamara K. Hareven have shown the extent to which family and community relationships—what Bodnar calls "the cultural content of the immigrant working class"—were not "simply infused into American society from abroad but [were] largely generated by the complex process of industrialization itself."[140] The strategies that enabled partly imported subcultures to grow and live semi-autonomously in a new country helped cushion conflicts, perhaps as much as the relative openness of the social system.

Social historians not only have provided a new explanation of the origins of ethnicity, but also have documented the many faces of ethnicity in different places in the country, the variety of circumstances encountered by the groups, and the changes that affected their destiny. The proliferation of these findings makes it increasingly difficult to talk authoritatively about ethnicity without immediately adjusting one's statements for local conditions and circumstances. It seems clear, for example, that immigrants had more opportunities— and hence could develop a more complex social structure—in western cities where they were often the first settlers. The Germans in Milwaukee were able to participate in the construction of the city itself and in 1858, as Kathleen Conzen has discovered, they with some justice proclaimed: "Have we not cleared the forest, drained the swamp, filled the hollow, levelled the hill, dragged the first log to the first cabin, carried the first stone to the first courthouse, set the first type, peddled the first wares?"[141] Under these conditions, German autonomy flourished and intra-ethnic mobility was encouraged. But in Boston at the same time, where the Yankees restricted the Irish role in the community, the social order was more rigid.[142]

These various advances make it difficult to return to the assimilationist view inherent in the majority of the mobility studies, but there are also limitations inherent in the view stressed more recently of a pluralistic America, fragmented into an endless number of autonomous communities. A plausible solution to this dilemma is to view these two perspectives as complementary, not contradictory. Enclaves exist, but they are only temporary, and thus ethnicity is best understood within a framework of generations. This answer, while certainly containing much truth, is nonetheless incomplete. Social historians are not utilizing effectively their expanding knowledge of ethnicity to understand assimilation, a process that will continue to elude us unless we examine it in the context of social change. The current discussion of the relationship between class and ethnicity suggests that we may, in fact, be moving away from understanding assimilation.

Class and Ethnicity

The controversy over the relationship of class and ethnicity is a case in point. Historians engaged in the debate over the role of class in American society advocate the merits of several different approaches, all of which limit the analysis of assimilation because they treat ethnicity as a secondary category. No doubt, defining class is one of the most difficult conceptual tasks facing the social historian. Marx himself left the topic of social classes open in the unfinished chapter of the *Capital*.[143] British labor historian E. P. Thompson made a very strong case that the proper usage of class is as a historical category, as a social process which evolves over time. As he put it, "class is defined by men as they live their own history, and, in the end, this is its only definition." Or more explicitly, he remarked, "class eventuates as men and women live their productive relations, and as they experience their determinate situations, within the 'ensemble' of the social relations, with their inherited culture and expectations."[144]

But he derived from this position an assumption which, I believe, has sent American social historians—eager to counteract an all too conservative "positivistic sociological tradition" where class can be "reduced to literal measurement"—off on the wrong track. For Thompson, class is inseparable from the notion of class struggle.[145] He maintains that it is in discovering the need for class struggle that class consciousness emerges. His years of reflection on English history have led him to conclude that "the wrong assumption is that classes exist and that they struggle because they exist; instead they come into existence out of that struggle." As a consequence, Thompson denies any value to literal quantitative measurement (the number of wage earners; the number of white-collar workers, and so on). And he reserves the word "class" for a *Klasse für sich* (class for itself), discarding out of hand a *Klasse an sich* (class in itself).[146]

Other Marxist scholars, as I have noted, do recognize the value of measurement but set intriguing limits to its proper use. This is evident in a recent exchange of ideas in the *American Historical Review* between Edward Pessen, Michael B. Katz, and Robert Wiebe.[147] The issues discussed go beyond those found in most mobility studies, which usually entail only the recognition of inequality in a land of promise and an evaluation of its extent, and center on the more complex problem of devising categories for social analysis. Katz—supported here by Wiebe—takes the position that there should be a strong differentiation between stratification, which he considers essentially a descriptive tool, and class, a category he reserves for the two great groups of the nineteenth century, the business class and the working class. This conceptual distinction differentiates the means used to describe a social structure in fine detail—stratification—from those used to analyze its dynamic—class. Pessen, on the other hand, treats class and stratification interchangeably, and in the tradition of

American sociology, places people on a scale of measurement according to a "crystallization" model. "Class," then, loses its potential as a historical force, becoming a mere collection of attributes which reflects particular levels of inequality.

The emphasis that underlies this exchange, on class as a sociological *and* mental category understood only in the context of experience, is a welcome refinement of Thompson's "cultural marxism." Stratification (for lack of a better name), however, has the potential to play a more significant role than we would gather from this debate. It has deep roots and precise functions in history. Counting wage earners, white-collar employees, and others allows the historian to take stock of both changes in numbers and in categories.[148] The rapid change of the United States in the nineteenth century saw with it the emergence of classes that did not exist before. Struggle was only a part of their experience. To return to the well-known example of Lowell, the struggle that the women workers waged against their employers was an indicator of the disjunctive thought patterns that characterized their lives; they attempted to preserve their conscious Republican heritage and to react against their proletarianization. Consciousness, however, emerged from the totality of their experience, not just the struggle.[149] As classes emerge, or are redefined by shifting constituencies and large-scale processes of change, they take on new forms. Labeling the variety of groups, ranking and ordering them according to multiple criteria, is in effect to study a process of change. Seen in this light, stratification is not mere description, but more properly, the identification of new categories.

Like the study of class, the study of ethnicity recognizes the dynamics of change and also involves the classification of individuals into categories. And as in class, over time some groups grow while others decline. The sometimes parallel histories of social and ethnic groups have led some historians to confuse class and ethnicity and treat these two categories interchangeably. According to the assimilationist vision offered by these historians, the relationship between class and ethnicity is simple. Although traces of ethnicity may be long lasting, ethnicity is essentially a temporary attribute, best understood in the context of the first generation. Since most immigrants entered this country at the bottom of the social ladder, ethnicity is identified as a working-class attribute. The consequences of the types of assimilation sociologist Milton Gordon distinguished—cultural, then structural—become apparent as workers/immigrants (or their children) improve their lot and are integrated into the larger society.[150] In other models, assimilation also entails diffusion of the ethnic group into the wider religious group, a pattern diagnosed as the "triple melting pot" in the 1940s by sociologists who saw religion gaining ascendency over ethnicity as a category of importance in American life.[151] These sociologists based their findings on increasing intermarriage not simply between different ethnic groups but rather within larger religious communities.

In contrast to this smooth interweaving of class and ethnicity, other historians, especially labor historians have touched on the conflicting hierarchies of class and ethnicity, but only as part of another effort. Labor historians, for instance, have studied ethnic subcultures in American society as part of an attempt to shed light on more pressing issues such as the source of class consciousness (as it emerged from German radicalism, for example) as well as the reaction to capitalistic exploitation (ethnicity provided an alternative to unionism). Thus Herbert G. Gutman finds the roots of class consciousness in the ethnic commitments of the Gilded Age.[152] Other historians see a more complex, integral relationship between these conflicting hierarchies; for example, John B. Jentz points to ethnicity as the source of class consciousness in his study of Chicago bakers: "Without the [German] neighborhood base and the control of the neighborhood bread bakeries, there would have been no journeymen bakers' union in Chicago in the Gilded age." But as he also points out, building "a strong interethnic city-wide union movement," which would require "the baker unionists . . . move out of the neighborhood," was a "feat" only sporadically achieved.[153]

Generally, however, these historians find that ethnicity is only a secondary attribute. Some of them have even dismissed ethnicity in favor of class as the only valid analytical category. Dawley in his study of Lynn shoemakers, a book on the formation of the American working class, mentions the Irish only in passing.[154] And Katz, in his most recent analysis of the social structure of Hamilton and Buffalo, presents a series of equations to show that ethnicity played a minor role in people's attitudes.[155] After elaborately defining the concept of class, he argues that ethnicity had little relationship to economic characteristics such as wealth when "occupation and property are kept constant." Katz is able to make this case because he never gives ethnicity its due. He treats it as a simple, uniform reflection of nationality and religion, not as a complex attribute worthy of careful definition.

The tendency to downplay ethnicity can be found in urban history as well. Theodore Hershberg and his associates, in their study of nineteenth-century Philadelphia, formulated an ecological model, placing the primary emphasis, not on cultural areas as the Chicago sociologists did, but on work sites.[156] They argued that "industry," not ethnicity dominated the spatial arrangements of the nineteenth-century city. Hershberg's study, valuable as it is on many other points, does not conclusively disprove the theory that the nineteenth-century American city was divided primarily along ethnic lines. Ethnicity is not found to be an important factor because the project concentrated on the material parameters of urban life rather than on cultural indicators. Dismissing ethnicity or subserving it to class analysis therefore impairs the serious treatment of assimilation in much recent social history.

Another danger is to subsume ethnicity, not to class but to power. A society is of course governed by a set of power relations. Some make decisions, and others abide by those decisions. Some influence the outcome of debates, and others don't. The reticence social historians have displayed when addressing political issues—a reticence that stems from their disillusionment with narrative political history, as well as an emphasis on the material parameters of life derived from a generation of Marxist historians—has brought sharp and welcome criticism from all camps including Marxists. In *Fruits of Merchant Capital*, Eugene D. Genovese and Elizabeth Fox-Genovese have remarked, "as admirable as much of the recent social history has been and as valuable as much of the description of the life of the lower classes may eventually prove, the subject as a whole is steadily sinking into a neo-antiquarian swamp presided over by liberal ideologues, the burden of whose political argument, notwithstanding the usual pretense of not having a political argument, rests on an evasion of class confrontation."[157]

Indeed, the history of the immigrant working class has become increasingly cultural in direction. American social/labor historians, addressing the problems of labor history, have often concentrated on the "particular experiences" of working groups or even individuals, have stressed consciousness, culture, ways of life, without determining the connections between the groups studied and others.[158] These social or labor historians are interested in politics but only in a limited sense. Their "radically de-institutionalized understanding of politics, in which the possible sources of working-class oppositional impulse are displaced from the recognized media of political parties and trade unions into a variety of non-institutional settings, embracing behaviour previously regarded as 'non-political' —e.g. crime, street violence, riots, industrial sabotage, mental illness, etc." is representative of what Geoff Eley and Keith Nield call "the post-Thompson florescence of social history."[159] This movement away from the traditional sphere of politics was reinforced by a renewed influence of ethnography on history.

In a parallel but unrelated trend, political historians themselves contributed to the depoliticization of social history. The ethnocultural school of electoral analysis represents a movement away from traditional politics. To be sure, political historians analyzed the very stuff of politics—elections—but the outcome, they told us, was not determined by political parties, economic issues, or specific political battles, but by cultural and religious affiliations. Voting reflected a clash of religious values "between those dubbed pietists or evangelicals and those dubbed liturgicals and ritualists."[160] Thus, much of what is meant by "the new political history" is a shift away from class and economic issues as well as the political logic of elections toward a cultural explanation of American politics.

In view of these developments, the Genoveses are right to assert that social historians have certainly not provided a comprehensive account of the role various social, ethnic, or socioethnic groups have played in the distribution of power. But the Genoveses' call for the study of the political antagonisms between rulers and ruled ignores much recent work in social history and, again, does not leave room for the role of ethnicity in power relationships. Recent studies have refocused our attention on elites and especially the ways in which elite groups interact with other power groups in the society. We now understand, for example, the relationship between Harvard-educated Mugwumps and Irish machine politicians in Boston, as well as the conditions that enabled New York Swallowtails to influence the Tammany machine.[161] Social history concerns itself with politics in other ways. By showing that members of the lower classes were not passive recipients of social change but had "lives of their own," social historians also showed that these people assumed responsibility for political decisions and set the limits within which they could effectively operate. For example, Ira Katznelson, recently summarizing many studies in urban and immigration history, offered perceptive observations on the consequences of the separation between home and work in American society, a society in which political parties build networks of loyalties in ethnic neighborhoods while labor unions perform the same task in the work place. "What needs to be explained," Katznelson notes, "is not the absence of class in American politics but its limitation to the arena of work."[162]

The lessons to be gained from the debate over ethnicity, class, and power are clear. Different schools interpret the past according to their theoretical perspectives and weigh factors accordingly. Social theory has an inescapable influence on historical interpretation as do political commitments. But a broad understanding of assimilation demands that we do not let social theory or political commitments exclusively guide our understanding of the balance of class, ethnicity, and power. Social theory is only a tool to understand social change and should not become a blinder. Yet, paradoxically, after stressing the cultural independance of minorities, social historians too often have downplayed the role of ethnicity in American life. I would argue that we can more effectively penetrate the process of assimilation in American society by defining those large-scale factors that cut across lines of ethnic, economic, or political loyalty to influence people's lives. For assimilation is not a constant but varies according to the interplay of outside conditions.

Toward Social Change

I suggested elsewhere, looking only at the history of Detroit from 1880 to 1920, that assimilation was affected by a shift from a dual to a single opportunity structure, a shift partly due to industrialization and the growth of corporate capitalism, and most visible around World War I.[163] A discussion of this shift can help us better understand the intricate interaction of social change with other historical processes such as assimilation and can also provide an illustration of the complex relationship between class, ethnicity, and power. The point is not to apply findings for one area to America as a whole but to search for a more complete assessment of social change.

Most nineteenth-century ethnic communities were sufficiently large and autonomous to provide their members with an alternative opportunity structure independent of the cities' main economic networks dominated by native white Americans. This alternative channel—reinforced by intra-ethnic family and associational life—was characteristic of the nineteenth century; was visible in the labor markets, in the organization of the neighborhoods, and in the acquisition of property, and was conducive to a form of ethnic semiautonomy. Ethnic enclaves existed in the midst of the larger society and strong intra-ethnic group channels for upward economic mobility were established within them.

My emphasis on ethnic entrepeneurship is hardly new; it is documented in classic immigrant novels, in the immigrant press, and in numerous public documents on the organization of work; other historians have studied the workings of ethnic businesses.[164] What is striking, however, is that ethnic enclaves were freer to grow in the midst of the larger society in the nineteenth century than in the twentieth. As a result, nineteenth-century immigrants encountered a greater variety of opportunities than their twentieth-century counterparts. With many skills, the Germans could work for large industrial concerns or could establish themselves as independent craftsmen, often employing a few men of their own. In many cities, ethnic groups dominated particular industries, not only as general laborers but also as manufacturers and wholesalers. Those members of the immigrant communities who were employed in white-collar occupations did not always have to enter the Anglo-Saxon world. Their rise could be contained within a social system based on complex intergroup relationships. Two qualifications are in order here. First, a pattern of ethnic semiautonomy does not imply consensus or the absence of conflict within communities. Second, the dual opportunity structure, which operated in many nineteenth-century cities, was only typical of large ethnic enclaves. And even within these large groups, those few who climbed to the top could elect not to remain within the group. The important point, however, is that they could elect to do so. In addition, communities often created channels for the political expression of mobility and independence.[165] In short, the ambiguities of a dual opportunity structure were more influential than either the assimilationist or autonomous tendencies that it encompassed. That two structures of daily life coexisted was more important than the existence of any one of them.

This duality partly disappeared as ethnic autonomy receded. By World War I, ethnicity was well under way to becoming a working class attribute. To put it differently, sociologists have described many times the ways in which middle class members of an ethnic group left the area of first settlement, but they have never said (to my knowledge) that this process became general sometime between 1910 and 1925. The transition from one sociospatial system, the ethnic neighborhood, to another, the working-class neighborhood organized around big factories, is indicative of the transformation that marked the American metropolis during this period. This significant change can aid us in understanding the assimilation pressures of modern America. America in 1910 or 1920 was very different from the land that welcomed the old immigrants in 1850. The difficulty that the new immigrant experienced was not simply a matter of geographic origin or literacy, but reflected the new, more restrictive environment they encountered. A poverty-stricken German of the 1850s was not better educated than a poverty-striken Hungarian of the 1920s. But he had access to economic opportunities within his own group. By the time an Italian or Slav joined his fellow immigrants to work for Carnegie or Ford, many such opportunities had disappeared.

In Detroit, in Pittsburgh, and in almost every major city that has been studied, a cohesive Anglo-Saxon elite gained control of the emerging corporate giants in the early twentieth century.[166] The changing scale of activities and the different forms of control exercised by this proprietary group greatly affected the relationship between class and ethnicity. Many avenues of mobility previously available within the semiautonomous ethnic group were now controlled by owners outside the group. The resulting homogenization of American society is a process still little understood despite its consequences for many social and psychological traits in modern American life.

To be sure, immigrants were not all neatly channeled within a single opportunity structure. Some industries remained in control of ethnic groups. But the immigrant industrialist felt greater pressures to assimilate than ever before. The creation of the movie industry in Los Angeles, which was almost entirely controlled by Jews of modest background, is an interesting case of the assimilation of ethnic entrepreneurs. Lary May argues that the element of "Yiddish folk culture," which encouraged "celebrations," including "music, singing, dancing, and . . . drinking"; which offered a conception of women as "sexual beings," despite a taboo on premarital sex; and which promoted in-

dulgence and "extravagance" in contrast to Protestant belief in fru-
gality, allowed them to realize the immense possibilities of the new
industry. The first movie magnates initially relied primarily on intra-
ethnic forms of borrowing, as ethnic financiers were more willing
to take the risk than others. These men soon broke away, however,
from their ethnic support, because success in the mass market required secularization. Many married gentiles and "each of these producers made films and statements filled with patriotism."[167] Although
their perspective as members of a minority enabled them to diagnose
the needs of a majority, they were forced to move outside the ethnic
community, away from the first neighborhood nickelodeons where
they started, in order to secure their gains.

The experience of these businessmen implies a significant change
in the relationship between class and ethnicity, a change brought
about by the transformations of social relations, by a changing
economy, and by the growing uniformity of American culture. In the
nineteenth century, the imbrication of class and ethnicity was less
complete. It was marked by a diversity of experiences and a greater
degree of autonomy for members of ethnic groups than in the twentieth when channels of upward mobility are more closely, more obviously related to a single opportunity structure.[168]

This interpretation of the transformation of American society during the period around World War I—stressing a shift from dual to
single opportunity structures—incorporates some of the divergent
views of assimilationists and pluralists but still it is incomplete. It fails
to account for all the participants of the organizational and social
change which occurred during these years, and as such reflects a
deficiency in the practice of social history. Most social historians have
looked at the social scene "from the bottom up" and "from the top
down," but not, if I may say, "out from the middle." In our hurry to
enshrine workers as heroes and to condemn robber barons as vil-
lains, we social historians have forgotten the powerful influences of
the middle classes. Yet the key to immigrant assimilation in this period might very well lie, not only in abstract changes imposed from
industrialists' offices or in the many persisting forms of ethnic autonomy, but in the re-formation of what we now call the middle
class.

Yet an examination which focuses on the activities of those filling the middle range of the social structure rather than of those occu-
pying extreme positions would give us a different view of assimila-

tion. At present there is a gap between the study of industrial elites, which we begin to know well, and the study of the working class. A few recent books have described middle-class attitudes in Jacksonian America, engendering much controversy over the meaning of the phrase middle class for this early period.[169] But there is almost nothing written about the middle class in the industrialization period. Michael B. Katz and his collaborators make clear that their two-class model applies to "the mid-nineteenth century, prior to the feminization of office work, the elaboration of very many organizational bureaucracies, or the widespread existence of department stores and supermarkets." Katz describes the social structure of the mid-nineteenth century at a unique and short-lived turning point, after artisans had lost their autonomy and before white-collar workers had grown in numbers. For the later period, he concedes the difficulty of "interpreting the class position of the great army of white-collar workers and salaried professionals who first appear in the late nineteenth century. . . . Here, bureaucracy takes the place of the factory as the paradigmatic form of organization."[170] Until recently, historians could only work backward from sociological classics on white-collar work written in the 1950s and 1960s, when the big corporation had already come of age. Other studies focusing on middle-class attitudes during the industrialization period were severely criticized. For instance, before the rise of social history, Robert H. Wiebe suggested that the severe social crisis of the 1880s and 1890s stemmed from the breakdown of local and regional systems of power and status, and the ambition of the middle class to fulfill its destiny through bureaucratic means. As he put it, "men and women [were] building a new structure of loyalties to replace the decaying system of nineteenth-century communities."[171] At the time, Wiebe's hypothesis was attacked on the grounds that a highly mobile society could not be fragmented into isolated units in the first place. This criticism was misdirected. We have developed a more sophisticated grasp of the mechanisms of population movements, and we know now that a highly mobile society can also maintain rigid structures. Despite this new awareness, Wiebe's main point has remained unverified in social history. After two decades of research mostly devoted to the working class, we still know virtually nothing on how the new bureaucratic order affected middle-class life. Because we thought we knew so much about a middle-class ideology (through sermons, speeches at business banquets, marriage literature, educational pamphlets, and so on), we have neglected to ask whether the new tempo of life affected the lives and the ideology of the middle class, and then spread to other segments of society.

Merely filling a gap in our current knowledge of social history will not of itself help us to understand assimilation. We must identify subgroups within the middle class most clearly associated with social change and determine their influence on other groups. Hopefully, such a study of linkages among members of the society will produce a new vision of assimilation, a vision free both from the assumption of internal consent and self-willed changes and from the ideas of coercion and manipulation. Some historians have already charted the way. We know that many members of the middle class transcended their loyalty to their employers to create independent professional organizations, to define new codes of life, new methods of conduct, and new rules of safety. Intellectual historians talk about a "matrix of specialization" taking place in the world of knowledge in the late nineteenth century.[172] This matrix extended beyond universities to all levels of production and distribution of goods, services, and even to the organization of hobbies. As Neil Harris put it, "if chemists, psychologists, and historians had their journals, so did retail merchants, hardware manufacturers, and advertising agents. . . . Increasing organization was a response to new levels of size as well as to advances in technology and management methods. An outpouring of catalogues, directories, and compilations of standards formed a reference literature as crucial and complex in its own right as the text of the new academic and professional disciplines."[173] The challenge to social history is to move beyond these interesting generalizations to uncover the process of social change behind them.

The work of Alfred D. Chandler, Jr., the historian of business, has also provided a basis for an extensive study of the middle class. Chandler rendered a great service to social history when he redirected business history, caught in subjective, sterile disputes which pitted "wealth" vs. "commonwealth," to issues of structure.[174] In the broad organizational revolution which he describes, big business not only took over the production of most goods and services and changed the tempo of life, it also provided most public services, including all forms of communications. The immense work of carrying out this innovative task fell to a new army of salaried personnel who played a major role in influencing policies not only within their own companies but also within professional organizations and the growing administrative state.[175] Altogether, a variegated group of white-collar workers—including executives, middle-level managers, sales personnel, clerical workers of both sexes, and federal employees—played an equally important role in promoting a new work culture and with it, social change. This group grew in number very rapidly. In 1903 Pierre du Pont, as treasurer of Du Pont, had twenty-five employees working under him; less than a year later, after reorganizing the company, his own office in Wilmington supervised over 200 employees. Most corporations followed the same pattern of growth. Everywhere in the country, salesmen held meetings and received directives from headquarters, while only a few years earlier, products were distributed by independent agents. At Du Pont, salesmen were told: "Don't forget you are a part of the organization just as much as the bass drum is a part of the orchestra—likewise, don't forget that bass drum solos are rather monotonous."[176] The sales meetings ended with patriotic songs and promotional couplets.

Chandler documented part of the organizational change underway. If he is correct, the new middle-class managers were important agents of social change during the industrialization process. These people carried an organizational revolution into many sectors of society several decades before "Taylorism" and scientific management formally imposed it on millions of workers. Our understanding of assimilation, therefore, should include a close study of this group of people, its relationship in the living environment to other segments of society, and its role in the creation of overlapping local and national bureaucracies. We need now to identify those segments of the middle class most clearly involved in social change. In my view, these segments of a new middle class embodied new values far removed from both the exclusiveness of the upper class and the autonomous tendencies of the immigrant working classes. The challenge, then, is to tell the story of how they undertook the job of industrializing the land and possibly homogenized it in the process. We need to discover how the emergence of a new class of managers translated into life styles (methods of counting, of buying, of building, of educating, and so on) that became America's dominant cultural form during this period and that contributed to blend the different segments of American society. Although industrialization obviously created enormous social tensions that often erupted in open class conflicts, organizational synthesis imposed a new, more homogeneous social order, capable of integrating people of various ethnic origins.

In contrast to Tönnies's vision of growing complexity, I would argue that America experienced a relative simplification of the social system during the industrialization period. As the society's economy and communication channels were growing more complex, there was a need for a simplification of mobility channels, and a need for a practical consensus. This need was urgently felt by middle-class Americans who, though threatened by pluralism, promoted new ways of working, living, and interacting with one another.

I developed this example only to stress that our understanding of assimilation—like that of other historical questions—needs to parallel that of large-scale social transformations. Assimilation is an important concept that can be understood only within the changing context in which it takes place. By locating the various agents of change in the social structure, by seeing how they might act as creators, implementers, and receivers of innovations, by paying greater attention to the process of class formation, in other words by studying social change, we can better understand the meanings of cultural transfers experienced by immigrants.

Conclusion

The continued fertility of social history depends on our ability to cultivate its achievements—defining the interplay of structural conditions within the immediate context of everyday life—while avoiding the American tendency to view history in terms of ideal types. At this point, we know a great deal about large structures that have characterized American society at different times in its history. We need now to focus on the change from one structure to the next and continue our investigation of the relationship between social change and the nature of national character. It is time to go beyond mere structural description.

Social history can successfully link the major changes that interest historians to the experiences of ordinary people. It can fuse in one integrated historical discourse the experiences of individual peoples with the broad social processes that characterize their age. But to do so, it must achieve a new level of analysis. It must abandon its single-minded emphasis on the study of discrete historical moments for the study of change through an extended series of moments. It must transcend the monographic framework suitable for study of small isolated locales to engage in more comprehensive, wider ranging studies. It can no longer be satisfied with partially drawn conclusions, leaving the task of full explanation to future investigators. Twenty years ago, social historians explicitly sought to replace the all encompassing explanations of the progressive and consensus schools of history by focusing on a great variety of concrete situations. In fact, they have complicated but not invalidated these large explanatory frameworks. Social history must now itself embrace an even more complex perspective. In its infancy, statements such as "people were highly mobile in the nineteenth century, therefore isolated communities did not exist" or "the majority of blacks lived in two-parent, therefore stable, households" seemed promising. They still contain an element of truth, but they seem now naive and unsatisfactory because they fail to account for the multitude of trends which shaped these patterns.

Furthermore, because analytical knowledge that social historians have uncovered is bound to specific historical periods, it does not conform to contemporary social theory. Social historians should now begin to free themselves from the theories of the social scientists and use the vast accumulation of historical social description to generate their own theories. Greater independence from social science will also make it easier for social historians to integrate their findings with those of political and economic historians and build sound explanatory frameworks. It will also permit the links between intellectual and social trends to be more readily perceived. Understanding how ideas contribute to the course of history is as crucial as understanding how history shapes ideas. I do not mean that social history should come to dominate all of history, imperialistically integrating the other fields into its own omniverous investigations. I mean simply that findings of social historians can and should have a much more obvious impact, easily understood in the context of changes studied in other sections of the history profession.

Twenty years ago, social history was absorbed by methodological issues and the discovery of uncharted territories. While it would be absurd to pretend that all methodological problems have been resolved and that we have reached the limits of history's absorption of new "objects" of investigation, it is fair to say that social historians have constructed an impressive arsenal of techniques and generated a great deal of knowledge. They are therefore in a position, never before achieved, to take full advantage of the possibilities inherent in their theories. By adapting other modes of historical analysis to social history and by practicing an integrated social history, one which emphasizes the full range of social change and changing consciousness rather than history from the bottom up, historians will develop a coherent explanation of social change, and will rewrite American history once again. How America achieved a balance of often conflicting social processes at any one point of its history is a major challenge for social history, a challenge too important to be reduced to the construction of a single formula of national character.

NOTES

1. See John Higham's new epilogue in *History: Professional Scholarship in America*, rev. ed. (Baltimore: Johns Hopkins University Press, 1983), 239–40; Elizabeth Fox-Genovese and Eugene D. Genovese, *Fruits of Merchant Capital: Slavery and Bourgeois Property in the Rise and Expansion of Capitalism* (New York: Oxford University Press, 1983), 179–212; Lawrence Stone, "The Revival of Narrative: Reflexions on a New Old History," *Past and Present*, no. 85 (November 1979): 3–24.

2. See André Burguière, ed., *Dictionnaire des sciences historiques* (Paris: Presses Universitaires de France, forthcoming).

3. Rush Welter, *The Mind of America, 1820–1860* (New York: Columbia University Press, 1975), 8.

4. Paul E. Johnson, *A Shopkeeper's Millennium: Society and Revivals in Rochester, New York, 1815–1837* (New York: Hill & Wang, 1978), 5, 9; Paul Boyer, *Urban Masses and Moral Order in America, 1820–1920* (Cambridge, Mass.: Harvard University Press, 1978), 12–23.

5. On this theme, see Dorothy Ross, "The Liberal Tradition Revisited and the Republican Tradition Addressed" in *New Directions in American Intellectual History*, ed. Paul K. Conkin and John Higham (Baltimore: Johns Hopkins University Press, 1979), 121–25, and more recently her essay, "Historical Consciousness in Nineteenth-Century America," *American Historical Review* 85 (October 1984): 909–28; see also John L. Thomas, *Alternative America: Henry George, Edward Bellamy, Henry Demarest Lloyd and the Adversary Tradition* (Cambridge, Mass.: Harvard University Press, 1983), 4.

6. Michael Kammen, *People of Paradox: An Inquiry Concerning the Origins of American Civilization* (New York: Alfred A. Knopf, 1972), 107; see also Karl Deutsch, *Nationalism and Social Communication* (Cambridge, Mass.: MIT Press, 1966); Edward Shils, *Center and Periphery: Essays in Macrosociology* (Chicago: University of Chicago Press, 1975).

7. Ernst Breisach, *Historiography: Ancient, Medieval, and Modern* (Chicago: University of Chicago Press, 1983), 366–67, 387; progressive history was itself a reaction against the conservative Germanic and Imperial schools. On the importance of the Beardian synthesis and its relevance for the current debate on history, see Thomas Bender, "In Retrospect, The New History—Then and Now: Charles A. Beard and Mary R. Beard, *The Rise of American Civilization*," *Reviews in American History* 12 (December 1984): 612–22.

8. See John Higham's review of Daniel J. Boorstin's book *The Genius of American Politics* in "The Cult of the 'American Consensus': Homogenizing Our History," *Commentary* 27 (February 1959): 95–99.

9. Seymour Martin Lipset, *The First New Nation: The United States in Historical and Comparative Perspective* (Garden City, N.Y.: Anchor Books, 1967); David Riesman, in collaboration with Reuel Denney and Nathan Glazer, *The Lonely Crowd: A Study of the Changing American Character* (New Haven: Yale University Press, 1950); Philip Gleason, "Identifying Identity: A Semantic History," *Journal of American History* 69 (March 1983): 923–26. The connection between prosperity and character is best established in David M. Potter, *People of Plenty: Economic Abundance and the American Character* (Chicago: University of Chicago Press, 1954).

10. For a thoughful discussion of the relationship between ideology and reality in a different context, see the essay by Jacques Julliard, "Sur un fascisme imaginaire: à propos d'un livre de Zeev Sternhell," *Annales: Economies, sociétés, civilisations* 39 (Juillet–Août 1984): 849–61.

11. Higham, new epilogue in *History*, 237–39.

12. For example, Alan Dawley, *Class and Community: The Industrial Revolution in Lynn* (Cambridge, Mass.: Harvard University Press, 1976).

13. See Daniel Bell, *The End of Ideology* (Glencoe, Ill.: Free Press, 1960).

14. John G. A. Pocock, *The Machiavellian Moment: Florentine Political Thought and the Atlantic Republican Tradition* (Princeton: Princeton University Press, 1975); see also Bernard Bailyn, *The Ideological Origins of the American Revolution* (Cambridge, Mass.: Harvard University Press, 1967), 85; Gordon S. Wood, *The Creation of the American Republic* (Chapel Hill: University of North Carolina Press, 1969). On Pocock, see Ross, "The Liberal Tradition Revisited."

15. See Samuel P. Hays, *American Political History as Social Analysis* (Knoxville: University of Tennessee Press, 1980), and the "comment and controversy" between Paul F. Bourke and Donald A. DeBats, "On Restoring Politics to Political History," J. Morgan Kousser, "Are Political Acts Unnatural?" and Hays, "Society and Politics: Politics and Society," *The Journal of Interdisciplinary History* 15 (Winter 1985): 459–99.

16. As in Eric R. Wolf, *Europe and the People Without History* (Berkeley: University of California Press, 1982).

17. A point well recognized by Potter, but not by Kammen; similar observations to mine can be found in Geoff Eley, "Nationalism and Social History" in *Social History* 6 (January 1981): 83–107.

18. Arthur Maier Schlesinger, *The Rise of the City, 1878–1898* (New York: Macmillan, 1933). And see Robert D. Cross's biographical notice on Arthur Maier Schlesinger in the *Dictionary of American Biography*, supp. 7 (New York: Charles Scribner's Sons, 1981), 675–77.

19. Frank Lawrence Owsley, *Plain Folk of the Old South* (Baton Rouge: Louisiana State University Press, 1949); Merle Eugene Curti, *The Making of an American Community: A Case Study of Democracy in a Frontier Country* (Stanford: Stanford University Press, 1959).

20. A point well made by Peter Friedlander, *The Emergence of a UAW Local, 1936–1939: A Study in Class and Culture* (Pittsburgh: University of Pittsburgh Press, 1975), xiii–xviii.

21. On this, see François Furet, "Beyond the Annales," *Journal of Modern History* 55 (September 1983): 389–410.

22. Jacques Julliard, "Political History in the 1980s: Reflections on its Present and Future," in *The New History: The 1980s and Beyond*, Studies in Interdisciplinary History, ed. Theodore K. Rabb and Robert I. Rotberg (Princeton: Princeton University Press, 1982), 29–44.

23. Charles Victor Langlois and Charles Seignobos, *Introductions aux études historiques* (Paris: Hachette, 1897); trans. as *Introduction to the Study of History* (New York: Henry Holt & Co., 1906).

24. Jacques Revel, "Histoire et sciences sociales: les paradigmes des Annales," *Annales: Economies, sociétés, civilisations* 34 (Novembre–Décembre 1979): 1371.

25. Emmanuel Le Roy Ladurie, *Le territoire de l'historien* (Paris: Gallimard, 1973), 14;

trans. as *The Territory of the Historian* (Chicago: University of Chicago Press, 1979).

26. Robert William Fogel and G. R. Elton, *Which Road to the Past: Two Views of History* (New Haven: Yale University Press, 1983), 25–26.

27. Alan McFarlane, Sarah Harrison, and Charles Jardine, *Reconstructing Historical Communities* (Cambridge: Cambridge University Press, 1977); see also Ian Winchester, "On Referring to Ordinary Historical Persons" and "A Brief Survey of the Algorithmic, Mathematical and Philosophical Literature Relevant to Historical Record Linkage" in *Identifying People in the Past*, ed. E. A. Wrigley (London: Arnold, 1973), 17–40, 128–30.

28. Marc Bloch, *Apologie pour l'histoire, ou métier d'historien* (Paris: Armand Colin, 1952), 4; trans. as *The Historian's Craft* (New York: Alfred A. Knopf, 1963), 26.

29. See Gordon Wood, "Star-Spangled History" (a review of Robert Middlekauff's *The Glorious Cause*), *New York Review of Books* 29 (August 12, 1982): 4–9.

30. On the influence of structuralism on history, see François Furet, "Les intellectuels français et le structuralisme" in *L'atelier de l'histoire* (Paris: Flammarion, 1982), 37–52; trans. as *In the Workshop of History* (Chicago: University of Chigago Press, 1984).

31. On urbanization, see also the pioneering work of Adna Ferrin Weber, *The Growth of Cities in the Nineteenth Century: A Study in Statistics* (New York: Macmillan, 1899).

32. William H. McNeill and Ruth S. Adams, eds., *Human Migration: Patterns and Policies* (Bloomington: Indiana University Press, 1978).

33. Wolf, *People Without History*, 355; see also Michael B. Katz, *The People of Hamilton, Canada West: Family and Class in a Mid-Nineteenth Century City* (Cambridge, Mass.: Harvard University Press, 1975); Gabriel Kolko, *Main Currents in Modern American History* (New York: Harper & Row, 1976), 68.

34. Daniel Scott Smith, "Migration of Colonial Militiamen: A Comparative Note," *Social Science History* 7 (Fall 1983): 475–79.

35. Charles Tilly, "Migration in Modern European History" in *Human Migration*, ed. McNeill and Adams, 48–72.

36. W. E. B. Du Bois, *The Philadelphia Negro* (Philadelphia: Publications of the University of Pennsylvania, 1899).

37. Elizabeth Hefkin Pleck, *Black Migration and Poverty: Boston 1865–1900* (New York: Academic Press, 1979), 64–67.

38. Tamara K. Hareven, *Family Time and Industrial Time: The Relationship Between Family and Work in a New England Industrial Community* (Cambridge: Cambridge University Press, 1982); for differences in migration patterns between Italians and Slovaks, see Josef J. Barton, *Peasants and Strangers: Italians, Rumanians and Slovaks in an American City, 1890–1950* (Cambridge, Mass.: Harvard University Press, 1975).

39. Stephan Thernstrom, *The Other Bostonians: Poverty and Progress in the American Metropolis, 1880–1970* (Cambridge, Mass.: Harvard University Press, 1973), 43–45.

40. Tilly, "Migration"; he also considers a fourth category, "Local migration [shifting] an individual or a household within a geographically contiguous market."

41. Lynn H. Lees and John Modell, "The Irish Countrymen Urbanized: A Comparative Perspective on the Famine Migration," *Journal of Urban History* 3 (August 1977): 391–407; this process of migration, bypassing (nonexisting) small towns in

Ireland, reverses the classic terms set by Brinley Thomas in *Migration and Economic Growth: A Study of Great Britain and the Atlantic Economy* (Cambridge: Cambridge University Press, 1954).

42. Orlando Patterson, "Migration in Caribbean Societies: Socioeconomic and Symbolic Resource," in *Human Migration*, ed. McNeill and Adams, 106–45; Dino Cinel, *From Italy to San Francisco: The Immigrant Experience* (Stanford: Stanford University Press, 1982); Kristian Hvidt, *Flight to America: The Social Background of 300,000 Danish Emigrants* (New York: Academic Press, 1975).

43. Louis R. Harlan, *Booker T. Washington: The Making of a Black Leader, 1856–1901* (New York: Oxford University Press, 1972); idem., *Booker T. Washington: The Wizard of Tuskegee, 1901–1915* (New York: Oxford University Press, 1983), 290–91.

44. Olivier Zunz, *The Changing Face of Inequality: Urbanization, Industrial Development, and Immigrants in Detroit, 1880–1920* (Chicago: University of Chicago Press, 1982), 320.

45. Graham Romeyn Taylor, *Satellite Cities* (New York, 1915; reprint ed., New York: Arno Press, 1970).

46. Six volumes under the editorship of Paul Underwood Kellogg: Elizabeth Beardsley Butler, *Women and the Trades, Pittsburgh, 1907–1908* (New York: Charities Publication Committee, 1909); Crystal Eastman, *Work Accidents and the Law* (New York: Charities Publication Committee, 1910); Margaret F. Byington, *Homestead: The Households of a Mill Town* (New York: Charities Publication Committee, 1910); John A. Fitch, *The Steel Workers* (New York: Charities Publication Committee, 1911); Paul Underwood Kellogg, ed., *The Pittsburgh District Civic Frontage* (New York: Survey Associates, 1914); Paul Underwood Kellogg, *Wage-Earning Pittsburgh* (New York: Charities Publication Committee, 1909–1914).

47. James Leiby, *Carroll Wright and Labor Reform* (Cambridge, Mass.: Harvard University Press, 1960); Lawrence A. Fuchs, "Immigration Reform in 1911 and 1981: The Role of Select Commissions," *Journal of American Ethnic History* 3 (Fall 1983): 58–85.

48. Samuel P. Hays, *The Response to Industrialism, 1885–1914* (Chicago: University of Chicago Press, 1957).

49. Thomas Bender, *Toward an Urban Vision: Ideas and Institutions in Nineteenth-Century America* (Lexington: University Press of Kentucky, 1975), 71–128.

50. Thomas Dublin, *Women at Work: The Transformation of Work and Community in Lowell, Massachusetts, 1826–1860* (New York: Columbia University Press, 1979).

51. Dawley, *Class and Community*, 70; for a recent and more sophisticated analysis of the impact of voting rights on politics and class consciousness, see Amy Bridges, *A City in the Republic: Antebellum New York and the Origins of Machine Politics* (Cambridge: Cambridge University Press, 1984).

52. Anthony F. C. Wallace, *Rockdale: The Growth of an American Village in the Early Industrial Revolution* (New York: Alfred A. Knopf, 1978), 172.

53. Jonathan Prude, *The Coming of the Industrial Order: Town and Factory Life in Rural Massachusetts, 1810–1860* (Cambridge: Cambridge University Press, 1983), 73–76.

54. Thomas Dublin, "Women's Work and the Family Economy: Textiles and Palm Leaf Hatmaking in New England, 1830–1850," *The Tocqueville Review* 5 (Fall-Winter 1983): 313; Franklin Mendels, "Proto-Industrialization: The First Phase of the Industrial Process," *Journal of Economic History* 32 (1972): 244–61.

55. Bruce Laurie and Mark Schmitz, "Manufacture and Productivity: The Making of an Industrial Base, Philadelphia, 1850–1880" in *Philadelphia: Work, Space, Family and Group Experience in the Nineteenth Century*, ed. Theodore Hershberg (New York: Oxford University Press, 1981), 43–88.

56. Philip Scranton, *Proprietary Capitalism: The Textile Manufacture at Philadelphia, 1800–1885* (Cambridge: Cambridge University Press, 1983), 139–61, 178–95.

57. Christine Stansell, "The Origin of the Sweatshop: Women and Early Industrialization in New York City" in *Working-Class America: Essays on Labor, Community, and American Society*, ed. Michael H. Frisch and Daniel J. Walkowitz (Urbana: University of Illinois Press, 1983), 94.

58. For Pittsburgh, see John Bodnar, Roger Simon, and Michel P. Weber, *Lives of Their Own: Blacks, Italians, and Poles in Pittsburgh, 1900–1960* (Urbana: University of Illinois Press, 1982); for Detroit, Zunz, *Changing Face*; for Amoskeag, Hareven, *Family Time*; for recent trends in labor history, see Herbert G. Gutman, *Work, Culture and Society in Industrializing America: Essays in American Working-Class and Social History* (New York: Alfred A. Knopf, 1976); David Montgomery, *Workers' Control in America: Studies in the History of Work, Technology, and Labor Struggles* (Cambridge: Cambridge University Press, 1979); Richard Oestreicher, *Solidarity and Fragmentation: Working People and Class Consciousness in Detroit, 1875–1900* (Urbana: University of Illinois Press, forthcoming); Hartmut Keil and John B. Jentz, eds., *German Workers in Industrial Chicago, 1850–1910: A Comparative Perspective* (DeKalb: Northern Illinois University Press, 1983); and Ronald W. Schatz, "Labor Historians, Labor Economics, and the Question of Synthesis," *The Journal of American History* 71 (June 1984): 93–100, a review essay of *Segmented Work, Divided Workers: The Historical Transformation of Labor in the United States* by David M. Gordon, Richard Edwards, and Michael Reich (Cambridge: Cambridge University Press, 1982).

59. Harold Barron, *Those Who Stayed Behind: Rural Society in Nineteenth Century New England* (Cambridge: Cambridge University Press, 1984).

60. See John Scott Strickland, "Traditional Culture and Moral Economy: Social and Economic Change in the South Carolina Low Country, 1865–1910" in *The Countryside in the Age of Capitalist Transformation*, ed. Steven Hahn and Jonathan Prude (Chapel Hill: University of North Carolina Press, 1985); Kathleen Neils Conzen, "Peasants into Pioneers: Patterns of Intra-Family Land Transmission Among German Immigrants in Rural Minnesota, 1856–1905" in *The Countryside*, ed. Hahn and Prude; idem, "Historical Approaches to the Study of Rural Ethnic Communities" in *Ethnicity on the Great Plains*, ed. Frederick C. Luebke (Lincoln: University of Nebraska Press, 1980), 1–13; Barbara Karsky, "Le paysan américain et la terre à la fin du XVIIIe siècle," *Annales: Economies, sociétés, civilisations* 38 (Novembre–Décembre 1983): 1369–91; Barron, *Those Who Stayed Behind*.

61. See Patrick Geddes, *Cities in Evolution* (London: William and Northgate, 1915); Lewis Mumford, *The Culture of Cities* (New York: Harcourt Brace, 1938); Sam Bass Warner, Jr., *The Urban Wilderness: A History of the American City* (New York: Harper & Row, 1972).

62. On the Connecticut Valley, see Stephen Innes, *Labor in a New Land: Economy and Society in Seventeenth-Century Springfield* (Princeton: Princeton University Press, 1983).

63. Stuart Blumin, *The Urban Threshold: Growth and Change in a Nineteenth-Century American Community* (Chicago: University of Chicago Press, 1976), 1.

64. Michael P. Conzen, "The American Urban System in the Nineteenth Century" in *Geography and the Urban Environment: Progress in Research and Applications*, vol. IV, ed. D. T. Herbert and R. J. Johnson, (New York: John Wiley, 1981), 339.

65. Alexis de Tocqueville, *De la démocracie en Amérique*, 3 vols. (Paris: Michel Luy Frères, 1865), 2:190–91.

66. Michael N. Danielson, *The Politics of Exclusion* (New York: Columbia University Press, 1976).

67. Kathleen Neils Conzen, "Immigrants, Immigrant Neighborhoods, and Ethnic Identity: Historical Issues," *Journal of American History* 66 (December 1979): 603–15; Olivier Zunz, "Residential Segregation in the American Metropolis: Concentration, Dispersion and Dominance" in *Urban History Yearbook, 1980* (Leicester: Leicester University Press, 1980), 23–33.

68. On leisure, see Roy Rosenzweig, *Eight Hours for What We Will: Workers and Leisure in an Industrial City, 1870–1920* (Cambridge: Cambridge University Press, 1983); on poverty, see Raymond A. Mohl, *Poverty in New York, 1783–1825* (New York: Oxford University Press, 1971); on education, Carl F. Kaestle and Maris A. Vinovskis, *Education and Social Change in Nineteenth-Century Massachusetts* (New York: Cambridge University Press, 1980); on religion, Gregory H. Singleton, *Religion in the City of Angels: American Protestant Culture and Urbanization, Los Angeles, 1850–1930* (Ann Arbor: UMI Research Press, 1977).

69. See Emmanuel Le Roy Ladurie, *Les paysans de Languedoc* (Paris: S.E.V.P.E.N., 1966); Michel Morineau, "Allergico cantabile," *Annales: Economies, sociétés, civilisations* 36 (Juillet–Août 1981): 623–41.

70. Although as economic history, demographic history is sometimes dubbed too technical, its scientific standards are well established. A further advantage of demographic history is that it has not been as heavily involved as economic history in moral debates such as the ones centered around the merits of the industrial revolution or the profitability of slavery. Overall, demographic history has inspired many branches of social history and given it much of its strength by its ability to encompass, or be itself incorporated into, other fields of inquiry.

71. The most complete list of budget studies is in Faith M. Williams and Carle C. Zimmerman, *Studies of Family Living in the United States and Other Countries* (U.S. Department of Agriculture, Miscellaneous Publication No. 223, December 1935). Two recent updates may be found in John Modell, "Patterns of Consumption, Acculturation, and Family Income Strategies in Late Nineteenth-Century America" in *Family and Population in Nineteenth-Century America*, ed., Tamara K. Hareven and Maris A. Vinovskis (Princeton: Princeton University Press, 1978), 206–40; Claudia Goldin, "Family Strategies and the Family Economy in the Late Nineteenth Century: The Role of Secondary Workers" in *Philadelphia*, ed. Hershberg, 277–310. See also Peter R. Shergold, *Working-Class Life: The "American Standard" in Comparative Perspective, 1899–1913* (Pittsburgh: University of Pittsburgh Press, 1982).

72. Byington, *Homestead* (1910; reprint ed., Pittsburgh: University of Pittsburgh Press, 1974).

73. Zunz, *Changing Face*, 227–40.

74. Ibid., 248–58.

75. Hareven, *Family Time*, 367; John Modell and Tamara K. Hareven, "Urbanization and the Malleable Household: An Examination of Boarding and Lodging in

American Families," *Journal of Marriage and the Family* 35 (August 1973): 471.

76. Hareven, *Family Time*; Tamara K. Hareven and Maris A. Vinovskis, "Patterns of Childbearing in Late Nineteenth-Century America: The Determinants of Marital Fertility in Five Massachusetts Towns in 1880" in *Family and Population*, ed. Hareven and Vinovskis, 85–125; Modell, "Patterns of Consumption"; Howard P. Chudacoff, "Newlyweds and Family Extension: The First Stage of the Family Cycle in Providence, Rhode Island, 1864–1865 and 1879–1880" in *Family and Population*, ed. Hareven and Vinovskis; Hershberg, ed., *Philadelphia*; Bodnar, Simon, and Weber, *Lives of Their Own*; Zunz, *Changing Face*.

77. Carl N. Degler, *At Odds: Women and the Family in America from the Revolution to the Present* (New York: Oxford University Press, 1980).

78. Zunz, *Changing Face*, 396.

79. Hareven, *Family Time*, 62.

80. Neil J. Smelser and Sydney Halpern, "The Historical Triangulation of Family, Economy, and Education" in *Turning Points: Historical and Sociological Essays on the Family*, ed. John Demos and Sarane Spence Boocock (Chicago: University of Chicago Press, 1978), 289; Byington, *Homestead*.

81. Byington, *Homestead*, 131–37.

82. Hareven, *Family Time*, 287–354.

83. Seymour Martin Lipset and Richard Hofstadter, eds., *Sociology and History: Methods* (New York: Basic Books, 1968), 3–53.

84. Pierre Vilar, *Une histoire en construction: Approche marxiste et problématiques conjoncturelles* (Paris: Seuil/Gallimard, 1982), 50.

85. Raymond Grew, "Modernization and Its Discontents," *American Behavioral Scientist* 21 (November-December 1977): 289–312.

86. Ibid.

87. Alex Inkeles and David H. Smith, *Becoming Modern: Individual Change in Six Developing Countries*, (Cambridge, Mass.: Harvard University Press, 1974).

88. Innes, *Labor in a New Land*.

89. On bonds and networks between migrants, see Hareven, *Family Time*, and Edward O. Laumann, *Bonds of Pluralism: The Form and Substance of Urban Social Networks* (New York: John Wiley, 1973).

90. Hays, *American Political History*, 268.

91. Gutman, *Work, Culture and Society*, 5.

92. Cinel, *From Italy to San Francisco*.

93. Oestreicher, *Solidarity and Fragmentation*.

94. Thomas Bender, *Community and Social Change in America* (New Brunswick, N. J.: Rutgers University Press, 1978).

95. John M. Murrin, "Review Essay," *History and Theory: Studies in the Philosophy of History* 11 (1972): 226–75.

96. Charles Tilly, "Food Supply and Public Order in Modern Europe," in *The Formation of National States in Western Europe*, ed. Charles Tilly (Princeton: Princeton University Press, 1975), 428.

97. Gary B. Nash, *The Urban Crucible: Social Change, Political Consciousness, and the Origins of the American Revolution* (Cambridge, Mass.: Harvard University Press, 1979), 77–78.

98. Michael Feldberg, "Urbanization as a Cause of Violence: Philadelphia as a

Test Case" in *The Peoples of Philadelphia: A History of Ethnic Groups and Lower-Class Life, 1790–1840*, ed. Allen F. Davis and Mark H. Haller (Philadelphia: Temple University Press, 1973), 58–61.

99. Ibid.

100. Roger Lane, *Violent Death in the City: Suicide, Accident and Murder in Nineteenth-Century Philadelphia* (Cambridge, Mass.: Harvard University Press, 1979); Eric H. Monkkonen, *Police in Urban America, 1860–1920* (Cambridge: Cambridge University Press, 1981). For a recent overview from the South, see Edward L. Ayers, *Vengeance and Justice: Crime and Punishment in the Nineteenth-Century American South* (New York: Oxford University Press, 1984), esp. 9–33.

101. Richard Hofstadter, *The Progressive Historians: Turner, Beard, Parrington* (Chicago: University of Chicago Press, 1968), 461.

102. For a good summary statement, see Morton Keller, *Affairs of State: Public Life in Nineteenth-Century America* (Cambridge, Mass.: Harvard University Press, 1977), 1–2; for a stimulating discussion of the impact of the Civil War, see William E. Nelson, *The Roots of American Bureaucracy, 1830–1900* (Cambridge, Mass.: Harvard University Press, 1982).

103. Oscar Handlin's review of Allan Nevins's *The Emergence of Lincoln in Nation* 171 (December 2, 1950): 512–23; cited in David M. Potter, *The South and the Sectional Conflict* (Baton Rouge: Louisiana State University Press, 1968), 100.

104. Leonard L. Richards, *"Gentlemen of Property and Standing:" Anti-Abolition Mobs in Jacksonian America* (New York: Oxford University Press, 1970).

105. Ira Berlin and Herbert G. Gutman, "Natives and Immigrants, Free Men and Slaves," *American Historical Review* 88 (December 1983): 1194–95.

106. See Michael F. Holt, *The Political Crisis of the 1850s* (New York: John Wiley, 1978).

107. Eugene D. Genovese, *Roll, Jordan, Roll: The World the Slaves Made* (New York: Pantheon, 1974).

108. James Oakes, *The Ruling Race: A History of American Slaveholders* (New York: Alfred A. Knopf, 1982).

109. Strickland, "Traditional Culture and Moral Economy."

110. Steven Hahn, *The Roots of Southern Populism: Yeoman Farmers and the Transformation of the Georgia Upcountry, 1850–1890* (New York: Oxford University Press, 1983), 100; see also Armstead L. Robinson, "In the Shadow of Old John Brown: Insurrection Anxiety and Confederate Mobilization, 1861–1863," *Journal of Negro History* 65 (Fall 1980): 279–97.

111. Whitney R. Cross, *The Burned-Over District: The Social and Intellectual History of Enthusiastic Religion in Western New York, 1800–1850* (Ithaca: Cornell University Press, 1950).

112. Johnson, *A Shopkeeper's Millennium*.

113. Mary P. Ryan, *Cradle of the Middle Class: The Family in Oneida County, New York, 1790–1865* (Cambridge: Cambridge University Press, 1981); the weight of the evidence is in favor of Ryan.

114. On this point, see François Furet, "Beyond the *Annales*."

115. For example, see Nick Salvatore, *Eugene V. Debs: Citizen and Socialist* (Urbana: University of Illinois Press, 1982).

116. Frisch and Walkowitz, *Working-Class America*. See also the essays by Charles C.

Bright, "The State in the United States during the Nineteenth Century" and Daniel R. Fusfeld, "Government and the Suppression of Radical Labor, 1877–1918" in *Statemaking and Social Movements: Essays in History and Theory*, ed. Charles Bright and Susan Harding (Ann Arbor: University of Michigan Press, 1984), 151–58, 344–77.

117. Pierre Vilar, "Histoire marxiste, histoire en construction. Essai de dialogue avec Althusser," in *Une histoire en construction*, 397–98, trans. in *New Left Review* 80 (July–August 1973): 79; see also Kathleen Neils Conzen, "Quantification and the New Urban History," *Journal of Interdisciplinary History* 13 (Spring 1983): 653–77. Read Gutman's attack on quantification while hailing Dawley's book, "Ladies Will Not be Slaves," *New York Times Book Review*, 12 June 1977; Gutman's attitude, however, is unclear since he employed quantification in his study of blacks but only for those calculations he could do manually as if a computer would have "spoiled" the data. See also Robert F. Berkhofer, Jr., "The Two New Histories: Competing Paradigms for Interpreting the American Past," *Organization of American Historians Newsletter* 2 (May 1983): 9–12.

118. Higham, new epilogue in *History*.

119. See "A Conversation with Sam Bass Warner, Jr." in *Journal of Urban History* 1 (November 1974): 85–110.

120. Bernard Bailyn, "The Challenge of Modern Historiography," *American Historical Review* 87 (February 1982): 1–24; Philip D. Curtin, "Depth, Span, and Relevance," *American Historical Review* 89 (February 1984): 1–9.

121. John Higham, "Beyond Pluralism: The Historian as American Prophet." (Paper delivered at the Seventy-Sixth Annual Meeting of the Organization of American Historians, Cincinnati, 6–9 April 1983).

122. Stone, "The Revival of Narrative"; see also C. Vann Woodward, "A Short History of American History," *New York Times Book Review*, 8 August 1982, 3–4.

123. Le Roy Ladurie, *Le territoire de l'historien*; Stone, "The Revival of Narrative."

124. Stone, "The Revival of Narrative."

125. Social change is a term with multiple related meanings. As used here, I mean it to refer to the modification of customary relationships, to the synthesis that, transcending existing social, economic, and political divisions, creates new norms, new behaviors, and new modes of thought. See the important distinction made by Henri Mendras and Michel Forsé between "changement de la société" and "changement dans la société," in *Le changement social* (Paris: Armand Colin, 1983), 9.

126. Oscar Handlin, *Boston's Immigrants, 1790–1880: A Study in Acculturation* (Cambridge, Mass.: Harvard University Press, 1941).

127. John Higham, "Current Trends in the Study of Ethnicity in the United States," *Journal of American Ethnic History* 2 (Fall 1982): 7.

128. Stephan Thernstrom, *Poverty and Progress: Social Mobility in a Nineteenth-Century City* (Cambridge, Mass.: Harvard University Press, 1964), 163–65; idem, *Other Bostonians*, 4, 247, 259; and "A Conversation with Stephan Thernstrom," in *Journal of Urban History* 1 (February 1975): 196; see also the review essay by Howard P. Chudacoff, "Success and Security: The Meaning of Social Mobility in America," *Reviews in American History* (Special issue: "The Promise of American History, Progress and Prospects") 10 (December 1982): 101–12.

129. Katz, *People of Hamilton.*

130. Daniel T. Rodgers, *The Work Ethic in Industrial America, 1850–1920* (Chicago: University of Chicago Press, 1978), 140–43; Michael Zuckerman, "The Nursery Tales of Horatio Alger," *American Quarterly* 24 (May 1972): 191–209.

131. Hartmut Kaelble, "Foreword by Guest Editor," *Journal of Social History* 17 (Spring 1984): 406.

132. Katz, *People of Hamilton,* 103–6.

133. Zunz, *Changing Face,* 177–95.

134. Montgomery, *Workers' Control.*

135. Kenneth L. Kusmer, "The Underclass: Tramps and Vagrants in Urban America, 1870–1920," unpublished paper, Symposium on Urban Development in the Age of Industrialism, Cologne, June 1981.

136. Lee Rainwater and William L. Yancey, *The Moynihan Report and the Politics of Controversy* (Cambridge, Mass.: MIT Press, 1967).

137. The most forceful critique of Frazier is Herbert G. Gutman, "Persistent Myths about the Afro-American Family," *Journal of Interdisciplinary History* 6 (Autumn 1975): 181–210. Elizabeth Hefkin Pleck originally adopted Gutman's position; see Pleck, "Two-Parent Household: Black Family Structure in Late Nineteenth-Century Boston," *Journal of Social History* 6 (Fall 1972): 3–36; she then reversed herself and presented a neo-Frazerian interpretation of the black family; see Pleck, *Black Migration,* 162–96. The most powerful but exaggerated argument against the breakdown thesis of the Black migrant is in James Borchert, *Alley Life in Washington* (Urbana: University of Illinois Press, 1980), 57–99. See also Kenneth L. Kusmer, *A Ghetto Takes Shape: Black Cleveland, 1870–1930* (Urbana: University of Illinois Press, 1976), and his important historiographical essay "The Black Urban Experience in American History," in *The State of Afro-American History: Past, Present, and Future,* ed. Darlene Clark Hine (Baton Rouge: Louisiana State University Press, forthcoming).

138. Cited in John Higham, *Send These To Me: Jews and Other Immigrants in Urban America* (New York: Atheneum, 1975), 204.

139. Sidney W. Mintz and Richard Price, *An Anthropological Approach to the Afro-American Past: A Caribbean Perspective* (Philadelphia: Institute for the Study of Human Issues, 1976), 21.

140. John Bodnar, "Immigrants, Kinship, and the Rise of Working-Class Realism in Industrial America," *Journal of Social History* 14 (Fall 1980): 59.

141. Kathleen Neils Conzen, *Immigrant Milwaukee, 1836–1860: Accommodation and Community in a Frontier City* (Cambridge, Mass.: Harvard University Press, 1976), 225.

142. Thernstrom, *Other Bostonians,* 131–35; compare with R. A. Burchell, *The San Francisco Irish, 1848–1880* (Berkeley: University of California Press, 1980).

143. See Vilar, *Une histoire en construction,* 421.

144. E. P. Thompson, "Eighteenth-Century English Society: Class Struggle Without Class," *Social History* 3 (May 1978): 146–50.

145. Ibid.

146. One will find similar observations in Craig Calhoun, *The Question of Class Struggle: Social Foundations of Popular Radicalism during the Industrial Revolution* (Chicago: University of Chicago Press, 1982), 19; the influence of Thompson's "cultural marxism" on American scholarship is still increasing. In a session at the 1984

Organization of American Historians meeting in Los Angeles devoted to "class formation," the participants concentrated their analyses on symbolic manifestations of class consciousness as seen through processions. Not once did we hear words like "social justice," "mobility," or "opportunity" that were at the center of the debate only a few years ago.

147. AHR forum on Edward Pessen's "Social Structure and Politics in American History," and rejoinder by Michael B. Katz and Robert H. Wiebe, *American Historical Review* 87 (December 1982): 1290–341.

148. On the meaning of numeracy, see Patricia Cline Cohen, *A Calculating People: The Spread of Numeracy in Early America* (Chicago: University of Chicago Press, 1982).

149. See Dublin, *Women at Work.*

150. Milton Gordon, *Assimilation in American Life: The Roles of Race, Religion and National Origins* (New York: Oxford University Press, 1964).

151. Ruby Jo Reeves Kennedy, "Single or Triple Melting Pot: Intermarriage Trends in New Haven, 1870–1940," *American Journal of Sociology* 49 (January 1944): 331–39; Will Herberg, *Protestant-Catholic-Jew: An Essay in American Religious Sociology* (Garden City, N.Y.: Doubleday, 1955).

152. This is the thrust of Gutman's opening essay in *Work, Culture and Society,* 3–78; on this point, see Higham, "Current Trends," 8–10.

153. John B. Jentz, "Bread and Labor: Chicago's German Bakers Organize," *Chicago History* 12 (Summer 1983): 35.

154. Dawley, *Class and Community.*

155. Michael B. Katz, Michael J. Doucet, and Mark Stern, *The Social Organization of Early Industrial Capitalism* (Cambridge, Mass.: Harvard University Press, 1976).

156. Hershberg, ed., *Philadelphia*; see also Sam Bass Warner, Jr., and Colin B. Burke, "Cultural Change and the Ghetto," *Journal of Contemporary History* 4 (October 1969): 182; Howard P. Chudacoff, "A New Look at Ethnic Neighborhoods: Residential Dispersion and the Concept of Visibility in a Medium-Sized City," *Journal of American History* 60 (June 1973): 79–93.

157. Fox-Genovese and Genovese, *Fruits of Merchant Capital,* 201.

158. Like Gutman's biographies of Richard L. Davis or Joseph Patrick McDonnell; see his *Work, Culture and Society,* 121–208, 261–92.

159. Geoff Eley and Keith Nield, "Why Does Social History Ignore Politics?" *Social History* 5 (May 1980): 267.

160. Allan J. Lichtman, *Prejudice and the Old Politics: The Presidential Election of 1928* (Chapel Hill: University of North Carolina Press, 1979), 17–18.

161. Geoffrey Blodgett, "Yankee Leadership in a Divided City: Boston, 1860–1910," *Journal of Urban History* 8 (August 1982): 371–96; David Hammack, *Power and Society: Greater New York at the Turn of the Century* (New York, 1982), 130–51. On the nonhegemonic character of New York elites, in the Gramscian sense, see Bridges, *A City in the Republic,* 144. On the need to connect social and political history, see Paul F. Bourke and Donald A. DeBats, "Identifiable Voting in Nineteenth-Century America: Toward a Comparison of Britain and the United States Before the Secret Ballot," *Perspectives in American History* 11 (1977–1978): 259–88; idem, "Individuals and Aggregates: A Note on Historical Data and Assumptions," *Social Science History* 4 (Spring 1980): 229–50.

162. Ira Katznelson, *City Trenches: Urban Politics and the Patterning of Class in the United States* (New York: Pantheon, 1981), 16.

163. Zunz, *Changing Face.*

164. Middle-class members of ethnic communites have been studied by many historians. See the recent synthetic essay by Kenneth L. Kusmer, "Ethnicity and Business Enterprise: A Comment" in *Making It in America: The Role of Ethnicity in Education, Business Enterprise, and Work Choices,* ed. M. Mark Stolarik and Murray Friedman (Lewisburg, Pa.: Bucknell University Press, forthcoming) and the methodological essay by David A. Gerber, "Ethnics, Enterprise, and Middle Ethnic History," *Immigration History Newsletter* 12 (May 1980): 1–7. On Jews, see Moses Rischin, *The Promised City: New York Jews, 1870–1914* (Cambridge, Mass.: Harvard University Press, 1962), 95–111; on Poles, see Caroline Golab, *Immigrant Destinations* (Philadelphia: Temple University Press, 1977), 141–48, and more recently John J. Bukowczyk, "The Transformation of Working-Class Ethnicity: Corporate Control, Americanization, and the Polish Immigrant Middle Class in Bayonne, New Jersey, 1915–1925" *Labor History* 25 (Winter 1984): 53–82; on Japanese immigrants, Edna Bonacich and John Modell, *The Economic Basis of Ethnic Solidarity: Small Business in the Japanese American Community* (Berkeley: University of California Press, 1980).

165. Katznelson, *City Trenches,* 70–71.

166. For a sense of regional variations, see Frederic Cople Jaher, *The Urban Establishment: Upper Strata in Boston, New York, Charleston, Chicago, and Los Angeles* (Urbana: University of Illinois Press, 1982).

167. Lary May, *Screening Out the Past: The Birth of Mass Culture and the Motion Picture Industry* (New York: Oxford University Press, 1980), 172–75.

168. The type of relationship between class and ethnicity which characterizes Spanish-speaking groups is an open problem. New research will show whether these newcomers will experience a repetition of the nineteenth-century pattern or whether their pattern will be more rapidly subsumed into the twentieth-century pattern.

169. See the aggressive review of Ryan's *Cradle of the Middle Class* by Robert A. Gross in the *American Historical Review* 88 (June 1983): 752–53.

170. Katz, *AHR forum,* 1334.

171. Robert H. Wiebe, *The Search for Order, 1877–1920* (New York: Hill & Wang, 1967), 129.

172. John Higham, "The Matrix of Specialization" in *The Organization of Knowledge in Modern America, 1860–1920,* ed. Alexandra Oleson and John Voss (Baltimore: Johns Hopkins University Press, 1979), 3–18.

173. Neil Harris, "The Lamp of Learning: Popular Lights and Shadows" in *Organization of Knowledge,* ed. Oleson and Voss, 431–32.

174. Alfred D. Chandler, *The Visible Hand: The Managerial Revolution in American Business* (Cambridge, Mass.: Harvard University Press, 1977).

175. On some of these issues, see Bright, "The State in the United States"; Thomas K. McGraw, *Prophets of Regulation* (Cambridge, Mass.: Harvard University Press, 1984); Stephen Skowronek, *Building a New American State: The Expansion of National Administrative Capacities, 1877–1920* (Cambridge: Cambridge University Press, 1982); William R. Brock, *Investigation and Responsibility: Public Responsibility in the United*

States, 1865–1900 (Cambridge: Cambridge University Press, 1984); and on problems of methods, the suggestive essay by Gerald N. Grob, "Sidney Fine on the Intellectual Origins of the General Welfare State: Or, What Happened to Social and Intellectual History?" *Reviews in American History* 12 (June 1984): 286–95.

176. Program of the Ninth Annual Banquet; Sales Convention and Dinner; E. I. Du Pont Cellulose Products Department. January 5, 1922. Hagley Museum and Library.

CHAPTER 3

BETWEEN GLOBAL PROCESS

AND LOCAL KNOWLEDGE

AN INQUIRY INTO EARLY LATIN

AMERICAN SOCIAL HISTORY,

1500–1900

BY WILLIAM B. TAYLOR

Latin America is difficult to master intellectually, not only because of its size and the great diversity of its land and people, but also because its history since 1500 seems so familiar on the surface. Historians have long studied the expansion of Europe and its many forms—military conquest, emigration, languages, religion, domesticated animals, technology, urban centers, African slavery, law, political institutions, certain habits of conception—and other patterns that resulted from European intrusion, such as devastating epidemics and organization of new economic activities through the exploitation

My thanks to Nancy Mann for many helpful suggestions on form and content; to Herbert Braun, Charles Gibson, and Stephen Innes for showing me where I should have made myself better understood; to David William Cohen, William T. Rowe, Charles Tilly, and Olivier Zunz for discussions and advice along the way; to Charles W. Bergquist for sending me his essays on the dependency literature as I began to organize this essay; to Paul Shankman for advice about current issues in anthropology; and to David Carrasco for his encouragement and his views on center and periphery. Fellowships from the John Simon Guggenheim Memorial Foundation and the Social Science Research Council made possible the research and thinking that went into the section on the state.

115

of labor. Latin America was more thoroughly within Europe's orbit from 1500 to 1900 than Africa or Asia, but the incorporation was never even or complete. Where we can break through the surface of great historical change during long and continuous European colonization, Latin America seems neither like Europe nor like a unit or a group of closely related units that had become quite what Europeans intended. Little of its history has been either self-contained or simply a product of European or North American action, despite the beliefs and best efforts of European conquerors and North American governments and businesses. The lines separating indigenous and western traditions are not clear except in those rare cases where the native population has been totally isolated or almost exterminated.

Although they did not use the term "Latin America," Spaniards and Portuguese thought of America in a unitary way, as a "New World" so different and unknown that it had to be invented, a place where legends about earthly paradises, Amazon women, Prester John, cities of gold, and millennial kingdoms might come true. These legends and fantasies of Latin America have continued to be reinvented in the form of romantic stories of island castaways like *Robinson Crusoe*,[1] and in glossy travel brochures inviting the foreign visitor to unspoiled island paradises and golden lands. The term "Latin America" apparently was coined in France in 1861, and was adopted by Napoleon III's government to emphasize a pan-Latin heritage of the former Iberian colonies and thereby justify French imperial ambitions in America.[2] The Monroe Doctrine, the Organization of American States, and other manifestations of the United States's national interest also have promoted the idea of a Latin America that requires partnership, protection, and direction from the north. Imperial ambitions and the desires of foreigners, then, have something to do with how and why Latin America is considered a unit.

If it is to be more than a convenient name for most of the Americas, the notion of a Latin America—or Ibero-America or Spanish America and Portuguese America—depends on the extent and clarity of a European imprint. But the notion of a history made from without has often revealed more about European beliefs and ambitions, and about the ideology of the interpreters than about that historical imprint. Some of the organizing concepts in the study of early Latin American history have been closely related to unitary thinking about Latin America and its corollary of Europe as subject/Latin America as object: Black Legend/White Legend; master/slave, servant, dependent; colonial heritage; and the problematic of dependence and underdevelopment in a Latin America conceived as the traditional economic hinterland of Europe and the United States. These ways of defining subjects for study evince distorting dichotomies, an oversimplified view of cause and effect, and too little attention to the many local, small-scale changes in social life, but the relation of Europe and the rest of the world to Latin America is indispensable to the area's history.

Latin America has been at the same time united and fragmented by its European history. Latin America does have a shared history of three centuries of Iberian colonization, enclave economies, and, long after the nominal political independence of most Latin American nations in the early nineteenth century, a common marginality to an emerging world economic system. But these are not homogeneous or timeless traits. Iberian institutions and demands did not spread uniformly or penetrate everywhere at once. The cities of Latin America have been self-consciously Europeanizing centers of authority, exchange, and values but their control over the vast countryside has been intermittent and uneven; and Latin American societies have been overwhelmingly rural until the last thirty years. Rural life breaks through at nearly every point of early Latin American history; yet it was little studied by historians before 1950.

Latin America is thought to share other historical traits and traditions connected to the area's incomplete gravitation into the European orbit. One is that Latin America has been a "conflict society," with a dialectical history of attempts at great redirections of social and economic relationships arising from moments of violent conflict and foreign intrusion: the Spanish Conquest, the Comunero Rebellions, the Tupac Amaru Rebellion, slave revolts, the Independence Wars, wars of reform, United States interventions, millenarian movements, and social and socialist revolutions.[3] Doctoral dissertations and other academic studies of Latin American history in recent years have continued to speak of "crisis" and "transformation" following an event or a violent clash of interests. The reader faces in this literature a bewildering series of very closely spaced "turning points" and overlapping periodizations; each author's change becomes the great change, producing "transformations" in the 1750s, 1790s, 1810s, 1820s, 1850s, 1870s, 1890s, and 1920s.

Another, less controversial trait that illustrates the impact of Europe and complicates the history of Latin America is that communities and other social groupings there cannot be grasped in purely secular terms. Local American versions of a broadly Mediterranean Catholic outlook imposed by the Spanish and Portuguese governments in the early colonial period did not accept quickly or cleanly the secularizing developments in Europe itself in the eighteenth and nineteenth centuries. The secular state and secular values in public life were on the rise before the Independence Wars, European liberalism and positivism were vital forces in Latin American political life in the nineteenth century, wars were fought to separate Church from State or to protect the Church against imminent danger to its position, and the priesthood gradually lost influence in public affairs, but Latin American nations were not close to being modern secular societies by 1900 (if they were "societies" at all). Catholic thought and the institutions of the Church remained vital forces throughout Latin America. States with names like Mexico, Colombia, and Venezuela were created in the early nineteenth century from the vast Spanish Empire long before "nation" had meaning to most of their subjects. There was little to hold these new countries together. Their capital cities aimed at being centers of national direction in all things, but the territorial boundaries of their control were vague and shifting, and the dedication of most provincial subjects to the idea of nation was, at best, weak and uncertain. And religion became a focal point of political and social conflict more than of cohesion. Disunity of sentiment and organization within as well as among new states became a common feature.

The list of common features in early Latin American history could be lengthened: degradation of the labor force, rural estates, village communities (many of which were "peasant" communities in the anthropologists' specialized meaning), Independence Wars, urbanization, and large-scale collective actions, among others. But do the common features signify one process in social history? In the sense of a halting tendency to centralize power, create states, and integrate the area into trans-Atlantic economies, probably so. However, the social results, direct or indirect, of capitalism and state-building were not simple or readily predictable.

Social history as it has been practiced for Europe and the United States during the last thirty years has had a large if diffuse impact on the way Latin American history is conceived today. Although there has been a general decline of narrative history in favor of analysis in recent writings on early Latin America, the effects of social history on the study of Latin America have been mostly indirect and influential mainly at the descriptive level. Before about 1960, historians did not ignore the topics typical of social history, but regarded them as secondary and did not research them systematically. Typically, groups such as women, servants, children, peasants, vagrants, and criminals were passed over with a brief paraphrase of the impressions of an early traveler or local notable. Such token attention offered no basis for establishing the patterns of change in the lives of these groups, or for relating one group to another outside the commonalities imposed by colonial and national leaders. Latin American social history generally has stood for the recognition of people in categories previously neglected, and for a rejection of traditional historical preoccupations with elites and "events," but it has not yet gone beyond these changes to the "new kind of history" predicted by Lucien Febvre— the study of social change over long periods of time; the study of how ordinary people in different places and of different fortunes "lived the big changes" of the rise of capitalism and state formation, as Charles Tilly puts it in his essay.

Not that European and North American social history has resolved for the *longue durée* these bedrock questions of what changed when and why (and not only large-scale changes in fundamental structures such as class, household organization, and kinship). Social historians have produced richly elaborated new kinds of history that examine whole communities, regions, and other large groupings of people and production in their routine affairs during decades, centuries, sometimes millennia. They have widened historical study to include many neglected people who had been taken as objects of history, perhaps stubbornly or heroically resisting change but not really making history or doing much for themselves. Long-term, often hidden social processes such as demographic changes or patterns of crime, or the social background of merchants and their place in public life, are aptly described by Bernard Bailyn as "latent history," which he distinguishes from "manifest history"—the large-scale events that contemporaries recognized as benchmarks.[4] Social history's rejection of the affairs of top-level political leaders who visibly directed public life, of the rule of law, and of the outcome of particular events, in favor of a democratization of history that gives some voice to the great majority of our ancestors, has important consequences. It has tended to separate latent from manifest history.

The historians who have used the surviving record to deal with submerged social groups have been better at describing structures and patterns of behavior at one point in time, or at compressing evidence from a lengthy period into regularities, than at describing a process or providing a clear description, much less explanation, of social change. Their works leave an impression of a "motionless history" of stability or of recurrent crisis and transformation. For Latin America, the broader syntheses of social change have deduced, more than demonstrated, what actually changed, or they have paid too little attention to great changes in state-building and relationships of production that transcend the area of study, whether that area is a fertile valley, a market system, a pilgrimage route, a nation, or Latin America as a whole.

Recent social history of Latin America, like social history of other areas, is often criticized for focusing on localities or groups and losing sight of systems. There is some truth to this criticism. Research on classes of people has tended to compartmentalize them in their functional role—workers working, lawyers in court—and to remove them from their associations outside the family and the work-place. In the last thirty years, many historians have undertaken local studies of short time periods, on the grounds that only in a manageable geographical area can the concrete relations of time and place between, say, Indian villages and *haciendas* before Independence be examined, in order to test large conclusions about the domination of *haciendas*. But studies of small geographical scope tend to be isolated, especially if they lack a specific hypothesis about historical process, or if they are restricted to one local group or institution like the *hacienda*, or if the written evidence is not rich enough to document change and continuity over a long or especially significant period of time, or if they are done in a way that makes comparison to other places impossible. With some outstanding exceptions, local studies have been most effective at challenging large conclusions and theories of historical change. They tend to generate few and sometimes contradictory conclusions, or their own large conclusions bear little relationship to the evidence. However, it is not as if the new local histories have displaced broad works of synthesis and theory for Latin America. On the contrary, the dependency perspectives, with their sights trained on world systems and theory have flourished at the same time as the detailed studies of small scope, though they have been accomplished without much reference to each other.

"In any given society," says E. P. Thompson, "we cannot understand the parts unless we understand their function and roles in relation to the whole."[5] The great challenge for Latin American social history today, as for social history generally, is to see localities or women, villages, slaves, merchants, bureaucrats, and the rest of the topics of social history as ways of approaching larger relationships and processes in history as a whole, as "bundles of relationships," to use Eric R. Wolf's expression. Contemporaries may have understood such groupings as their own, but they were not self-contained, isolated, independent entities. This challenge—of putting more history into social history, and asking what holds groups of people together and what pulls them apart—is contained in Bailyn's call for a joining of latent and manifest history, Charles Tilly's view of social history as "the study of connections between large, structural changes and alterations in the character of routine social life," and Eric R. Wolf's bold conception of "processual and relational history"—"processes that transcend separable cases, moving through and beyond them and transforming them as they proceed," and "how socially organized populations produce to supply their polities."[6] These three scholars, all deeply interested in historical social change, approach it from different academic homes in history (Bailyn), sociology (Tilly), and anthropology (Wolf), and exemplify a fruitful convergence of the interests and methods of historians and social scientists in the United States in the last generation.

Here is a daunting challenge, but one that historians have encountered for generations—to write whole histories as well as to treat large groups and long periods. We are not approaching an end to the interests that have propelled the new social history for nearly twenty years—discovering new subjects and unexplored places, finding seats at the banquet of history for great gatherings of forgotten people, and applying new techniques to unlock the mysteries of serial records of birth, death, marriage, property, contract, and crime in which these people appear. What is passing is the sense that the suggestive comparisons and small or loose connections of the pioneering work are enough for now.

This essay seeks to describe some of the work that has been done so far or might be done in early Latin American social history before 1900 with the challenge of a more connected history in mind. It does not attempt to discuss most of the important recent work of historians on social groups, regions, the routines of daily life, and other topics of social history, or to duplicate or amplify Magnus Mörner's state-of-the-art essays on the major subjects of slavery, immigration, elites, and landed estates—subjects for which there have been important cumulative results.[7] Nor will it do justice to the achievements of all of the works cited or to the fact that some of them combine elements of several approaches and topics; and it leaves out some of the most interesting work on the social history of the colonial period, such as James Lockhart's use of notarial records and documents written in Nahuatl, and important new work on demographic changes and their effects, and cultural ecology.[8]

Sections of the essay are devoted to dependency perspectives and connections between the state and society. This approach to Latin America before 1900 is incomplete but not altogether arbitrary. Dependency perspectives constitute a serious effort to address the large structures and process of Latin American history in terms of the social organization of production and domination by Atlantic economies. They represent an approach with clear political overtones that has engaged leading Latin American historians as well as foreigners, and is certain to influence the agenda of Latin American social history for years to come. State and society has been little studied recently, but, as the study of institutionalized political power's bearing on social relationships, beliefs, desires, and fears, it offers a joining of research in anthropology and history that promises to illuminate networks other than those of the market in early Latin America and to allow a simultaneous consideration of latent and manifest history. This subject, too, opens out to other recent research, especially on elites, the Church, mentalités, agrarian structures, collective action, and the Independence period.

Two points are emphasized about the ways in which recent research in social history has changed the periodization of Latin American history between 1750 and 1900. First, there has been a close connection between great economic and social changes since the last third of the nineteenth century—a relationship that will come as no surprise but that recent studies have confirmed independently for many parts of Latin America. These studies are a reminder that in historical scholarship, the surprises and advances often come in the details more than in the conclusions, and in resolving specific issues of correlation and chronology where a sketchy literature had permitted contradictory conclusions and inconclusive debate. Second, I question the idea that long-term continuities make the years from roughly 1750 to 1850 a decisive period in Latin American social history, and I make a preliminary case for returning one series of events—the Independence Wars—to a prominent place in the chronology of Latin American social history.

For these subjects there is an unavoidable geographical imbalance in the essay. More of the social history of Latin America has been written for the areas that were central to Spain's colonial empire: Mexico and the western highlands of South America. These were the areas of greatest population, wealth, and political influence before 1810. No one area or country is typical of Latin America, and I have not attempted to consider them all. My purpose is different and less ambitious. It is to explore possibilities for a more connected social history from 1500 to 1900, using examples mainly from the geographical areas that were central in the colonial period. Behind the convenient references to regions—in terms of market areas, cities and their hinterlands, provinces, Audiencia and Intendancy districts, bishoprics, parishes, nations, viceroyalties, and world systems—that appear in the essay is the unresolved matter of appropriate as well as convenient territorial units of study in social history.[9] The idea that the only proper unit for studying social history is the whole world begs the question of where decisive regional relationships and institutions were centered, except as a chastening reminder that regions are not isolated things. Recognizing that the unit that accounts for the most relationships or the most important ones may vary over time, within Latin America, and between Latin America and other parts of the world, we will have to see the relationships that make up a wider social history as part of a process, and in a way that attends to the influence of other overlapping or encompassing units. Recent scholarship describes a notable fluidity of communities—much leaving and returning, some movement across lines of rank, ethnicity, and class, and vague and permeable boundaries—and significant regional variation in structural changes and institutions that should make us less certain than we have been about what social relationships existed and how they worked.

Dependency Perspectives

The most influential approach to a broad, connected social history for early Latin America that has appeared in the last fifteen years is the concept of dependency.[10] Dependency "perspectives"—there is no accepted theory of dependency, and interpreters of the concept in Latin America, Europe, and the United States now disagree about approaches and conclusions as much as they agree on certain broad outlines of historical process—begin with Latin American history as a common process of underdevelopment, domination, and class formation that unfolds with the expansion of Europe after 1492. The long arm of the world market, with its demands from European and North American centers and inequalities of exchange, determines the organization of regional production in Latin America that, in turn, determines social classes and their relationships. Latin America is treated as the underdeveloped West, a periphery of an emerging world capitalist system. The formation of social relationships in the area derives from the needs of the world market: unequal exchange of wealth between developed and underdeveloped capitalist nations and colonies since the sixteenth century. Social history becomes a branch of economic history, and the underdevelopment of the region, the degradation of the labor force, and other forms of inequality are seen as functions of the area's peripheral, dependent position in the world capitalist system.[11]

As inconclusive as they have been—which is expected when a new approach does not spring from the monographic literature—dependency perspectives on the causes of underdevelopment have advanced the study of social history in Latin America. They have the virtue of drawing attention to problems of domination as well as facts, to how the parts of a world system are related to the whole, and how what happened in distant markets affected local prices, supply, and demand, and changed the material life of ordinary people. This focus on large systems of exchange and states is especially appropriate for Latin America, where European expansion has had profound and lasting effects. Dependency perspectives have offered a way to relate the formation of colonial and neocolonial societies in Latin America to what Europe sought and gained in the New World. *Dependentista* studies also have helped to draw the attention of social historians to class issues, the economic structure behind the relationships of groups, the social effects of economic changes, the importance of markets, and the commercialization of agriculture as an integral part of the history of *haciendas* and Indian village "subsistence" communities, and to challenge the old dichotomy of subsistence sector/market sector. But as an approach to early Latin American social history, dependency perspectives have presented special problems:

1. The dependency studies present capitalism as a single system of meaning, and take dependency as a given from the Spanish Conquest to the present. Although the authors of the *dependentista* studies make a broad, sequential distinction between mercantile or commercial capitalism and industrial capitalism, they have paid little attention to the differential effects of the two capitalisms on social relationships in various places and times, as if mercantile capitalism determined these relationships as effectually as industrial capitalism would later on. In this, the maturity and importance of commercial capitalism in the colonial period may be overemphasized; an overemphasis that results more from reasoning backward in time about the functions of peripheries in international capitalism—what anthropologists call "upstreaming"—than from close historical study. For example, *dependentista* approaches have not considered whether small-scale peasant market activities in colonial Oaxaca or other highland areas were a way to resist wage labor and peonage on *haciendas* that would have reduced the villagers' participation in a world system directed by commercial capitalism.

2. A flexible economic determinism generally also is taken as given. Rather than documenting social changes and charting them over time, the dependency approach has made its first priority the identification of economic networks and structural changes in national economies, to be followed by investigation of the social changes that presumably resulted. Social history, then, becomes bracketed into time periods that follow economic changes (economic changes that themselves are not yet well documented for many parts of Latin America). Unless the social changes for these periods are clearly shown not to antedate the presumed economic changes, this line of investigation tends to deduce its conclusions about social change from an undemonstrated assumption. Without paying close attention to the complex and variable precapitalist, pre-Conquest social forms and relationships of production in different localities, and to changes in these relationships at different times after the Conquest, it is impossible to establish what social changes resulted largely from mercantile capitalism and the new external dependencies.

3. By viewing the history of domination in terms of the spread of capitalist relationships of exchange from Europe, dependency perspectives generally have minimized the place of institutions of the state in shaping social and economic inequalities and subordination. The state in early Latin America is passed over as secondary, or as-

sumed to result from economic transformations and to be mainly the expression of the interests of a capitalist class, or is studied as a competitor in an international system of states without much attention to domestic relationships. Little attention has been given to whether the colonial state and early national governments depended on local groups and villages for support and therefore had an interest in preserving their integrity (the next section of the essay, "Connecting State and Society," addresses these issues).

4. *Dependentista* and some Marxist studies have generally assumed, not only that economic change is primary, but that it was imposed from outside, by European colonizers on powerless natives.[12] To describe local social structures, integration, centralization, and standardization only in terms of capitalism and external dependencies neglects the role of local modes of thought and practice and local arrangements of power in forming those dependencies. It removes attention from local elites and collective action, leaving the impression that colonial Spanish American economies were directed only toward exports, and that all centers of economic decision making were located outside Latin America.[13] To the extent that dependency perspectives have dealt exclusively with the way in which the requirements of European capitalism determined social organization for the colonial period (and not all do so), they have promoted a new Black Legend that substitutes thoroughgoing economic control by the export economy for the extravagant personal brutality of Spanish masters and the omnipotence of viceroys, priests, and "feudal" *encomenderos* and *hacendados*. In either legend, black or white, Europeans are the real subjects of history. They create and manipulate the relationships of inequality as they wish. Wealth becomes equivalent to power; those without great wealth are powerless objects of the export economy.

One consequence of the *dependentista* focus on external relationships and the controlling influence of the world market is the general proposition that the mining economy was the bone and blood of the colonial system. Along with the activities of merchants, it determined the social relationships of production throughout the viceroyalties of New Spain and Peru.[14] From the European vantage point the gold and silver mines certainly were the heart of the colonial economy. And mining was not an isolated, enclave activity.[15] It required hides, food, and labor, and it stimulated the production of other goods and services that drew in a capacious hinterland. The mines also pro-

moted a money economy (although recent studies of financial transactions and markets suggest that money was always in short supply,
and little of the gold and silver mined in Mexico or Peru circulated in
markets there).[16] Still, it remains to be demonstrated how mining
shaped colonial society in its regional variations; how commercialized colonial Latin America was; and how the tributary system or
village farming and ranching in New Mexico, the Sierra de Puebla,
and hundreds of other places in highland Latin America were "by-
products" of the mining economy.

5. In the *dependentista* view, the sweeping influence of capitalism,
once it penetrated, left little room for regional variation except in
the timing of that penetration and in the amounts of labor and capital needed to extract different raw material. Yet some regions or
countries whose economic and social histories are reasonably well
known, like Argentina or Mexico in the first half-century after Independence, do not seem to fit the dependency models well, despite
their contacts with capitalism and world markets. Regional differences have not attracted much attention from leading *dependentistas*
(Frank, for example, sees a general uniformity and inevitability of
essential relationships once mercantile capitalism has penetrated an
area, so that regional differences below the national level hold little
interest). Where they have, there is a tendency to explain the differences in terms of diffusion—areas differ in social relationships in pro-
portion to the extent of their contact with the capitalist world system.
There has been little recognition that commercial agriculture, as in
the cultivation of cochineal, does not necessarily transform peasant
land tenure or community relationships.

In dismantling modernization theory and its misleading dichotomy
of traditional and modern societies, dependency perspectives have
substituted other simplicities that may obscure more than they reveal. Metropolis and satellite, core and periphery, and the sustained,
controlling influence of a world market system are as much homogenizing categories as "traditional" society, and the nation may not be
the only or even the proper unit of analysis for explicating dependent
relationships in a world system.[17] Even within one geographical area
in the central areas of Spanish America there could be several economies, not all of them the inevitable, direct products of exchange in a
world market. The plantation and *hacienda* owners, their dependent
staffs, and landless wage laborers belonged, in their different ways, to
a system of commercial agriculture that tied them to urban markets

in the vicinity or province and, directly or indirectly, to international markets. By comparison, Indians in corporate landholding villages, where agriculture was practiced more nearly at the subsistence level and where labor service was intermittent and largely stimulated by a need for cash to meet tax obligations, were largely removed from the major markets so important to dependency perspectives. Between these two extremes came various intermediate situations of involvement in the market economy—*rancheros*, perhaps paying rent in money but supporting themselves and their extended families from the produce of their holdings and occasional trading ventures; or agricultural workers who exchanged a portion of their labor for a plot of farmland. The coexistence of what appear to be different ways of life does not mean a "dual" society. These groups were not static; they overlapped and penetrated each other as parts of the same agrarian structure; and they were all connected to a money economy in one way or another.

While early writings on dependency emphasized that their approach was "historical-structural,"[18] their interest in history derived from a critique of modernization theory as an explanation of economic inequalities in Latin America today, a concern with contemporary underdevelopment, and a commitment to change the "oppressive reality" of Latin America. Close historical study was a secondary matter in this "committed"[19] criticism of capitalist exploitation. Fernando H. Cardoso and Enzo Faletto's *Dependencia y desarrollo en América Latina* (1969 and later expanded editions), which is widely regarded as the first emphatically *dependentista* study, started with the proposition that "the historical specificity of the situation of underdevelopment derives from the relationships between 'peripheral' and 'central' societies" but barely touched on the past. The Great Depression after 1929 is the book's watershed. The colonial period is passed over entirely; the brief section on the nineteenth century derives from one book, Tulio Halperín Donghi's *Historia contemporánea de América Latina*, and mainly summarizes national trends and events.[20]

The other early *dependentista* book, André Gunder Frank's *Capitalism and Underdevelopment in Latin America* (1967) devoted about one-third of its text to characterizing historical stages in the economy and society of Latin America. Focusing on the terms of exchange in an international market system dating from the sixteenth century, Frank argues strongly against the idea of a single ladder of economic and social development from traditional to modern, from backward to progressive, from *Gemeinschaft* to *Gesellschaft*; and against the Europocentric view of foreign economic and cultural penetration of Latin America as altogether positive. But he does not systematically develop the conclusion that unequal relations simply reproduce greater inequality, and in this and subsequent writings his historical propositions are asserted more than demonstrated:[21] that mercantile capitalism was the "motor" driving social change in Latin America from the sixteenth century; that colonial Indians were fully integrated into a mercantile capitalist system; that agriculture in the highlands of Mexico and South America was a "by-product" of a colonial economy based on silver and gold mining; that the colonial economy, even in the seventeenth century, was "an open economy . . . determined above all by its relationship to . . . this virtually world-embracing [mercantilist] system";[22] that political initiatives to change economic relationships in the eighteenth and nineteenth centuries simply "ratified" prior changes in the world economic system; and that foreign investment necessarily drains as much capital as it injects into Latin America and provides no real benefits to the local population.

The early *dependentista* writings of Cardoso and Frank were not without their progenitors. Frank acknowledges a debt to Paul Baran's writings on surplus and backwardness; Cardoso acknowledges the influence of economists at the U. N. Economic Commission for Latin America in the 1950s and 1960s, who criticized the rosy view that economic development in Latin America was producing sustained growth, eventual national autonomy in key economic decisions, and middle-class societies, and pointed to the unequal relationships between advanced capitalist centers and backward peripheries. Sergio Bagú and Silvio Frondizi seem to be more distant intellectual precursors from the 1940s.[23] Above all, the center-periphery materialism of dependency perspectives has older roots in the writings of Marx, Lenin, and Trotsky. *Dependentistas* of all kinds have been influenced by Marx's writings, whether they consider themselves Marxists or not. Marx is cited often in the dependency literature, no matter where it is produced and despite its obvious departures from Marx's approach to material inequalities.

Yet it is a mistake to speak of dependency perspectives in general as Marxist. In fact, the sharpest criticism of the dependency literature on Latin America has come from Marxist scholars. On the level of political commitment, they have condemned it as a reformist "anti-imperialism that becomes class collaboration"[24]—a refurbishing of old "formulations of bourgeois ideology" comparable to the thinking of nineteenth-century Russian Narodniks, with a "historically regressive meaning for the socialist process."[25] And at the level of theory, they charge that it focuses on nations as the units of analysis and on superficial aspects of international trade, without due attention to class and the relationships of production.[26] Above all, Marxists generally have distanced themselves from non-Marxist *dependentistas'* emphasis on the distribution of surpluses among international groups. This emphasis they consider an excursion into a cul-de-sac that slights the social relationships of production. Marxist writers have praised the attention that non-Marxist dependency perspectives attract to materialist issues and to the effects of capitalism on the unequal accumulation of wealth worldwide, but they find in this literature no unified theory, a tendency to reduce all interaction to the exchange of goods and services, and—in the practice of North American social scientists—a loose and indiscriminate application to empirical research of a poorly developed concept.[27]

Dependency studies are only beginning to become good history, as Charles W. Bergquist has remarked.[28] Their propositions about the impact of markets on the relations of production and class formation have not often been systematically tested by historians, and contradictory developments such as peasants "seceding" from the world economy have not been addressed. Essays and books informed by dependency perspectives and deep historical knowledge were published as many as fifteen years ago by Tulio Halperín Donghi, Stanley and Barbara Stein, and Ciro F. S. Cardoso, but these are general treatments usually grounded in a spotty secondary literature and concentrated on the nineteenth century.

Halperín's synthesis of modern Latin American history, *Historia contemporánea de América Latina* is often cited by dependency writers to support their historical interpretations.[29] This book shares with dependency perspectives an interest in the growth of capitalism worldwide and a view of the colonial heritage that stresses inequalities in material relationships—inequalities related to the impact of gold and silver mining, the power of landed estates (though he recognizes that possession of land did not equal control of wealth), and requirements imposed by Europe on peripheral economies. Halperín's view of the Independence Period (1810–1825) as a great economic and social crisis, and of early national history to 1850 as a period that accentuated semi-independent rural structures more than economic dependency on the world system, departs from the dependency view of the years 1750 to 1850 as a fairly unified period of dependent underdevelopment. But his periodization for the late nineteenth century is compatible with the outline of stages used by dependency writers.[30] As part of his "long wait" for a new order after national independence, Halperín sees a transition to a "neo-colonial" order beginning at mid-century with the increased capacity of the world market to absorb Latin American exports and with the growth of the capital supply in Latin America, thanks to foreign loans to national governments, the establishment of branches of European banks, and foreign investment in the local economy. After 1880, with "the maturity of the neo-colonial order," Latin America experienced the direct impact of industrial capitalism in the form of British and United States investment, production of raw materials for the world market on a new scale, railroads, and the proletarianization of part of the work force. Despite its compatibility with some of the literature on dependency, Historia contemporánea is no bible for theorists in search of a dependentista or Marxist explanation of process in social history. While it is attentive to economic forces, Historia contemporánea is more a grand work of synthesis, influenced by Braudel's version of "total history" but without the close attention to geography, and evincing a determined interest in political reform, intellectual life, institutional history, and nations, and an affection for old-fashioned histoire événementielle. It touches on a great many institutions and views them in new and deep ways from top to bottom (the Church is one of many examples), and is a rich source for subjects and connections in need of further study. However, Historia contemporánea is little concerned with the details of social history, and is intentionally short of statistical evidence of material relationships (there are no tables and very few figures in the text).[31]

In English, the most important work of historical synthesis on early Latin America from a dependency perspective remains Stanley and Barbara Stein's The Colonial Heritage of Latin America: Essays on Economic Dependence in Perspective. While it follows Frank's emphasis on silver mining and the export economy, the Colonial Heritage is also a compelling inquiry into the internal structures of colonial economies, labor, and social relationships. Nor does it neglect the complexities of the state's participation in the degradation of the labor force and its largely indirect but effective system of rule in the colonial period. It contains many ideas about specific connections among economic, political, and social processes in early Latin America that still provide a valuable agenda for the field. In the late 1960s there were few case studies or fully documented works on regional society and economy to draw on (beyond Stanley Stein's own work on a Brazilian coffee county and the textile industry of Brazil in the late nineteenth century), and the Steins made no claim to fill that void or account for regional differences in the Colonial Heritage. More recent research into particular places and times would modify their view of law in society, latifundios and debt peonage as formative institutions of dependency from the sixteenth century, and the unbroken continuities of economic dependence on Europe in the first half of the nineteenth century.[32] Also, the shaping of colonial social and economic relationships by export agriculture and the production of silver remains to be demonstrated for most parts of Latin America. Still, the Steins did not simply derive their history from theory or use "dependency" as a label, and they rethought that history into an interpretation that still challenges other historians to produce a general view of early Latin America that accounts for as much.

Since the early 1970s, scholars have begun to take up the challenge of elaborating a social history for Latin America through Marxist theory as an extension of dependency perspectives. Ciro F. S. Cardoso's work on nineteenth-century Central America and Mexico is representative of this recent scholarship. His own researches have been combined with his supervision of many graduate theses at the Universidad de Costa Rica, and with his coordination of seminars there and at the Centro de Estudios Históricos of the Instituto Nacional de Antropología e Historia in Mexico City. These seminars have led to the publication of wide-ranging books in the tradition, if not on the scale, of Daniel Cosío Villegas's Historia moderna de México, which grew from seminars in the Colegio de México. One example of this collective work under Cardoso's direction is México en el siglo XIX (1821–1910): historia económica y de la estructura social, published in Mexico in 1980.[33] In this socioeconomic interpretation of Mexican history, Cardoso and his eleven coauthors are concerned primarily with the transition to dependent capitalism in the late nineteenth century. While Mexico's place in the world capitalist system is central to the conception of this book, the authors reject the Frank and Immanuel Wallerstein approach to dependency as a function of exchange, preferring to emphasize structures of production and internal developments. They characterize Mexico as precapitalist until the

Porfiriato, and divide the text into two parts by period: 1821–1880 and 1880–1910. Except for skirting Halperín's "crisis" of the Independence Period in order to emphasize the "fundamental continuity [of the first half of the nineteenth century] with colonial structures," this chronology follows the *Historia contemporánea* periodization into "the long wait," the decisive transition in the 1850s, and consolidation of the new order after 1880. The economic changes of each period and subperiod are carefully described and justified in rewarding detail. Identifying the Liberal-Conservative civil wars of the 1850s and 1860s as the point of crisis in the transition to dependent capitalism makes good sense in terms of banking, agricultural exports, mining, the beginnings of railroads, and national economic policies, although the privatization of much community land decades before 1850, the end of the Indian legal status in the 1820s, and the population growth from 1750 to 1850 could also justify a view of the 1850s as more of a political crisis than an economic watershed.[34]

Where *México en el siglo XIX* falls short of its goal of "socioeconomic" history is in the connections between economic changes and social structure. "Social structure and social movements" are separated out of the analysis as thirty-page chapters (in a text of 507 pages), one for each of the two time periods; the twenty-two page introduction on colonial structures devotes one page to society and simply describes it as an ethnic-estate hierarchy; and the pages on society have a much weaker statistical base than the economic history sections. The conclusion points to three changes in a social structure that remained "massively agrarian" and rigidly stratified: (1) the emergence of dynamic new sectors of the dominant class; (2) the proletarianization of artisans and peasants; and (3) the destruction of community structures. In this treatment of society, people seem to act only as members of economic classes. The authors discuss changes in class relations almost as an afterthought after they have established the economic changes, assuming rather than demonstrating that social change results from changes in economic structure, and necessarily glossing over social changes that may have coincided with the Independence wars. Wealth is equated with the "dominant class"; the clergy is presented as having been eliminated from this dominant class in the 1850s; and religion is said to be no longer important, despite the "religious clichés" of worker ideology thereafter. By considering only those "social movements" that were led by the "dominant classes and middle strata," on the grounds that those were the ones that involved real power, the authors conveniently dismiss most of the collective actions of *campesinos*.[35]

Beyond these significant entries into the general history of dependency relations in Latin America, the last five years have seen important publications influenced by dependency and more definite Marxist perspectives that reach past general propositions and suggestive examples to test and demonstrate the process of dependent relationships and the formation of specific social and economic structures with solid evidence rooted in a manageable region and a carefully justified period of time. Three recent books can serve to illustrate this trend: Steve J. Stern's *Peru's Indian Peoples and the Challenge of Spanish Conquest: Huamanga to 1640*; Claude Morin's *Michoacán en la Nueva España del siglo XVIII: crecimiento y desigualdad en una economía colonial*; and Laird W. Bergad's *Coffee and the Growth of Agrarian Capitalism in Nineteenth-Century Puerto Rico*.[36]

Peru's Indian People examines a highland region of agricultural communities with overlapping ethnic affiliations and hereditary chiefs and commercial relations. Conquered and loosely incorporated into the Inca Empire after 1460, the area was then organized into the economic and political hinterland of the important colonial town of Huamanga after the Spanish Conquest. Stern uses administrative and judicial records to reveal the development of Spanish-Indian relations and the social organization of colonial Indian communities in terms of the political economy of the region as it was linked to a precapitalist world market. The book concentrates on the systematic extraction of Indian labor for agriculture and mining—then the principal means of generating wealth—in the expanding commercial economy of the early colonial period. Stern locates three overlapping but successive systems of extracting Indian labor: a traditional indigenous system that characterized the first decades of colonial rule to the 1560s; a centralized state system of forced labor, organized by Viceroy Toledo in the 1570s with the nucleation of the Indian population in *reducciones*; and a gradual transition to private forms of securing labor by 1640 in which Indian laborers increasingly depended on patrons and employers for their subsistence. Stern connects these stages to Indian responses to Spanish rule and the formation of closed, corporate Indian communities. During the first period, local Indian leaders (*kurakas*) became the mediators of colonial labor relations, mobilizing laborers through traditional channels but now for service to the Spaniards. By the 1560s, resistance to Spanish demands, previously expressed in *kuraka* influence on the terms of the labor supply, grew into millenarian movements and a social crisis that were out of *kuraka* control. The "profound demoralization" of native Andean societies after the failure of these popular movements for moral purification allowed Viceroy Toledo to undertake a systematic reorganization of labor for the mining economy and a consolidation of the colonial regime. By the early seventeenth century, Stern argues, the colonial state exercised a "pervasive hegemony over the indigenous peasantry." While Stern sees class as the motor of historical change, he specifically addresses the interplay of Indian peasants and the Spanish legal system, and how the state intervened between a world market system and the periphery. The "effective network of state power" over labor, "reduction" of Indians to Spanish-style settlements, and the rise of individual labor contracts were accompanied by the development of resilient corporate communities that pursued "closed" strategies in their relations with Spanish masters as an Indian accommodation to the reality of defeat. Stern suggests that these reconstituted communities and local solidarities were as much a product of internal struggles over increasing inequalities of wealth between Hispanicized Indian notables and impoverished peasants— accentuated, if not created, by colonial demands for labor—as they were resistance movements that asserted native traditions and limited colonial appropriations of land and labor.[37] In this sense native Huamangans participated in their own oppression.[38]

Michoacán en la Nueva España deals with the regional economic development of the territory encompassed by the Bishopric of Michoacán, Mexico—another important agricultural and mining zone within one of the highland core areas of colonial Spanish America—during the last century of Spanish rule. It gives less attention to labor and social relationships and agricultural production for a limited local market than do *Peru's Indian People* or Karen Spalding's *Huarochirí*, but provides a fuller documentation of the short- and long-term movement of production, trade, land tenure, financial activity, the economic and social impact of taxation, the relationship of mining to agriculture, and local differences within Michoacán. This difference in focus is partly a function of sources, partly a matter of the authors' interests, and partly a reflection of inherent differences between Mexico and Peru and between the sixteenth and eighteenth centuries.

Morin argues that economic dependency was deeper and growth slower for his region in the eighteenth century than in earlier times.

Virtual monopolies and trade privileges of the merchant guilds, and the export of silver, greatly restricted the general circulation of money and the supply of liquid capital in the eighteenth century; Mexico was "bombarded" with manufactured goods from Europe; agricultural production increasingly was geared to provincial and international markets. Morin speaks of a "hemorrhaging of money" to Europe and China, caused partly by increases in royal taxes that outstripped the substantial growth of production in agriculture and mining.[39] He demonstrates that economic growth was confined to parts of Michoacán in the eighteenth century, and that the enrichment of the crown should not be equated with general prosperity. This book is a valuable if indirect elaboration on the place of silver mining in the colonial economy; unfortunately, Morin goes on to speak with little elaboration or evidence of "retrograde changes" in society and "frozen" social relations resulting from these dependency relationships.

Coffee and the Growth of Agrarian Capitalism examines dependency relationships in commercial agriculture in the late nineteenth century, still in a colonial setting but at a time when agrarian capitalism relying on wage labor can be said to have taken hold.[40] It deals both with the rise and fall of coffee production in two highland municipalities and with the history of commercial agriculture and wage labor in Puerto Rico as a whole. Like Morin, Bergad is more concerned with the economic organization of his region, with market forces in a world economy, and with when and how commercial agriculture took hold than with internal social relationships outside of markets or with the role of the state in the social relationships of production. But his extensive use of notarial and administrative records permits a detailed description of the changing organization of production in coffee—Puerto Rico's principal export from 1850 to 1900—and its general effects on the island's society: a decline in subsistence agriculture, the simultaneous rise of a free labor market, and control of the coffee industry by foreign merchants turned planters. The land pressures of an expanding coffee industry combined with population growth and a consequent oversupply of laborers to proletarianize subsistence farmers, renters, and sharecroppers. Bergad goes beyond the transition to wage labor which has preoccupied some Marxist scholars to consider in rich detail the historical pattern of land use, capital accumulation and its place in the expansion of coffee production, income distribution, and trade. Puerto Rico appears as a classic example of late nineteenth-century dependent underdevelopment in Latin America: coffee *fincas* became "modern capitalist enterprises for the era" rather than seigneurial estates; the long-term boom and bust cycles were fueled by the organization of international trade more than by the characteristics of production; foreign investment attracted to agricultural activity was directed toward foreign markets; much of the capital generated by coffee was exported; and a new generation of estate owners grew up who had been the merchant creditors and middlemen in the early years of the industry. In his conclusion comparing Puerto Rico to other Latin American coffee producers Bergad makes it clear that Puerto Rico is a classic example, not a typical one. Puerto Rico was still a colony in the coffee period. It is not surprising that much of the capital left the island, or that the merchant-planter entrepreneurs did not think of themselves as Puerto Ricans.[41]

The dependency approaches' emphasis on capitalism as the "motor" driving Latin American society from the sixteenth century on inevitably leads back to disagreements about whether the Latin American economy and resulting social relationships were feudal or capitalist. Marcello Carmagnani, for example, has viewed early Latin America as a "feudal system" with a "feudal" mode of production. He means by this that the system was not primarily capitalist because it depended on the intensive exploitation of servile labor in various forms and on the extensive exploitation and redistribution of natural resources (land and mines) by personal concession from the crown.[42] In this limited conception, a feudal system of production with "dominant" (*haciendas*, mines) and "indirect" (landholding villages) parts can exist without a predominance of isolated manorial communities, and with private property and a partially monetized market economy geared to exports. Frank and more empirical dependency writers, of course, do not claim that the mode of production must be capitalist to be shaped by a capitalist world system. Precapitalist modes of production may long survive contact with capitalism because they are congruent rather than in conflict with an international division of production and exchange. As long as peripheral areas produce their raw materials for capitalist centers, there is little pressure to move quickly into a "free" labor system.[43]

The feudalism-capitalism debate, then, tends to move at two different levels. Neither side of the debate excludes the possibility of several modes of production existing in the same place simultaneously or intermittently even though one is said to dominate, but the feudal-ism thesis for early Latin America emphasizes relationships of production while the capitalism thesis tends to emphasize relationships of exchange. But, as Hermann Rebel cautions, it is not enough to investigate whether classes or orders, feudalism or capitalism predominated in a complex situation that was not all one or the other. It is also important "to discover the way they interact with each other in mutually supportive as well as in contradictory ways." Capitalism and feudalism "often together create unique social systems that undergo their own development and historical transformations without being dominated by either one or another kind of organization of production."[44]

Eric R. Wolf has proposed another way to conceive of social relationships of production before the rise of industrial capitalism without calling them either capitalist or feudal (with all that feudalism necessarily implies about vassalage and Spanish culture at the time of the Conquest, in addition to servile labor and patriarchal politics) that seems to work for the most populous areas of early Latin America. Wolf speaks of a tributary mode of production, in which labor is mobilized and surpluses are extracted from primary producers by political more than economic means, largely in the form of tribute—the taxes and services owed to the lord.[45] The various resources of the state, more than market forces, determined how labor was mobilized and how land was assigned. Mercantile activities and a money economy could have an important place in this mode of production, as they did in Spanish and Portuguese America, but merchants in a tributary system primarily were agents for the distribution of surplus after its extraction by the state. And ideally (from the government's point of view) their success depended on concessions from the crown through monopoly contracts (like the *asiento* slave trade or the commercial companies of the eighteenth century) or on membership in the *consulados* (merchant guilds) controlled by the crown. In fact, merchants were not simply powerless functionaries. The relationship of merchants and the state was complicated by the crown's dependence on their expertise and by the commercialization of goods and services, which could weaken the basis of tributary power. But substantial merchant activity and money begetting more money do not mean Latin American societies in general were determined by a system of "mercantile capitalism" in the colonial period. Tributary states had a clear interest in subjecting merchants to political supervision and impeding the development of free markets in their empires. They were not always successful, but tributary states left a deep imprint on the economies of early Latin America.[46]

Wolf sees capitalism not as an outgrowth of merchant wealth— which he considers important mainly to the growth of markets, money exchange, and what he calls the "prehistory" of capitalism— but as a transformation in the social relationships of labor and property, so that wealth is used to control the means of production and to buy the labor power of propertyless workers.[47] This transformation is connected with the beginnings of industrialization, from the late eighteenth century. One of the virtues of this conception, which places capitalism's influence late in the history of Latin America, is that it can account for the similarity between the colonial system and pre-Conquest states in the highlands, in production and in the extraction of surplus. Tribute mechanisms, while not identical before and after the Conquest, were an essential feature of the production and distribution of wealth in those areas until the mid-nineteenth century. The possibilities of Wolf's theory, and his interest in the history of "the people without history" and the extent to which the colonial system in the highlands lived off peasant surpluses, are strangely at odds with his specific characterization of the colonial Spanish American economy and society in terms of external forces and coercion. In Wolf's version of colonial society, Spaniards have seized the land and water, the basis of wealth in the countryside; haciendas loom large as the populous centers of power and agricultural production, coercing the labor of masses of displaced Indians and seasonal workers from villages; Indians are victims, separated from their lands and resettled by the state in new communities, with little about their lives they can call their own; mining "reshapes" the colonies because the Spaniards want gold and silver; and society is rearranged by a coercive state to produce for the mines and towns.[48] Wolf's call for a broadly conceived materialist history that goes beyond the dependency perspectives' absorption in how the core subjugated the periphery to a "processual, relational history" of workers, ideology, and the social relationships of production and distribution is not achieved for early Latin America in *Europe and the People Without History*. But his book represents a promising way of thinking about Latin American history, influenced by *dependentista* and world systems approaches as well as by Marxist theory and the large body of scholarship without theoretical pretensions that has begun to appear in North American empirical studies of early Latin America and that seeks to discover and explain large patterns in the history of social relationships without deducing them from social theory.[49]

Connecting the State and Society

By emphasizing interactions at the level of economic domination in a world capitalist system, dependency perspectives have the advantage of reaching beyond the isolation of national, provincial, and local boundaries, the split distinctions of rural/urban, ruled/rulers, internal/external, Gemeinschaft/Gesellschaft, and Indian/Spaniard to focus attention on processes of material inequalities. But the dependency perspectives so far have not been adequate as a way of seeing early Latin American history whole: of discerning as far as possible the relationships among individuals and groups, and of understanding how the lives of subjects were controlled both directly and indirectly and how resources were distributed (resources in the broad sense of knowledge, control of symbols, patronage, force, communication, and mediation of all kinds as well as material wealth). In particular, dependentistas generally have treated the state as little more than a vehicle of coercion in the economic interests of a ruling class, another category to be treated separately as superstructure rather than as an integral, indispensable part of the process of inequality.

Much of the dependentista literature has taken its point of departure from the concept of class popularized by Marx—social classes as the fundamental structures of historical change organized by the division of labor and other relationships to the factors of production—and given class an international context for the history of capitalism. The social changes to which this literature has been drawn are transitions to a free labor market, wages, and new situations of economic dependency. The remainder of this essay treats social divisions in Latin America to 1900 with less reference to capitalism and in a less precise way that I believe is truer to that time in the old centers of native population. This conception of inequality accepts the importance of conflict and divisions of society in terms of their relationships to the process of production, but it recognizes other relationships of domination within "peripheral" Latin America before 1900 that do not seem to be determined mainly by the process of production.[50]

Of the two great structural changes occurring in Europe and influencing the Europeanizing areas of the world after 1500—capitalism and state formation[51]—the institutions of the state, in their ordering of social relationships, had an earlier, more direct, and deeper impact on the central areas of Spanish America, at least until the last quarter of the nineteenth century. Centralizing states directed from Spain, and to a lesser extent from Portugal, operated long before the growth of capitalism in Latin America or the influence of European industrial capitalism over Latin American economies. (Of course, such a broad generalization will not hold good everywhere in Latin America. The history of mining and tropical plantation areas—coastal Brazil, the Caribbean Islands, mining and plantation enclaves on the mainland of Spanish America that relied much more on immigrant labor—does conform more closely to dependency perspectives, and the mainland enclaves often shaped production and distribution of wealth far beyond their immediate zones of production.)

In suggesting that the state in early Latin America cannot readily be identified simply as superstructure I do not mean that the state can be separated from economic relationships. I do mean that in the core areas of Spanish America the new political relationships organized under the Spanish state were more far-reaching than the change in mode of production—basically tributary both before and after the Conquest, with the state taxing its subjects, requisitioning labor and shaping the supply of labor indirectly, and overseeing the political peace that allowed for access to complementary ecological niches and stimulated markets. Again, this is a sweeping statement that requires qualification. Spanish rule changed the timing and territory of markets, introduced export-import relationships, found new and often greater uses for labor, increasingly viewed labor as a commodity to be demanded or bought and sold, monopolized and licensed various enterprises, and led to a drastic decline of the population that changed the scale of production and the organization of colonial communities in the countryside.[52] Still, one of the peculiarities of early Latin American history is that the state became important before thoroughgoing mercantilism or industrial capitalism from Europe had much effect. It makes little sense to speak generally of a Latin American working class in a capitalist system much before 1900. Even more than in most European societies, in rural Latin America the horizontal solidarities and vertical antagonisms of class were less evident than the vertical bonds of patronage and religion, the institutional and ideological links between centers of society and peripheral areas, and the horizontal antagonisms of competing local interests.

The historiography of early Latin America, especially for the colonial period, offers little guidance on how social changes and the structure of large, intertwined societies can be examined through the history of the state, as an alternative to or an extension of dependency and Marxist perspectives. Recent social history has routinely eschewed the study of national events, the rule of law, and the affairs of top-level leaders in favor of groups of ordinary people and their informal lives; earlier works tacitly assumed that the colonial state was all powerful, or at least took little interest in its contingencies. Clarence Haring's *The Spanish Empire in America*, a distinguished synthesis of the best thinking about the colonial period up to the mid-1940s, exemplifies this older emphasis on formal institutions as the subject of Latin American history.[53] There were good reasons for social historians to turn away from approaches that were tinged with a nineteenth-century providential nationalism, and that focused more on portraying colonial rulers as tyrants, for patriotic reasons, than on examining the institutional expressions of social relationships. Ricardo Palma's engaging tales of old Peru, *Las tradiciones peruanas*, written in the decades after his country's national independence, are filled with just such all-powerful colonial curates and magistrates.[54] Regardless of the author's political sympathies, Indians were treated in this early literature from Palma to Haring like flakes of gold: inert, easily molded, and valuable objects, to be gathered up and spent by *encomenderos*, *hacendados*, miners, merchants, and royal officials.

In reaction to this tradition, much recent social history has shifted its attention from rulers to subjects (as if such a neat dichotomy were possible), and has shown that production and power were contested, that ordinary people had feelings, values, and leverage, too. In the process, formal institutions and political events have receded into the background or disappeared altogether. The groups to be studied, whether Indian villages, merchants, *hacendados*, or even slave communities, are regarded as more or less autonomous, or at least are treated without much reference to their relationships to other people. The state and formal institutions are "weak and spotty," "fragmented, with limited resources."[55]

This turning away from the state in society neglects an obvious pattern of Latin American history that Kalman Silvert pointed out in his criticism of a causal chain from economic change to occupational shift to social change to politics:

> This single-line chain is always questionable; in Latin America it is untenable. To the contrary, one of the manners in which social change has occurred in Latin America is along the following line: change of ideology in Europe, carry-over to Latin America and readaptation by local intellectuals, translation of the notions into political terms, change in the political institution, and then a political attempt to implement economic and social policies. There have been many processes at work but the ability to import a notion and then use tutelary politics to implement it is a long-standing tradition of the area.[56]

Here is dependency of a different kind. Silvert's chain of change is too neat to represent social and economic change in many Latin American places before 1900, but his emphasis on conscious changes and political ideas working through institutions of the state is well placed. One example, the social and political effects of the eighteenth-century Bourbons' single-minded determination to extend absolutism through a more secular state, will appear later in this section. Similar transfers of ideas also took place after independence from Spain, even during the decades of weak national and state government in many new Latin American countries before the 1870s. For example, the rapid decline of community landholdings in former Indian *pueblos* of western Mexico in the 1820s and 1830s, in favor of more private ownership, was directly inspired by decrees of the Spanish Cortes of Cádiz, issued in 1812 and 1813 and designed to stimulate production and integrate Indians into society by weakening village ties and turning over ownership of the village patrimony to local families. These decrees served even after independence as models for state laws and judicial acts in Jalisco, Mexico, that were widely if incompletely implemented, especially in communities that had already begun to divide up corporate lands among their members before 1810. The new laws did not independently "cause" the privatization of land, and other economic changes were underway at the same time,[57] but these laws accelerated the process in many *municipios* decades before agrarian capitalism could have reorganized the social relations of production there. The redistribution of land and other community property before the 1850s reduced or eliminated the estates held by *cofradías* and required adjustments in religious

celebrations—either the elimination of some cult practices, more individual sponsorship, or some new form of community contributions—that would have preceded more than followed the influence
of capitalism there.

At the opposite extreme in the recent literature from this inatten-
tion to the affairs of the state, justified on the grounds that politics
had little to do with long-term changes in the lives of common people, is a return to the idea that the colonial government was nearly
omnipotent. This new work inquires into the ways in which the state
created and preserved social inequalities. Starting with the premise
that "Latin American society cannot be understood without the historical force of the state," this approach has tended to see the state
in terms of coercion and all-or-nothing control: "The colonial state
was able to consolidate an overall domain through the implementa-
tion of detailed, centralized mechanisms for the division of labour
and the use of resources," and "power was effectively vested in the
King of Spain's representatives," presented as controlling the lowliest
villager's life.[58] By emphasizing the power of the state, this interpretation criticizes the dependency perspectives while retaining their
emphasis on an imperial system operating in a world economy. Its
proponents tend to forget that the scope of government in the eighteenth and nineteenth centuries was quite limited by today's standards. Poor communications, poor transportation, illiteracy, and limited resources all hindered any universal diffusion of the ideal of
central state authority or the traditions necessary to uphold it. Perhaps in the sixteenth and eighteenth centuries Spanish rulers had an
interest in imposing a single culture on all villages within their territories, but the relationship of the colonial state to "its" villages always
was too limited and contingent to accomplish such a homogenization. It could be said with equal accuracy that the state in Latin
America took little interest in what went on within the village. This
last statement, like its opposite, contains only a kernel of truth; and,
by itself, it does not advance our understanding of the connections
between state and society. It treats societies as things, seeing villages
and patrimonial rulers as closed worlds located at the poles of Robert
Redfield's folk-urban continuum.

For now, there are few published works on state and society in
Latin America from 1700 to 1850 that do not start from one of these
two positions—the state as an autonomous actor and independent
variable, or the state as weak and fragmented, a passive arena of

competing interests.[59] This divergence is a sign of the early stage of research and thinking about the subject. It is also a sign that the eighteenth and early nineteenth centuries, parts of which have been studied intensively and well in the last fifteen years, currently are undergoing substantial re-vision.[60] We seem to be in the middle of a sort of free-for-all, before a more comprehensive interpretation achieves some degree of consensus or the period and subject lose their appeal.

One approach to research on state and society in early Latin America that is faithful to what is known (and probably can be known) would set aside the hidden dichotomies of ruler/ruled, omnipotent state/weak state, outside world/local community, secular/religious, and think of communities and institutions more as Eric R. Wolf proposes—as bundles of relationships among people rather than as things or units that lead lives of their own, interacting with other units but not bound to them except perhaps one-to-one. In this way it is easier to see that most people are in some sense both rulers and ruled, and that power relationships may be intermittent, incomplete, and complicated by many conflicting obligations and loyalties; and to recognize that there was not a single, unified, coherent ruling class. The recent scholarship on agrarian structures in early Latin America leads toward this way of asking questions about the state and about relationships of inequality. In most central areas of colonial Spanish America, great haciendas and their owners did not dictate the affairs of the rural people in their vicinity, monopolize the means of production, or serve as the only important connectors between rural communities and the "outside world." If the idea of the all-powerful landlord no longer is tenable as a general rule, the inward/outward dualism becomes less useful and we need to pay more attention to political maneuvering within a complex and contingent system of social control.

This approach need not deny the place of coercion in the operation of Latin American states since 1500. For the nineteenth century the use of brute force, the figure of the caudillo, the armed overthrow of governments, and the militarizing of many provinces and new nations are familiar historical themes. We should remember, however, that coercion and force became more prominent rather than less so with the collapse of the centralizing colonial Spanish states. There were no standing armies until the late eighteenth century, and then mainly to defend borders against invasion and illegal trade. Juan

Linz's observations about Spain after 1800 as a divided nation of political violence apply in a general way to Latin America as well:

> Perhaps the explanation lies in the fact that Spanish state-building went on before the age of nationalism and that the era of nationalism coincided with a period of crisis of the Spanish state, bitter ideological conflicts, loss of its colonial empire, and economic backwardness and uneven development—a period in which the center, Madrid and its government, had little to offer to the periphery and limited resources for a successful policy of Castilianization.[61]

Nevertheless, Spanish colonization had begun with the threat of armed conquest, and Cortez, Pizarro, and the small host of founders of provincial centers of the Spanish empire were well remembered by succeeding generations of local people, whatever their station in life. State power in the colonial period was exercised more through magistrates and priests than through soldiers, but the threat of coercion was evident in the enforcement of laws designed to disarm all but the Spanish population, in the definition of Indians as perpetual minors ("children with beards," as one priest put it), in the characterizaton of *castas* as dangerous and untrustworthy by nature. Much of the deference of public life could have been disguised coercion more than genuine humility—at least, the officials who complained that Indian subjects exhibited only a false humility implied that they thought more coercion was needed. But coercion that took rural Indians, or what they produced, out of their villages often was less direct than taxation, forced labor, or outright confiscation. For example, coercion partly explains the movement of eggs from Indian villages in the Sierra de Puebla to Mexico City in the eighteenth century, but it was not as if colonial officials removed the eggs at gunpoint. Under the *repartimiento de mercancías* the villagers were obliged to accept cattle or other monopoly trade goods from the *alcalde mayor* or his lieutenants, paying for these goods on a daily or weekly basis in eggs. The tribute and other taxes that were levied in cash had an important added result that drew villagers out of their homes and fields: Even if otherwise meeting their subsistence needs, villagers had to find a cash market for their surplus produce or, more likely, find a seasonal employer who would pay cash for their labor.

One entry into the state and relationships of power across social classes that seems fruitful, partly because it is documented in the great collections of administrative and judicial records for the colonial period and lends itself to configurations based on hundreds or thousands of individual cases distributed over many years, is through personal mediation. That is, we may examine interactions of state institutions with local society and politics at the points of face-to-face contact between people with different interests and different resources, usually but not always including officials of the government: district judges or their lieutenants and the people within their jurisdictions; parish priests and their parishioners; lawyers in the administrative towns and the people they represented; traders, producers, and consumers in a market system. And we may also examine the relationships among these priests, judges, traders, and others who exercised authority or mediated between policy makers and the objects of policy.[62] Among these "others" who were in a position to make, interpret, or enforce policy were owners or managers of private estates; village officials; village secretaries; and other purveyors of knowledge, news, and rumor that reached beyond the local place, such as tavernkeepers, traders, and the small literate population.

This approach to the maintenance and exercise of systems of power through concrete personal mediations expands the concept of the state beyond the usual meaning of centralized institutions of the sovereign authority to encompass a larger field of institutional expressions of social relationships that have to do with the regulation of public life. It is meant to suggest that the state was, as E. P. Thompson has said, the "institutional expression of social relationships," not just rulers and their offices. Many of the concrete relationships and their structures have yet to be described for early Latin America. In addition to the hierarchy of royal officeholders, the state included local elites and priests (and their relatives), as well as semiformal brokers like notaries, supernumeraries, attorneys, messengers, and others who were personally connected to magistrates, priests, generals, and tax officials and who could influence these officials' decisions through advice or the timing of their own actions. Without stretching "the state" to the point where it becomes another word for society, this conception does, at least potentially, involve everyone who participated in some identifiable behavioral interaction connected with state actions. But it does not encompass all social relationships or all people all the time or all forms of power (taking power to mean all social relationships that resulted from patterns of control, and were reciprocal).[63] Successful research of this kind does, however, depend on reaching beyond the dyadic relationships of priest and parishioner, judge and judged, to the networks of contacts that were activated by these relationships or that influenced when and how these formal relationships were established.

Studying the careers of any of the groups of people who could be considered power brokers is a convenient place to begin research. It will give an indication of the activities, education, interests, experiences, wealth, and social background of a class of people who could influence the lives of others by their office, training, or knowledge, and allow the activities of individuals to be measured against the group. More important and more difficult than prosopography for the study of power and social change is the task of connecting these groups of brokers, seeing their overlapping responsibilities and constituencies, establishing when and where they appeared or disappeared, how their influence changed in other ways, and how they were affected by and participated in decisions about production. The aim is to see these people not only according to their job descriptions in law and custom and in professional resumés (for bureaucrats and priests these often exist as *relaciones de méritos y servicios*), but also as actors in the local economy and public life, and as links to distant markets and higher centers of formal power. Their relationships to centers, whether district capitals, cathedrals, marketplaces, or high courts, are most likely to be documented; the challenge here is to detect how direct, continuous, and intense the relations to these centers were, and how they changed over time.

Parish priests occupied critical intersections between the majority of rural people and higher authorities. As bellwethers of changing relationships between state and society in the eighteenth and nineteenth centuries, they are excellent subjects for this kind of investigation. Their special importance stems from the intimate connection between colonial sovereignty and religion. It was through Catholicism that people learned their place in society, and the Church was one of their main sources of attachment—however limited—to larger collectivities. As Eric J. Hobsbawm has noted for preindustrial Europe, "religion remained inseparable from the ideology of common people and provided the main language for its expression."[64] It was the Catholic Church that served to "spiritualize the material"[65] in Spanish America with a theory of organic, familial, hierarchical associations. State authority and the connected meaning of symbols in the altarpieces of early colonial churches, like the famous Huejotzingo *retablo* in Mexico, took the same form: divinely ordered, unified triangles narrowing to one figure at the top. The pastoral letters of colonial bishops to their clergymen and Christian families invoke father and mother and the respect owed by children to parents as metaphors for authority and society. God is the father of piety, Mary the mother of mercy; kings, under the divine protection of God, are to be loved and revered as fathers of the state and its members; the Church is their mother. Rulers and the rich are enjoined to exercise prudence, piety, and charity; subjects and the poor are instructed to be patient, tolerant, and humble.[66] Like God, the king was a distant, aloof and shadowy father who could be approached mainly through benevolent intercessors.

From the beginning of Spanish colonization, curates were the natural local representatives of their Catholic king. It was the curates who were instructed to live among Indians, charged with supervising their conversion and civilization in settled farming communities. There was no clear line dividing secular and religious life and, until the mid-eighteenth century, the curate operated quite freely as the keeper of public morality, punishing adulterers, gamblers, and drunkards with the whip and reporting serious offenses to royal judges. He and his vicars were also expected to report to the higher levels of government on agricultural conditions, natural disasters, local disturbances, and political news; to record the population; to supervise the annual elections of village officers in communities within the parish; and to aid in social control in other ways (such as using their personal suasion and spiritual office to disperse the angry mobs that formed against colonial officials bearing unpleasant news of new taxes or defeat in land litigation). As a moral and spiritual father and literate local resident able to speak the native language of his parishioners, the curate was well placed to represent the requirements of the state to rural people and interpret their obligations, as well as to carry their interests to higher authorities. The curate, as local defender of the Indians, who more often visited outlying places and resided outside the district capital and usually depended on individual fees for his living, was more likely to speak up for his parishioners' interests and to enjoy their confidence. This was a reciprocal relationship. He could usually fulfill his calling and gain wealth and respect from his superiors as well as from his neighbors by serving the village. Of course, curates were not omnipresent, continuously powerful figures in local affairs. Many were distanced from their parishioners by their

education and their yearnings for the high culture, good conversation, and recognition of the city or even the humble district seat.
Their morality was not always that of their parishioners or that of
their calling; it would be unwise to assume that what the rural curate
taught was identical to what was understood by his parishioners; and
there are many recorded instances of formal complaints by villagers
against the curate, or of curates ridiculed, taunted, and ignored.

The curates' position, career patterns, and vows made them both
strangers and patrons in their parishes, and particularly important
"hinge-men" or mediators in these societies.[67] They belonged to the
outside world and were morally separated from their village parishioners by principles of asceticism and celibacy; yet they lived among
their flocks, ideally as teachers and platonic parents, and their knowledge could be used by the villagers. That colonial rulers and local
communities both were prepared to assign a person such a position
during much of the colonial period suggests that the curate filled a
major gap in rural society in the core areas of Spanish America thanks
to the Spaniards' legal conception of the *pueblo* as a semiautonomous
entity, the place of state religion in public life, and the development
of a variety of "closed, corporate" ideologies in many villages. His
influence as a power broker with his peasant parishioners depended
on his success with higher levels of the state, and vice versa. Though
he was likely to favor one or the other, he had to do something for
both in order to continue filling the gap.[68]

For much of the colonial period the local priests were regarded by
the royal government as counterweights to the *corregidores* and their
lieutenants. A curate who understood his prominent place in public
life to be partly independent of the *corregidor's* authority, especially in
Indian affairs, could be counted on to report abuses of that authority
to the bishop or the Audiencia. Audiencia judges spoke of the countervailing powers of curates and *corregidores* as working best when
these officials were neither openly hostile to each other nor in col-
lusion.[69] The balance would make it more likely that the grievances
of rural people would be heard. Such a balance was, of course, more
an ideal than reality—one or another may have dominated; the natural affinity between Spaniards stationed in remote places may have
united them against the natives; or neither may have had much to do
with the other or with the local population. In any case, the relationships between curates and *corregidores*, studied in many concrete cases,

can begin to reveal ways in which social relationships were ordered through institutions.

Regional studies and collective biographical studies of the lower clergy are beginning to reveal some of these complexities in their role, in time as well as place.[70] It is becoming clear that the Bourbon reforms directed toward centralizing and secularizing the state altered at all levels the relationships of the Church and the moral-political order of society. This change was not unique to Spanish America. Tawney's description of the process in Europe would apply to America as well: Organized religion changed "from the keystone which holds together the social edifice into one department within it."[71] But the central areas of Spanish America were not Europe. Priests there were more important to the bureaucratic operations of the state; in general, their place in local affairs had not eroded gradually as it had in Europe. There was no loss of religious fervor before the Bourbon reforms. If anything, religious beliefs were more intense, and local cults were spreading.[72]

The effects of the eighteenth-century Bourbon reforms on curates in the Latin American countryside are less well known than those of the expulsion of the Jesuits or the narrowing of the Inquisition's activities, but they were equally profound. In principle, the curate was now to be a spiritual specialist, his public duties and his role as an agent of the Christian monarch sharply curtailed. Royal edicts forbade him to use corporal punishment, to certify election results, to undertake repairs of church buildings without royal license, or to manage the property and finances of lay brotherhoods in his parish. Primary schools were to be established, and curates could not be the teachers. The district magistrates alone were to deal with adultery, gambling, and drunkenness. The results of these reforms reached beyond the formal powers of priests to begin to dismantle the judicial state, a state that had preserved its aura of legitimacy through case judgments combining principles of natural law, royal power to make law, and sensitivity to local customs and beliefs about right relations between subjects and the sovereign.

Unwittingly, the Bourbons would contribute to the national revolutions of the nineteenth century by cutting themselves loose from divine purpose. In a literal sense, power was being desacralized and increasingly separated from traditional patterns of attachment, convenience, and consent. More village leaders in the late eighteenth century began to speak of Spanish rule as if it were a naked assertion of superiority. District governors more often were military men or short-term appointees with little knowledge of the law and local customs, and a bent for summary judgments. They were less judges than enforcers of royal orders, eager to regulate the disorder of local fiestas and other old habits that had never threatened the government. The rising demands of villages to separate from the district seat and become headtowns themselves, was a response to Bourbon centralization and the seemingly arbitrary acts of the new district officials as much as it was an expression of a long-standing ideology of local autonomy.

Where it occurred, the diminution of the curate's public power in the late eighteenth century meant a withdrawal of his patronage from the village. A curate who confined his public activities to administering the sacraments, or who withdrew to the district seat or cathedral city, had less claim on the allegiance of his parishioners and was more likely to be criticized by them for personal faults and illegal acts. There were fewer chances for country people to play one district authority against the other, depending on the curate to side with the village. Without the countervailing authority of the curate, district governors and their minions were freer to operate as they wished. If the curate did not accept his new place in public life, he was likelier to become estranged from the district governor and his allies in the community even to the point of violent conflict. Lieutenants burst into church during the Mass to arrest Indians, sometimes shouting obscenities and insulting the priest if he objected. Proud curates were ridiculed in public by the lieutenants, and sometimes responded in kind. In the late eighteenth century, curates were more often accused of leading unruly protests against the acts of royal officials.

Religion supported the state not only through the concrete mediations of priests but through mentalités or popular beliefs and their ceremonial expressions: symbolic behavior and attitudes toward authority that are embedded in everyday life and shared by large groups of people across social classes—what E. P. Thompson has called "the popular mentalities of subordination."[73] This interest in ideas in the process of subordination derives in large measure from Antonio Gramsci's "hegemony"—what rulers espouse and which many subjects also hold sacred—and how states can establish their cultural and moral superiority. In this view, ideas about and representations of what is proper in unequal social relationships that go largely unquestioned, and consent to reciprocity and cooperation can be powerful ingredients in political power and exchange, and are not neatly explained by relationships of production (any more than they can be separated entirely from relationships of production). Priests, especially country curates, would have been among the most important of Gramsci's "traditional intellectuals" connecting institutions of the state and royal subjects at the level of consent and legitimacy by controlling important services and rites that represented religious ideology and its central place in the colonial enterprise, as well as directly mediating a variety of political relationships with royal officials, the church hierarchy, and their parishioners.[74]

States in early Latin America before independence enjoyed a remarkable level of acceptance, even though wealth and power were very unequally distributed. As research has moved closer to the history of rural Latin America on its own terms, it has become clear that villagers, landless laborers, and small ranchers were not politically inert; nor were their histories confined to the rhythm of the seasons and the life cycle, or to the horizon seen from their stone fences and cactus curtains. There was much coming and going, sometimes permanently; there were changes in institutions and practices; and there were thousands of violent collective actions, mainly against new taxes or other encroachments on local resources. The relative stability of Spain's rule in America was not simply the product of extremely low levels of mobilization, poor communications, or the heavy hand of force. It had as much to do with the consent of the subjects, and with their ingrained beliefs about legitimacy—like the politics of paternalism that Thompson identified as the primary basis of ruling class control in England before the nineteenth century.[75] I do not mean that consensus can be studied alone as the key to social relationships, even though Edward Shils has done just that. By extension, Shils's richly elaborated insights into the diffusion of traditions from "centers" to achieve legitimating consensus contribute to a deeper understanding of power and inclusive structures of society in early Latin America, but Shils admits that he has slighted other aspects of power —conflict and material inequalities as integral features of continuing control[76]—and the idea that politics is about "competition and the confrontation of interests."[77] Allegiance was nearly always conditional and incomplete, and it could express the fear of coercion as much as active belief. And beliefs about legitimacy could generate protest and collective action, as well as acquiescence.

Here we enter the realm of culture as anthropologists generally have conceived of it since the 1940s, that is, as structures of belief, values, shared understandings. Sidney W. Mintz and Richard Price have defined culture in this way and with a sensitivity to historical change in the Americas (but without asserting an idealist determinism): culture is "a body of beliefs and values, socially acquired and patterned, that serve an organized group (a 'society') as guides of and for behavior."[78] The challenge for historians is not only to identify these beliefs and values and to avoid the tacit assumptions that culture was compartmentalized by groups and isolated from material life, but to establish where the beliefs and values came from and when; how they were communicated and applied; how they changed; and how they were related to other changes. Latin American historians, with exceptions like Jacques Lafaye, Irving Leonard, and Inga Clendinnen, have given little attention to these questions and to the history of sacred matters in society beyond religious objects and institutions. North American historians who have lately taken up the study of cultural symbols and rituals for other parts of the world sometimes find inspiration in the concepts, if not the methods, of the anthropologist Clifford Geertz.[79] Geertz's interest in "local knowledge" and "thick description" leads him to a close, almost textual analysis of rituals like the Balinese cockfight that seem to sum up a group's unconscious principles and assumptions about social relationships. His approach looks for symbolic behavior and sees this behavior as a way for participants to establish social relationships and to make statements about those relationships. Geertz eloquently shows that ideas are more than ideology, that beliefs in their local settings are of consequence, and that questions of status and ceremony as well as command should be taken seriously in studying the state; but, as a way to illuminate developments in society otherwise difficult to identify, Geertz's writings on "webs of meaning," "deep play," and "thick description" are used by historians mainly as metaphors and an invitation to ponder the structure of local events. The temptation for Latin American historians inspired by Geertz's writings is to overinterpret poorly described symbolic acts, to concentrate on internal descriptions and explanations of particular cases, and to skirt the issues of power (beyond power as a structure of thought), prosaic changes, and material relationships beyond the locality that are raised in dependency and Marxist perspectives, among others.

We need to examine symbolic behavior in early Latin America in relation to the political processes of state formation, colonization, and control, without building in the antinomy of idealism versus materialism. Subtle interpretations of a single act—a celebration in honor of the Archbishop's arrival in Mexico City in 1622, or the feast of the patron saint in Tulancingo in 1751—will not carry us far toward an historical inquiry into the association (or lack of association) between religious symbols and political action. Above all, we need accurate descriptions of popular religious practices and other expressions of belief in various places at different times. As yet we have too little sense of what changed and when. Once that is accomplished, the challenge will be to find the significance of these beliefs and how they changed, and to examine the possibility of social or political messages in the symbols and religious activities of groups professing common beliefs.

The cult of the Virgin Mary of Immaculate Conception in Mexico is one example of the problems and possibilities of a social history of belief and the *mentalités* of subordination. Studying the symbolism of Mary is more difficult than studying priests or land systems. There is no convenient section of any public archive that contains much information on any particular religious cult over time. Except for occasional investigations of a local cult, the administrative and judicial records of a diocese or the Inquisition yield fragments and incidental information rather than the core of a whole history. The published works of priests sometimes treat Mary directly, as Lafaye has shown, but they cannot be assumed to represent popular beliefs, and they rarely contain evidence that bears on the political significance of religious beliefs. Revealing expressions of belief set in their social context are documented here and there in unlikely places: in criminal trials, reports on rebellions, baptismal records, civil suits, records written in native languages, and *cofradía* (sodality) documentation.

A second, more purely intellectual difficulty is the problem of transcending existing historiographical views about the Virgin's importance in Latin America. There is a tendency in the historical and anthropological literature to accept a metaphor of cultural crystallization, with its tacit assumption or active presumption that key colonial institutions, practices, and beliefs hardened toward the end of the sixteenth century and remained largely unchanged—or that if they changed thereafter, the change was like smashing or dissolving a crystal. For Mexico, the cult of the Virgin of Guadalupe—that most powerful of national religious symbols—has been treated as if it emerged shortly after the Conquest as a universal syncretic Indian cult synonymous with worship of the Virgin Mary, changing little in later years except to grow beyond its Indian constituency. This view of the cult of Guadalupe is fundamentally ahistorical, serving a providential patriotism that validates a powerful Mexican tradition by making it appear older, more popular, and more closely connected to a message of Indian liberation than it was. Focusing on the dark Virgin, Guadalupe, as the "spiritual aspect of protest against the colonial regime"[80] obscures the fact that the Virgin Mary was introduced by Spanish masters as their own patroness, that she appeared in hundreds of different images, that the specific cult of Guadalupe was originally strongest in some of the most urban and the least Indian parts of Mexico, and that the Virgin stood ambiguously for several meanings which were subject to change long before the Industrial Revolution and which may or may not have moved people to action.[81]

What appear as peculiarly strong indigenous folk beliefs about the Virgin Mary actually were much like the popular beliefs of contemporary Spaniards. It is true that in the high formal religion of the Catholic Church, the Virgin Mary carried a variety of symbolic connotations—virgin, bride, queen, mother, and intercessor[82]—and that in rural Latin America she was worshipped mainly as protective intercessor and fertile mother. But it would be a mistake to present the religion of Spanish rulers only as formal and doctrinaire. What Indians understood about the Virgin directly from the first Spaniards was also communicated in less intentional, almost offhand ways. To sixteenth-century Spaniards she was not mainly a remote or regal figure, but rather a beloved intercessor who worked to deflect or soften the harsh judgments of a stern God the Father.[83] At one point in Bernal Díaz's narrative of the Conquest, Cortez tells the Indians of Cempoala that they, too, should look upon Mary as their "lady and intercessor." Mary in Spain was closely associated with the land and fertility and Cortez encouraged Indians at Tenochtitlan to pray to the Virgin Mary for rain.[84] The point here is not that the meaning of the Virgin Mary to Indians in colonial Mexico was simply borrowed from Spanish folk beliefs—beliefs change in the borrowing and acquire distinctive qualities. It is that Spanish conceptions of the Virgin were not only abstract and formal while Indian conceptions were informal and syncretic. There were not neatly separable great and little traditions.

In Mexico the local cults of Mary Immaculate (of whom Guadalupe

was one of many representations) were especially strong in the territories assigned to the Franciscans and Augustinians in the sixteenth
and seventeenth centuries, where hospital chapels founded in Indian
villages were dedicated to her image. These local cults, dedicated to
many different representations of Mary Immaculate and associated
with the protection and destiny of a particular village, developed in
the seventeenth and eighteenth centuries well after the supposed
crystallization of colonial culture. This was a time when Indian *pueblos*
stabilized and took on distinctive forms that promoted community
attachments. Several of these images of Mary gained a wider following: the Virgin of Los Remedios, the Virgin of Candelaria at San Juan
de los Lagos, the Virgin of Zapopan, and especially the Virgin of
Guadalupe.

The cult of Guadalupe, which grew dramatically in the seventeenth
and eighteenth centuries, has a somewhat unexpected history. Syncretic cults of Guadalupe and other mixtures of Mary with local
mother goddesses may well have existed in parts of central Mexico
from the sixteenth century. Perhaps the early Indian worship of Guadalupe coincided with the communities that had worshipped To-
nantzin at Tepeyac before the Conquest. However, most of the many
colonial Indians throughout Mexico who had a special attachment
to the Virgin Mary apparently did not express their devotion to her
in the form of Guadalupe.[85] The consciously providential version
of Guadalupe's apparition apparently first took hold among creole
clergymen in the seventeenth century, and it centered in the viceregal
capital of Mexico City more than in Indian villages.[86] By 1629, when
she was reported to have held back flood waters that nearly destroyed the capital, Guadalupe was well on the way to becoming the
patroness of Mexico City. By the late seventeenth century the large
tezontle church at Tepeyac was under construction. From the 1650s,
copies of Guadalupe's image found their way into other parts of
Mexico: first, apparently, to the city of San Luis Potosí, then to Que-
rétaro (where the first temple to Guadalupe outside the Valley of
Mexico was completed in 1680), Oaxaca, Zacatecas, and Saltillo. By
the early eighteenth century Tepeyac probably was the major pilgrimage site in New Spain, although it was not without rivals. By the 1770s
there were reports of apparitions of the Virgin of Guadalupe in western Mexico. Clearly, Guadalupe was on the minds of more people in
more places. Although we may never know much about who made
pilgrimages to the shrine of Guadalupe at Tepeyac, something of a

spiritual geography of Mexico can be recovered from baptismal records and land litigation that indicate where and when parents named their daughters and sons after Guadalupe, and where and when settlements and estates were named for her. A preliminary inspection of baptismal records from parishes in two parts of Mexico—Oaxaca and Jalisco—suggests that the name Guadalupe gained popularity in district head towns and provincial cities in the second half of the eighteenth century, but that the name was not common in Indian districts and rural villages outside the vicinity of Mexico City until after the Independence wars (1810–1821).

Three patterns are fairly clear from what is known about the expansion of this cult: (1) that its greatest pull was from Mexico City, the Valley of Mexico, and places within a few days' travel from the sanctuary; (2) that it was centered in large towns and cities as it expanded further; and (3) that it spread outside the Valley of Mexico first and most broadly to the north (the least Indian part of New Spain). To say that the Virgin of Guadalupe was only a metropolitan symbol goes too far, but it does seem likely that this is a case of the great preindustrial city as style center, as Paul Wheatley calls it, the place from which values are disseminated and specialized expertise provided.[87] In any case, historians have missed the close connection between the cult of Guadalupe and the history of the city by seeing the cult first as an Indian-based crystallization of the early colonial period and treating it in protonational terms.

Whether we consider Guadalupe separately or as the most widely revered of many images of the Immaculate Conception, the messages of the symbol of Mary Immaculate bear on the question of cultural hegemony and how Spaniards ruled in America. It is especially as mother and intercessor that Mary Immaculate contains one of the master principles of both religious life and political relationships within the colonial system. Mary retained her special hold on popular piety partly because God had not been softened in Spanish America; and because the great gulfs in the social and political hierarchy had not been bridged. There was need of her intercession with her son and his father to bring healing and consolation to the living. For rural Mexicans she was perhaps less a broker in the journey after death—although her place in the journey to personal salvation was very important—than a mother and protector in this life. Part of her appeal was that she did not seem to play favorites. She was a helping mother to all, while the saints appeared more as special advocates for particular people and special purposes. The figures of the Immaculate Conception assume the posture of prayer, the instrument of both her intercession with God and believers' appeal to her.

This central meaning of the Virgin Mary in Indian Mexico as mother and intercessor carries paradoxical messages for colonial political life and the idea of cultural hegemony. Most scholars who have considered the Virgin's political significance see revolutionary and messianic messages. The Virgin was the only mortal to have escaped the stain of the sins of Adam and Eve. Her purity carried the promise of redemption; her child was the source of a new beginning. For Indians this could be understood as liberation in the widest sense— spiritual salvation, a new intimacy, liberation from taxes, an end to oppressive labor service, and rebellion against alien power. Mary, then, could be a symbol of Indian interests, her faithful a chosen people. In effect, devotion to the Virgin was a rejection of Spanish values and a guide to action—a "confrontation of Spanish and Indian worlds."[88]

The other clear political message superficially contradicts this symbolism of liberation: as intermediary, the Virgin was a model of accommodation to and acceptance of colonial power. The success of Spanish rule in Mexico for three centuries without a standing army depended on a system of administration and justice that worked through intermediaries and specialists, defusing or postponing independent action by aggrieved subjects. The political system succeeded largely because the elaborate hierarchy of colonial judges was, in the end, believed to be just. Village Indians in colonial Mexico were inclined to take their complaints over land and taxes to the courts, and to appeal to a higher authority within the colonial structures if the verdict went against them. The images of the Virgin were intermediaries, too, who would intercede with higher authorities on behalf of the believer. Ritually, the Virgin was approached as the colonial authorities were—humbly, hat in hand.[89] One had to trust in her and give her time, just as one had to accept that justice came slowly in the colonial courts.

This political message of accommodation worked especially well as long as priests had the king's support for their moral and political, as well as spiritual, leadership in their parishes. Where she had not been appropriated by the local community or used against the authority of the priest, the Virgin Mary was part of the priest's domain and many times curates displayed her image as a way to stop local uprisings against colonial tax collectors and Spanish governors. Where curates lost much of their moral authority in the late eighteenth century, or where they chose to identify more closely with their parishioners than with the cathedral chapter or the king, the Virgin's message of reconciliation and stability was jeopardized.

The apparent contradiction within the Virgin's role as intercessor, between the message of reconciliation and the message of rebellion, was not perceived as such. The importance of each message waxed and waned, but neither meaning disappeared. Mary's message of liberation dominated the years after 1810, during the struggle over independence. As in the Conquest, she became a warrior again, a patroness of partisans in an armed struggle. But the tables were turned; she had become the Mexican patroness, not the protectress of Spaniards. The Virgin of Guadalupe in particular was taken up as the natural ally of common people after the war broke out, partly because of a subtle change that had been in the making for many years. Gradually the Virgin Mary had come to be a general protectress, not only a specialist in dialogue with a judging God. She was approached for aid against hated new taxes, and in other ways that had political meaning for an ideology of community autonomy and protection of the poor. In forgotten times and places in central Mexico during the decades before 1810, the Virgin of Guadalupe became attached to an idea of millennial reconquest. In a regional Indian uprising in the jurisdiction of Tulancingo during 1769, the leaders called for death to Spanish officials and creation of an Indian priesthood. They dreamed of the day when bishops and *alcaldes mayores* would kneel and kiss the rings of the native priests. Their new theocratic utopia was led by an Indian who called himself the New Savior, and by a consort who was reputed to be the Virgin of Guadalupe.

During the chaotic first months of the Independence struggle, the Virgin of Guadalupe was used not only by leaders like Hidalgo but also by small bands of rebels to legitimate their acts of violence. In December 1810, Father Hidalgo ordered the Indians of Juchipila (in the state of Zacatecas, directly north of Guadalajara) not to sack the estates of the local Spanish tax administrator. The Indians refused to obey, even after a direct order from their parish priest. They did it, they said, with the permission of the Virgin of Guadalupe. What was unthinkable months before could now be accomplished under the higher authority of the Virgin.

Still, by concentrating on the Virgin of Guadalupe, some of the complex and contingent meaning of religious symbols at the time of the Independence struggle has been lost. Father Hidalgo planned his uprising to coincide with the fair of the Virgin of San Juan de los Lagos, not with the feast of Guadalupe. The areas of central and western Mexico where Indians did join the Hidalgo movement in large numbers had been evangelized by the Franciscans and had strong local beliefs in Mary Immaculate. Guadalupe, as an image of the Immaculate Conception with a large following among the creole religious, townspeople, and some country people in areas north of Mexico City, could have served as the bridge between these proto-Mexicans and villagers who worshipped their own local images of Mary Immaculate. If this was so, Guadalupe's importance as a national symbol for Indians and common people may have been more a result of the war—an attachment that emerged during the course of the fighting and migrations of country people—than a motivating force in it. Even if the national cult of the Virgin of Guadalupe was more result than source of mobilization in the Independence wars, she was the natural symbol for the beginnings of national identity in the nineteenth century. Unlike the small host of images of the Virgin that appealed to local groups, the cult of Guadalupe provided a loose and incomplete but still important network of connections between formally separated groups and places—and precisely those groups and places that seem to have taken part in the war: some urban creoles, especially in the Bajío region north of Mexico City; some rancheros, hacendados, and estate managers; lower clergy; and deracinated mestizos and Indians in the Bajío and some parts of central Mexico. Guadalupe had a special appeal in places where people thought of themselves as Mexicans, or as members of a social category without privileges, or as members of a group whose privileges had been lost—notably creoles, lower clergy, and Indians.

The idea that one symbol can stand for both submission to authority and liberation will not surprise most students of the history of religions. Twenty-five years ago Victor Turner discussed the "multivocality" of religious symbols—their various contradictory meanings.[90] Female sacred images, in particular, have had many different meanings—simultaneously nurturing, protecting, terrifying, and destroying.[91] But it is essential not only to recognize the existence of these split meanings but also to examine their history. For Mexico, the surfacing over time of different messages of the Virgin Mary of the Immaculate Conception and the changing circle of believers may eventually be related by historians to wider changes in colonial society. First, redemption and justice through mediation, prayer, and deference may have occupied a crucial place in the formation of a way of thinking among Indians that accepted Christianity and colonial rule in the generations after the Conquest. Second, the rise in the seventeenth and eighteenth centuries of a close association between the Virgin Mary of the Immaculate Conception and an ideology of village autonomy in Indian *pueblos* where the Virgin came increasingly to be a corporate protector and intercessor seems to be connected in time and place with the gradual reconstitution of Indian peasant communities in "closed, corporate" villages. Third, the increased emphasis in the late eighteenth century and during the Independence wars on the Virgin's millenarian message of a new age, reversal of social order, and rebellion against the people of privilege seems connected to the Bourbon reforms to alter the Church's position in public life, as well as to the general economic and demographic changes of the time, to weakening of corporate community ties in some regions, and to a growing sense of membership in larger groups such as "Indians" or "Americans." But these changing beliefs in Mary Immaculate in the early nineteenth century also contain durable ways of thinking about cycles of time that spanned social groups in Latin America and resisted the advancing belief in linear history and the easy acceptance of change.

Another approach to state and society that can complement the study of mediators and of cultural symbols as ideology is the historical study of the operation of law in relationships of inequality. The virtue of all these approaches is that they can examine politics without (as sometimes happens where politics is seen as ideas, leaders, or formal institutions, with little attention to relationships of power from top to bottom)[92] leaving out most of the population as "unpolitical." Law does not have to be the "ordered irrelevancy" it has become in Latin American social history, if our questions are not limited to whether or not rules and decrees reflected social realities, whether or not they were enforced, whether or not law was a tool of oppression. These dichotomous ways of thinking about early Latin America have been shaped by earlier scholarship that tacitly took laws to have determined social behavior or to be a rough approximation of the social reality—an excessive legalism in Latin American history written out of the *Recopilación* (seventeenth-century compilation of laws)—and the recent reaction against these assumptions, which proceeds as if written law and its administration say nothing important about the operation of social relationships.

How much law was there, and how did it vary across regions and time? What matters did the state take an interest in regulating? To what extent was the state capable of doing what its leaders wanted? To what extent was policy transformed into action? What social situations did not produce either dispute or intervention by the state? These questions relating to the practice of law can be asked without denying that social realities may be obscured by legal classifications; and these questions make it possible to concentrate on the actual connections between lawmakers, administrators, judges, and objects of the law. A useful treatment of law as a process connected to social change is The Behavior of Law by Donald Black. Black views law as governmental social control ("the normative life of a state and its citizens, such as legislation, litigation, and adjudication"), only one of several kinds of social control (including violent force, custom, and gossip, among others).[93] He offers a clear but complex set of hypotheses about how the amount of law varies from one political system to another and within single systems over time. For instance, he posits a direct relationship between law and stratification (the more stratification and wealth in a society, the more law), and between law and culture (the more literacy and education the more law); an inverse relationship to the presence of other kinds of social control; and a curvilinear relationship to relational space (law is less active and custom is more active among intimates and among the most distant parts of a legal system).[94] These abstract relationships, if they are valid, do not imply that the amount of law became fixed at some point or changed little over time. Custom was always important, especially in frontier areas of early Latin America like Paraguay or New Mexico, but custom was never sufficient to regulate local affairs there. And the rule of law in New Mexico, at least, increased rather than decreased in the decades after 1810, when the colonial and national states were unstable.[95]

One recent book on early Latin America that centers on legal and institutional history and suggests some of the possibilities for research on state, law, and society is Justice by Insurance: The General Indian Court of Colonial Mexico and the Legal Aides of the Half-Real by Woodrow Borah. Drawing upon the author's four decades of investigation in primary sources on Spanish-Indian relations, this book is more than an institutional history of the General Indian Court from 1585 to the end of the colonial period. It is a history of the issue of Indian justice, the adjustments between native subjects and European rulers, and the accommodation of laws and legal procedures to the exploitation of the native population (and to the drastic decline in its numbers during the sixteenth century), in the context of a tributary mode of production. The General Indian Court and the legal aides were established to provide trained legal advice and quick and effective legal remedies for natives in need of special protection. Indians made great use of their rights in court, but Borah shows that the judicial system functioned as a colonial school of proper conduct as well as a place to settle disputes. The legal advisers were face-to-face intermediaries between rural villagers and the highest levels of colonial government in Spanish America. Borah lays the foundation for asking the same questions about them that were proposed earlier in this section for other intermediaries in the study of state and society. His study suggests that royal absolutism and the system of justice were historical forces in their own right during a period that saw the "steady development of a more inter-penetrated society and economy."[96] As Borah demonstrates, there were at least three competing conceptions of Indian policy in the early colonial period, and the crown worked more through *ad hoc* decisions than a teleological program, but the General Indian Court did have two broad purposes from its inception: to strengthen the state and to moderate between exploiting the Indians and insuring their survival.[97]

One other approach to state and society that has attracted attention for early Latin America in recent years, especially in the United States, and has much potential for a more connected social history concentrates on elites as dominant social groups.[98] Compared to writings on the colonial period that have focused separately on the circumstances of single, large elite groups such as merchants, conquerors, miners, governors, judges, nobles, and *hacendados*, studies of nineteenth-century elites have given more attention to family and personal relationships that defined and linked political and business elites across generations within single families, and linked regional families to foreign entrepreneurs and to state and national political elites.[99] Most of the studies confirm the continuity of strong family networks and the power and wealth of old families, despite the political and economic changes of the nineteenth century and a growing orientation toward business enterprises rather than traditional professions during much of the nineteenth century. But political officials and businessmen are not the only elites worth studying for social history and state and society. Studying members of professions that were in transition (such as priests, lawyers, and physicians in the nineteenth century) and their connections to their publics may provide clues to broader social changes in the family, community, and state.[100] The nineteenth-century studies are leading to a clearer view of the relative power and fortunes of particular regions—establishing where bundles of important relationships were centered geographically and how they changed—as well as their relationships to national governments and foreign investors. Still, the job of establishing who really composed the elite networks and how they were influential has just begun. Little has yet appeared that would clearly establish the relationship of powerful families to the people over whom they exercised power—the full range of vertical as well as horizontal relationships—or changes in those relationships.[101]

While these four examples of brokers, mentalités of subordination, law, and elites are far from all there is to the state and power, they do offer different angles of inquiry into the special importance of the state in the social history of early Latin America in terms of relationships and structures that mediated between local groups and global processes, relationships and structures that often were hidden behind what would appear on a chart of offices and duties. The conceptions of law and mentalités of subordinations used in this essay are intended to suggest that the "bundles of relationships" among unequals in early Latin America have as much to do with rights as with rules; with hegemony and complex, intertwined connections that were shaped and constrained by formal institutions of state power but that often were made far from Madrid, Lisbon, Mexico City, Lima, Bahia, Rio, and the provincial centers; and with what was understood as proper for formal institutions of power, which is not always the same as what was decreed.

The range and intensity of connections of local magistrates, laws, and elite families and occupations to state power, subordinate people, and a system of production and exchange are reasonably clear from the literature. Less clear and particularly important for early Latin America is how the sacred also was involved in the development of the state and relationships of power. As long as Latin American historians see the history of the Church and religion as subjects separate from others in social history, and in terms of paired opposites of secular/religious, thorough conversion of native Americans to

Catholicism/little meaningful conversion, and compulsion by Iberian masters/resistance by "the people," and with little attention to complex face-to-face relationships and the actual practice of the religion, it will be difficult to determine how the formal and folk religions of Spaniards and Portuguese were communicated to and understood by peasants, slaves, and urban laborers, and how religious practices related to state power. By describing the religion of Indian peasants through devotion to the Virgin Mary as a kind of applied Christianity or continuing reinterpretation that was connected in some surprising ways to the Catholic priesthood and state power as well as to local beliefs and conditions, I have suggested how apparent contradictions in the religious and political history of Latin America—of curates being both strangers and patrons, of Iberian colonial states encompassing huge, unprecedented territories in America but controlling them as much through separation as integration, and of the official religion as a model of patron-client bonds of consent, deference, and reciprocity while Catholic images and the content of the religion also dominated the rhetoric of revolution—helped to shape highly unequal social relationships in that time and place and to provide subject people with a basis for judging those relationships.[102]

Conclusion

In suggesting that a more connected social history for the central areas of early Latin America should give greater weight to reasons of state, cultural hegemony, and the activities of government elites and bureaucracies, I am not arguing for the "autonomy" of politics or the idea that politics commands economics. In obvious ways the centralizing colonial state did direct production and distribution and other aspects of material life through monopolies, taxes, price-fixing, and other regulations, and colonial judges and governors were as much concerned wih regulating economic affairs as with the stability of Spanish rule in Old Regime terms and the protection of bureaucratic interests. The state, by both its strengths and its weaknesses, was a major force in the lives of early Latin Americans, but it was not an altogether independent force. Government actions were affected by international conditions and markets and by a desire to accumulate wealth and power as Europeans understood them, and often reflected the interests of an upper class of Spanish colonial merchants, miners, landowners, and bureaucrats. During the colonial period, and in many cases down to the 1850s or the 1870s, the presence and growth of market-oriented enterprises connected to Atlantic economies greatly influenced the division of labor, the intensity of labor demands, and the land tenure system. However, in this essentially precapitalist period many rural areas in this largely rural part of the world were subject mainly to tributary demands by the state and church and to the seasonal labor requirements of *haciendas*, mines, and other employers—by which elites enriched themselves without drastically changing the local economy—leaving room in most areas of highland Latin America for local decisions and social structures based on personal relations, local knowledge, and particular characteristics of local economies. Indeed, the decline of the centralized state and its cultural hegemony in most of Spanish America in the decades after Independence seems to have led to more autonomy for many local places and, in the short run, less influence by market-oriented forces. But by the late nineteenth century, when political power began to coalesce in national governments in most Latin American countries, these governments were following more than leading the relationships of production,[103] and they were more obviously the instruments of an economic class, their actions shaped by international markets. At the same time, markets, class interests, and new systems of labor and production began to challenge (but could also be congruent with and did not often sweep aside) village communities, paternalism, organized religion, and other traditional relationships in the social order.

If economics, politics, nations, villages, and world markets are not to be treated as closed categories—or in Eric R. Wolf's words as "billiard balls" with a cue ball sending the others in various directions—it will be necessary to ask how these factors (and others) combined to produce history. Surely we may assume that "the rationality of history exists!" as Jacques Le Goff recently exclaimed, without making history too orderly, or diminishing what is unique to time, place, and individual, or asserting connections that can never be demonstrated, or denying the weak predictability of historical study. Class, ethnicity, governments, and the rest, as Thompson, Wolf, and others before them have told us, are relationships, not things. The history of these relationships is "a process, not a product." To say that societies are structured in terms of productive relations is not to say that economics and other strictly material considerations determine everything else. One of the weaknesses of Latin American social history is that it has become too fixed on general economic conditions of the *longue durée* as explanations for rebellions and other great events. This is "the thick molasses of social history" to which G. R. Elton rightly objects. This essay has emphasized the relation between state and society in early Latin America not only because relationships in the state were important to the kinds and degrees of connections among people then, but because state and society has not been much studied in recent Latin American social history or has been treated in categorical ways.

Until more is known about the extent and timing of change in the routine affairs of organized groups, the major advances in Latin American social history will continue to be made (as they have been made in studies of land and labor systems, rural collective actions, elites, slavery, and regional history) not at the level of theory, synthesis, and great connections to capitalism and the state,[104] nor at the level of the actual collection of data, but in a middle range. Within this middle range, there have been three particularly fruitful kinds of connections: (1) cross-disciplinary studies that combine the inductive, contextual, documenting preoccupations of traditional historical study with questions and leads to hypotheses about specific processes in the works of other kinds of historians, anthropologists, sociologists, political scientists, economists, and geographers; (2) studies connecting two or more documented patterns of long-term behavior in particular places, such as patterns of homicide set next to demographic patterns or land and water tenure in farming villages; and (3) studies comparing or connecting two or more groups, such as examinations of the relationships of merchants and *hacendados* in several places, and the process by which a particular community or district or region was alienated from the Church. In order to make these middle-range connections, we must first establish when long-term shifts of behavior and attitude among particular social groups took place (shifts that are real, not the result of rearrangements of labels in the records or new ways of counting or enforcing). For example, we need to determine when the structure of an Indian language changed; when individual sponsorship of religious fiestas developed in villages; when property was privatized; when "free" wage labor came to predominate; when and where cults of the Virgin and other religious images took hold and how they were propagated; when bilateral kinship became important; when parents used the name Guadalupe for their children; and when patterns of fertility, longevity, death, and settlement changed. Answering such questions and completing more of the middle-range connections between place and process will help to test rather than assume a providential nationalism, and the precedence of economic or political changes. And the resulting new knowledge will challenge the metaphors and dichotomies that have taken root in the literature on early Latin America: conquest, crystallization, decay, dissolution, and crisis; traditional/ modern, feudal/capitalist, urban/rural, external/internal, Black Legend/White Legend, Indian/Spaniard, secular/religious, *Gemeinschaft/ Gesellschaft*, Europe as subject/Latin America as object, accommodation/resistance, rulers/ruled, and metropolis/satellite.[105]

We still know little about which social processes were comparatively static, gradual, and rapid in their transformation. It has always seemed natural to think of the history of Latin American elite groups and European immigrants in terms of families, generations, and inheritance. But by the second half of the nineteenth century the more rapid pace of change may justify a more explicitly generational approach to the history of most social groups. Luis González's *Pueblo en vilo*, which mainly examines the history of a rural ranching town from its founding in the late nineteenth century, suggests that while core values such as religion can be maintained in the face of most material changes, important modifications in activity and outlook are still possible, and they seem to happen in increments of generations.[106]

Recent attention to the nature and pace of changes in economic and social life is leading to revised (but still uncertain) ideas about periodization in early Latin American history.[107] The Spanish Conquest remains a fundamental watershed—ushering in epidemic diseases and the great dying; reorienting economic activity toward mining, ranching, new plants, and exports; introducing new technology with the wheel, iron and steel tools and weapons; breaking off the development of native states and civilization; introducing writing, a new religion, and new genetic stocks; and more—but recent work on colonial Indian perceptions of the Conquest, Indian languages, and local and regional studies of economic activity and social life before and after the Conquest indicate that there were powerful continuities as well, and that many of the changes, especially in language, habits of conception, community life, and mode of production occurred gradually and well after the time of the Conquest.[108]

Much of the historiography for the colonial period treats 1580 to 1750 as Spanish America's *histoire immobile* (from the consolidation of representative colonial institutions and culture to the grand project of the late Bourbon reforms and commercial capitalism). Yet there are indications that this was the time when Indian peasant adjustments in closed, corporate villages were realized. And Peter J. Bakewell and others have suggested that the history of mining and agriculture in seventeenth-century Latin America probably does not justify the label, "century of depression." Other significant changes were at work then, too. Frances Karttunen finds that the colonial Nahuatl language began to adopt elements of Spanish grammar and to borrow Spanish verbs directly only after the mid-seventeenth century.[109] Village institutions in Indian communities such as *cofradías*, hospitals, and cults of the Virgin developed especially during this time, as did *haciendas*, which were changeable in their own right—heavily mortgaged, and subject to sale, consolidation, and division.

There is a consensus based on extensive research that during the last third of the nineteenth century, at the time agrarian capitalism and other classic circumstances of modern underdevelopment took hold, there was a great redirection of production, politics, and social relationships, with national governments, local entrepreneurs, and foreign investors forming alliances for economic growth and against local interests. Old attachments to locality and family were complicated and sometimes overwhelmed and absorbed into wider associations of class, province, and country by railroads, privatizing of community lands, nation-building, wage labor, and more production for export, but the gaps between regions and social groups also widened as the new economic growth bypassed many places and people.

In a chronology shaped by the concentration of research in the colonial period and the late nineteenth century, the orphan period of early Latin American social history would seem to be the first half of the nineteenth century. Thanks to dependency perspectives and social history's suspicion of political boundaries and its interest in long-term patterns, the mid-eighteenth century to the mid-nineteenth century has come to be seen as one long, homogeneous stage of Latin American history. In early nineteenth-century Latin America, after the separation of Spain and Portugal from their colonies, notorious political instability coexisted with a good measure of social stability and continuity in Latin America's economic relationship to world markets. Other continuities include the decline of the judicial state, the promotion of public primary education,[110] miscegenation, *caciquismo* (local boss rule), and the aggregation of people into larger, more diffuse groups (which is evident in the spread of religious cults like that of the Virgin of Guadalupe, and growing consciousness of villagers in some regions as "Indians" or creole Spaniards as "Americans").

Yet there is reason to think that, underlying continuities in economic structures and in the rise of the secular state, the Independence wars brought changes that require investigation: changes in social behavior, state and society, property, community, and religion, particularly in rural areas. The political events, laws, and institutional changes of the period led to social change even when economic structures and modes of production were not much altered. For example, in rural areas of peasant villages, the abolition of some privileges based on ancestry and Indian *pueblo* status contributed to plundering of communal lands, privatization of holdings, greater inequality within villages, and "exposure to far greater exploitation,"[111] which in turn required adjustments such as more migration, wage and debt labor, and individual sponsorship of feastday celebrations if basic family, neighborhood, and village institutions were to continue.[112] Above all, the period of the Independence wars seems to have contributed greatly toward violent conflict in social relationships thereafter.[113] Firearms and knives were owned and carried openly without license by virtually anyone for the first time; firearms and other means of force no longer were controlled largely by one group; the legitimacy and mediating authority of the state had been seriously weakened; and banditry, according to Tulio Halperín Donghi,[114] became endemic only after the wars. Whatever the cause, a surprising pattern in the incidence of homicides that suggests more violence in social relationships is revealed in death records for nineteenth-century Mexico: Homicides grew dramatically in number from 1810 to 1821 and maintained this new level thereafter, through most of the century.[115]

These puzzles and refinements in periodization stimulated by recent social history suggest the complexity of the processes of change in early Latin American history as much as they point to what is not yet known about routine social life in the past. While capitalism, other economic structures, and the state conditioned social life, they did not simply determine it. The reciprocal (which is not to say equal) connections described in this essay depended on local responses and conditions—not just relentless pressure of external de-

velopments and authority—as much as violent resistance did. As social history takes account of the varieties of experience within and
between particular places, becomes more concerned with the limits
of change and choice, and examines more thoroughly what lies between changes in social life and their likely origins, historians of early
Latin America will have to confront the model of "acculturation" that
has influenced the way we have thought about social change in the
areas of dense native settlement. Acculturation (and its related concept of syncretism as "a special kind of acculturation in which elements in interaction are similar in structure, function, and form")[116]
centers attention on changes that result from the contact between
people of two cultures. Both cultures change in the process, but one
dominates. While it seems right to speak in these categorical terms
for the first generation of contact between Europeans and native
Americans, the process of change incompletely described here for
popular religion and one group of mediators seems like negotiations,
struggles, and reinterpretations among unequals who had historical
relationships and expectations about each other, as much as like repeated meetings of two cultures from separate worlds.

NOTES

1. Even a casual reading of first-hand accounts of castaways ought to sober readers of Defoe. A good example of the real thing is Maese Joan's account of his eight grim years stranded on the wastes of the Serrana Keys. It was translated into English with an introduction by Lesley B. Simpson as "The Spanish Crusoe: An Account by Maese Joan of Eight Years Spent as a Castaway on the Serrana Keys in the Caribbean Sea, 1528–1536," *Hispanic American Historical Review* 9 (August 1929): 368–76.

2. John L. Phelan, "Pan-Latinism, French Intervention in Mexico (1861–1867), and the Genesis of the Idea of Latin America," *Conciencia y autenticidad históricas: Escritos en homenaje a Edmundo O'Gorman* (Mexico: Universidad Nacional Autónoma de México, 1968), 279–98.

3. A good example of Latin American time viewed in terms of irregular cycles of destruction and Latin American history as an "oppressive reality" is Gabriel García Márquez's novel, *One Hundred Years of Solitude*, trans. Gregory Rabassa (New York: Harper & Row, 1970). Latin American history as a violent dialectic of explosive contradictions and unfinished syntheses is not a view limited to dialectical materialists in Latin America. Idealists like Octavio Paz have a similar outlook in their political writings. See his *The Labyrinth of Solitude* (New York: Grove Press, 1962) and *The Other Mexico: Critique of the Pyramid* (New York: Grove Press, 1972). Writings on Latin American history are filled with figures who epitomize political coercion and violence: Cortez, Pizarro, Lope de Aguirre, Boves, Facundo, Pancho Villa, and many more. But these men are metaphors of historical imagination more than irreducible facts that represent Latin America. Conquest was a technique that worked mainly in the Spaniards' encounters with a few developed native states, and even there it was not simply subjugation by force but alliance, unequal balance of interests and, essentially, a coup d'état.

4. Bernard Bailyn, "The Challenge of Modern Historiography," *American Historical Review* 87 (February 1982): 1–24.

5. E. P. Thompson, "Eighteenth-Century English Society: Class Struggle Without Class?" *Social History* 3 (May 1978): 133–66.

6. Eric R. Wolf, *Europe and the People Without History* (Berkeley: University of California Press, 1982), 9, 17, 355; Charles Tilly, *As Sociology Meets History* (New York: Academic Press, 1981), 44 and passim.

7. Published separately, these essays appeared together with a new introduction as *Historia social latinoamericana (nuevos enfoques)* (Caracas: Universidad Católica Andrés Bello, 1979). Most recent of these surveys by Mörner is "Economic Factors and Stratification in Colonial Spanish America with Special Regard to Elites," *Hispanic American Historical Review* 63 (May 1983): 335–70.

8. A separate, equally long, and perhaps more valuable essay could be limited to the publications of national and regional centers of cross-disciplinary historical study that have been organized in various Latin American countries during the last twenty years. One of the most recent of these centers is the Colegio de Michoacán in Mexico, which has brought historians and anthropologists together to study popular culture and its connections to economic, political, and social

change. Interview with Luis González y González, President of the Colegio de Michoacán, published in *Uno Más Uno*, 29 March 1980, 18.

9. One will find a comprehensive overview for the colonial period in a new book, *Early Latin America: A History of Colonial Spanish America and Brazil*, by James Lockhart and Stuart B. Schwartz (Cambridge: Cambridge University Press, 1983), that is certain to stimulate constructive debate and influence the terms in which Latin American history is understood. There is a growing literature on concepts of regional history for Latin America. Recent inquiries include Aristides Medina Rubio, "Teoría, fuentes, y método en historia regional," *Relaciones* 15 (Summer 1983): 88–108; Carol A. Smith, "Local History in Global History in Global Context: Social and Economic Transitions in Western Guatemala," *Comparative Studies in Society and History* 26 (April 1984): 193–228; and Carol A. Smith, ed. *Regional Analysis*, 2 vols. (New York: Academic Press, 1976).

10. Charles W. Bergquist, "Latin America: A Dissenting View of 'Latin American History in World Perspective,'" in *International Handbook of Historical Studies*, ed. Georg Iggers and Harold T. Parker (Westport, Conn.: Greenwood Press, 1979), 371–86; Charles W. Bergquist, "Recent United States Studies in Latin American History: Trends Since 1965," *Latin American Research Review* 9 (Spring 1974): 3–37. Latin American historiography still needs the kind of thorough evaluation of the dependency literature that Frederick Cooper has written for Africa in "Africa and the World Economy," *African Studies Review* 24 (June–September 1981): 1–86.

11. Fernando H. Cardoso and Enzo Faletto, *Dependency and Development in Latin America* (first Spanish language edition in 1969, expanded and emended edition, Berkeley: University of California Press, 1979), 17.

12. As in Maurice Godelier's statement, "Deprived of their traditional social hierarchies, expropriated, impoverished, enslaved to masters having a foreign language and culture, the Indian communities either disappeared or retired into themselves," *Perspectives in Marxist Anthropology* (Cambridge: Cambridge University Press, 1977), 65.

13. Sidney W. Mintz, who has made many important contributions to the history of material relationships in the Caribbean, notes that New World societies are divided not only by class differences "but also by perceptions, values, and attitudes," in "Time, Sugar and Sweetness," *Marxist Perspectives* 2 (Winter 1979–1980): 7. As Woodrow Borah recently reminded me, the drain of assets from Latin America by Latin Americans themselves has played an important part in the shortages of capital and economic dependence on foreigners.

14. André Gunder Frank puts it simply: The colonial economy was "based on" mining of precious metals and "Mexican agriculture" was a "by-product" of the mining economy, *Mexican Agriculture, 1521–1630: Transformation of the Mode of Production* (Cambridge: Cambridge University Press, 1979), 2. This point is accepted by other leading students of capitalism in Latin American history: Angel Palerm, *Sobre la formación del sistema colonial en México: Apuntes para una discusión* (mimeograph, 1976); Eric R. Wolf, *Sons of the Shaking Earth* (Chicago: University of Chicago Press, 1959), 82.

15. Peter J. Bakewell and David A. Brading published the outstanding studies of colonial mining regions in Mexico in the early 1970s: *Silver Mining and Society in Colonial Mexico, Zacatecas, 1546–1700* (Cambridge: Cambridge University Press,

1971); *Miners and Merchants in Bourbon Mexico, 1763–1810* (Cambridge: Cambridge University Press, 1971). Recent efforts to broach the question of capitalist mining's influence over social and economic change in a wider geographical context are Carlos Sempat Assadourian, Heraclio Bonilla, Tristan Platt, *Minería y espacio económico en los Andes* (Lima: Instituto de Estudios Peruanos, 1980); Carlos Sempat Assadourian, *El sistema de la economía colonial. Mercado interno, regiones, y espacio económico* (Lima: Instituto de Estudios Peruanos, 1982); and Gwendolyn Cobb, *Potosí y Huancavelica: bases económicas del Perú, 1545–1640* (La Paz: Academia Boliviana de la Historia, 1977).

16. Claude Morin, *Michoacán en la Nueva España del siglo XVIII: Crecimiento y desigualdad en una economía colonial* (Mexico: Fondo de Cultura Económica, 1979); Richard B. Lindley, *Haciendas and Economic Development: Guadalajara, Mexico, at Independence* (Austin: University of Texas Press, 1983); Richard L. Garner, "Exportaciones de circulante en el siglo XVIII (1750–1810)," *Historia Mexicana* 31 (abril–junio 1982): 544–98.

17. Non-Marxist dependency writers are most likely to use the nation-state as their unit of study because of their interest in the development of national capitalism, according to Ronald Chilcote, "A Question of Dependency," *Latin American Research Review* 13 (1978): 60. But Marxist streams of the dependency literature also have dealt in nations more than in other regional groupings that may be more closely connected to production, e.g. Ronald Chilcote and Joel C. Edelstein, eds., *Latin America: The Struggle with Dependency and Beyond* (Cambridge, Mass.: Schenkman, 1974).

18. Cardoso and Faletto, *Dependency*, 16–17; Larissa A. Lomnitz uses "historical structuralism" as a synonym for dependency writings, *Networks and Marginality: Life in A Mexican Shantytown* (New York: Academic Press, 1977), 36.

19. André Gunder Frank, *Capitalism and Underdevelopment in Latin America: Historical Studies in Chile and Brazil* (New York: Monthly Review Press, 1967).

20. Cardoso and Faletto, *Dependency*, 17; Halperín Donghi, *Historia* (Madrid: Alianza Editorial, 1969).

21. Especially in his *Mexican Agriculture*.

22. Frank, *Capitalism and Underdevelopment*, 35.

23. Ronald Chilcote, ed., *Dependency and Marxism: Toward a Resolution of the Debate* (Boulder: Westview Press, 1982), x.

24. Ronaldo Munck, "Imperialism and Dependency: Recent Debates and Old Dead-Ends," in *Dependency and Marxism*, ed. Chilcote, 163.

25. Carlos Johnson, "Dependency Theory and the Processes of Capitalism and Socialism," in *Dependency and Marxism*, ed. Chilcote, 55–81.

26. David Barkin, "Internationalization of Capital: An Alternative Approach," in *Dependency and Marxism*, ed. Chilcote, 156–61.

27. Ronald Chilcote, "Issues of Theory in Dependency and Marxism," in *Dependency and Marxism*, ed. Chilcote, 6; Wolf, *Europe*, 297. A crucial first matter, still largely unresolved, is the timing and extent to which parts of Latin America were incorporated into and affected by world trading systems issuing from mercantile activities and industrial capitalism in Europe and the United States. Differing views of eighteenth- and early nineteenth-century developments are summarized in an exchange between D. C. M. Platt and Stanley and Barbara Stein published in *Latin American Research Review* 15 (1980): 113–30, with Platt claiming that "domestic

circumstances" shaped Latin American economies in the nineteenth century and the Steins arguing for the dominant influence of the international economy and "foreign trade as the *raison d'être* of Spanish America since the conquest" (p. 135). Both sides of this exchange seem to accept nation-states as the primary unit for discussing Latin American economic and social structures in the nineteenth century.

28. Bergquist, "Latin America: A Dissenting View."

29. For example, F. H. Cardoso and Faletto, *Dependency*; and Bergquist, "Latin America: A Dissenting View."

30. A standard outline of stages of dependent underdevelopment in Latin American history—colonial, nineteenth century, neocolonial—by a non-Marxist dependency writer is José A. Silva Michelena's "Diversities Among Dependent Nations: An Overview of Latin American Developments," in *Building States and Nations: Analyses by Region*, ed. S. N. Eisenstadt and Stein Rokkan (Beverly Hills: Sage, 1973), 2:232–49.

31. For Halperín's view of dependency perspectives, see his "'Dependency Theory' and Latin American Historiography," *Latin American Research Review* 17 (1982): 115–30, which dismisses Frank's and Cardoso and Faletto's early books for their "brutal simplicity" and static treatment, and praises several richer, deeper, subtler works by Latin American Marxist historians who have escaped the "blunt reductionism" of their theoretical views.

32. Stanley Stein and Barbara Stein, *The Colonial Heritage of Latin America: Essays on Economic Dependence in Perspective* (New York: Oxford University Press, 1970); see p. 81 for their view of law in society.

33. Cosió Villegas, *Historia moderna de México*, 7 vols. (Mexico: Editorial Hermes, 1955–1965); Cardoso, ed., *México en el siglo XIX* (Mexico: Editorial Nueva Imagen, 1980); see also his edited volume, *Formación y desarrollo de la burguesía en México, siglo XIX* (Mexico: Siglo Veintiuno Editores, 1978); "Los modos de producción coloniales; estado de la cuestión y perspectiva teórica," *Estudios Sociales Centroamericanos* 4 (1975): 87–105; "Características básicas de la economía latinoamericana (siglo XIX): algunos problemas de la transición neocolonial," *Revista de Historia* (Heredia, Costa Rica) 2 (1977): 47–66. Other leaders in this field working in Mexico are Enrique Florescano, *Estructuras y problemas agrarios de México, 1500 a 1821* (Mexico: Secretaría de Educación Pública, 1971); "La época de las reformas borbónicas y el crecimiento económico, 1750–1808," with Isabel Gil Sánchez in *Historia General de México* (Mexico: El Colegio de México, 1976), 2:185–301; Carlos Sempat Assadourian, *El sistema de la economía colonial. Mercado interno, regiones, y espacio económico* (Lima: Instituto de Estudios Peruanos, 1982); and Enrique Semo, *Historia del capitalismo en México: los orígenes, 1521–1763* (Mexico: Ediciones Era, 1973); *Historia mexicana: economía y lucha de clases* (Mexico: Ediciones Era, 1978).

34. C. F. S., Cardoso, ed., *México en el siglo XIX*, pp. 50–51 on "the long wait"; p. 239 speaks of the Reforma as the period when the traditional property system disintegrated.

35. Ibid., 227–43.

36. Steve J. Stern, *Peru's Indian Peoples and the Challenge of Spanish Conquest: Huamanga to 1640* (Madison: University of Wisconsin Press, 1982); Morin, *Michoacán*; Laird W.

Bergad, *Coffee and the Growth of Agrarian Capitalism in Nineteenth-Century Puerto Rico* (Princeton: Princeton University Press, 1983). There are other examples to choose from in English, including Charles W. Bergquist, *Coffee and Conflict in Colombia, 1886–1910* (Durham, N.C.: Duke University Press, 1978); Florencia E. Mallon, *The Defense of Community in Peru's Central Highlands: Peasant Struggle and Capitalist Transition, 1860–1940* (Princeton: Princeton University Press, 1983); Gilbert Joseph, *Revolution from Without: Yucatan, Mexico, and the United States, 1880–1924* (Cambridge: Cambridge University Press, 1982); John H. Coatsworth, *Growth Against Development: The Economic Impact of Railroads in Porfirian Mexico* (DeKalb: Northern Illinois University Press, 1981); Guillermo de la Peña, *A Legacy of Promises: Agriculture, Politics and Rituals in the Morelos Highlands of Mexico* (Manchester: Manchester University Press, 1982); Arturo Warman, *"We Come to Object": The Peasants of Morelos and the National State* (Baltimore: Johns Hopkins University Press, 1980); and Karen Spalding, *Huarochirí: An Andean Society under Inca and Spanish Rule* (Stanford: Stanford University Press, 1984). Now, fifteen years after its publication, John Womack's *Zapata and the Mexican Revolution* (New York: Alfred A. Knopf, 1969) still stands alone as a compelling narrative history recounting human actions with purposes rooted in the issues of dialectical materialism and dependency.

37. Stern, *Peru's Indian Peoples*, 57, 77, 119, 188; similar approaches stressing the importance for early colonial adjustments in Peru of social and political units poised between the Inca Empire and the ethnic *ayllu* are Carlos Sempat Assadourian, "Dominio colonial y señores étnicos en el espacio andino," *Diálogos*, no. 108 (November–December 1982): 29–41, and Karen Spalding, *De indio a campesino* (Lima: Instituto de Estudios Peruanos, 1974). At this stage of knowledge of Spanish-Indian relations it would be inappropriate to draw a close comparison between Peru and Mesoamerica, where closed corporate communities have been most extensively described historically and where the term was first used by Eric R. Wolf in the 1950s. To all appearances the tribute system in Peru was far heavier, the *repartimiento de mercancías* and other types of forced purchase and sale more excessive, *corregidores* more abusive, and judicial protection of Indians less effective. This point is made in Woodrow Borah, *Justice by Insurance: The General Indian Court of Colonial Mexico and the Legal Aides of the Half-Real* (Berkeley: University of California Press, 1983), 411.

38. Stern here borrows (p. 182) from the anthropological literature on civil-religious hierarchies in Mesoamerica, which posits—with little evidence—that individual sponsorship of religious fiestas was the practice in emerging closed corporate villages by the seventeenth century. This view currently is undergoing revision. See Jan Rus and Robert Wasserstrom, "Civil-Religious Hierarchies in Central Chiapas: A Critical Perspective," *American Ethnologist* 7 (February 1980): 466–78; John K. Chance and William B. Taylor, "Cofradías and Cargos: An Historical Perspective on the Mesoamerican Civil-Religious Hierarchy," *American Ethnologist* (forthcoming); and Olinda Celestino and Albert Meyers, *Las cofradías en el Peru: región central* (Frankfurt a/M: KD Vervuert, 1981). Another advance, within a Marxist framework, in placing Indian peasants actively into the historical process of capitalism for early Latin America is Florencia Mallon's study of traditional patron-client relationships which lasted long into the development of capitalism in

the Jauja Valley of Peru after 1860 because they were temporarily congruent with the economic changes, "Murder in the Andes: Patrons, Clients, and the Impact of Foreign Capital, 1860–1922," *Radical History Review* no. 27 (May 1983): 79–98.

39. Morin, *Michoacán*, p. 186; Richard L. Garner, "Exportaciones" supports this point, indicating that less than ten per cent of silver produced in Mexico between 1752 and 1776 stayed there as specie and that exports of silver thereafter grew faster than the value of silver registered at the royal mint. For all its strengths, Morin's book has an arbitrary starting point. The "region" of Michoacán is, for most purposes, the Bishopric of Michoacán. Why this is appropriate—why an administrative territory organized under the Church might be the basis of regional social and economic history—beyond the fact that the church records are the source of most of the information used, is not made clear.

40. An important collection of historical essays on agrarian capitalism in Latin America that bears on dependency issues in Latin American social history has been published as *Land and Labour in Latin America: Essays on the Development of Agrarian Capitalism in the Nineteenth and Twentieth Centuries*, ed. Kenneth Duncan and Ian Rutledge (Cambridge: Cambridge University Press, 1977). See especially the essays by Juan Martínez Alier, Ciro F. S. Cardoso, and Jaime Reis.

41. Some other countries had larger coffee estates or moved more slowly into wage labor or generated an indigenous capitalist elite from their periods of boom in monoculture; see Michael Gonzales, "Capitalist Agriculture and Labour Contracting in Northern Peru, 1880–1905," *Journal of Latin American Studies* 12 (November 1980): 291–315. Little work has yet been done on precisely what social changes the "new economic order" after the 1870s brought about or what the internal structures of regional economies were like at different times. New work on Bolivia is beginning to clarify this process. Erick D. Langer has established how railroads, the revival of silver mining in the 1870s, and especially the later development of the mining enclaves disrupted the regional economy of Cinti Province and old commercial networks: wine and sugar produced by Indian villages as well as by many *haciendas* gave way to cheaper imported sugar from Argentina and wine from Santa Cruz. While the regional agricultural production in general declined, two *haciendas* producing subsistence crops did prosper, expand, and mechanize. There was a glut of labor and the *haciendas* sought to phase out unnecessary reciprocal relationships with local workers and simply hire labor for wages. They succeeded only in part ("Peasant Labor and Commercial Agriculture in Cinti, Bolivia, 1880–1930," paper presented at the Tenth National Meeting of the Latin American Studies Association, Washington, D.C., 1982). Erwin P. Grieshaber has pointed to regional variations in the survival of populous, landed Indian villages in Bolivia in the nineteenth century. He contrasts the *altiplano* departments of Oruro, La Paz, and Potosí, which had 80 percent of the national Indian population in the late nineteenth century, where tributary rule during the colonial period had not radically changed indigenous forms of exploitation, and where only low-value crops grew, with much of the temperate department of Cochabamba, where the Indian population had long been smaller and had been displaced from fertile lands by market-oriented *haciendas* that produced grains for the large urban market of Potosí. See his "Survival of Indian Communities in Nineteenth-Century Bolivia: A Regional Comparison," *Journal of Latin American Studies* 12 (November

1980): 223–69. Tristan Platt makes a detailed study of nineteenth-century Chayanta where indigenous communities largely succeeded in forestalling a transformation of land tenure, tribute, and the *ayllus* by agrarian capitalism and national laws, in *Estado boliviano y ayllu andino. Tierra y tributo en el norte de Potosí* (Lima: Instituto de Estudios Peruanos, 1982). For the Colombian frontier, Catherine C. LeGrand clarifies the relationship between export agriculture and change in peasant society in "Land Acquisition and Social Conflict on the Colombian Frontier, 1850–1936," *Journal of Latin American Studies* 16 (May 1984): 27–49.

42. Marcello Carmagnani, *Formación y crisis de un sistema feudal: América Latina del siglo XVI a nuestros días* (Mexico: Siglo XXI Editores, 1976), 26. John Coatsworth points out that what the state-directed colonial economy of Spanish America had most in common with feudal Europe was an inefficient economic organization and institutions that were not geared to free enterprise or entrepreneurial activity, "The Limits of Colonial Absolutism: The State in Eighteenth-Century Mexico," in *Essays in the Political, Economic, and Social History of Colonial Latin America*, ed. Karen Spalding (Newark: University of Delaware Latin American Studies Program, 1982), 25–52.

43. De la Peña, *A Legacy of Promises*, (Manchester: Manchester University Press, 1982), 51, speaks of capitalism as a mode of production in early Latin America, positing a transition to free labor in Morelos in the late eighteenth century. "Agrarian capitalism" in terms of commercial monoculture on Jesuit estates that used wage labor and money transactions is documented by Nicholas P. Cushner for seventeenth- and eighteenth-century Ecuador in *Farm and Factory: The Jesuits and the Development of Agrarian Capitalism in Colonial Quito, 1600–1767* (Albany: State University of New York Press, 1982).

44. Hermann Rebel, *Peasant Classes: The Bureaucratization of Property and Family Relations Under Early Habsburg Absolutism, 1511–1636* (Princeton: Princeton University Press, 1983), 16–17.

45. Wolf, *Europe*, chap. 3.

46. The organization and regulation of markets at various levels by state authorities in early Latin America has been described by Rosemary D. F. and R. J. Bromley, "The Debate on Sunday Markets in Nineteenth-Century Ecuador," *Journal of Latin American Studies* 7 (May 1975): 85–108; in Carol A. Smith's discussion of "administered solar" and "dendritic" market systems in Guatemala, *Regional Analysis* 2:335–41; and by John Coatsworth, "Obstacles to Economic Growth in Nineteenth-Century Mexico," *American Historical Review* 83 (February 1978): 80–100, and "The Limits of Colonial Absolutism."

47. A similar Marxist conception of the growth of capitalism (but also ascribing a deeply conservative nature to merchant capital and emphasizing the domination of "absolute private property" as well as wage labor) is found in the writings of Eugene D. Genovese, most recently in *Fruits of Merchant Capital: Slavery and Bourgeois Property in the Rise and Expansion of Capitalism*, co-authored by Elizabeth Fox-Genovese (New York: Oxford University Press, 1983).

48. Wolf, *Europe*, 135, 143. Considering together all of Wolf's important work on Mesoamerica, chap. 3 of *Europe and the People Without History* does not fulfill the intent of this latest book or of his earlier thinking about the forces that have moved Latin American history. Beginning with articles on Latin American peas-

ants, *compadrazgo*, and closed corporate communities in the 1950s, Wolf has been concerned with political as well as economic forces in a "processual" history, and with the meaning of symbols for public life: "Types of Latin American Peasantry: A Preliminary Discussion," *American Anthropologist* 57 (June 1955): 452–71; "Closed Corporate Communities in Mesoamerica and Java," *Southwestern Journal of Anthropology* 13 (Spring 1957): 1–18; "The Virgin of Guadalupe: Mexican National Symbol," *Journal of American Folklore* 71 (January–March 1958): 34–39.

49. Scholars consciously influenced by Marx and Marxist writings and emphasizing labor systems and oppression have had the lead in this. For example, Spalding, *Huarochirí*; Stern, *Peru's Indian Peoples*; Florencia E. Mallon, *The Defense of Community in Peru's Central Highlands: Peasant Struggle and Capitalist Transition, 1860–1940* (Princeton: Princeton University Press, 1983); and Brooke Larson, "Caciques, Class Structure and the Colonial State in Bolivia," *Nova Americana* 2 (1979): 197–235.

50. A useful introduction to the history of the class concept by a scholar who knows Latin America is Peter Calvert, *The Concept of Class: An Historical Introduction* (London: Hutchinson, 1982). He concludes with the sobering observation that "however far we stretch our taxonomy of definitions we will never find a concept of class that is universally acceptable," 209.

51. Tilly, *As Sociology*, p. 44; and Wolf, *Europe*, chap. 1.

52. John Coatsworth discusses the intervention of the Spanish state in the late colonial economy in "The Limits of Colonial Absolutism."

53. Clarence Haring, *The Spanish Empire in America* (New York: Oxford University Press, 1947).

54. This providential tradition is represented in a large literature and popular ideas about Latin American history, e.g. Victor Manzanilla Schaeffer, "La propiedad rural durante la colonia española," *Revista de la Facultad de Derecho de México* 15 (1965): 395–412.

55. James Lockhart, "The Social History of Colonial Spanish America," *Latin American Research Review* 7 (Spring 1972): 6–46. The separation of everyday lives of ordinary people from the history of power and formal institutions allows G. R. Elton gleefully to dismiss social history as an academics' peep show: "The dedicated social historian, second cousin to the tabloid journalist, now pursues even the obscure into parlor and bedroom. Tired eyes light up as details of sexual practices or malfunction rise from the record. Eager hands tremble as the veils drop from privacy," in "Happy Families," *New York Review of Books* 31 (14 June 1984): 39.

56. Kalman Silvert, *The Conflict Society: Reaction and Revolution in Latin America* (New York: Harper & Row, 1968), 8.

57. Lindley, *Haciendas*, 94, has shown that some English capital and goods from Jamaica came directly into Jalisco through Panamanian merchants after 1814.

58. De la Peña, *Legacy*, 16; Enrique Florescano, "El poder y la lucha por el poder en la historiografía mexicana," Mexico: n.d. (Cuadernos de Trabajo 33, INAH Departamento de Investigaciones Históricas), 17–18. *Legacy* is a particularly forceful treatment of these issues that is attentive to regional differences and historical process, within a framework that is critical of dependency perspectives.

59. An extensive, documented overview of state and society for late colonial

Central America—although it deals more with government, fiscal matters, and elites than society as a whole—is Miles Wortman's *Government and Society in Central America, 1680–1840* (New York: Columbia University Press, 1982). A good example of recent work at the regional level that connects power and class in personal terms is David W. Walker, "Kinship, Business and Politics: The Martínez del Río Family in Mexico, 1824–1864," Ph.D. diss., University of Chicago, 1981. A stimulating introduction to the study of rural politics through patron-client relations, peasant collective action, regionalism, and local-national interaction is Catherine C. LeGrand, "Perspectives for the Historical Study of Rural Politics and the Colombian Case: An Overview," *Latin American Research Review* 12 (1977): 7–36.

60. An important reconsideration of the state in the economic and social life of eighteenth-century Mexico has been started by John Coatsworth in "Limits of Colonial Absolutism." This article offers a clear, well-supported case for the state constraining economic growth and extracting a surprisingly large amount of colonial resources by taxation. It is less convincing on two other hypotheses: that hegemony had little, if anything, to do with relationships to the state ("Most Mexicans in the colonial period, and for decades thereafter, viewed their government as alien, if not illegitimate, to be avoided and evaded wherever possible." 36); and that the colonial state rarely made contact with rural people and had little impact on political and administrative activity outside of economic affairs. The impact of bureaucratization on rural society, which Rebel studied for Hapsburg Austria in the sixteenth and seventeenth centuries, will have to be considered more systematically for various places and periods in colonial Ibero-America before the limits of state autonomy can be well understood. Rebel describes a new "self-contradictory" politics for Austrian peasants in which "the peasantry continued to assert its independence and acquired a reputation for refractoriness, [while] it also learned to accept and act within the narrow bounds of estate management and state politics" (*Peasant Classes*, 6). Rodolfo Pastor has another recent evaluation of rural communities and the state in Mexican history that views the relationship as one of cycles of alliances and conflicts with the state, "La comunidad agraria y el Estado en México: Una historia cíclica," *Diálogos*, no. 108 (November–December 1982): 16–26.

Anthropologist Carol A. Smith recently published a promising historical interpretation of how local-level processes simultaneously have helped shape and been shaped by regional and national structures in western Guatemala, "Local History in Global Context: Social and Economic Transitions in Western Guatemala," *Comparative Studies in Society and History* 26 (April 1984): 193–227. But her conclusion that distinctive, closed corporate peasant communities developed there because of Indian resistance in the face of a weak state ("this made it much more difficult for the state to break the community apart later," 199) assumes that the colonial state intended to break up these communities and misses the possibility of a more active state whose interests could be compatible with the existence of such rural "Indian" communities.

61. Juan Linz, "Early State-Building and Late Peripheral Nationalisms Against the State: The Case of Spain," in *Building States*, ed. Eisenstadt and Rokkan, 2:99.

62. Carol A. Smith notes that most studies of brokers and personal networks

across levels in complex societies operate in an organizational vacuum and provide "no explicit methodology for distinguishing types and levels of linkages that may differ from institution to institution and from region to region," *Regional Analysis*, 2:16. As Smith says, it will be essential to place these personal mediations into the "societal routes or paths" through which they moved and were expected to move, to establish the "system" of organization that integrated complex societies. For early Latin America, the "system" is becoming better understood at the level of political institutions as well as markets. See the references in notes 96 and 97.

63. Richard N. Adams, *Energy and Structure: A Theory of Social Power* (Austin: University of Texas Press, 1975), 22.

64. Eric J. Hobsbawm, "Religion and the Rise of Socialism," *Marxist Perspectives* 1 (Spring 1978): 14.

65. R. H. Tawney, *Religion and the Rise of Capitalism* (New York: Penguin Books, 1940), 36.

66. A good example, recently republished in facsimile, is Juan Palafox y Mendoza's *Carta Pastoral*, 1649 (Mexico: Editorial Innovación, 1979).

67. The term "hinge-man" is Peter Brown's in *Society and the Holy in Late Antiquity* (Berkeley: University of California Press, 1982). The idea of such mediators and brokers of power in history is not new, but Brown's treatment and those of Richard N. Adams in *Energy and Structure*, and Dwight B. Heath in "New Patrons for Old: Changing Patron-Client Relationships in the Bolivian Yungas," *Ethnology* 12 (January 1973): 75–98, are particularly suggestive.

68. Adams, *Energy and Structure*, 52, speaks of a "janus point" down a scale of power where the broker favors the interests of higher authorities rather than lower ones. Historians dealing with uncertainties and contingencies might prefer to think of it as a range of points where the broker may well turn either way.

69. Archivo Judicial de la Audiencia de la Nueva Galicia, Civil 117–4–1249; Gonzalo Aguirre Beltrán, "Delación del cura de Acayucan, Don Joaquín de Urquijo," *México Agrario* 4 (January–March 1942): 63–73; Alberto de la Hera, ed., "Juicios de los obispos asistentes al IV Concilio mexicano sobre el estado del virreinato de Nueva España," *Anuario de Historia del Derecho Español* 31 (1961): 307–26.

70. Recent work on the eighteenth and nineteenth centuries includes Raymond P. Harrington, "The Secular Clergy in the Diocese of Mérida de Yucatán, 1780–1850: Their Origins, Careers, Wealth and Activities," Ph.D. diss., the Catholic University of America, 1983; Dennis Paul Ricker, "The Lower Secular Clergy of Central Mexico: 1821–1857," Ph.D. diss., University of Texas at Austin, 1982; Adriaan van Oss, "Catholic Colonialism: A Parish History of Guatemala, 1524–1821," Ph.D. diss., University of Texas at Austin, 1982; Gene A. Muller, "The Church in Poverty: Bishops, Bourbons, and Tithes in Spanish Honduras, 1700–1821," Ph.D. diss., University of Kansas, 1982; Rodolfo Pastor, "Los religiosos, los indios y el estado en la Mixteca, 1524–1810: Sobre el trasfondo y función social de la ideología," paper presented at the VI Conference of Mexican and United States Historians, Chicago, 1981; David A. Brading, "El clero mexicano y el movimiento insurgente de 1810," *Relaciones* 2 (Invierno de 1981): 5–26; and Brading's "Tridentine Catholicism and Enlightened Despotism in Bourbon Mexico," *Journal of Latin American Studies* 15 (May

1983): 1–22. For late colonial Peru, Christine Hunefeldt addresses the central issues of curate-community relationships in "Comunidad, curas y comuneros hacia fines del período colonial," HISLA: Revista Latino-americana de Historia Económica y Social 2 (1983): 3–32.

71. Edward Shils, Center and Periphery: Essays in Macrosociology (Chicago: University of Chicago Press, 1975), xx.

72. The basis for contrast to Europe is in Jean Delumeau, Catholicism Between Luther and Voltaire (Philadelphia: Westminster Press, 1977), and E. P. Thompson, "Patrician Society, Plebeian Culture," Journal of Social History 7 (Summer 1974): 390.

73. Thompson, "Patrician Society," 387.

74. Gramsci's formulations of intellectuals (except for occasional statements that they were simply the "dominant group's 'deputies'") and hegemony are useful in thinking about relationships of power in early Latin America but his own brief allusions to Latin America do not fit well. In the Prison Notebooks he underestimates the size and importance of the "traditional intellectual" group in Latin America, and speaks of priests as attached to a feudal landed aristocracy as if hacendados dominated early Latin American societies, and an early colonial "crystallization" of hegemonic relationships, Selections from the Prison Notebooks of Antonio Gramsci, ed. Quintin Hoare and Geoffrey N. Smith, (New York: International Publishers, 1971), 7, 14, 17, and 22.

75. Thompson, "Patrician Society."

76. Georges Balandier, Political Anthropology (New York: Pantheon, 1970).

77. See especially Edward Shils's collected essays, Center and Periphery (Chicago: University of Chicago Press, 1975) and Tradition (Chicago: University of Chicago Press, 1981). One of Shils's particular interests has been symbols of the center and of order, "the locus of the sacred [in relationship to specific objects] that confers legitimacy." Shils's "center" bears comparison to cultural hegemony in Gramsci's terms: "conscious attachment to or agreement with core elements of a society"; "an agreement powerful enough to deflect divisive forces arising from conflicting interests." Shils is criticized for concentrating too much on the center (as well as on consensus)—on the ideas of the elites who seek to control—and too little on the periphery, but he is right in saying that continuity and tradition need explanation as much as change does. By tradition he means "the pattern that guides reenactment" (Tradition, 7). However, it would be unwise to think of early Latin America in Shils's terms without the major qualification that relationships between unequals (such as "Spaniards" and "Indians") contain a fundamental oppression (with great variation) and both "mutuality" and "brutality," as the Genoveses put it in Fruits of Merchant Capital. Domination through symbols is discussed at length by Pierre Bourdieu, Outline of a Theory of Practice (Cambridge: Cambridge University Press, 1977), especially 191–92. Calling it "gentle violence," "gentle, hidden exploitation," Bourdieu sees cultural hegemony darkly as "the form taken by man's exploitation of man whenever overt, brutal exploitation is impossible." There is little in this conception of Gramsci's faith in "the popular creative spirit" and the possibility of "civil society" and communitas that Gramsci sets off against political society (coercion, direct domination), Prison Notebooks, 12, Letters from Prison, ed. by Lynne Lawner (New York: Harper & Row, 1973), 80.

184   William B. Taylor

78. Sidney W. Mintz and Richard Price, *An Anthropological Approach to the Afro-American Past: A Caribbean Perspective* (Philadelphia: Institute for the Study of Human Issues, 1976).

79. Jacques Lafaye, *Quetzalcoatl and Guadalupe: The Formation of Mexican National Consciousness, 1531–1813* (Chicago: University of Chicago Press, 1976); Irving Leonard, *Baroque Times in Old Mexico* (Ann Arbor: University of Michigan Press, 1959); Inga Clendinnen, "Landscape and World View: The Survival of Yucatec Maya Culture under Spanish Conquest," *Comparative Studies in Society and History* 22 (July 1980): 374–93. While Clifford Geertz is concerned with the nature and basis of sovereignty and "the intricacy of the balance of power" he acknowledges that his model of social and cultural process is a "conceptual entity, not an historical one," *Negara: The Theatre State in Nineteenth-Century Bali* (Princeton: Princeton University Press, 1980), 9. For recent evaluations of Geertz's writings, see Ronald E. Walters, "Signs of These Times: Clifford Geertz and Historians," *Social Research* 47 (Autumn 180): 537–56; William Roseberry, "Balinese Cockfights and the Seduction of Anthropology," *Social Research* 49 (Winter 1982): 1014–28.

80. Lafaye, *Quetzalcoatl and Guadalupe*; Victoria R. Bricker, *The Indian Christ, the Indian King: The Historical Substrata of Maya Myth and Ritual* (Austin: University of Texas Press, 1981); Michael T. Taussig, *The Devil and Commodity Fetishism in South America* (Chapel Hill: University of North Carolina Press, 1980).

81. Victor Turner, *The Forest of Symbols* (Ithaca: Cornell University Press, 1967); Victor Turner and Edith Turner, *Image and Pilgrimage in Christian Culture* (New York: Columbia University Press, 1978); James J. Preston, ed., *Mother Worship: Theme and Variations* (Chapel Hill: University of North Carolina Press, 1982).

82. Marina Warner, *Alone of All Her Sex: The Myth and the Cult of the Virgin Mary* (New York: Alfred A. Knopf, 1976).

83. As William Christian shows in *Apparitions in Late Medieval and Renaissance Spain* (Princeton: Princeton University Press, 1981), a truly extraordinary devotion to Mary blossomed in Spain about the time of the Conquest of Mexico with reports of numerous apparitions that were "eminently social visions, validated by widespread public devotion." During that time she eclipsed all other saints and heroes of the Church. Roughly two-thirds of all reported miracles were attributed to Mary in her various forms.

84. Robert C. Padden, *The Hummingbird and the Hawk: Conquest and Sovereignty in the Valley of Mexico, 1503–1541* (Columbus: Ohio State University Press, 1967), 192.

85. Even in the early twentieth century, when the cult of Guadalupe had achieved truly national dimensions, only about one in seven of the chapels and churches dedicated to the Virgin Mary was associated with Guadalupe. Lafaye mentions a total of 1,756 places of the Virgin—a large number, but far from comprehensive, because the old hospital chapels do not seem to have been included. Of these, Guadalupe accounts for 256. In the colonial period the worship of the Virgin by Indians would have been even less unified by one image than these figures indicate.

In contrast to Europe, early Latin America lacks a substantial base of historical writings on pilgrimages and the social history of Christianity other than the "Spiritual Conquest" and Jesuit missions. Little of the work outlined by Delumeau in 1971 has been undertaken for Latin America; nor are there studies comparable to

S. J. Connolly's *Priests and People in Pre-Famine Ireland, 1780–1845* (New York: St. Martin's Press, 1982).

86. Lafaye, *Quetzalcoatl and Guadalupe.*

87. Paul Wheatley, *The Pivot of the Four Quarters: A Preliminary Enquiry into the Origins and Character of the Ancient Chinese City* (Chicago: Aldine, 1971).

88. James B. Greenberg, *Santiago's Sword: Chatino Peasant Religion and Economics* (Berkeley: University of California Press, 1981), 43.

89. That Spanish officials actively promoted this symmetry between acts of deference toward royal officials and religious images is copiously documented. For example, Diego de Vargas, reconqueror of New Mexico, made the following entry in his journal on November 19, 1692: "I told him to silence them [the Indians], for did they not remember that, when they were Christians, a saint or the Virgin was received with much devotion and on bended knee, not shouting, and that they should fall upon their knees? And through the divine will I succeeded in having them do so." This text is quoted in Ronald L. Grimes, *Symbol and Conquest: Public Ritual and Drama in Santa Fe, New Mexico* (Ithaca: Cornell University Press, 1976), 213.

90. Turner, *Forest of Symbols* and Turner and Turner, *Image and Pilgrimage.* Stanley Tambiah has observed similar multivocality of symbolic structures in Buddhism, which he calls "pulsation between modalities," and has examined how religion and politics interrelate in *World Conqueror, World Renouncer: A Study of Buddhism and Polity in Thailand Against a Historical Background* (Cambridge: Cambridge University Press, 1976).

Another ubiquitous Christian symbol that can be studied this way is Santiago. Although he was more clearly a symbol of conquest, the Spaniards' patron in war, his representations in sculpture and painting were acquired and carefully preserved by villagers all over the heartlands of colonial Spanish America. Always shown on horseback, sword in hand, Santiago represented coercive power. But worshipping him was not necessarily an act of submission to Spanish rule. Scattered references for rural Mexico suggest at least three other possibilities of "multivocal" meaning: (1) the symbolism of St. James was not always public and political. In a more personal and private way his fierce image also was a model of manhood and competency to males individually; (2) the horse sometimes was revered more than its rider. Separated from its rider, the horse became a potent mystical force in its own right, believed to protect the community from attack; and (3) Santiago could be used as a foil for expressing village autonomy. In some places, the common spectacle on the day of St. James of a mounted horseman loping through the plaza brandishing his sword against the "moors" ended with the people surging forward to "kill the saint." Sometimes the luckless rider was seriously injured and a criminal trial ensued.

91. Preston, *Mother Worship.*

92. As does G. R. Elton, *Political History: Principles and Practice* (New York: Basic Books, 1970).

93. Donald Black, *The Behavior of Law* (New York: Academic Press, 1976).

94. John H. Kautsky provides a long discussion of the amount of politics between aristocrats and peasants before the rise of merchant capital in *The Politics of Aristocratic Empires* (Chapel Hill: University of North Carolina Press, 1982), 73 and passim. Factors in the intensity of exchange—economic, social, and ideological—

are discussed for a Mexican urban family over several generations in Larissa A. Lomnitz and Marisol Pérez Lizaur, "The History of a Mexican Urban Family," *Journal of Family History* 3 (Spring 1978): 405–8.

95. Notwithstanding the sweeping and largely justified criticism of the uses of anthropology in recent social history by Elizabeth Fox-Genovese and Eugene D. Genovese (*Fruits of Merchant Capital*, ch. 7), anthropologists working lately in the study of power or "political anthropology" have thought about the law and politics of complex societies in terms of process, change, consent, and confrontation of interests, and have much to offer to historians concerned with agrarian societies like early Latin America. For a critical introduction to promising recent work, see Sherry B. Ortner, "Theory in Anthropology Since the Sixties," *Comparative Studies in Society and History* 26 (January 1984): 126–66. Abner Cohen, for example, in *Two Dimensional Man* (London: Routledge & Kegan Paul, 1974), treats power relationships and symbolic action as interdependent but "relatively autonomous." Cohen studies the political implications of symbols and symbolic activities of custom and ritual, suggesting how a custom may continue although its function and symbolic meaning change, and how symbols may stand ambiguously for disparate meanings and may or may not impel people to action. In his view, power and symbolism are aspects of nearly all social relationships. They should be studied through specific interest groups that made up local societies and their connections in the political order of land tenure, patron-client relations, and exchange and distribution of goods and labor. By connecting power and symbolic action in political terms, Cohen provides a way to ask questions about cultural symbols that does not isolate the study of inequality.

Sally Falk Moore, in *Law as Process: An Anthropological Perspective* (London: Routledge & Kegan Paul, 1980), is equally interested in the contingency of power relationships, the place of reciprocity and mechanisms to contain abuse, and their susceptibility to change more than regularity and coherence. However, she focuses on law more than symbolic action and follows a conception of law similar to that of Black. This focus on the instability of political systems over time, rather than on traditional societies in structuralist isolation, is common to all these works in political anthropology.

Richard N. Adams combines state, law, and market as "partially independent" forces in power relationships that reach beyond pure coercion. See his "Power in Human Societies: A Synthesis," in *The Anthropology of Power: Ethnographic Studies from Asia, Oceania and the New World*, ed. Raymond Fogelson and Richard N. Adams, (New York: Academic Press, 1977), 387–410. He sees the state not only as repressive power but as a potentially contingent social control by governments that is affected by a range of independent and dependent power relationships. The relative importance of a symbolism of reciprocity, patron-client relations, brokers who span the gaps between lawmakers, law enforcers, and objects of the law, and cultural hegemony in a system of power, says Adams, depends on the existence of clients who have some control over the means of production. Once they have nothing to offer but their labor, as in a developed capitalist system (which Adams calls "the world's most powerful control system" today), they are worthless as clients. For Adams, the actions of the state, whether its power is expanding or contracting, are as important to the history of rural collective actions as capitalism. Much of the literature on the anthropology of power not touched upon in this essay is discussed in Joan Vincent, "Political Anthropology: Manipulative Strategies," *Annual Review of Anthropology* 7 (1978): 175–94. See also S. Lee Seaton and Henri J. M. Claessen, eds., *Political Anthropology: The State of the Art* (The Hague: Mouton, 1979); Ian Hamnett, ed., *Social Anthropology and Law* (New York: Academic Press, 1977). Historians have also entered the subject of power relationships and consent through Gramsci's writings; for example, E. P. Thompson (works cited earlier) and Elizabeth Fox-Genovese and Eugene D. Genovese, *Fruits of Merchant Capital*, ch. 12. A convenient summary of Gramsci's writings on hegemony is found in Joseph V. Femia, *Gramsci's Political Thought: Hegemony, Consciousness and the Revolutionary Process* (Oxford: Clarendon Press, 1981).

96. Borah, *Justice by Insurance*, p. 120.

97. Other major works that straddle the boundary between legal and social history are Magnus Mörner, *La corona española y los foráneos en los pueblos de indios de América* (Stockholm: Almqvist & Wiksell, 1970); Stuart B. Schwartz, *Sovereignty and Society in Colonial Brazil: The High Court of Bahia and Its Judges, 1609–1751* (Berkeley: University of California Press, 1973); and Ramón A. Gutiérrez, "Marriage, Sex, and the Family: Social Change in Colonial New Mexico, 1690–1846," Ph.D. diss., University of Wisconsin, 1980. Connecting legal and social history will require the rediscovery of the *Anuario de Historia del Derecho Español*, and early studies of the colonial state composed by Latin Americans such as Mario Góngora, *El estado español en el derecho indiano* (Santiago, Chile: Instituto de Investigaciones Histórico-Culturales, Universidad de Chile, 1951).

98. Frank Safford examined the social bases of political affiliation in "Social Aspects of Politics in Nineteenth-Century Spanish America: New Granada, 1825–1850," *Journal of Social History* 5 (Spring 1972): 344–70. For the colonial period, merchants are the best known group: for example, Brading, *Miners and Merchants*; Susan M. Socolow, *The Merchants of Buenos Aires, 1778–1810: Family and Commerce* (Cambridge: Cambridge University Press, 1978); Louisa Hoberman, "Merchants in Seventeenth-Century Mexico City: A Preliminary Portrait," *Hispanic American Historical Review* 57 (August 1977): 479–503; Ralph L. Woodward, *Class, Privilege and Economic Development: The Consulado de Comercio of Guatemala, 1793–1871* (Chapel Hill: University of North Carolina Press, 1966); John E. Kicza, *Colonial Entrepreneurs: Families and Businesses in Bourbon Mexico City* (Albuquerque: University of New Mexico Press, 1983). We also have works in which conquerors, high royal officials, clergymen, cabildo officers, nobles and *hacendados* are studied in social context: J. I. Israel, *Race, Class and Politics in Colonial Mexico, 1610–1670* (Oxford: Clarendon Press, 1975); James Lockhart, *The Men of Cajamarca: A Social and Biographical Study of the First Conquerors of Peru* (Austin: University of Texas Press, 1972); Lindley, *Haciendas*; Ann Twinam, *Miners, Merchants, and Farmers in Colonial Colombia* (Austin: University of Texas Press, 1982); John Tutino, "Power, Class, and Family: Men and Women in the Mexican Elite, 1750–1810," *The Americas* 39 (January 1983): 359–81; Doris M. Ladd, *The Mexican Nobility at Independence, 1780–1826* (Austin: University of Texas Press, 1976); Peter Marzahl, *Town in the Empire: Government, Politics, and Society in Seventeenth-Century Popayán*

(Austin: University of Texas Press, 1978); Stephanie Blank, "Patrons, Brokers, and Clients in the Families of the Elite in Colonial Caracas, 1595–1627," *The Americas* 36 (July 1979): 90–115; Margaret Chowning and Frederick P. Bowser, "Socio-Economic Power and Political Change in Mexico: The Case of Michoacán, 1650–1910," paper presented to the VI Conference of Mexican and United States Historians, Chicago, 1981; Paul Ganster, "La familia Gómez de Cervantes: linaje y sociedad en el México colonial," *Historia Mexicana* 31 (October–December 1981): 197–232; Jacques Barbier, "Elites and Cadres in Bourbon Chile," *Hispanic American Historical Review* 52 (August 1972): 416–35.

99. See Linda Lewin, "Some Historical Implications of Kinship Organization for Family-Based Politics in the Brazilian Northeast," *Comparative Studies in Society and History* 21 (April 1979): 262–92; Mark Wasserman, "Foreign Investment in Mexico, 1876–1910: A Case Study of the Role of Regional Elites," *The Americas* 36 (July 1979): 3–21; Allen Wells, "Family Elites in a Boom-and-Bust Economy: The Molinas and Peóns of Porfirian Yucatán," *Hispanic American Historical Review* 62 (May 1982): 224–53; Mark Wasserman, *Capitalists Caciques, and Revolution: The Native Elite and Foreign Enterprise in Chihuahua, Mexico, 1854–1911* (Chapel Hill: University of North Carolina Press, 1984); Richard P. Hyland, "A Fragile Prosperity: Credit and Agrarian Structure in the Cauca Valley, 1851–1887," *Hispanic American Historical Review* 62 (August 1982): 369–406; Stuart F. Voss, *On the Periphery of Nineteenth-Century Mexico: Sonora and Sinaloa, 1810–1877* (Tucson: University of Arizona Press, 1982); María Teresa Huerta Preciado, "La familia Yermo, 1750–1850," *Relaciones* 14 (Spring 1983): 46–65; Thomas Flory, *Judge and Jury in Imperial Brazil, 1808–1871: Social Control and Political Stability in the New State* (Austin: University of Texas Press, 1981); Roderick and Jean Barman, "The Prosopography of the Brazilian Empire," *Latin American Research Review* 13, 2 (1978): 78–97; Robert Oppenheimer and Diana Balmori, "Family Clusters: The Generational Nucleation of Families in Nineteenth-Century Argentina and Chile," *Comparative Studies in Society and History* 21 (April 1979): 231–61; Diana Balmori, Stuart F. Voss, and Miles Wortman, *Notable Family Networks in Latin America* (Chicago: University of Chicago Press, 1984); Frank Safford, *The Ideal of the Practical: Colombia's Struggle to Form a Technical Elite* (Austin: University of Texas Press, 1976); Thomas F. O'Brien, *The Nitrate Industry and Chile's Crucial Transition, 1870–1891* (New York: New York University Press, 1982), chap. 6; Mary L. Felstiner, "Kinship Politics in the Chilean Independence Movement," *Hispanic American Historical Review* 56 (February 1976): 58–80; Eul-Soo Pang and Ron Seckinger, "The Mandarins of Imperial Brazil," *Comparative Studies in Society and History* 14 (January 1972): 215–44; and Richard Graham, "Political Power and Landownership in Nineteenth-Century Latin America," in *New Approaches to Latin American History,* ed. Richard Graham and Peter H. Smith (Austin: University of Texas Press, 1974), 112–36.

100. For example, physicians as a new professional group in Latin America in the nineteenth century promoted a concept of hygiene that helped create a new image of women as monogamous housewives and mothers in Brazil after 1830, according to Dain Borges, "Physicians in Bahia, Brazil, 1830–1930," Ph.D., diss., Stanford University, 1983.

101. Ralph L. Woodward examines one aspect of relationships between politicians and peasants in nineteenth-century Guatemala in "Liberalism, Conservatism,

and the Response of the Peasants of La Montaña to the Government of Guatemala, 1821–1850," *Plantation Society in the Americas* 1 (February 1979): 109–30.

102. Eugene D. Genovese, *Roll, Jordan, Roll: The World the Slaves Made* (New York: Pantheon, 1974), 162, 280–83, is an example of how religions of the oppressed can be understood as a reciprocal process that is full of these kinds of contradictions.

103. Friedrich Katz, *The Secret War in Mexico: Europe, the United States, and the Mexican Revolution* (Chicago: University of Chicago Press, 1981), discusses how politics followed economic changes in the late nineteenth century; especially p. 5.

104. In this sense it is just as well, as Tulio Halperín puts it, that "actual [Latin American] historiography is usually either better or worse than the theoretical assumptions that sustain it, and maintains a surprising degree of independence from these assumptions," in "Dependency Theory," 129.

105. A recent example of scholarship that goes beyond dichotomies of slave labor/wage labor and accommodation/resistance is Rebecca Scott, "Gradual Abolition and the Dynamics of Slave Emancipation in Cuba, 1868–1886," *Hispanic American Historical Review* 63 (February 1983): 449–77.

106. Luis González y González, *Pueblo en vilo; microhistoria de San José de Gracia* (Mexico: El Colegio de México, 1968).

107. Based on recent scholarship, Woodrow Borah provides a challenging appraisal of the three standard divisions in Mexican history: the Conquest, the Independence period, and the Revolution of 1910 in "Discontinuity and Continuity in Mexican History," *Pacific Historical Review* 48 (February 1979): 1–25. He concludes that the Conquest was the only really deep discontinuity in Mexican history and suggests that 1760 to 1877 and 1877 to the present are significant periods.

108. See the essays in *The Inca and Aztec States, 1400–1800: Anthropology and History,* ed. George A. Collier, Renato I. Rosaldo, and John D. Wirth (New York: Academic Press, 1982), especially those by James Lockhart, "Views of Corporate Self and History in Some Valley of Mexico Towns: Late Seventeenth and Eighteenth Centuries," 367–93, and Frances Karttunen, "Nahuatl Literacy," 395–417.

109. Karttunen in *Inca and Aztec States,* ed. Collier, Rosaldo and Wirth.

110. Dorothy Tanck de Estrada, *La educación ilustrada, 1786–1836: educación primaria en la cuidad de México* (Mexico: Colegio de México, 1977).

111. Borah, *Justice by Insurance,* 412.

112. The importance of the Independence wars in rural social change can easily be overemphasized. Carol A. Smith seems to regard wage labor for partial peasant subsistence, cash economy, migration out of *pueblos* and privatization of common lands as all beginning in western Guatemala after the Independence wars, "Local History in Global Context," 203–4. These processes were accelerated by the wars but probably did not begin with them.

113. This point also is developed by John Tutino in his paper, "Agrarian Social Change and Peasant Rebellion in Nineteenth-Century Mexico: Chalco, 1840–1870," presented to the 1982 Social Science Research Council symposium on peasant rebellions in Mexican history.

114. Tulio Halperín Donghi, *The Aftermath of Revolution in Latin America* (New York: Harper & Row, 1973), 1–3.

115. William B. Taylor, "Patterns of Homicide in the District of Tlacolula, Oaxaca, 1700–1880: A Preliminary Examination of Death Records," unpublished paper, July 1982.

116. Hugo Nutini, "Syncretism and Acculturation: The Historical Development of the Cult of the Patron Saint in Tlaxcala, Mexico (1519–1670)," Ethnology 15 (July 1976): 301–21.

CHAPTER 4

DOING SOCIAL HISTORY
FROM *PIM'S* DOORWAY

BY DAVID WILLIAM COHEN

In Kenya today, many women and men affectionately recall the figure pim.[1] In the period of her transition from marriage to infirmity, pim came into the Luo household (Kenya) from a considerable social and geographical distance. She lived with and nurtured the young girls and boys of the household, the compound or enclosure, and sometimes the neighborhood. Boys stayed with pim for several years, leaving her charge when it was seen that they were too old to sleep among the young girls. Girls stayed much longer, often going from pim's care directly into marriage. And there, in this new residence, pim herself found shelter, food, support, companionship, and protection.

Pim and her charges lived together in the siwindhe, the nursery, located within the enclosure or compound. The siwindhe materialized as a cohort of children who had advanced into the years when they should not sleep with their parents. Some enclosures had the resources and a budding young population of sufficient size to sustain a

Without obligating them to assume any responsibility, I would like to acknowledge the very helpful counsel, criticism, and aid of Helmut Bley, Fred Cooper, Donald Crummey, Charles Feigenoff, Ashraf Ghani, John Godfrey, Richard L. Hall, Jr., Shula Marks, Hans Medick, Sidney W. Mintz, Richard Price, Christopher Steiner, and Robert Tignor, and of members of the African seminars at Dalhousie University and the School of Oriental and African Studies, the Social History seminar at the University of Virginia, and the General Seminar in Atlantic History, Culture, and Society at Johns Hopkins. I especially appreciate the critical counsel of Olivier Zunz and the other contributors to this volume. A German Academic Exchange Service (DAAD) fellowship permitted me to work on this chapter at the Max-Planck Institut für Geschichte in Göttingen.

191

siwindhe for a long period of time. But in many settings a few children from here and there would be passed to the care of a *pim* in a nearby enclosure. The *siwindhe* dematerialized as the population of the compound aged, or disappeared.

The *siwindhe* was usually indistinguishable from other domiciles in the compound; however, the interior of the *siwindhe* is recalled as a structure of transition from infancy to maturity. It was within the *siwindhe* that much of the essential social intelligence of the Luo world has been imparted by *pim* to those with little experience or knowledge of that world.

Children learned about the past from *pim*. They drew upon her wisdom. They learned about the people, the groups, and the settlements around them. They learned a geography of succor and a geography of danger. They learned about sexuality and about childbirth. Using her ranging social knowledge *pim* both broadened and delimited the fields of possible and optimal marriages. From *pim*, children learned about health, illness, misfortune, and death. They learned about interest, opportunity, and obligation that would both open and restrict their lives. As *pim* nurtured and instructed her charges, joined them to the mature world, the material she brought from outside the enclosure neighborhood and from outside the patri-group provided the young with an array of referents extending far beyond the patrilineage and gave the young the elements of an intimate understanding of a complex and physically remote social universe.

In a broad sense, in taking up the care of her first charges, *pim* embraced a pattern of nurturing which is held to have descended from far in the past. Pim learned her critical role within the *siwindhe* of her own childhood; yet *pim* was assuming a new role which called upon all her experience beyond the *siwindhe*: in marrying, in gathering valuable domestic materials, wild foodstuffs, and condiments from the field margins and scrubland, in organizing the cultivation of foods, in cooking and serving, in treating illness, in producing and marketing ceramic and fiber wares, in handling childbirth and young children, in visiting and helping friends and relations, in coping with dangerous conditions and forces, in identifying and securing refuges in times of war, famine, and epidemic, in caring for the ancestors, and in discovering pleasures and interests. And in taking possession of her new role as *pim*, the elderly Luo woman also protected herself from a "social death." She would not be abandoned to starve amidst a famine or left without companionship and protection.[2]

It was this sometimes helpless and dependent figure whose knowledge and experience pierced the fences of the enclosure and the
walls of the *siwindhe* and transformed the social intelligence of the
young from that of the enclosure and the immediate patri-group to
that of marriage and adulthood and the many associations, alliances,
dangers, and opportunities lying beyond the enclosure. The circulation of social knowledge from *pim* through the *siwindhe* literally extended the horizon of young Luo speakers and made it possible to
meet various contingencies, whether in an area twenty kilometers
away or over much greater distances in Kampala, Nairobi, and Mom-
basa. In fact, one of the better known of the last *pim* was Granny
Muzungu, who was considered to be very knowledgeable about European ways and about Nairobi's society, thus the name "Muzungu."[3]
The rich materials of history, of past contacts, of alliances, of old
marriages, coalitions, and descent which *pim* imparted to members of
a household later facilitated travel for trade and for social visits. Pim's
knowledge contributed to the social expertise carried along on fishing expeditions and marketing enterprises on Lake Victoria. The
learning in the *siwindhe* produced an invaluable basis for individual
and household migrations and for the settlement of new areas. Pim's
teachings also fostered new activities, relationships, marriages, and
mobility that continued the process of extending knowledge for people across western Kenya. Given the importance of social knowledge
in the construction of middle-distance and long-distance relations
in western Kenya, the role of childhood socialization—the work of
pim—in the generation of a regional consciousness and corporateness
is pivotal. Assembled, this knowledge and the social activity that it
animated gave form to the broader *oganda* associations and was part
of the base upon which an active Luo identity—a "national" identity
rather than a clan or neighborhood identity—developed.

Before 1930, there may have been thousands of *siwindhe* in western
Kenya. But after 1930, there were few. Kisumu, Nairobi, and Mom-
basa, along with both rural and town schools, promised greater opportunities for nurturing the young, while the changing shape of
the rural household economy made the feeding of an elderly and
dependent woman coming from outside the home more problematic. When in the late 1960s and early 1970s, a sociolinguist, Ben G.
Blount, did research on the acquisition of language of Luo children in
western Kenya, he found that a "young girl ... of five or six may
become the principal caretaker for a young sibling, assuming the re-

sponsibility for feeding the child, protecting him from harm and danger, and catering in general to his needs."[4] Without access to the memory of pim and to the material on the evident transformation of childhood socialization in this century Blount accepted this absence of adult supervision as "characteristic of the Luo and closely related Nilotic groups." One is reminded of how easy it is to accept the present and observed social world as given and traditional.

Pim's nurturing was an almost invisible crucible of Luo culture and society, and consequently, its critical activity has been missed, as anthropologists and historians have attended to the form and play of "larger," and in a sense "masculine" structures and segmentary processes in Luo society. Until recently, the historical process of development of Luo society in western Kenya has been seen as a process of repetitive, methodical budding, branching and expansion of segments of patrilineal units, a steady segmentation process from a narrow base.

Having recognized the role that pim plays in nurturing the young, we now stand on the verge of comprehending a far more complex process, one that incorporates and reworks knowledge from outside of the patrilineage and that puts this knowledge of relations, alliances, and opportunities to active social use. The ideology of patrilineal segmentation is not therefore the overarching system defining identity and constituency as has been thought. The ideology of segmentation in Luo thought and speech is but one means of conceptualizing and animating complex social activity over time. It has an elegance and a methodical quality that make it a commonly evoked premise in everyday discourse. Pim, most often coming to the household from outside the patrilineage, provided the young with elements of understanding of a social universe that diverges far from the model of segmentation which many social scientists and many Luo have carried so comfortably for so long.

The camp where my research in Siaya (Kenya) and on pim was based was used as an archaeological camp from time to time, and during different periods of my stay, trays of artifacts, pieces of pottery and stone tools, were pulled out of storage by members of my staff who had also worked on the excavations. Fragments and shards were examined and columns of data were entered in a registry book. Pieces were handled and discussed, and I received an education on the Late Stone Age and Early Iron Age activity in the vicinity of our camp. At the time, it occurred to me that the material on pim and her work could be seen as a fragment or shard from which projections of the complete object or social complex might be made, projections that would in turn illuminate a much wider social process. Indeed, the identification of an arena of social production where knowledge from outside the patri-group residence reorganized knowledge within it provided a means to comprehend the formation of Luo society.[5]

The case of pim and the siwindhe of the late nineteenth and early twentieth century makes one wish to have access to still deeper layers of learning and socialization such as have been revealed in Françoise Zonabend's study[6] of childhood in Burgundy. Unlike the siwindhe, where an "outsider" was often brought in to nurture and educate, in Minot, "throughout childhood and even beyond it, the grandparents played a leading part in the process of socialization, a part that was long unsuspected as it was on the sidelines, in the shadow."[7]

It is not the point to introduce a comparative analysis of fostering in Agulu—where one well-known pim resided—and Minot though there is an implication that a contextually far broader, social intelligence may have been brought into the lives of the children of the siwindhe than into those of Minot.[8] The point is that there are critical areas in the shadows, critical silences in the social worlds we study. They are there not because we are few in number and sources are recondite, but because the attentions of anthropologists and historians tend to follow the visible wake of the past, ignoring the quiet eddies of potentially critical material that form at the same time.

It is perhaps a violation of the praxis of synthesis to open a treatment of the "history of society in Africa" with a popular description of an elderly nurse who lived with her young charges within a rustic compound far from the contentions of the slave trade, colonial domination, the emerging city, and capitalist development. Social history has, after all, found its sustenance in the study of the transformations of the lives of ordinary people, under capitalism and in Europe and North America,[9] while it has found its mission in questioning theories of broad social change and their unmediated application to specific experiences of ordinary people. But pim, along with her charges, serves the purpose of social history because she helps us understand the interior architecture of African society. Pim challenges us to comprehend, visualize, and disinter certain routines of behavior at their source, to understand the intimate structure of thought and activity through which simple routines become powerful reper-

toires, to see how these are given meaning and impulse. She challenges us to observe how this little social mechanism—aggregated
thousands of times in ways pims in their siwindhes over generations
each evolved—produces life and gives it order and logic and direction.

This presentation of pim and her work in part reflects the ways
older Kenyans today speak of pim and recall their experiences and
learning within the siwindhe. Both their reflections on pim and the
presentation here, which intentionally follows those reflections, are
full of sentiment. These reflections reveal otherwise undocumented
aspects of Luo home life and childhood. And because they are subjective accounts of the past, they are instructive in another way. The
nostalgic, timeless, and idealistic form in which pim and the siwindhe
come down to us in these reports exemplifies the way historical reflections are composed within African knowledge of the past.

This knowledge, with its idealistic and timeless thrust, has had, in
turn, a powerful influence on the literatures of anthropology, sociology, economics, and history. African historians must comprehend
critically and sympathetically the intellectual processes that give the
historical knowledge of Africa its idealistic and timeless quality. At the
same time, we must extract the gritty sediment of the lives of our
subjects and their forebears which these idealistic, sentimental, and
normative statements or texts often hide. The warm memories of pim
as well as the actual teachings of "Granny" Muzungu and other pims
may have helped many young Africans in this century move effectively along the branches of society leading to remote centers of
domination, arenas of employment, and capitalism.[10] Understanding
this may help the historian disclose the ways ordinary lives are linked
to world capitalism.

But pim's work may also remind us that for pim and her children,
knowledge began not with a remote world-system but with the vista
seen just beyond the doorway of the siwindhe. Pim and her charges
may encourage us in our quest for a composition not to lose sight of
each tiny multiple-edged fragment that constitutes knowledge of the
African past, nor to ignore the yet to be studied areas of silence.

An Apparatus

There is an approach here, a perspective, the beginnings of a theoretical apparatus, directed toward the investigation of what Charles
Tilly[11] has termed "collective encounters with social change." A starting point is the tension between this interest in "collective encounters" and Tilly's bolder agenda, that "social history deals with the
interplay of large processes, big social structures, and whole populations." One might remark that understanding the emergence of major
cultural groupings, the development of African empires and kingdoms, the formation of relations between African kings and European agencies, the impact of the slave trade on Africa, the coupling of
Yao, Dyula, Ga, Ibo, and Swahili trading congeries with the world
economy, the movements of resistance to colonialism, the underdevelopment of Africa, the proletarianization of African peasantries, the
militarization of independent African states, the paths to consciousness of African laborers, and the enravelment of neocolonialism has
been the program of historians of Africa since 1960.

In Nyamwezi caravans . . . a young man often used the wages
earned on safari (which were usually paid in cloth) to begin
trading on his own account. On his second or third expedition
he might carry two small tusks of his own; with experience, he
might become a caravan guide (kiongozi) and eventually he
might become rich enough to fit out a caravan of his own.[12]

There is, after a quarter century of research and publishing, an
extraordinary historical literature that has the general feel of social
history. And yet, African historians have, with rare exceptions, made
no claim of being on the cutting edge of social history, and few historians even seek to label their work as "social history." Over the past
five hundred years, the historical study of Africa has evolved without
the regulation of dense, centripetal intellectual networks such as have
given form to the historical literatures of Europe and North America.
Consequently, important investigations of African society are being
generated outside the discourse of formal social history as practiced
in Europe and North America.
    The past of Africa is brought down to us through a myriad of

sources that emerged because, for centuries, the social worlds of the African continent have attracted observation and have challenged comprehension. Indeed, perhaps the major issue in the reconstruction of the African past is, and has been for some years, the question of how far voices exterior to Africa shape the presentation of Africa's past and present. Certainly, the exterior voices have had a major influence on how we as historians—Americans, Europeans, and Africans—know Africa. The traveler in his tale grappled often unsuccessfully or inconclusively with the unusual, the remote, the exotic. Sometimes such an early report or observation passed from "observer" to "observer" until finally recorded in a journal or a history. Often, such "knowledge" as early European travelers constructed influenced the shape of subsequent observations.[13]

They [the Fula] come determined to ferry this army across the river [the Gambia], but having no boats for this purpose, the river being at that point one league wide, they filled it with rocks in such a way that the whole army crossed. Many aver that the army was so great that it was unnecessary for each soldier to carry more than one rock. Be that as it may, they blocked the river, and the whole army crossed with its baggage, which was great because they had numerous horses, camels, donkeys, and cows . . . they carried hives of bees, which they let loose upon their enemies when the wind was favorable. This was a terrifying army. Never was another of equivalent size seen among these nations, destroying and laying waste everything, passing through the territory of the Mandingas, Cassangas, Banhuns, and Buramos, a distance of more than 150 leagues, until they came to the Rio Grande, the country of the Beafadas, where the Fulas were defeated.[14]

Early travelers and writers from the Christian and Islamic worlds produced pictures of an African continent full not only of large armies and powerful kingdoms but also of great resources. A desire to discover and capture these resources—the gold, ivory, spices, hides, fragrances, and exotic woods—turned the eyes of travelers, traders, and mercantile companies toward Africa. By the end of the seventeenth century, as slaves entered the inventories of trade, the

West African coast was visited with great frequency by European ves-
sels. Considerable numbers of Europeans were established at stations
and in forts along the West African coast from Arguin Island to the
Bight of Benin. They were on the coast to trade to amass wealth, and
through this trade, through the collection of intelligence bearing on
trade, and through the formation of working relations and alliances
with local artisans, laborers, and rulers, they accumulated an impressive knowledge of the African worlds around them. The agents of
European mercantile enterprise in the seventeenth and eighteenth
centuries assembled observations on production, exchange, markets,
health, governance, town organization, housing, consumption, and
law.

The towns which lie towards the interior of the country are
richer in goods and gold than the border (that is, coastal)
towns, and have more houses and are more populous than the
sea side towns; they also have wealthier merchants who conduct more trade than those in the coastal towns whose inhabitants are the interpreters, boatmen, pilots, officials, fishermen,
and slaves of the inhabitants of the interior towns. . . . The inland towns are extremely large compared to the coastal towns
. . . but I have learned from the Blacks that further inland still
are larger towns containing multitudes of people.[15]

In the eighteenth century, the Atlantic slave trade became the
central fact of relations between Europeans and Africans, and forces
generated within Africa by the demand for African manpower in
the slave societies of the Americas had enormous influence upon
the most densely populated areas of the continent. Few states in
west and west-central Africa could escape the effects of this demand
for labor.[16] The slave trade made misery the daily lot for millions
of people. Immeasurable changes were produced across much of
Africa.

Whydah is the greatest trading Place on the Coast of Guinea,
selling off as many Slaves, I believe, as all the rest together; forty
or fifty Sail (French, English, Portuguese, and Dutch) freighting

there every year. The King is absolute as a Boar; making sometimes fair Agreements with his Country Neighbours, it being often the Interest of Traders to be honest (perhaps the only reason that makes them so) but if he cannot obtain a sufficient
number of Slaves that way, he marches an Army, and depopu-
lates. He, and the King of Ardra adjoining, commit great Depre-
dations inland.[17]

Within this context, of Europeans and Africans capturing, assem-
bling, trading, and transporting human beings, the images and intelligence that one party—the numerous European companies and ad-
venturers on the West African coast—gathered about the other—the
numerous African groups variously situated in the trade—were reshaped. Some of these images fixed the European language of description of Africa for more than a century and influenced the new
information brought forward to the historian. This can be seen in the
debates that began in Europe in the late eighteenth century over the
legitimacy of the slave trade, which produced still more findings on
trade, agriculture, artisanry, manufacture, disease, mortality, and governance, and in the abolitionists' arguments about the destructive
effects of the slave trade on African social and economic life and in
them plans to protect nonslave production in both Africa and the
New World.

These images are also found in the data on markets, labor, and
production that so-called free traders and firms collected in the nineteenth century. European governments sought, at mid-century, to
stimulate overseas commercial enterprises while holding down the
costs to the nation of such enterprises. Consequently, European traders and trading companies were sometimes pressed, sometimes left
free, to arrange political and economic relations with the rulers and
administrations of African states. These relations were intended, first,
to generate new or increased levels of production of palm oil, rub-
ber, ivory, hardwoods, groundnut oil, coffee, and gum; and, second,
to ease and cheapen their supply. Throughout the nineteenth century, the growth in African consumption of European and American
manufactures and products—metal goods, including guns, textiles,
salt, rum, and gin—rose hand in hand with commodity production
and became an effective motor of economic and social change. Afri-

can commodity production was stimulated, and new areas came into production, while large numbers of Africans drew new income as laborers, collectors, carriers, coastal merchants, and country traders.

Yet the nineteenth-century spurt in commodity production for the world market and attendant new patterns of consumption were not to the advantage of many Africans. African manufacturers of metal ware and cloth faced stiff competition as many Africans developed new and enduring tastes for European goods. Older entrepreneurial and transport groups in Africa and a newer generation of merchants were here and there squeezed out of central roles in the transactions of trade. Privileges were rescinded, treaties were abandoned or abrogated, European credit advances to African merchants and firms were pinched or withdrawn, as—from the mid-nineteenth century—European traders and companies found it possible and profitable to advance more directly into the markets fifty, a hundred, two hundred kilometers from the coast.

The reworked consumption patterns and the expansion of commodity production introduced other forces into the African setting. The returns from commodity production for European and American markets brought changes in the management of commodity production, as rulers of African states and African merchants sought to gain control of the production. In some areas, chiefs,[18] big men, and the state organized slave production, while in other settings producers managed to defend the labor of their household and still draw income from commodity production. And while at some moments the alliances formed between African rulers and European agents and companies enhanced the power of the rulers, at other moments these relations among Europeans and Africans made the authority of the African rulers more brittle and more likely to be resisted. The promotion of "legitimate" commerce did not dissolve the rapacity and inhumanity of the Atlantic system's method of extracting African commodities. New struggles for power were introduced to the African terrain; yet these contests of control and resistance followed the course of older struggles over the regulation of life and the control of labor. The events of these contests, which continued into the twentieth century, generated new records and memories among both Europeans and Africans.

The nineteenth century was also an era of evangelical revival in Europe and with this came the promotion of a civilizing and Christianizing mission in Africa. This mission was seen by its promoters as part of the movement against the slave trade and slavery, which included the stimulation of "legitimate" production and commerce. In the late nineteenth century, a tremendous wave of European missionaries fanned out across Africa, pushing inland from a number of secure stations long established on the African coasts. Through regular reports, journals, and correspondence, missionaries in the nineteenth and twentieth centuries relayed information and assessments of social conditions and social behavior to supporters at home, ofttimes colored by a combination of courage, hope, and ethnographic zeal, racism, and frustration.

Undoubtedly the races of Africa with whom we have come into contact have been so miserably low, intellectually and morally, in the scale of humanity, apparently so dull and unimpressionable, that to persons who take no account of the generating power of the Holy Spirit, it must seem a thing incredible that many of them should become intelligent Christians.[19]

These reports constitute an immense file of observations and impressions on Africa in the last decades before the colonial period and through much of the colonial era. Closely read, they reveal much about the structure of conversion efforts in African communities. Missionaries edged close to African rulers and courts, seeking the influence and patronage that court entry promised. At the same time, their stations served as centers for outcasts and refugees, the human product of political and economic conflicts and dislocations. Over much of Africa, missionaries were responsible for the establishment of the first European educational institutions and for the establishment of authoritarian patterns of teaching and curriculum which have persisted for over a century. Early Christian converts constituted new and very active political parties in a number of settings. Here and there, some parties of converts took up arms to fight for their new faith, to defend its political or social status, or simply to defend themselves. Religious wars displaced the ambiguous political and economic treaty in many parts of Africa as the epitome of early colonial experience.

To begin with, isolated cases were dealt with as isolated cases of disobedience. But as more and more cases occurred of this Christian disobedience, Kabaka Mwanga, who had succeeded in 1884, seems to have realised that these Christians were forming a seditious group within his kingdom which was dangerous, not least because it consisted of some adherents of his court. Such dangers were given added urgency both because these Christians might prove the agents and abettors of a European invasion of Buganda, and because their activities threatened to disrupt the united front which it was essential that Buganda should present to any European advance. It is not surprising therefore that mass executions took place.[20]

As the Christian church pressed its claims upon the religious and moral lives of Africans, new struggles opened up within the churches and missions themselves. Africans demanded full admission to the priesthood, greater toleration of African rituals, beliefs, and moral codes, control of missions and schools, and occasionally a greater role for the Christian church and congregation in the wider colonial society. Church ritual and church-defined standards of conduct became the center of broader debates over the meaning of conversion and the ultimate objectives of the European colonial presence in Africa. These debates were considerable and produced remarkable African articulation of Christian dogma.

Churches became places of residence, centers of social activity, and political affiliation, as well as houses of prayer. Crowds of converts moved to the mission station and church and made the African church a more complete universe than the most energetic missionary ever intended. From the first days of mission activity, there was a sense among African converts that the European presence was but transitory and that Africans would rise to command the faith. When the opportunities to participate in Christian practice were not fulfilled, Africans began to struggle for control of the churches. The struggles often leaped out of the early churches. Established Christian institutions were, here and there, taken over and transformed into popular institutions by African Christian leaders, and independent churches were established by discontented Africans and African prophets in virtually every location where missionaries were established. The independent churches and prophetic movements often became the vehicles of broad social and political protest against colonialism, and the colonial administrations and European mission organizations tried desperately to suppress them. Often, however, these attempts only enriched the enthusiasm of African Christian revivalism. The waves of independent and prophetic Christianity attracted astonishing numbers of converts, making the established churches and missions sometimes secondary in the spread of Christianity in Africa.

---

the Prophet [Harris] appeared on the veranda with a crowd of people. He told the priest, "I tell you, you have to send away all of the people who I brought to you. I am going to make my own church." "There are the stairs," said Father Stauffer, gesturing with his hand.[21]

In many settings, the first generation of African readers and writers came from this first group of converts, and a robust literature written in an African hand began to emerge about Africa. Early African writers published records of their own history, sometimes presented as ethnohistory, sometimes as chronicle, sometimes as petition, sometimes as autobiography, a literature often reflective and revealing of class interests in the encounters between Africans and European colonialism. The coupling of high status (and authority) with literacy came out of the first and second decades of mission teaching in many areas of Africa, and the coupling constituted a very powerful element in the African political landscape throughout the late nineteenth and twentieth centuries.

I started the collection of the three Rs [rupees] tax. I realized how poor we were because it was difficult for people to get three Rs. It was decided that people should pay two Rs in cash and the third as a bag of flour of dried Matoke, but it was still difficult to get two Rs. The government therefore decided that

those who could not get two Rs could pay by presenting a
python, or bunches of processed sisal, pepper, a male sheep,
maize, sim-sim, etc. One man named S. Munaku of Singo
brought a python once. This all illustrates how poor Buganda
was.[22]

Yet another element in the picture of Africa was contributed by
colonial administrations in the present century. They encouraged the
production of detailed studies of political organization, agriculture
and land use, and indigenous law, with the general objective of making "native administration" less costly, more efficient. Advocates of
"colonial reform" in rural Africa and in the metropoles collected evidence on the working and living conditions of African labor and on
the effects of colonial labor laws and tax programs on social life.
Anthropologists sought to combine an interest in preserving African
institutions with wider analyses of political power, of kinship, of religious belief and practice, of conflict in colonial society, and of economic growth. Urbanologists attempted to comprehend and even to
slow the tumultuous growth of African towns and societies and, in
the process, assembled data on the conditions that they felt shifted
population from rural to urban areas.

Starting in the 1960s, social scientists explored the contours of social and economic stratification that were beginning to be perceived
as deeply etched into the nations of the continent. In addition, novel-
ists, poets, playwrights, and filmmakers have begun in the past fifteen
years to explore actively and fluently the political, economic, and
social forces and processes shaping African society. They have drawn
portraits of African social worlds of enormous interpretative power,
portraits that are often accessible to popular audiences in Africa concerned with the crises in their own lives and the course and meaning
of their own past.

The office fills up as the day clerks enter, first the small boys
and messengers, then the other clerks. About nine-thirty the
Senior Service men come in each with his bit of leftover British
craziness. This one has long white hose, that one colonial white
white. Another has spent two months on what he still calls a

study tour of Britain, and ever since has worn, in all the heat of Ghana, waistcoats and coats. He would have made a good Obedient Boy of the Empire on a Queen's Birthday.[23]

In the same period African historians have made a commitment to record the memories, narratives, and testimonies of older Africans and to reconstruct the African past from these sources. This effort, aimed at producing another past for Africa other than a colonial past, had, and in some ways still has, substantial support from African governments, from international organizations, from publishers, from intellectuals, schools, and universities within Africa, and importantly, from those who are sometimes coldly referenced as "informants" in the historical studies of the African past. The use of massive and difficult bodies of evidence derived from oral testimonies has attracted considerable attention to the methodologies of African historiography, as well as to both the utility and limitations of these materials. These oral materials have been seen by some as, at best, an evocation of social constitutions, by others as cells containing objective detail, and by still others as evidence of social concourse and conflict in the past. These oral materials nevertheless reveal much about the formation of those African states and societies that European explorers and colonial authorities encountered in the late nineteenth century. In a hundred precolonial settings, from the eastern Cape of southern Africa, where the European settlements and sheep farming compressed the African population, to seventeenth- to nineteenth-century Buganda and the organization of bureaucratic administration, to the civil wars of nineteenth-century Ethiopia, to the Islamic revolutions of eighteenth- and nineteenth-century West Africa, oral materials have revealed historical experience otherwise closed to present observation and have augmented—and sometimes opened—a critical dialectic with written documentation.

While this program of reconstructing the noncolonial past of Africa has largely been carried forward by the guild of historians, clearly much significant work has been produced outside the historical profession; recently, the social sciences have come to consider the past of great interest, and much social scientific work now being done on Africa has an historical orientation. Historians of Africa today do not control an "intellectual property." Importantly, Africans outside the professional historical guild are actively producing, in both ordinary and extraordinary settings, their own records of the past in the form of oral texts, local histories, and literary treatments. A substantial base of the professional historian's history of Africa, however, rests upon a multitude of small fragments of such interior knowledge. In the past, the *griot*, the storyteller, the elder, the father, indeed pim's work, was a part of that interior production of knowledge. The guild of professional historians has only begun to plumb the riches of these interior reservoirs of social intelligence in which records of the past are located. This first accession of such material has often involved the collection of the essentially "official" and "national" accounts and formal narrative traditions of the past of a state or population or group. As elders with the knowledge, capability, and interest to recite formal narratives are passing from the African scene, historians, ethnohistorians, and historical anthropologists have begun to consider the abundant material from and on the past—on parentage, marriage, property, moral codes, production, joking, cuisine, nomenclature, ritual—the stuff of discourse and behavior in everyday life. The materials on the past still to plumb may be extraordinarily rich, if the historian is able to read the "unconscious" records of past from the "texts" being produced by individuals every day.

The Tribe of African Historians[24]

While social history has been in Europe and North America a product of segmentation of larger academic congeries, in Africa the critical mass necessary to produce subprofessionalization is not there (though African economic historians have appropriated an identity and something of a specialized field of work)[25] Another aspect of the critical mass question concerns the individual African historians who are likely as not to find themselves temporary visitors (and to find that they are objects of a good deal of ambivalence) in the area and country of research. The challenge at the moment is, therefore, to understand the trends and tendencies within African historiography more generally. A comprehensive explanation for the movements that African historians (of the guild) have made to address particular questions at certain moments awaits a major study or studies of the history of African historiography. While only small sections of such a history have been developed,[26] a tentative explanation of the paths taken lies in the national segmentation of African historiography, in the tensions created by anticolonial sentiment within the descendant lines of historiography, and in variations in the "social texture" of much of what the African historian works with—lineages, villages, age stratification, pastoralists, cultivators, gender relations, clienteles, ethnic conflicts, and chiefdoms.

It can also be said that the highly segmented nature of African historical enterprise and the very difficult nature of much historical fieldwork undertaken in Africa mean that a certain disarray is part of the structure of the field. Nonetheless, each new research project has the promise of introducing new methods and new questions. The experience within a given narrow field might be applicable to a larger frame of reference as may other externally evolved questions or approaches.

But African historians are not *autonomes*, nor is the field altogether inchoate. It is possible to offer a few thoughts concerning the shifting directions which African historians have taken over the past three decades. In the 1950s and 1960s, historians of Africa tended to concentrate on certain phenomena because of their high visibility (kingdoms and empires, religious wars, European agencies and African kings, guns and slaves). With the independence of African countries came a tendency to focus on issues of considerable, though momentary ideological weight (religious revolutions, resistance movements, slavery and the slave trade, racism, and proletarianization). While many African historians marshaled their efforts to fill perceived "gaps in the historical record" (for example, the early history of Africa), there was a welling up of interest in current political and economic problems. Attempts to analyze the origins and elaborations of underdevelopment have begun, and in some ways African historians have moved into (or, better, backed into) terrain held by European and North American social historians and by counterparts working on the history of the Caribbean, Latin America, and Asia,[27] particularly in areas of "peasantries" and "proletarianization."

The Contours of Our Analytical Terrain

Working upon a rich and diverse base of historical literature on Africa, historians today have been pushing several important renovations in the traditions of historical inquiry. A first challenge is to become—at one instant—more conscious of and more able to control the definition of analytic unit. Much early research on Africa was defined by notional, consensual boundaries and usually around the entity of district or ethnic group. Such definitions most often fell between what Edmund Leach once saw as two prevailing modal definitions of the social unit of study: "any convenient locality" and the "self-contained political unit."[28] As the historian began to learn that the meanings of such units as the "Yao," "Kikuyu," "Bakedi," and "Hausa" were socially constructed in time and that the collective unit could only be defined "in motion," so earlier studies, as they were read more critically, raised new problems for the students of the past. Were the early students of African culture fully aware of the considerable heterogeneity of most precolonial African populations? Were they aware of the social and ideological processes that established "boundedness" and the basis of collective action not as the starting point of the history of the group but as, essentially, the extended history of the formation of a group, continued into the present?[29]

In interesting ways, the African historian has been pressed to mediate between the most general levels of description of the continent and the intimate arenas of field research. On large scale maps and satellite photographs and in general textbooks, the continent is viewed as a quilt-work of large, distinctive ecological zones. These are seen, for most of the continent, as running east and west, wet tropical forest in the equatorial belt, woodland and grassland to the north and south of the wet forest, dry savanna and desert to the north and south of the woodland and grassland, and a moister vegetational belt at the northern and southern tips of the continent. On the eastern side of the continent, the strong rise in elevation associated with the rift system stretching from the Red Sea to south-central Africa is responsible for a somewhat more complicated arrangement of general zones oriented along a north-south rather than east-west axis.

Demographically, these two patterns are important because the densities of population tend to rise in consonance with the moisture levels, except in the strongest bands of moist tropical forest, which have resisted until recently intensive settlement by human populations. The general continental features have their own history, for we understand today that over the past six to eight thousand years, Africa has been undergoing a general process of desiccation, an effect of large climatic change, compounded by the work of man, his agriculture, and his industry.

One witnesses from occasional airplane trips the disappearance of woodland from the western Kenyan upland (for new cultivable land and for fuel) and from West Africa (by drought, foraging animals, and fuel gatherers), the immense and tumultuous expansion of urban settlement in Addis Ababa, Dakar, Kinshasa, Kano, Johannesburg, Nairobi, and Lagos, and the gigantic scale of recent agricultural schemes such as the project along the confluence of the White Nile and the Red Nile in Sudan. One begins to understand the meaning of the expression "imbalanced growth," and one begins to think about the ways human experience in Africa has not been distributed neatly across the continent, but rather has reflected and reinforced patterns of significant concentrations of human activity in the urban developments along the West African and eastern African coastal littorals, in the gold-producing and agrarian region of the West African forest, in the densely populated agricultural zones of the higher elevations of eastern Africa, in the state systems of the Lakes Plateau region and of the lower Zaire River and the southern savanna, in the agrarian regimes of the Ethiopian highlands and northern and southern tips of the continent, and in the urban and mercantile systems of the upper, middle, and lower Niger River valleys.

But even the most general levels of description and differentiation of the continent's resources give African historians reason to pause. In the case of one-field study, distinctions in microenvironments or in the play of seasonal conditions or in the vagaries of climate have great significance. The field historian becomes a witness to the deprivation and hunger that Africans experience at the end of a long dry season, even in areas of substantial annual moisture. The field historian witnesses the way in which population concentrations seem to defy considerably the notional "carrying capacities" of the land, as in the rapid twentieth-century growth of the grassland "town" of Kano into a peri-urban and urban center of perhaps two millions. The field historian witnesses the critical importance of seasonal population movements, marketing activities, and other forms of exchange between close and marginally distinct ecological and microecological zones.[30] These variations and the departures "from norm" begin to take on an importance greater than those features boldly demarcated on the large classroom maps of the continent.

It is not a simple matter to reconcile the large picture of Africa with the historian's comprehension of a particular narrow terrain. Today, historians are attempting to reconceptualize the spatial organization of Africa's past by deploying various modes of regional analysis and by developing larger and less exclusive definitions of their analytical tools. Grand spatial definitions such as the "West African forest," the "Middle Niger," the "Niger-Benue," "Senegambia," the "Sahel," the "Atlantic islands," the "Maghreb," the "Nile Valley," "the Horn of Africa," the "Zaire basin," the "east coast of Africa," "Upper Guinea," the "southern savanna," the "Lakes Plateau," and "Southern Africa" have now become conventions of discourse for African historians.

African historians have also tried to adapt the methods of regional analysis developed for China and Latin America.[31] They have had mixed results, because much of regional analysis is oriented toward urban-centered spatial organizations. Yet the act of challenging older, consensual, and often imperial definitions of social domains (even if, again, they have a consensual quality) has placed into suspension many of the precepts concerning general structure and process on the African continent.

In a recent important work, Ray A. Kea has given us multiple images of the Gold Coast, a critical region of contact between Europeans and Africans from the sixteenth to the eighteenth century.[32] Seen from one perspective it appears a large region of towns knit together by commercial and administrative hierarchies. From another it is the arena of contact between the European traders and administrators based in seaboard forts and towns and the Africans living around them. And from still another perspective, it epitomizes the process by which interior markets expanded to incorporate the opportunities offered by the European-managed coastal traffic. The towns that developed along the seaboard, some continuing pre-European settlements, reflected the diverse and often conflicting characteristics associated with each of these several frameworks. The difficulties of realizing a "region" are evident.

But the problems of defining the processes by which regions evolve and take on new shape under such obvious conditions as the presence and influence of European commercial agencies are still larger when we view Kea's data more closely. The seaboard towns grew dramatically in population from the late sixteenth to the early eighteenth century (from less than 1,000 persons in a typical town to more than 5,000), and they began to take on new forms, quite different from the functional requirements of expanding commercial hierarchies of the interior and from abroad.

The coastal and subcoastal towns had "inns" (in the singular, *herbergerie*), which were located in the residences of landlord-brokers (in the singular, *herberger* or *huisvester*), and "dancing houses." They also had occupational corporations or guilds—artisan guilds, military guilds, and merchant-broker guilds. Further, there were places where prostitutes, "common whores" (*publyke hoer*), could be found and where the "brotherhood" (*confrater/broederschap*) of nobles (*edellieden*) was based. The large expenditures in money, trade goods, and provisions which were associated with membership in the "brotherhood" were made in the towns.[33]

As traders and people of differing social status flowed into these seaboard towns, the towns came to look less and less like the functional entities described by the European and interior authorities. Their *quartiers* and towns began to reflect multiple interests. Artisanry, domestic production, marketing, and recreation took on a local, immediate character and served the growing population assembled at the edge of the strict functional nexus of the Atlantic trade. By the nineteenth century certainly, and probably by the beginning of the eighteenth, the web of seaboard towns had taken on a continuous cultural shape, which in the conventional view was seen as mediating the distinct pools of European and African interests. The challenge here is to see this continuous cultural shape not simply as an outgrowth of functional position between Europe and Africa but as a complex social production, in service of external and internal authorities, but also in conflict with these extractive pressures, and, importantly, as evolved through the indirect and unmediated expression of interests and pleasures of a large immigrant population flowing through the grasslands and forests into the towns of the littoral.

A further example of this remodeling of an African landscape is the case of Kano in Nigeria. Between 1820 and 1970 the population of the Kano "close-settled zone" grew from about 40,000 to about three million. The Kano region, at 1,500 meters altitude, is a fragile ecological zone, with a mean annual rainfall of about 1,270 millimeters. This rainfall occurs mainly from June to September, with almost no precipitation in the long dry season, which begins in October. The rainy season begins a few weeks earlier in the southern part of the Kano zone than in the north and continues a bit longer into October in an average year. While under a similar rainfall regime, the country of Upper Volta has a population density of twenty-five persons per square kilometer, the Kano "close-settled zone" carries a population of around 1,200 per square kilometer. Its demographic growth was a consequence of continuous immigration, and its attraction was its role as a major religious, cultural, and administrative center for northern Nigeria, for its cosmopolitan character, and for the security and opportunity that folk from across the savanna region of northern Nigeria believed possible there.

When we evaluate the predictable connections between the "carrying-capacity" of a region and a region's actual population, all our understandings are overturned by the course of Kano's growth. The question is not simply how a peri-urban area manages to produce ever-increasing surpluses of foodstuffs for a large and rapidly growing urban population, but how a densely packed peri-urban population produces sufficient food stocks for itself? How can a fragile environment be made to support such an enormous rural population?

What is observed in the Kano region is a decisive transition from a situation in which outlying regions had produced a surplus for direct consumption by a growing urban center to a situation in which the city and countryside became reciprocally integrated through a series of profound adjustments in agriculture, domestic manufacture, landholding, marketing, and labor utilization. The adoption of Islamic tenure law produced more individualized tenure and land fragmentation, easing the settlement of new population and facilitating rational transfer of land. Lightly utilized common land was brought under more intensive use as manuring and intercropping displaced fallowing as methods of managing the quality of land. The manuring of land became incorporated into the transportation of firewood in Kano, as the firewood sellers carried night-soil back into the gardens of the peri-urban zone. Landholders occasionally hired additional labor to achieve greater returns from their gardens, while they hired themselves and members of their household out to raise additional income for the household. From the nineteenth century to the present, observers of Kano have witnessed an extraordinary elaboration of part-time occupations or secondary activities—weaving, wage labor, leatherwork, marketing, woodworking, and laundering—as a means of increasing household income. During a century and a half of small adjustments in the domestic routine, in the fabric of law, in the accommodation of new population, the Kano "close-settled zone" has experienced an urban and agrarian revolution.[34] It has not been a "revolution" that has resulted in the greater production of an export commodity—as with cocoa in Ghana and Nigeria, or coffee and cotton in Uganda—and it has not been a "revolution" that has created great wealth for its elite; rather, it has been a revolution that reworked a society in its entirety (and without the intervention of planners or managers) with the aim of achieving greater integration of rural and urban activities, greater accommodation of new population, and a more equitable and, in some ways, more rational management and distribution of fragile and scarce resources. From the cumulus of little and often intimate activity, a region has been produced. As in the towns of Kea's Gold Coast, or South Africa's Soweto, the play of interest, initiative, and innovation defied the predictable functional elements of the social setting.

The organization of new social landscapes in Kano and the Gold Coast reminds us of the enormous mobility of population on the continent and of the contextual force of mobility in the elaboration of political organizations, productive forces, and cultural forms. Such mobility cannot be seen as simply the flux of specific imperial forces and conditions developing in the late nineteenth and twentieth centuries, but as a central element in African social structure and social process. Part of the knowledge imparted to the young by pim in the siwindhe concerned locations at a distance where the young might seek marriage partners, establish new settlements, find work and marketing opportunities, and gain safety in times of war and hunger. The knowledge imparted was a stimulus to migration in western Kenya, just as tales of the bright lights and economic opportunities of Lagos and Nairobi inspired heavy migration in the colonial era. The information pim and other trusted tutors conveyed gave the migrants special intelligence. They were not simply following their wanderlust.

High rates of migration were not necessarily voluntary. In Busoga, Uganda, in the precolonial period, discontent at home, political miscalculations, intrigues, and dangers, and civil wars and the effects of tribute-gathering campaigns in Buganda fueled migration.[35]

The . . . record of migration reveals that located close to one another on a hillslope above the Nabisira were, in 1830, individuals whose antecedents had resided on the floating papyrus islands of the Mpologoma River system, had fished in and traded across Lake Victoria waters, had managed an environment offering 140 centimeters of rainfall per year and one providing but sixty, had carried the status of members of the ruling family of a small state, had participated in a movement to overthrow the king of Buganda, had crossed the Nile, had empowered charms and amulets for the rulers of the Bukono state, had resided immediately next to the courts of kings as well as in worlds without kings, and had experienced a loss of place amidst the expansion of the Luuka state.[36]

Across much of Africa, slave-raiding and tribute-raiding caused large populations to take flight and closed off areas to settlement. Likewise desiccations, epidemics, and infestations engendered large-scale migrations. Migrations, big and small, transformed the locational geography of Africa, building concentrations of population here, leaving empty corridors there. Changes in land tenancy, service, marriage, household organization, inheritance, livestock keeping, land management, and community governance were consequences of the demographic effects of migration. Migrations challenged the authority of rulers and the ideological models of lineage and extended family. And migrations held the potential of constituting active and residual regional and ethnic organizations.[37]

The varied and multiple efforts to comprehend the "region"— using the examination of shared or continuous culture, market networks, cult distributions, arenas of social movements, growth processes, migration tracks, the organizing media of "town and country" and "country and town"—have taken us far from the view of state and society as congruent. African historians are now better able to evaluate the performance of the state upon a wider tableau. A fuller sense of the uneven incorporation of region and population by the precolonial and postcolonial state is now emerging, and we are beginning to understand how the state can be simultaneously weak and strong. Perhaps African historians will move from the rather historicist and sometimes evolutionist concern for the measure of the state's control over a region to an understanding of how people in Africa model their own landscapes and give meaning to sections and nodes in their own social geography.[38]

[Njwiywila was a whispering campaign ...] ... through the whole country it sprang. A man met another, stopped him and said, "I have a message, a special word to tell you. But first you must give me one pice." Then on receiving the pice he said, "Bring your ear closer," and said he should not tell anybody, it was secret. We all continued whispering behind their (the German's) back ... The movement (Maji Maji) had brought together war bands and their leaders, thereby improving communication and coordination.[39]

In the first decade of the twentieth century, individuals and groups overcame ethnic distinctions, considerable distances, and a colonial divide-and-rule program in German East Africa, to organize a movement of resistance to colonial rule—Maji Maji.[40] At the core was a "whispering campaign," njwiywila, organized among intimate friends and close relations, a campaign which established a new and formidable scale of collective intelligence and activity.[41]

In West Africa, a populist Christian movement, forming around the prophet Harris, spread across the frontiers of Liberia, the Ivory Coast, and the Gold Coast, raising the anxiety of established church officials and colonial administrators alike, and reiterating, almost unconsciously, a deep, continuous Akan cultural and social world.[42] In the Lakes Plateau region, centers of kubandwa religious activity spread across the boundaries of precolonial states, creating a distinctive framework of organization, refuge, and resistance capable of both influencing and resisting political capitals.[43] In this century, the activities of separatist and insurgent Christian movements, similar to the Harris movement, defined new spheres of continuous social and religious movements in eastern, central, and southern Africa.[44] At another level, it is perhaps better understood now than ever before that "Africa" itself is an invention, and that the formation of a spatial construct embued with enormous ideological power is itself worthy of historical study and suggests the ways in which the specific processes of domination and resistance give meaning to less grand spatial and social labels.[45]

Time

A second general renovation has been a conscious loosening of the
temporal boundaries used to order the discussion and presentation
of the African past. Whereas the view of process as "era-bound" was
implicit in so much work on Africa, historians find value in the perception of greater "temporal disarray." They realize that what matters
is the process in situ, and that institutions, forces, behaviors, and values have incredible powers of reproduction and persistence through
what appear on the surface to be very different eras of economic,
political, and social organization.

In the dance called *banji* the people make a society of two
camps for dance-competitions. One camp is called *goboreni* and
the other is called *seneda*. They build a hut and buy lengths of
calico and sew a sail . . . and they put it up with pieces of wood.
In the middle of the canopy they put a flag. When they have
fastened the hut . . . they place stools and the men and women
are invited.[46]

In one view, particular exchanges—for example, treaty signings—
are seen to define new eras, but in the other, the disparate pace
and character of different realms of activity suggest uneven lines of
change. A powerful example of this latter view is Terence O. Ranger's
study of the *Beni ngoma* of eastern Africa.[47] He found that military and
ceremonial paraphernalia of European colonialism, including battle-
ships, were brought within the public expression and entertainments
of Africans closely witnessing and sometimes participating in the organization of early colonial domination. Here, a discourse among
Europeans and Africans over the forms and meanings of popular
entertainment—drumming societies and their audiences—became a
discourse on tradition, on rights, and on power. The campaigns of
the drumming societies to preserve a traditional or neotraditional
order become contexts of social aggregation and sociability over considerable distances. Time in this sense passes as through a prism. It is
not simply a chronological measure but a central part of a struggle to
control one important discourse on the definition of tradition and

another discourse on the social rights of those feeling most actively the brunt of colonialism.

When the perspective of the explorer or colonial consul is dropped, temporal forms take on new shapes. For the occupants of the European forts on Kea's Gold Coast in the seventeenth century, the construction of the forts inaugurated a new era in that section of the littoral. For many who flowed into the towns arranged around the forts, the fort was seen as something already familiar and viewed in the context of activities going on elsewhere. While we open the temporal boundaries that we have used (and that have also divided us), we should try to understand how concepts of period and tradition and modernity gather meaning and power within social discourse in Africa. The loving recollections of older Luo of the pim of their childhoods are at the same time implicit critiques of the present society and the present situation of children in Kenya, and these are perhaps the most affecting of critiques.

Anthropologists and Historians

The early *abirempon* were essentially developers: they put gold to work by using it to procure labour, and they put the labour to work to clear the farmland without which the communities of settlers could neither sustain nor reproduce themselves.[48]

One of the important contributions of African historiography over the past twenty-five years (and it has taken nearly the full duration) has been to achieve the understanding that social structures in Africa are not permanent, everlasting, or given, but socially and culturally constructed by real people, through real activity, in real time.[49] The African historian's break with social anthropology—a break which was powerful and involuted in the 1950s and 1960s—resulted from the observation that social anthropologists had not attended to the past of the societies and institutions which they were studying. Thus, anthropologists were seen as explaining the existence of structure through the analysis of function without reference to the past. A charge more suggestive than correct,[50] this view divorced many historians from the literature of social anthropology at the very moment when such engagement might have had the greatest and most productive effect on the evolution of African historiography. The work of social anthropologists was not always ignored, but the distance from which some historians read anthropology gave the literature an unwarranted mystery and power, as if the anthropologist's portrait of society and culture *were* African society and culture. The larger problem was that in the absence of serious discourse, the historian sometimes used tools and concepts of the anthropologist—matriliny, patriliny, extended family, bridewealth, pawnship—without really understanding how these tools and models acquired utility and significance for the anthropologist.

Only recently have historians attended to the geometry of relations between the two disciplines working upon common terrain, and in doing so they have joined or stayed a step ahead of their counterparts working on other parts of the world.[51] Far from taking notional structures as given, African historians have, through both naive curiosity and formidable ingenuity, devoted attention to the questions of how social, political, and economic forms were built upon the African landscape. Wilhelm Peukert[52] and James de V. Allen[53] have produced important arguments against perspectives which have held that African societies, here in Dahomey and the Swahili-speaking coast of East Africa, were "built from the outside in." Eric R. Wolf has treated this issue on a global scale.[54] At a microcosmic level, Megan Vaughan has shown European and Africans manipulating concepts of mental illness in the setting of mental institutions in Malawi.[55] Often without engaging in higher discourses on the concept of social structure, African historians have moved through or around what they have sensed to be valuable in ahistorical studies.

Some African historians have, as well, become dissatisfied with the concept of "institution" and with such other borrowed concepts as "family," "clientship," "kingship," "feudality," "clanship," "bureaucracy," "caste," and "state," and they have recognized that, at best, these concepts are friendly conveniences that make possible professional discourse over great distances and across great differences, while, at worst, these concepts close off deeper inquiry. "Modes of production" approaches seem to disclose even less. Though there is an intent to demonstrate how various arenas of social activity are conjoined, the approach tends to underplay the less obstrusive details of social life such as the products of pim's instruction and the indirect and unmediated social production that shaped the towns of the Gold Coast littoral. In efforts to simplify the complexity of Africa for the benefit of a more distant observer, much is left in the shadows.

Social Process

A further renovation has involved a general reconceptualization of long-run social process. The most comfortable position has been that recent change and development evolved from an old base in which the fundamental requirements of life were easily catered to by a salubrious environment that allowed for extended family units to evolve in a relatively self-contained, self-subsistent way. Early European visitors to the Lake Victoria region saw it as a region of great abundance and great promise for the production of tropical commodities. They saw verdant gardens from one end of the country to another and enormous quantities of food and beverage entering markets and chiefly courts. These travelers and the social scientists who followed them two generations later saw a subsistence food economy that relied on the fecundity of nature. They saw it losing ground under colonial pressure and under commercialization. What was perhaps not so well understood by these observers was the extent to which the generation of plentitude and the image of tropical abundance in the past rested not on nature but on elaborate forms of coercion— taxation, tribute-gathering, pillage and theft, unequal exchange, administered production, and dependent relations of production.[56]

This position—that contemporary Africa has been transformed only recently from a stable subsistence base—was carried, consciously and unconsciously, through all sorts of historical and social scientific work and is especially influential in research which focuses on relatively recent history. It is a "comfortable position" because it views the past as a relatively simple tableau and assumes that the forces and processes which changed it can be observed within a "present context." Many historians today are excising this view from the "historical vision" and are in their reconstructions of the past bringing attention to the real difficulties of environment, to the regional interrelations of production and survival, to the ways in which both present and early states on the continent have been involved in the regulation of production and consumption, to the flow of labor from domestic household toward centers of production, and to the critical nature of labor supply in the evolution of the domestic unit, community, and state in the past.

Clan identity on Ijwi (Zaire today) . . . finds its clearest expression in the ritual of kingship. In general, those clans most central to the ceremony have the strongest corporate feeling. . . .[57]

Now, the "extended family" is not seen as being bombarded by "new forces"; rather, the household's work of planning, appropriating, producing, and maximizing is viewed as critical, as external pressures and opportunities pervade the compound, residence, or neighborhood.[58] This was just as true in Buganda of the eighteenth century—when the scale and work of the kin groups expanded with, and not against, the state—as it is true in twentieth-century Kenya, Nigeria, Zaire, and Southern Africa. A perspective is evolving which holds that new conditions, conflicts, and forces were not simply triggered by the penetration of new elements from outside Africa—the "impact of Europe on Africa paradigm"—nor were they the result of African management of the new elements which entered the landscape—the acculturative model. The new view is that these are extraordinarily complex processes, incapable of being conceptualized in terms of continental process, but rather contextual in nature.

A certain Okoth Ka Opiyo, an Uhanya (Kenya) man, used to be (Lord) Delamere's herdsboy, one of the many, in the 1920's. When he returned home he decided to supply two bottles of milk a day constantly to an Indian shopkeeper at Ndere known as Ogonji (Govindji Karsandas Karia). Because Okoth could supply milk all year round, and be paid by Ogonji for it, the analogy was that he was doing as well as Delamere. So he acquired his present name, Okoth Ouro Dalmia.[59]

The notion that characteristics of society, economy, and politics in Africa can be ascribed in any part to the power of custom has for a long time been under attack; yet it often remains the last resource of explanation. Present-day historians of Africa are seeking to relocate the discussion of custom, institution, pattern, routine, and structure within the discussion of ideological structures, regulative forces, controlling coteries and centers, production, and particularly, process. Some historians now hold that much discourse over social and cultural praxis, over rights and obligations, over customary roles and duties—over what essentially has been the stuff of much anthropological and historical literature—is really a discourse on domination, subordination, and resistance.[60] As in the case of my work with the recollections of pim, historians are attempting to learn to use the riches of earlier literatures—however inflected by an assumption of the power of custom—while struggling to comprehend the work of dominant forces in the construction of African society.[61]

Domination

It is this conscious concern with domination that has brought African historians most boldly into the work of social history, into the elaboration of the tools of study of the society. A few examples might make this point clearly. The first example concerns the formation of alliances between agents of European imperialism and African states. Historians are looking at the central place that emerging class held in the evolution of the African negotiating position, and the drama of external domination is now seen as enclosing a very important process of internal domination.

Less spectacular (than ivory), but in the long run much more significant, were the regular food surpluses produced by countless comparatively obscure peoples, either for sale to passing caravans, or as a means of obtaining essential raw materials from neighbouring regions.[62]

Second, institutions of slavery in Africa have captured the attention of African historians and other social scientists. To a certain extent, this has been evolved as a critical link to New World slavery studies and to the study of the Atlantic slave trade.[63] Third, more studies are appearing that reveal early processes of agrarian transformation[64]— both before European partition and under European pressure—and that illuminate the connections among the state, consumption, exchange, and production.[65] The central place of labor—new routines of gathering and managing labor—is revealed among the more traditional discussion of new crops, technology, and demand.[66] And here attention is being given to the ways in which labor, or peasants, participate in the construction of a system of production and extraction, and thereby limit their own domination.[67]

Historians have developed a more complex understanding of the relationship between the regulation of labor under slave regimes and the regulation of labor in postslavery colonial systems.[68] And closer and closer attention has been brought to the social conditions and forces underlying revolts, rebellions, and revolutions in Africa—including jihads, Maji Maji and other early resistance movements, Mau Mau, labor strikes, the Algerian war, the Biafran secession, and so on. Not only are more cogent explanations of their generation being set forth, but also layers and sections and descriptions of social conditions and social processes are being unveiled in greater detail and with greater sensitivity.

After a time his (Kakumba's) master died, and he told us that he wished to come and serve, i.e., "senga" us. This we allowed. Now people only go to "senga," i.e., serve, a chief or person of authority in the country, and our allowing young men and boys to stay at the mission gave the chiefs, who were always listening to the slanders of our Arab enemies and others, the impression that we wished to gain a position of power and influence in the country by attaching a number of followers to ourselves.[69]

The enhancement of social historical work on Africa created by the focus on domination is brought home most powerfully when one examines the brilliant work being done on social conditions, social forces, and social processes in South Africa—on conditions of labor, on community, on social aggregation, on indigenous ideology and consciousness, on material conditions of life, on strife and revolt.[70] This work provides a preview of the course of future work on the continent. The uneven terrain it reveals suggests the strengths, weaknesses, and directions of more general study of Africa. It is around the close examination of specific contexts of domination that the work of evolving an historical comprehension of society in Africa is likely to develop an early fluency and a mature competence.

Rethinking the Interpretative Process

African historiography has moved far from a four-part periodization of the continent's past, far from a thousand cell Murdockian cultural map, and far from the perspective of five or six imperial theaters. The transformation of a field of knowledge has, in twenty-five years, been nothing less than revolutionary, and all the more powerful for the difficulty of the sources at hand. That there has been an historiographical revolution does not mean, however, that there is some new clarity, that the past of the "dark continent" is now brightly lit. That there has been a movement toward a few common and important problems and toward more collective discourse over the issues of underdevelopment does not mean that the problems which lie before the African historian are well defined.

It can be said, for instance, that the frames of reference that have been developed have not done well in the prediction or analysis of more recent developments in Africa. One view is that entirely new conditions in Africa have been created by new outside circumstances (which perhaps for recent years, can be categorized as the gigantic petroleum price increase and the world depression, and for earlier periods, the slave trade and imperialism or earlier depressions). Another is that accumulation of violence, due in part to an internal African arms build-up, joined to primordial divisions and conflicts have unleashed in Africa a pathology of wild and unpredictable behavior (today, and also in the eighteenth and nineteenth centuries). To the extent that these explanations of change have been internalized in our discourse and in that of colleagues in conjoint fields, they draw attention to notional forces and "large processes" outside the continent.

These large explanatory frameworks of our time, which "descend" from world-system explanations of historical time, are extraordinarily powerful tools, for they are arresting in their simplicity, encompassing in their scale, and exculpating in their assignment of cause, or blame, outside Africa. These frameworks lead to a methodological circularity; a disproportionate interest develops in the effect of outside influences on forces that in turn become the matrix of explanation. Only occasionally has logic been served by the careful detailing of what is meant by "external" and by the close study of those identified external details among all other elements, forces, and interests operating within an arena of Africa, as Kea has done in his study of the Gold Coast. But this is more than a problem of method. The "study" of large world processes and the effects upon Africa has become a judgmental discourse over cause and victim, and such study has left Africa no less ill economically; it has, however, left it noiseless, undifferentiated, uninteresting, and unknown.

It is a strange and nearly paralyzing paradox that the brilliant work of reconstruction of the African past has led some authorities to the view or their readers to the implication that the details of Africa's past, in the face of these overwhelming pressures from outside, do not really matter. Though Tilly would surely not claim this position, the logic of his agenda to pursue the "interplay of large processes, big social structures, and whole populations" leads, with respect to Africa, in this very direction.

The story of the African past that historians have produced over the past twenty-five years shows us the surface textures in many areas.[71] Structures and processes have some clarity and the variations seem at one moment to contradict the logic we bring to the study of Africa and at another to reveal still more of the past. Superficial similarities and differences dissolve into more complex, and often more revealing matter, as we linger over our material or look more closely across the garden wall.[72]

Interpretative routines lie beneath the surface of our studies. Variations in our interpretations, sometimes boldly demarcated, sometimes barely discernable, form a simple, bipolar architecture of historical discourse about the continent's past. First, African historiography has internalized seemingly incompatible ideas—that Africa's past has its own meaning and that Africa is located on the periphery of the world system.[73] We understand that the interior past of Africa matters, that internal structures contain and resist external forces, and that structures and processes are supported and reproduced from within. The participation of Africans in the slave trade is a notable expression of the sense that Africa's past cannot be understood without understanding interior processes. At the same time, we understand that external forces and processes have given Africa its "next form." Our language of discourse has such familiar phrases as "the impact or effect of . . . on Africa," "the penetration of . . . into Africa," and "the coming of . . . to Africa," as if Africa has been substantially composed from the outside in. The Atlantic slave trade is commonly discussed as having produced a substantially reconstructed Africa.[74]

A second area of tension in our discourse is between notions of reproduction and notions of transformation. On the one hand, Africa is understood in terms of its deep cultural base or deep structure, enduring institutions, constant rules and forms, social formations, modes of production, custom, and systems. But on the other hand, we see culture as processual,[75] as "socially constituted and socially constituting."[76] We speak of knowledge being reorganized, of the interpretation and manipulation of rules, norms, and tradition.[77] We speak of innovation and change.

A third area of tension exists between the notion of the invasive state and the notion of the weak state. On the one hand, we see the state policing household and community, organizing the economy. We speak of despotism and the weak following of the whims of autocrats. We see the colonial state emerging dominant and able to stimulate production and generate returns through the manipulation of markets, lower level officials, and consumption pressures. But on the other hand, we maintain that household and community resist the impulses, planning, and programs of the state, while holding that the household has the capacity to organize independently of the domains of state activity.[78] We view the colonial state as undermanned and undercapitalized and show workers and peasants heroically opening space for themselves. Labor participates in the political and regulatory definition of the conditions of work.[79] People at large evolve their own social, economic, and political strategies. The township of Soweto, for instance, is viewed as an enclosure within a system of racial domination, while it is also considered as a space allowing the recomposition and defense of the lives of the dominated. Folk, and not the state, are reckoned as the critical agencies of change.

The emphasis on external causes does not imply that equatorial African society was static or that it was capable of reacting only to initiatives from others. The European traders could do no more than come to the coast; it was African initiative that forged trade routes seventeen hundred kilometers into the interior and developed the marketplaces and diplomatic machinery for long-distance trade. African traders could not have undertaken this initiative had not the basic institutions and concepts necessary for trade and capitalist activity already existed in equatorial African society. Trade had existed for a long time, and so had the practices of renting out capital goods and paying wages in kind. The international economy provided opportunities for expanding and strengthening the mercantile and capitalistic elements that already existed in riverine society; it did not create them.[80]

Some readers, and most African historians, will anticipate how these tensions have appeared in our analyses and interpretations and will be familiar with some of the routine ways they are mediated in the historian's presentations of the past—most often by the historian moving into some synthetic middle ground. The point here is that such tensions or polarities mark out the edges, surfaces, and trajectories of our present discourse. These tensions or polarities have other lives outside our contemporary search for ways of presenting the African past. Far more important than our mediations are those of Africans, whose everyday lives were marked by these tensions. It was in their lives that routines were worked or reworked, knowledge sifted, knowledge reorganized, efforts mobilized, emotions handled, decisions made, little solidarities dissolved and constructed, and interests affirmed. It was in their lives that distant forces were noted, evaluated, and answered. It was within their lives that the state was evaluated, its presentation of itself recomposed. To understand the tensions in their lives, as opposed to those in our work, we must see how casual or sometimes critical and often intimate concerns gather and appropriate significance from moments in the past. We must see how people compose their own lives in order to understand the composite forces around them.[81] We must see how little routines have gathered into arrays, and how they rework the forms of social life. We must see how these forms are given meaning, and how force is imparted to them, and how they generate or rework still newer arrays of routines.

A teacher once put a map of Africa on the classroom wall with South Africa at the top and North Africa at the bottom, suggesting to his students the mundane often can play a role in how we see a subject, think about it, act upon it. The unearthing of pim's work has a similar didactic function but doubly so, for we can recognize the possibility not only that the inconsequential can have significance in the construction of society but also that it can illuminate our understanding of it. As a colleague has argued, "prominence and visibility no longer constitute a prima-facie case of historical significance. On the contrary, the value of every subject depends entirely upon how much it reveals about larger historical processes."[82] Returning to the siwindhe, we might see that pim's work is socially and culturally centered as a locus in the social and cultural education of children, in the formation of marriage linkages, in the elaboration of broader affinal networks, and in the formation as knowledge of a still broader social geography. If in our work on Africa's past, we rush too quickly toward an agenda which deals with the relations of "larger processes, big social structures, and whole populations," we risk losing sight of the intimate areas of social life where real contradictions are managed and actual structures are enraveled, and we risk falling into a falsely placed confidence that we have managed them in our own discourse.

NOTES

1. In 1978, Grace and Allan Ogot suggested that I open research on several sites within the area of Alego, Siaya District, western Kenya. In our discussions, Grace Ogot encouraged me to give attention to the cultural and social formation of children, to see what historical research might illuminate concerning past childhood. She and Allan were among a number of Kenyans who spoke of their own *pim* with great interest and affection. A first look at *pim* and at the implications of *pim*'s work for the processes of construction of relations and groups was presented to a conference on the "History of the Family in Africa" organized at the School of Oriental and African Studies, London, in September, 1981.

2. Some older Luo have related that widows without protection were occasionally seized and sacrificed to assure the well-being of a new Lake Victoria transport or fishing craft.

3. "Muzungu" was not the Luo word for a European or a person of another culture but is, rather, a Bantu term drawn jokingly into Luo parlance. Granny is not so much an adaptation of English references to "Grannies" or "Nannies" but seems, rather, simply a Luo speech play on her knowledge of European ways.

4. Ben G. Blount, "Aspects of Luo Socialization," *Language and Society* 1 (1979): 247–48.

5. David William Cohen, "Pim's Work: Some Thoughts on the Construction or Relations and Groups—the Luo of Western Kenya." Paper presented to a conference on "The History of the Family in Africa," School of Oriental and African Studies, London, September 1981.

6. Françoise Zonabend, "Childhood in a French Village," *International Social Science Journal* 31 (1979): 492–507.

7. Ibid., 498.

8. This may remind us that in Africa, perhaps more than in other regions of the world, there has been an extraordinary interiorization of structure, through the retention, aggregation, and reorganization of social intelligence, including historical knowledge. Among pioneering studies of African childhood is Otto F. Raum's *Chaga Childhood: A Description of Indigenous Education in an East African Tribe* (London: Oxford University Press for the International African Institute, 1940), Lorene K. Fox's *East African Childhood: Three Versions* (Nairobi: Oxford University Press, 1967), and Esther N. Goody's *Parenthood and Social Reproduction: Fostering and Occupational Roles in West Africa* (Cambridge: Cambridge University Press, 1982).

9. Charles Tilly, *As Sociology Meets History* (New York: Academic Press, 1981), 46, in presenting an agenda for sociological history, uses the phrases " . . . the analysis of power, of participation, or rebellion as historical problems, ultimately (linked) to the expansion of capitalism and the growth of systems of national states. . . . Capitalism and statemaking provide the context for a historically grounded analysis of collective action—of the ways in which people act together in pursuit of shared interests."

10. Gavin Kitching, *Class and Economic Change in Kenya: The Making of an African Petite Bourgeoisie, 1905–1970* (New Haven: Yale University Press, 1980), takes up this story and shows the ways Kenyans used ingenuity and intelligence to move forward within the Kenya labor market.

11. Personal communication to editor of this present collective project, April 5, 1983.

12. Andrew Roberts, "Nyamwezi Trade," in *Pre-Colonial African Trade: Essays on Trade in Central and Eastern Africa before 1900*, ed. Richard Gray and David Birmingham (New York: Oxford University Press, 1970), 67.

13. Philip D. Curtin, *The Image of Africa: British Ideas and Action, 1780–1850* (Madison: University of Wisconsin Press, 1964).

14. Alvares de Almada, *Tratado Breve dos Rios de Guiné do Cabo Verde* (1594; reprint ed., Porto: Typographia commercial portuense, 1841), quoted in translation in Walter Rodney, *A History of the Upper Guinea Coast, 1545–1800* (Oxford: Clarendon Press, 1970), 12.

15. Pieter de Marees, *Beschryvinghe* . . . (reprint, Gravenhage, Netherlands: M. Nijhoff, 1912), 80; cited in translation in Ray A. Kea, *Settlements, Trade, and Polities in the Seventeenth-Century Gold Coast* (Baltimore: Johns Hopkins University Press, 1982), 23.

16. This is not to say that because the slave trade became the central tangent between Europeans and West Africans in the eighteenth century that it was therefore the central issue for all West Africans. The simple fact that so much of our knowledge of West Africa in the period comes from Europeans who were directly involved with the trade has led most writers to assume that it was also the central issue for Africans. A number of historians of Africa have begun, in recent years, to evaluate changes in diet, health, opportunity, and social life for those Africans not transported to the Americas while others have become interested in estimating the scale of the Atlantic trade—imports, exports, services, and dislocations in production and marketing—relative to, or within, the more differentiated, regional African economies which the demands and pressures of the Atlantic trade were penetrating in the seventeenth and eighteenth centuries.

17. John Atkins, *A Voyage to Guinea, Brazil and the West Indies in His Majesty's ships, the "Swallow" and "Weymouth"* . . . (London: C. Ward and R. Chandler, 1735; reprint ed., London: Frank Cass, 1970), 168.

18. The Atlantic slave trade persisted through most of the nineteenth century and slavery within Africa was used, paradoxically, as one means of extracting "civilizing" and "legitimate" products for the world markets.

19. W. S. Price, *My Third Campaign in East Africa: A Story of Missionary Life in Troublous Times* (London: William Hunt, 1891), 22–23, cited in Thomas O. Beidelman, *Colonial Evangelism: A Sociohistorical Study of an East African Mission at the Grassroots* (Bloomington: Indiana University Press, 1982), 128.

20. D. Anthony Low, *Religion and Society in Buganda* (Kampala: East African Institute of Social Research, c. 1957), 7.

21. "Father Stauffer's Journal," cited in Gordon M. Haliburton, *The Prophet Harris: A Study of an African Prophet and His Mass-Movement in the Ivory Coast and the Gold Coast, 1913–1915* (New York: Oxford University Press, 1973), 71.

22. Samwiri Mukasa's unpublished "Record of My service . . . ," cited in D. Anthony Low, *The Mind of Buganda: Documents of the Modern History of an African Kingdom* (Berkeley: University of California Press, 1971), 59.

23. Ayi Kwei Armah, *The Beautyful Ones Are Not Yet Born* (London: Heinemann, 1969), 109.

24. One of the challenges of teaching African history is overcoming the existing

popular knowledge of Africa, the most common centerpiece of which is the notion that "Africans live in tribes." This view is fed by such supportive details as the newspaper report that "Tribesmen from all over Rhodesia are going to the polls today. . . ." Inhering within the notion of "tribe" is, first, a presumption of common descent; second, a concept of a "tribal person" who shares with all others of his, or her, "tribe" (or, for some, with all people of all "tribes" everywhere) one "world-view" or one common behavioral order; and, third, a technical, cultural, and social level somehow and somewhat lower than that claimed by the person using the term "tribe." The use of the term here is a play on the common usage and an opportunity to bring attention to the issue. Recently, historians of Africa reconstructing the precolonial past have worked with a considerable variety of sources, including oral material, to demonstrate the complex social, cultural, and economic processes which have produced African "societies," "peoples," "ethnic groups"—or, simply, Tiv, Acholi, Luba, and Basoga—that have the look of groups with a common origin or common view of the world. See note 45 below.

25. For the moment, African historians are unlikely to find value in organizing a subprofession of "African social history."

26. See Christopher Fyfe, ed., *African Studies Since 1945: A Tribute to Basil Davidson* (New York: Holmes & Meier, 1976); Arnold Temu and B. Swai, *Historians and Africanist History: A Critique* (London: Zed Press, 1981); and Robin Law, "In Search of a Marxist Perspective," *Journal of African History* 19 (1978): 441–52.

27. Where links formed they have been productive ones: (1) in the effort to form some quantitative estimates on the scale of the trade in slaves across the Atlantic: Philip D. Curtin, *The Atlantic Slave Trade: A Census* (Madison: University of Wisconsin Press, 1969); Patrick Manning, "The Enslavement of Africans: A Demographic Model," *Canadian Journal of African Studies* 15 (1981), 499–526; Herbert S. Klein, *The Middle Passage: Comparative Studies in the Atlantic Slave Trade* (Princeton: Princeton University Press, 1978); Paul Lovejoy, "The Volume of the Slave Trade: A Synthesis," *Journal of African History* 23 (1982): 473–501; (2) in the comparative study of African slavery: Frederick Cooper, "The Problem of Slavery in African Culture," *Journal of African History* 20 (1979): 103–25; and C. Meillassoux, *L'esclavage en Afrique pré-coloniale* (Paris: Maspéro, 1975); and (3) in the study of the history of African labor: Richard Sandbrook and Robin Cohen, eds., *The Development of an African Working Class* (Toronto: University of Toronto Press, 1975); Charles van Onselen, *Chibaro: African Mine Labour in Southern Rhodesia, 1900–1933* (London: Pluto Press, 1976); Robin Cohen and Jean Copans, eds., *African Labor History* (Beverly Hills: Sage, 1978); and Shula Marks and Richard Rathbone, eds., *Industrialisation and Social Change in South Africa. African Class Formation, Culture and Consciousness, 1870–1930* (London: Longman, 1982).

28. Edmund R. Leach, *Political Systems of Highland Burma: A Study of Kachin Social Structure* (London: G. Bell, 1954), 5–6.

29. See David William Cohen, "Precolonial History as the History of Society," *African Studies Review* 17 (September 1974): 467–72.

30. For an important historical study which develops a picture of complex social and economic exchange among several microecological zones in one small setting, see Steven Feierman, *The Shambaa Kingdom: A History* (Madison: University of

Wisconsin Press, 1974). Conrad Kottak, "Ecological Variables in the Origin and Evolution of African States: The Buganda Example," *Comparative Studies in Society and History* 14 (September 1972): 351–80, has presented a model of the formation process of the Buganda state which centers on exchanges across boundaries of marginal ecological variation. For a study of precolonial Busoga, Uganda, see David William Cohen, "The Face of Contact: A Model of a Cultural and Linguistic Frontier in Early Eastern Uganda," in *Nilotic Studies. Proceedings of the International Symposium on Languages and History of the Nilotic Peoples, Cologne, January 4–6, 1982*, ed. Rainer Vössen and Marianne Bechhaus-Gerst, (Berlin: Dietrich Reimer, 1983), 339–55.

31. Ivor Wilks, *Asante in the Nineteenth Century: The Structure and Evolution of a Political Order* (Cambridge: Cambridge University Press, 1977); Allen Howard, "The Relevance of Spatial Analysis for African Economic History: The Sierra Leone-Guinea System," *Journal of African History* 17 (1976): 365–88; Kea, *Settlements, Trade, and Polities*; and Philip D. Curtin, *Economic Change in Precolonial Africa: Senegambia in the Era of the Slave Trade* (Madison: University of Wisconsin Press, 1975).

32. Kea, *Settlements, Trade, and Polities*.

33. Ibid., 40.

34. See M. J. Mortimore, "Land and Population Pressure in the Kano Close-settled Zone, Northern Nigeria," *The Advancement of Science* 23 (1967): 677–86.

35. David William Cohen, *Womunafu's Bunafu: A Study of Authority in a Nineteenth Century African Community* (Princeton: Princeton University Press, 1977).

36. Ibid., pp. 67–68. For work on mobility, see William Beinart, "Joyini Inkomo: Cattle Advances and the Origins of Migrancy from Pondoland," *Journal of Southern African Studies* 5 (April 1979): 199–219; Richard Roberts and Martin Klein, "The Banamba Slave Exodus of 1905 and the Decline of Slavery in the Western Sudan," *Journal of African History* 21 (1980): 375–94; Richard Roberts, "Long Distance Trade and Production: Sinsani in the Nineteenth Century," *Journal of African History* 21 (1980): 169–88; James B. Webster, ed. *Chronology, Migration, and Drought in Interlacustrine Africa* (Halifax: Dalhousie University Press, 1979); Abner Cohen, *Custom and Politics in Urban Africa: A Study of Hausa Migrants in Yoruba Towns* (Berkeley: University of California Press, 1969); Kitching, *Class and Economic Change*; Colin Murray, *Families Divided: The Impact of Migrant Labour in Lesotho* (Cambridge: Cambridge University Press, 1981); Enid Schildkrout, *People of the Zongo: The Transformation of Ethnic Identities in Ghana* (Cambridge: Cambridge University Press, 1978); and Robin Palmer and Neil Parsons, eds., *The Roots of Rural Poverty in Central and Southern Africa* (Berkeley: University of California Press, 1977).

37. Carole Buchanan, "Perceptions of Ethnic Interaction in the East African Interior: The Kitara Complex," *International Journal of African Historical Studies* 11 (1978): 410–28.

38. For example, John Godfrey, "Invented Regions and Created Landscapes: The Shawya of Morocco in the Nineteenth Century," paper presented to the annual meetings of the Social Science History Association, Washington, D.C., October, 1983; Richard Werbner, ed., *Regional Cults* (New York: Academic Press, 1977); and Gwyn Prins, *The Hidden Hippopotamous. Reappraisal in African History: The Early Colonial Experience in Western Zambia* (Cambridge: Cambridge University Press, 1980); and

for a valuable example from colonial America, Rhys Isaac, *The Transformation of Virginia, 1740–1790* (Chapel Hill: University of North Carolina Press, 1982).

39. G. C. K. Gwassa, "Kinjikitile and the Ideology of Maji Maji," in *The Historical Study of African Religion*, ed. Terence O. Ranger and I. N. Kimambo (Berkeley: University of California Press, 1972), 202–17.

40. O. B. Mapunda and G. R. Mpangara, *The Maji Maji War in Ungoni* (Nairobi: East African Publishing Press, 1972).

41. Gwassa, "Kinjikitile and the Ideology of Maji Maji."

42. Haliburton, *The Prophet Harris.*

43. Iris Berger, *Religion and Resistance: East African Kingdoms in the Precolonial Period* (Tervuren, Belg.: Musée royal de l'Afrique Centrale, 1981).

44. See, for example, Bengt G. M. Sundkler, *Bantu Prophets in South Africa* (London: Oxford University Press for the International African Institute, 1961); Bethwell A. Ogot and Frederick B. Welbourn, *A Place to Feel at Home: A Study of Two Independent Churches in Western Kenya* (London: Oxford University Press, 1968); and S. W. Cross, "The Watch Tower Movement in South Central Africa, 1908–1945," D. Phil. thesis, Oxford, 1969.

45. For reconceptualizing work on the problematics of ethnic definitions and handed-down labels, see David William Cohen, "Precolonial History as the History of Society"; C. A. Kratz, "Are the Okiek Really Masai?" *Cahiers d'Etudes Africaines* 20 (1980): 355–68; John Lonsdale, "When did the Gusii or any other Group Become a Tribe?" *Kenya Historical Review* 5 (1980): 355–68; James de V. Allen, "Swahili Culture and the Nature of East Coast Settlement," *International Journal of African Historical Studies* 14 (1981): 306–34; B. M. Masquelier, "Ide as a Polity: Ideology, Morality, and Political Identity," *Paideuma* 25 (1979): 41–52; and Wim M. J. Van Binsbergen, "The Unit of Study and the Interpretation of Ethnicity: Studying the Nkoya of Western Zambia," *Journal of Southern African Studies* 8 (October 1981): 51–81. See also note 24 above. On regional analysis, see Werbner, ed., *Regional Cults*; Richard Roberts, "Long Distance Trade and Production"; Curtin, *Economic Change in Precolonial Africa*; Howard, "The Relevance of Spatial Analysis"; Joseph C. Miller, *Kings and Kinsmen: Early Mbundu States in Angola* (Oxford: Clarendon Press, 1976); and Wilks, *Asante.*

46. Swahili text on the early Beni Ngoma dance companies of eastern Africa, quoted in Terence O. Ranger, *Dance and Society in Eastern Africa, 1890–1970: The Beni Ngoma* (Berkeley: University of California Press, 1975), 36–37.

47. Ibid.

48. Ivor Wilks, "The State of the Akan and the Akan States: A Discussion," *Cahiers d'Etudes Africaines* 22 (1982): 231–49.

49. Ivor Wilks, "Land, Labour and Capital and the Forest Kingdom of Asante," in *The Evolution of Social Systems*, ed. J. Friedman and M. J. Rowlands (Pittsburgh: University of Pittsburgh Press, 1977); and David William Cohen, *Womunafu's Bunafu.*

50. See Joan Vincent, *Teso in Transformation: The Political Economy of Peasant and Class in Eastern Africa* (Berkeley: University of California Press, 1982).

51. Hans Medick and David Sabean, eds., *Interest and Emotion: Essays on the Study of Family and Kinship* (Cambridge: Cambridge University Press, 1984), 1–27; and Sidney W. Mintz and Richard Price, *An Anthropological Approach to the Afro-American Past: A*

Caribbean Perspective (Philadelphia: Institute for the Study of Human Issues, 1976).

52. Wilhelm Peukert, *Der atlantische Sklavenhandel von Dahomey, 1740–1797* (Weisbaden: Steiner, 1978).

53. James de V. Allen, "Swahili Culture and the Nature of East Coast Settlement," *International Journal of African Historical Studies* 14 (1981): 306–34; and "The 'Shirazi' Problem in East African Coastal History," *Paideuma* 28 (1982): 9–27.

54. Eric R. Wolf, *Europe and the People Without History* (Berkeley: University of California Press, 1982).

55. Megan Vaughan, "Idioms of Madness: Zomba Lunatic Asylum, Nyasaland, in the Colonial Period," *Journal of Southern African Studies* 9 (April 1983): 218–38.

56. For a fuller presentation of this argument, see David William Cohen, "Food Production and Food Exchange in the Precolonial Lakes Plateau Region," in *Imperialism, Colonialism, and Hunger: East and Central Africa*, ed. Robert I. Rotberg (Lexington, Mass.: Lexington Books, 1983), 1–18.

57. David S. Newbury, "Clan Alterations and Political Centralization on Ijwi Island, Zaire, ca. 1780–ca. 1840," *Cahiers d'Etudes Africaines* 22 (1982): 452.

58. Jane Guyer, "Household and Community in African Studies," *African Studies Review* 24 (April 1981): 87–137; and Thomas C. McCaskie, "State and Society, Marriage and Adultery: Some Considerations Towards a Social History of Pre-colonial Asante," *Journal of African History* 22 (1981): 477–94.

59. E. S. Atieno-Odhiambo, "The Movement of Ideas: A Case Study of Intellectual Responses to Colonialism among the Liganwa Peasants," in *History and Social Change in East Africa*, ed. Bethwell A. Ogot (Nairobi: East African Publishing House, 1976), 165–85.

60. See Colin Murray, "Migrant Labour and Changing Family Structure in the Rural Periphery of Southern Africa," *Journal of Southern African Studies* 6 (April 1980): 139–56, and *Families Divided*; and Frederick Cooper, *From Slaves to Squatters: Plantation Labor and Agriculture in Zanzibar and Coastal Kenya, 1890–1925* (New Haven: Yale University Press, 1980).

61. See, for example, Kea, *Settlements, Trade, and Polities* and Frederick Cooper, "Peasants, Capitalists, and Historians: A Review Article," *Journal of Southern African Studies* 7 (April 1981): 284–314.

62. John Tosh, "Lango Agriculture during the Early Colonial Period: Land and Labour in a Cash-crop Economy," *Journal of African History* 19 (1978): 415–39.

63. Cooper, "The Problem of Slavery," reviews a good deal of this literature.

64. Wilks, "Land, Labour, Capital"; and Tosh, "Lango Agriculture."

65. See, especially, Robin Palmer and Neil Parsons, eds., *The Roots of Rural Poverty*; Terence O. Ranger, "Growing from the Roots: Reflections on Peasant Research in Central and Southern Africa," *Journal of Southern African Studies* 5 (October 1978): 99–138; and Cooper, "Peasants, Capitalists, and Historians."

66. See, for example, W. Gervais Clarence-Smith, "Slaves, Commoners, and Landlords in Bulozi," *Journal of African History* 20 (1979): 219–34; John Tosh, "Lango Agriculture" and "The Cash Crop Revolution in Tropical Africa: An Agricultural Reappraisal," *African Affairs* 79 (January 1980): 79–94; Emmanuel Terray, "Long Distance Exchange and the Formation of the State," *Economy and Society* 3 (August 1974): 315–45; Wilks, "Land, Labour, Capital"; and Cooper, *From Slaves to Squatters*.

67. Cooper, *From Slaves to Squatters*; "Africa and the World Economy," *African Studies*

Review 24 (April 1981): 1–86; and "Peasants, Capitalists, and Historians."

68. See Cooper, *From Slaves to Squatters.* For a different kind of study, see R. Roberts and Klein, "The Banamba Slave Exodus"; also, Frederick Cooper, ed., *Struggle for the City* (Beverly Hills: Sage Publications, 1983).

69. Low, *Religion and Society in Africa*, 5, citing Robert P. Ashe, *Two Kings of Buganda* (London, 1889).

70. Shula Marks and Anthony Atmore, eds., *Economy and Society in Pre-Industrial South Africa* (London: Longman, 1980); Shula Marks and Richard Rathbone, eds., *Industrialisation and Social Change*; Charles van Onselen, *Studies in the Social and Economic History of the Witwatersrand, 1886–1914*, 2 vols. (London: Longman, 1982); and the *Journal of Southern African Studies* more generally.

71. Richard Rathbone, "The People and Soweto," *Journal of Southern African Studies* 6 (October 1979): 124–32, has eloquently placed a challenge to historians concerning the detailing of "texture." See Guyer, "Household and Community in African Studies," for a review of work on social life and family organization.

72. For example, Hans Medick, "Village Spinning Bees," in *Interest and Emotion*, ed. Hans Medick and David Sabean, 317–39; Vaughan, "Idioms of Madness"; and Ben G. Blount, "Agreeing to Agree on Genealogy: A Luo Sociology of Knowledge," in *Sociocultural Dimensions of Language Use*, ed. Mary Sanches and Ben G. Blount (New York: Academic Press, 1975), 117–35; pim show us ways of discovering extraordinarily important matter under the surface of our observations.

73. See Wolf, *Europe and the People Without History*; Walter Rodney, *How Europe Underdeveloped Africa* (London: Bogle-L'Ouverture, 1972); Peukert, *Der atlantische Sklavenhandel*; Frederick Cooper, "Africa and the World Economy"; and Allen, "The 'Shirazi' Problem" and "Swahili Culture and the Nature of East Coast Settlement."

74. See John D. Fage, "Slaves and Society in Western Africa, c. 1445–c. 1700," *Journal of African History* 21 (1980): 289–310; and Peukert, *Der atlantische Sklavenhandel*.

75. For other parts of the world, see the discussions by William Roseberry, "Balinese Cockfights and the Seduction of Anthropology," *Social Research* 49 (Winter 1982): 1012–28; Hans Medick and David Sabean, eds., *Interest and Emotion*, intro.; and, more generally still, Wolf, *Europe and the People Without History*, 377–88.

76. Roseberry, "Balinese Cockfights and the Seduction of Anthropology."

77. David William Cohen, "Reconstructing a Conflict in Bunafu: Seeking Evidence outside the Narrative Tradition," in *The African Past Speaks: Essays on Oral Tradition and History*, ed. Joseph C. Miller (Hamden, Conn.: Archon, 1980), 201–20.

78. See John Lonsdale and Bruce Berman, "Coping with the Contradictions: The Development of the Colonial State in Kenya," *Journal of African History* 20 (1979): 487–506, for one view, and Gerd Spittler, "Administration in a Peasant State," *Sociologia Ruralis* 23 (1983): 130–44, for another. See also David William Cohen, *Womunafu's Bunafu*.

79. See Cooper, *From Slaves to Squatters.*

80. Robert Harms, *River of Wealth, River of Sorrow: The Central Zaire Basin in the Era of the Slave and Ivory Trade, 1500–1891* (New Haven: Yale University Press, 1981).

81. For a more detailed exposition of this argument, see Carlo Ginzburg and Carlo Poni, "La micro-histoire," *Le Débat*, no. 17 (1981): 133–36.

82. Jack P. Greene, "The New History: From Top to Bottom," *New York Times*, 8 June 1975, 37.

CHAPTER 5

APPROACHES TO MODERN

CHINESE SOCIAL HISTORY

BY WILLIAM T. ROWE

For most historians of China "social history" remains essentially lower case—it describes not so much a methodological movement as simply an orientation to addressing problems of society and social change. Indeed, for many of us I suspect there remains considerable doubt regarding what this much-heralded "social history" revolution is all about. If by this term we mean the application of social science quantification on the macrosocietal level, then we in the China field have seen relatively little of it. A few pioneering works of the 1950s and 1960s by Ho Ping-ti and Chang Chung-li come to mind, but problems of data and doubts about generalization on an empirewide scale have worked to discourage similar efforts since that time.[1] If on the other hand social history means depicting the impact of large structures and structural change on the lives of ordinary individuals, then examples are even harder to find. Within the monographic literature, Jonathan Spence's The Death of Woman Wang, that highly literary reconstruction of daily life in the seventeenth century, stands almost alone.[2] The specific models and techniques developed by participants in the social history revolution in European and American studies have only rarely been applied to the study of China, and even more rarely applied with ingenuity. More often than not the poorly thought-out attempt to apply social history models has marred rather than enriched otherwise sound empirical studies (Fei-ling Davis' appropriation of Eric J. Hobsbawm's ideas in her Primitive Revolutionaries of

The author wishes to thank Paul A. Cohen, Joshua A. Fogel, Susan Mann, Mack Walker, Olivier Zunz, and the other contributors to this volume for helpful comments on an earlier draft of this chapter.

236

China is an unfortunate example); in a very few cases such as R. Bin Wong's use of Charles Tilly's work on food riots a particularly close fit of historical circumstances allows the borrowing to pay off.[3] More generally, however, the methodological innovations of giants such as Emmanuel Le Roy Ladurie and Lawrence Stone have had virtually no effect. We represent, in short, an underdeveloped field.

There are many reasons for this. The difficulty of acquisition of East Asian language skills by Western historians of China, and their cloistering in "regional studies" institutes have combined to inhibit their keeping up with disciplinary colleagues who study parts of the world closer to home. The obvious problems since 1949 of access to archival sources have affected not only Western and Japanese scholars, but Chinese as well. The normative concerns of Confucian historiography and its preoccupation with personality, imperial politics, and cyclical change did not encourage Chinese historians to develop an early social history tradition of their own. When this tradition did arise, in the 1920s, it was dominated from the start by the politicization that has continued to handicap the field. Demands for orthodoxy by Chinese Nationalist and Communist ideologues, the witch-hunts of the McCarthy era (which dissuaded a generation of American scholars from seriously considering the role of social forces in Chinese history), and the radical anti-intellectualism of the Great Proletarian Cultural Revolution, all took considerable toll.

In the most general sense, however, the past two decades have indeed seen a social history revolution in Western studies of modern China, in the form of a marked increase in the willingness to look beyond macropolitical markers—the Manchu conquest of 1644, the Opium War of 1839–1842, the Republican Revolution of 1911, and the founding of the People's Republic in 1949—and concentrate instead on longer-term, more gradual processes of change in the society and economy. As Paul A. Cohen has recently pointed out, this has been accompanied by a parallel trend to find the significant aspects of modern Chinese history to be those indigenous to China, rather than those relating to its contact with the West.[4] This shift of emphasis has begun to show some satisfying results, most especially in the area of local case studies. It has also brought with it a burgeoning interest in many of the same concerns that have occupied Western social historians. For example, some of the most creative recent work has been done in the areas of demography, family history, folk religion, popular culture, and popular movements.[5] For the most part this interest has come less as a deliberate response to work done on Europe or America as much as it has been home-grown, the result of a fresh empirical look at the evidence of Chinese history. In this regard it has been spurred by the recent reopening to scholars (Chinese as well as foreign) of various archives in the People's Republic— what is new here is not so much sources on major political events, which have long been available in Taiwan and elsewhere, but rather vast quantities of the routine, local records that are the stuff of social history. And it is in the handling of this new wealth of data that a more sophisticated appreciation of the methodologies of Western social history can be expected to be of use. It is by all measures a most exciting time to be studying modern China.

Stagnation, Periodization, and the Impact of the West

If a single overriding question could be identified at the heart of modern Chinese social history, it would probably be this: Was China "stagnant" prior to its encounter with the expanding West? In the formulation stated first by John Stuart Mill and popularized recently by Eric Wolf, did pre-Western contact China have a history at all? Or, to ask the same question in the form in which it has most often appeared within the field itself, when did "modern" China begin? What, in other words, does "modernity" mean in the Chinese case?

While there are any number of possible answers to this question, three views have been most common. Conventional wisdom in the West and orthodox Marxist historiography in China and elsewhere converge on the position that modern (Chinese: chin-tai, Japanese: kindai) China dates from the signing of the first unequal treaty with the West, the Sino-British Treaty of Nanking, in 1842. Most Western scholars, tending to view the European impact on balance in favorable terms, have adopted the view of imperial China advanced early in this century by Max Weber.[6] For Weber China remained, for all its acknowledged uniqueness, a "traditional" society analogous to the precapitalist West. Yet for a complex set of reasons, unlike the West it was "stationary," unable to make its own transition to a "rational" modernity until receiving a transformative shock from without. Weber's ideas on China, like the general worldview of which they were a part,

pervaded Western thinking for a half century. In the decades following World War II they were gradually elaborated into that orgy of
American self-congratulation, "modernization theory."[7] Against this
theoretical background developed the body of historical scholarship
that essentially comprised American China studies in the 1950s and
1960s, the "China's Response to the West" school of Harvard University and John K. Fairbank, whose contributions to sinology in the
United States are unparalleled and enormous. Moreover, by comparison to stricter modernizationists he offered a view of China that was
less constrained by ethnocentric value judgments and held a greater
appreciation for the empire's unique politicocultural achievements
and its nineteenth-century predicament of cultural crisis. And yet, it
seems to me, the view he imposed on the field through his writing of
textbooks, training of teachers, and supervision of Harvard's energetic program of monograph publication, remained largely devoid
of a sense of process or dynamism within the indigenous society.
His celebrated characterization of Communist China as the "People's
Middle Kingdom" perhaps epitomized the stress he has placed on
the continuity of traditional culture, society, and polity.[8]

During the era of the Vietnam war there arose a radical critique of
American China studies, which drew from Marxist tradition a view of
Western influence in China that was as negative as the modernization
theorists' view was rosy. (This critique, of course, owed more to Lenin than to the historical Marx, that rather smug European who de-
rided nineteenth-century China's "hereditary stupidity" and "barba-
rous and hermetic isolation from the civilized world.")[9] In the wake
of normalization and post-Maoist policy shifts in China, the impas-
sioned anti-imperialism of younger scholars which poured forth in
the pages of the *Bulletin of Concerned Asian Scholars* has given way to the
more detached Wallersteinian "world-economy" perspective argued
with some sophistication by Frances Moulder and others.[10] In all its
forms, however, the radical critique in America remains essentially
the other side of the same coin as the "China's Response" school,
insofar as the two share a view of the external shock as the single
dominant event of importance in China's history of the several centuries prior to socialism, and a presumption of (at least relative) stagnation within the indigenous order.

A very different perspective on modernity in China was advanced
in the early part of this century by the pioneering Japanese sinologist
Naitō Konan, founder of the influential Oriental studies program at

Kyoto University. Rather than as a latecomer to modernization, Naitō depicted China as precocious. The key to modernity for him was the replacement of an hereditary aristocracy by a dominant "middle class" whose status was achieved rather than ascribed. He located this transition in China in the ninth and tenth centuries, with the establishment of the civil service examination as the primary vehicle for upward mobility and the roughly concurrent rise of mercantile wealth. China thus anticipated Europe's modern age by several hundred years. But for all the respect it seemingly paid to the East Asian mother culture, there was implicit in Naitō's theory a patronizing view of China's stagnation *since* this medieval breakthrough, which postwar scholars have tended to see as providing the ideological underpinning for militant Japanese expansion onto the continent.[11] Quite possibly, then, Naitō's overbroad, nonmaterialist conception of modernity obscured more than it revealed, since in some fashion unexplained by him industrialized Europe and Japan had clearly reached a level of material civilization surpassing China by the later nineteenth century.[12]

A third, intermediate, view has recently been emerging in Western historiography of China, based largely on postwar researches done in Japan and the People's Republic. This position, which I share, sees a major social transformation occuring in the last century of the Ming dynasty (1368–1644), and continuing on into the early Ch'ing. Frederic Wakeman, Jr., tentatively stated the case in 1975 as follows:

> Gradually, social historians began to realize that the entire period from the 1550s to the 1930s constituted a coherent whole. ... The urbanization of the lower Yangtze, the commutation of labor services into money payments, the development of certain kinds of regional trade, the growth of mass literacy and the increase in the size of the gentry, the commercialization of local managerial activities—all these phenomena of the late Ming set in motion administrative and political changes that continued to develop over the course of the Ch'ing and in some ways culminated in the social history of the early twentieth century.[13]

Like Naitō's thesis, this position takes indigenous causes of change as more significant than those imposed from without, and thus avoids the ethnocentric pitfalls of both the modernization and imperialism perspectives. It also shares with Naitō the awkward problem of dealing with subsequent transformations such as industrialization, the invasion of foreign capital and ideas, and political revolution. Perhaps, like historians of Europe, we may eventually settle upon the label "early modern" to describe the era from the sixteenth century to whatever later set of changes we judge as most fundamentally transformative.[14]

We shall return to these competing proposals for periodization in the course of our discussion. In what follows, I propose to look in turn at four general questions around which social history of modern China has appeared to be organized: the agrarian regime, the local community, state and society, and commerce and capitalism. I make no claims to be exhaustive of the range of issues being addressed by scholars in the field. Indeed, in at least one case—rebellions and popular movements—I have been led to avoid deliberately any sustained discussion because a recent and expert historiographic survey already exists.[15] I have chosen to concentrate on these four topics not only because they have been among the most enduring and basic areas of inquiry by students of Chinese society, but also because looking at the way thought on these subjects has evolved seems to me to reveal a great deal about the progress of the field as a whole. For this reason I have made an effort in each case to trace the intellectual origins of the problematic—in other words, to consider why these particular questions have seemed so important to ask about Chinese history.

The Agrarian Regime

Most of us in the West seem to begin with an undifferentiated mental image of agrarian China, bequeathed to us by John L. Buck, R. H. Tawney, Fei Hsiao-t'ung, and other social scientist reporters of the 1920s and 1930s.[16] Radically simplified, this picture might incorporate the following elements: (1) free peasant households as the basis of farm management, making independent decisions on such matters as crop selection, budget, and labor allocation; (2) an orientation toward subsistence, but with a fair amount of production for the market; (3) concentrated village living, with scattered and highly fragmented plots; (4) ownership of land by the cultivator legally possible and frequently achieved, but with high rates of tenancy the norm; and (5) landlordism of the rentier type, with large holdings customarily divided for lease to tenants on a small household scale. While many would see this system as oppressive, it is hardly likely to suggest feudalism. Yet by many historians, especially Chinese and Japanese Marxists, the agrarian regime of pre-Communist China is in fact routinely described as "feudal." In this section let us look briefly at the general questions of freedom of property and person (both assumed in the above model to exist), examine variations from the conventional depiction over time and space, and then reconsider the issue of Chinese feudalism.

It is probably not extravagant to claim that in late imperial China there existed a concept of real property more closely resembling that of the modern West than that of other imperial states, such as India and Japan. Recognized rights of private ownership included those of utilization, inheritance, and alienability. The Ming and Ch'ing codes explicitly distinguished between private arable land (min-t'ien) and several other categories (imperial, official, military, tribal, and so on) over which the state claimed special jurisdiction, but at least during the Ch'ing there was a steady trend for more and more land to fall into the private sector. According to one estimate, whereas around 1700 better than 27 percent of all arable land was classed as official land (kuan-t'ien) and about 9 percent as military, by the end of the dynasty virtually all of this had been privatized.[17] Chinese historians frequently identify the "single-whip" tax reforms of the seventeenth century, which merged labor service taxes into the land tax and affixed the fiscal burden equally to the unit of the land regardless of the status of its owner, as a decisive step in the state's recognition of real property as a freely marketable commodity. And indeed it is clear that the free market in land became increasingly active over the last several centuries of imperial China.

There were nevertheless limitations on private rights of disposition, imposed locally by customary law. Most pervasive was recognition of the household rather than the individual as the unit of ownership. As Fei Hsiao-t'ung pointed out, individuals who were not heads of household were usually accorded rights of possession over consumable goods only.[18] Moreover, even households were frequently held accountable by kinsmen for the disposition of their property, and inheritance in cases of death without issue was usually decided by a lineage group. Rights of intervention of neighbors and fellow villagers might also be recognized, but were generally rather weak. Another limitation on private ownership was the widespread institution of mortgage (tien) or conditional sale (tien-mai), a complex and variable practice which accorded previous owners in some cases the option of reclaiming certain rights over their land.[19]

Most interesting were the provisions for multiple proprietorship between landlord and tenant-cultivator, which operated in different areas of the country under such terminology as two lords per field (*i-t'ien-liang-chu*), surface and subsurface ownership, and rights of permanent tenancy (*yung-tien*). Such institutions, which generally came into being under conditions of short labor supply or where considerable overhead investment of labor was required of the prospective tenant, might guarantee the cultivator security from eviction, rights of inheritance, or even free sublease or sale of his cultivation rights. Under these circumstances it was possible to develop any number of strata of claims on a given piece of land, as in fact occurred in highly commercialized agricultural regions like the Yangtze delta, where secondary markets in such cultivation rights appeared. Research done on these phenomena by Chinese and Japanese scholars has revealed the remarkable flexibility and potential for economic development they allowed. For example, subsoil rights (which implied only a claim to rent) were frequently traded on the market by urbanized absentees in a manner similar to stocks and bonds; entrepreneurial "permanent tenants," on the other hand, could acquire relatively large tracts of property to farm with hired labor for commercial profit, without the unnecessary overhead of outright purchase.[20]

The issue of personal freedom of the peasantry in late imperial China has been probably the biggest question in Japanese sinology, and finds echoes in scholarship elsewhere.[21] The Kyoto school (Naitō Konan, Miyazaki Ichisada) argues that the early imperial system of serfdom, undermined by the destruction of the aristocracy and the rise of commerce, had been "totally destroyed" by the end of the tenth century and replaced by a purely contractual nexus of landlord-tenant relations. Terms of contracts varied widely, determined by the free markets in land and labor, but although residues of Confucian paternalism survived, servile status had disappeared. In the more advanced regions such as Kiangnan an intermediate managerial stratum began to insert itself between landlord and cultivator, thus bringing about the split between capitalist investor and professional manager characteristic of "modernity" in both China and the West.[22]

More widely accepted at present is the contrasting view associated with the Tokyo school (Katō Shigeshi, Sudō Yoshiyuki, Niida Noboru) and popularized in the West by Mark Elvin.[23] Katō in 1917 chose the term manor (shōen, Chinese: chuang-yuan) to refer to the conjunction under a single lord of a directly managed demesne (chuang) and indirectly managed outlying holdings. It was this system, rather than the small peasant capitalism of the Kyoto school, that Katō and his followers saw succeeding the old aristocratic estates in the T'ang-Sung era. The general position of the Tokyo school is that the post-T'ang system embodied feudal production relationships and servile labor, which only incrementally disappeared much later (in the view of some, only in 1949). However, in the process of defending their views against attacks of their rivals, Tokyo scholars have introduced several qualifications into Katō's simplistic picture that (to this writer at least) throw the basic conception of manorialism into some question. For example, Sudō conceded that Katō's manor rarely if ever constituted a unified property, but usually comprised a collection of widely scattered plots. He also accepted a modified version of Miyazaki's managerial stratum, whose role may appear closer to that of independent small-scale entrepreneurs than to that of feudal domain overseers (for example, they usually paid land tax directly to the state on holdings under their jurisdiction).

It is acknowledged that most manors were operated using a combination of types of labor, including a tiny minority of legal slaves (nu-li), some freely hired labor, and most frequently tenants (tien) and bondservants (nu-p'u) under written contract. The key questions—as yet far from resolved—would seem to concern the relative proportions of the latter two groups and the reality of the status distinction between them. We know that from Ming times on bondservants were legally allowed only to state officials, not private landlords, but how effectively was this enforced? Bondservants were responsible for performance of a wide variety of personal services, whereas tenants were liable only for contractually stipulated rent payment, but how generally was this difference observed in practice? How real was the freedom to leave upon expiration of contract, in either economic or extraeconomic terms? Bondservants as well as tenants were usually assigned to specific plots of land; how free were members of either group from interference in managerial decisions regarding their plots? In other words, are the Tokyo and Kyoto schools simply arguing over semantic differences in regard to the same real situation?

This situation, of course, continued to develop after the T'ang-Sung transition, as scholars everywhere have come increasingly to recognize. In recent scholarship, a second key turning point has come to be identified from the late sixteenth to the early eighteenth century, associated with the political turmoil and commercial intensification of the era. Work done by Fu I-ling and others has emphasized the active role of bondservants in the late Ming peasant rebellions, and the consequent dying out of this institution in the early Ch'ing.[24] Recent studies by Wu Liang-k'ai and Liu Yung-ch'eng point out the repeated attempts by early Manchu emperors to legislate against servile agrarian relations, and the substantive efforts of local magistrates to enforce these laws.[25] Few of these writers would claim that extra-economic obligations between landlord and tenant disappeared altogether after this time, or that relations of dependency eroded. Indeed, the apparent growth of usurial domination guaranteed the economic entrapment of most peasants, freeholders as well as tenants. Nevertheless, at least by the late eighteenth century the fully contractual basis of the Chinese tenancy system seems to have been generally established in fact as well as in principle.

Spatial variations in the late imperial land system were probably at least as significant as were changes over time. It should be pointed out that the overwhelming majority of the pioneering works so far described—those of Fei, Miyazaki, Sudō, Niida, Fu I-ling, and so on—concentrated on a single region, the lower Yangtze. This region certainly justifies scholarly attention due to its commanding position in the economy and society of the empire as a whole, but for this very reason it can hardly be considered typical. Let me here attempt to vary this depiction somewhat, at least as regards conditions from the eighteenth to the mid-twentieth century.[26] Although it is abundantly clear that drastically different agrarian regimes might pertain in adjacent counties, or even in villages of the same county, it still seems possible to identify four broad zonal variants: those characteristic of north and northwest China, of the lower Yangtze, of the southeast, and of later developing areas throughout the empire.

North China.[27] Irrigated dry-field agriculture characterized this zone. Individual plots were large, perhaps averaging three times the size of those in the south, but nevertheless produced lower yields per plot. In comparison to other zones, cultivation concentrated on staples for home consumption (wheat, millet, sorghum), but there was also diversified production of tobacco, cotton, silk, peanuts, livestock, and so on, for local marketing. Since the Ming, certain favored areas like

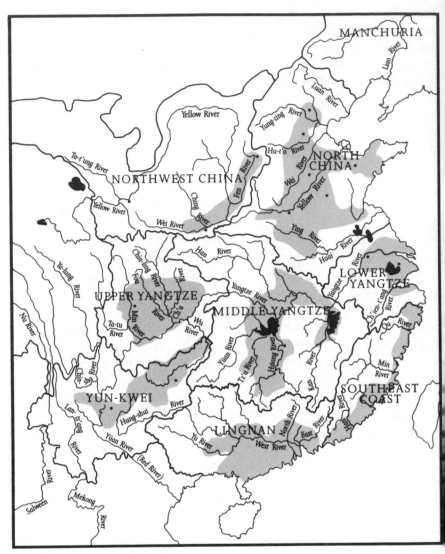

Map 1. Physiographic Macroregions of Agrarian China in Relation to Major Rivers with Regional Cores Indicated by Shading. Adapted from The City in Late Imperial China, edited by G. William Skinner, with the permission of the publishers, Stanford University Press. © 1977 by the Board of Trustees of the Leland Stanford Junior University.

Map 2. Physiographic Macroregions in Relation to Provinces, Showing Metropolitan Cities, 1843. Adapted from The City in Late Imperial China, edited by G. William Skinner, with the permission of the publishers, Stanford University Press. © 1977 by the Board of Trustees of the Leland Stanford Junior University.

the route of the Grand Canal in western Shantung had seen increased production for urban and interregional markets; in the twentieth century this spread to areas newly served by railroad lines.

Probably because of the lower productivity of its agriculture, the land system of North China approached what might be termed the "yeoman farmer" type. Land and labor were freely traded. Concentration of landholding was relatively low: in a typical northern Anhwei county during the 1930s the wealthiest 3 percent of the population owned but 18 percent of the land, and in a Shensi village of the 1940s the top 7 percent likewise controlled only 18 percent.[28] More remarkable were the low rates of tenancy. John Buck's surveys from 1921 to 1925 suggested that throughout North China a mere 10 percent of the farm population were full tenants; rates in most districts ranged between 20 percent for the most commercialized to near zero for the more remote. Because of the low incidence of tenancy rents too remained lower than elsewhere, and already by the eighteenth century were often fixed in cash—a sign of the greater monetization of the rural economy in this zone.

The dominant regime in most of North China was farming by owner-operator households. Buck's surveys showed that more than three-quarters of northern peasants owned *all* the land they tilled, and more localized studies in general support this claim. Most holdings were farmed by family labor, but hired labor was also quite widespread. Depending on locality full-time hired workers might constitute from 5 percent to 20 percent of the population, but hired labor was actually far more pervasive than this. In the North, freeholders of insufficient land characteristically opted to reach subsistence by sale of surplus family labor rather than leasing of additional plots. This was true both of less and of more commercialized areas, though in the latter the scale of hiring was obviously greater. It was, in fact, in commercialized western Shantung that Ching Su and Lo Lun discovered what they termed in 1959 managerial landlordism (ching-ying ti-chu), or the farming by contractual hired labor of individual holdings up to 100 acres, under the direct supervision of profit-oriented resident landlords.[29] In these authors' view this constituted agrarian capitalism, which they saw emerging in the sixteenth century; yet the validity of this characterization and the geographic extent of this atypical form of labor organization remain open questions in Chinese as well as Western academic circles.

The Lower Yangtze. The land system of this zone, whose agriculture was the most commercialized in the empire, was in many ways the antithesis of that in North China. Long a chief supplier of paddy rice to the empire's administrative and military headquarters in the north, it became increasingly involved after the sixteenth century in the production of cotton and silk to serve interregional markets. High productivity apparently spawned greater differentiation of classes here than in other areas, and concentration of landholding was pronounced. A Japanese field study of one Kiangsu village in 1940 found only 11 percent of arable land owned by the cultivator; Buck's surveys suggest that this was extreme but not wholly unrepresentative of the region overall.[30] Hired labor was less significant than in the north, while tenancy was much more widespread. David Faure has found that in the highly commercialized prefectures of Soochow and Sungkiang during the late nineteenth century as many as 90 percent of all peasants were primarily tenants.[31] On the other hand, tenant security was greater here than elsewhere—in the Soochow village studied by Fei Hsiao-t'ung in the 1930s virtually all tenants held contractually stipulated rights of surface ownership.[32] In other words, while individual holdings in the lower Yangtze could be very large, the basic managerial units remained minute: the autonomous peasant household that practiced commercial agriculture for subsistence, not profit, and merely paid rent to an impersonal landlord.

The reasons for both the pervasiveness of rentier landlordism and tenant autonomy were the same: an unusually high rate of absenteeism. In the Japanese village study noted above, for example, only 17 percent of cultivated land was owned by village residents.[33] From the Sung period on the lower Yangtze had been the most urbanized region in China. Beyond the recreational pleasures and commercial opportunities offered by life in such cities as Soochow, Hangchow, Nanking, and (later) Shanghai, large numbers of landlords were apparently induced to urbanize by the rural class warfare of the seventeenth century and of the Taiping rebellion (1851–1864), which affected this area more deeply than any other in China. The decreased labor supply brought about by the carnage and out-migration of these periods seems also to have played a role in the securing by remaining tenants of rights of permanency.[34]

The greater autonomy of the lower Yangtze tenant-cultivator was reflected in the style of rent assessment and collection. According to Liu Yung-ch'eng's recent statistical analysis of eighteenth century data, sharecropping was far less prevalent here than elsewhere (13.3 percent of his sample cases), and fixed rents correspondingly higher, indicative of landlords' abrogation of decision-making responsibilities. On the other hand, these rents were most often fixed in kind, suggesting an emphasis on procurement of urban food supplies and raw textiles for urban artisans.[35] The entire set of phenomena associated with urbanized rentierism reached a new level of sophistication with the emergence in the post-Taiping decades of landlord bursaries (tsu-chan), especially in the Soochow area. By means of these agencies urbanites of varying scales of wealth relieved (for a fee) of all responsibilities of land management, tenant recruitment, and even rent collection, were able to invest a portion of their savings in agriculture. The bursaries, whose geographical spread seems to have remained rather restricted, thus represented a new level of depersonalization of agrarian economic relations.[36]

South China. The land system of South China bore some resemblance to that of the lower Yangtze, but had several peculiarities of its own. Throughout the modern period this had been an area of rentier landlordism, high tenancy (by the 1930s more than 60 percent of cultivated acreage in Kwangtung was leased),[37] and relatively little use of hired labor. Rents were probably the highest of any part of China, supported by the rich double- and triple-crop paddy rice agriculture of the tropical south, and most often fixed in kind. This reflected not only absenteeism, as in the lower Yangtze, but absenteeism of a type peculiar to this region with its maritime orientation. At least by the sixteenth century both Fukien and Kwangtung had become heavily tied in to the Southeast Asian trade, with wealthy landowning merchants dwelling both in domestic coastal ports and commercial enclaves overseas collecting grain rent for storage in their urban warehouses.[38] Whereas in Fukien rents seem to have remained fairly stable and tenants retained some contractually guaranteed security, in Kwangtung rights such as permanent tenancy seem to have died out by the beginning of the nineteenth century.

The reason may be related to a second peculiarity of Cantonese society, the extraordinary economic role of kinship associations. Corporate landlordism was known throughout China, but was endemic in Kwangtung. Whereas, for example, the northwest China village studied by Hinton in the 1940s had 13 percent of its land owned by temples and lineages, and the lower Yangtze county of Wu-hsi in the 1930s had some 8 percent of its land owned by clan estates, in Kwangtung the provincial average was 35 percent and in some Pearl

River delta counties reached 60 percent.[39] According to Han-seng Ch'en, this derived from lineage restrictions on the sale of members' land, and from the unique inheritance practices of the area. As elsewhere throughout China generational succession was accompanied by equal partition among male heirs, but in Kwangtung clan corporatism often dictated that not the land itself, but rather shares of rent from an undivided familial estate be thus divided. After many generations and partitionings in this fashion, what resulted was numerous shareholders (often émigrés) and numerous tenants tied into a corporation managed ostensibly in the collective interest by a few clan elders. By Ch'en's reckoning, more than 80 percent of Cantonese peasants in the 1930s dwelt in kinship communities, reflecting their at least partial dependence upon this ancestral land.[40] Ch'en has frequently been criticized for the extreme negativism of his view of Kwangtung rural society, and his political motivations are fairly plain, but his depiction is nevertheless based on close and competent observation and is generally convincing.

Later Settled Areas. This dispersed zone incorporates lowland grain producing areas such as southwestern Anhwei, the Hsiang River valley and Tung-t'ing lakeshore of Hunan, and the plains of Taiwan, which for one reason or other were densely settled (or resettled) only in the modern period.[41] It also includes highlands in all these provinces, as well as in Hupeh, Kiangsi, Fukien, and so on. In these areas a variety of land-tenure systems took hold, but they shared certain attributes common to pioneer areas. While not necessarily representative of China as a whole, these areas are extremely intriguing; one is in fact tempted to concur in Fu I-ling's recent judgment that, paradoxically, capitalist agrarian relations "did not appear first in the economically developed riverine and coastal areas but in some economically backward, mountainous, and rural feudal locales."[42]

Both lowlands and highlands in this zone were cleared, reclaimed, and irrigated largely with commercial ends in mind—in the case of Hunan and Taiwan lowlands to develop export rice, and in the highlands for tea, indigo, timber, wood-ash fertilizer, and other products habitually not grown on land suitable for grain cultivation. Tenancy was widespread in these areas, but it was tenancy of a special sort. A common feature was a highly developed system of multiple ownership, which stemmed from the combination of very cheap land available to the first arrivals and the high cost of rendering this land productive. The usual pattern would be for a frontier entrepreneur (*k'en-*

shou, shan-chu, or other such term) to acquire title to vast stretches of virgin terrain, then recruit tenants willing to finance the clearing or reclamation of smaller sections of this land. These "capitalist tenants" (to use Fu's phrase) would then subdivide their leasehold for rent to later arrivals, who paid rents to both primary and secondary landlords. Someone, very often the tenant-developer himself, would establish markets for collection of the local product for export, as well as processing facilities such as tea refineries or paper mills.

Reflecting the heavily commercialized nature of this agriculture, rents in this zone were often fixed directly in cash. There was also an abnormally high incidence of rent deposit (*ya-tsu*).[43] The demand for a large, often nonrefundable, up-front cash payment from a prospective tenant had been known since the Sung was found throughout China. However during the eighteenth century it became especially common in frontier areas, owing to such factors as high absenteeism by the primary owners, the desire of such owners to guarantee stability in their tenants, the need for heavy initial investment in the land, and the desire of both primary and secondary landlords to acquire cash for commercial investment.

Because of the character of recruitment of settlers (usually through old native-place ties), the need for large-scale work organization in land development, and the exigencies of frontier justice, large-scale social organizations were common in these areas: kinship associations, polder communities, and paramilitary forces of many types. Exploitation of later arrivals could be severe, and this as well as more general disputes over "turf" offered continual provocations for social conflict. Tensions escalated as continued immigration and population growth strained the productivity of the land, and as short-sighted practices of early settlers (deforestation, slash-and-burn agriculture, encroachment on natural floodwater receptacles) eventually yielded a deteriorating agrarian ecology. In the Han River highlands of northwestern Hupeh, in fact, such pressures seem to have played a large part in the outbreak of the White Lotus Rebellion in the 1790s.

Given the nature and the diversity of the Chinese agrarian regime, how is it that so many writers have characterized it as "feudal?" Most historians are willing to grant the existence of a more-or-less feudal society at some point in China's past; the difference, based of course on one's definition of "feudalism," lies in when one chooses to locate its demise. Generally speaking, four alternatives have suggested themselves. The first, common among Western and Chinese non-Marxist

historians, identifies the transition around the time of the founding of
the empire in the third century B.C. Adherents of this view stress that
imperial China was a centralized bureaucratic state, totally lacking the
system of contractual bonds of vassalage that characterized European
and Japanese feudalism. The second view, that of Kyoto school, is
based on somewhat broader sociopolitical criteria, and sees the end
of feudalism in the T'ang-Sung destruction of the aristocracy and establishment of meritocratic official recruitment.

Few partisans of the third and fourth views, however, would deny
that late imperial China lacked a feudal political superstructure; they
base their claim rather on the organization of the economy. The third
view, held by less orthodox Marxists within the Tokyo school (and
somewhat tentatively it appears by several economic historians in the
People's Republic) sees feudalism's demise with the collapse of the
manorial economy and the disappearance of serflike bondservice between the sixteenth and the eighteenth centuries. Some problems
with this point of view have already been pointed out, and when
these writers make their case for "feudalism" these problems begin to
multiply. For example, even among the most vociferous proponents
of the survival of the medieval manor, there are few who would claim
that this entailed the manorial rights identified by Bloch and others as
the essence of European feudalism: manorial justice, the right to private military retinues, and the independent authority to levy taxes. In
China these remained the formally claimed and periodically enforced
monopolies of the state. Largely in recognition of this fact, the Tokyo
school's chief exponent in the West, Mark Elvin, explicitly seeks to
disassociate Chinese manorialism (*régime seigneurial*) from true feudalism (*régime féodal*).[44] This disclaimer finds something of an echo in the
work of recent Chinese writers who distinguish between the feudal
lord economy (*ling-chu ching-chi*) of ancient China and medieval Europe and the landlord economy (*ti-chu ching-chi*) of the late imperial
period; while both are variants of the "feudal mode of production,"
the latter is a more advanced stage.[45]

It is of course this last point—the mode of production—upon
which orthodox Marxists in China and elsewhere base their view of
the survival of feudalism or "semi-feudalism" up through the "liberation" of the 1940s and 1950s. This fourth viewpoint grew directly
out of the debates on revolutionary strategy of the Republican era.[46]
The initial application of the term "semi-feudal" to China came from
Lenin in 1912; eight years later at the Second Comintern Congress

he introduced the formula "semi-colonial and semi-feudal." During the Soviet leadership struggle and the intimately related debates on United Front strategy of the 1920s, the issue of feudalism was hotly debated in Moscow and China. Briefly, Trotsky in opposing any alliance with the bourgeoisie argued that China was thoroughly dominated by world capitalism; Stalin in accepting this alliance argued that feudal China still called for a bourgeois-capitalist revolution. Mao Tsetung, who had demonstrated adherence to the Stalinist "feudal" line as early as his famous 1927 report on the peasant movement in Hunan, made the "semi-colonial semi-feudal" formula official upon his assumption of Chinese Communist Party leadership in the 1930s, and it remains official to this day.

In leftist Chinese academic circles, these leadership and policy struggles were reflected in the so-called social history debate of the late 1920s. Those historians who argued the case that contemporary society remained feudal did so in general on the following grounds: (1) that China still had a predominantly agrarian economy, within which the "structure of exploitation" took the form of extraction of surplus from the producers by a landholding elite; (2) that a "natural economy" of small-scale peasant agriculture remained the norm, with the peasant household the basic unit of production, and self-sufficiency the primary orientation; (3) that rentier landlordism predominated; and (4) that landlord-tenant relations still retained a strong element of personal dependency and "extraeconomic" obligation.

There are a number of obvious problems in the orthodox case for the survival of feudalism in Ch'ing and Republican China, beyond the question of political organization, with which historians in the People's Republic still continue to wrestle. First, as indicated above, most evidence clearly points to the alienability and free market in land. Second, the predominance of the small peasant economy is itself potentially troublesome, since no less an authority than Marx saw this as symptomatic not of feudalism but of its dissolution.[47] Third, the claimed discovery of "managerial landlordism" (as well as evidence from North China in general) undermines the assumption of universality of a rentier elite. Fourth, new research into the erosion of personal dependency bonds and servile status in the early Ch'ing suggests to some historians fundamental changes in production relationships. (According to one recent writer, contractual landlord-tenant relationships without "extraeconomic" obligations are by definition nonfeudal).[48] Finally, it seems difficult to reconcile any notion of a feudal "natural economy" with increased evidence of the high level of commercialized agriculture in late imperial China.

The issue of feudalism is thus by no means resolved, nor has a detailed consensus been reached on most of these problematical areas by historians either in China or outside of it. What is perhaps most encouraging is the interest recently displayed by scholars in the People's Republic regarding the details of feudal institutions in Europe and Japan.[49] With a common ground for discussion, historians of China worldwide may be in position to make major strides in interpreting continuity and variation in the history of agrarian China.

The Local Community

Two defense lines were built around the village, the outer one consisting of removable mines—iron tubes filled with powder and scrap iron and connected by wire. The villagers knew where they were and how to pass through the line safely, but a stranger could not enter the village without being trapped by the wires which exploded the mines. . . . The second line, built within the limits of the village, consisted of a number of fortifications, lane gates, and gun placements on the backyard walls. At night, the young men were assigned, first, to lay the explosive mines and wires for the outer line, and then to patrol the streets, lanes, and strategic points. Meanwhile, several other teams were on guard in two or three places in different parts of the village. . . . The village had not been attacked since the organization of the defense.[50]

So wrote anthropologist Martin C. Yang in a study of his native Shantung village in the years prior to the Japanese invasion. To what extent was the mentality of village solidarity, so graphically portrayed here, a basic factor in the social history of modern China?

It is clear that, for the most part, Chinese villages held little common land. They lacked not only collective cultivated fields but also common pastureland (as in Europe) and common woodland (as in Japan). In contrast to Japanese villages, those of China also engaged in very little interhousehold labor exchange. However, as was emphasized as early as 1898 by the missionary sociologist Arthur H. Smith, at least some villages practiced cooperation in a wide range of critical activities: maintenance and operation of irrigation works, extension of credit, finance and management of religious events, crop watching, and militia organization.[51] Research activities of the Japanese South Manchurian Railroad and pioneer ethnographic studies by Chinese anthropologists during the Republican era provided additional rich data on village cooperative institutions. As a result, a number of general theories of village solidarity have been passed into our general stock of lore on rural Chinese society.

We might identify the first of these in the work of Fei Hsiao-t'ung, who proceeded from his important field studies of individual villages to spin out a more general picture of Chinese social organization which became enormously influential both in China and in the West.[52] A pioneer in functionalist anthropology, Fei brought to his work the influence of Emile Durkheim, of his mentors Bronislaw Malinowski and Robert Park, and of his friend and colleague Robert Redfield (whose theory of the "folk culture" owed much to observations shared with him by Fei). In his model of village society Fei began with several assumptions which today seem open to question: an extremely low degree of geographic mobility, relatively little extra-local contact or cooperation, and a clear and fundamentally important rural-urban gap. Fei stressed the significance of village-level groups like crop-watching societies (which, he noted, were usually organized by and for the elite), as well as the role of customary law in enforcing solidarity among village residents. For example, in his lower Yangtze village study Fei pointed out that whereas subsoil landownership had largely passed into the hands of urbanized absentees, social pressure had prevented the alienation of surface ownership from the villagers themselves, in effect allowing outside investment without sacrificing local control over cultivation practices and rights.[53] In his work of the late 1940s, Fei largely backed away from his emphasis on residence to a view of kinship as the most important principle of social organization. While still characterizing rural China as intensely localistic (ti-fang-hsing), he argued that peasants held an ego-centered "network consciousness" more strongly than an omniscient "group-consciousness"; the priority of territorial groupings he came to identify as distinctive of a type of modernity which China had not yet achieved.[54]

A second body of theory arose at about the same time in Japan, like Fei's growing ultimately out of the European sociological tradition of the late nineteenth and early twentieth centuries, but filtered through very different processes of transmission. This theory centers around the notion of *kyōdōtai* (community, communalism), a Japanese neologism coined to translate—depending upon the user—the *Gemeinde* of Marx or the *Gemeinschaft* of Tönnies and Weber.[55] An enormous literature on *kyōdōtai* has been built up in Japan since the 1930s, both as general theory and as applied to the historical civilizations of the West, of South Asia, of China, and of Japan itself.[56]

The debate over application of *kyōdōtai* ideas to China has had an especially long, varied, and politically resonant history.[57] In the prewar years *kyōdōtai*-analysis was seen generally as a subset of the theory of "Oriental despotism" (see the following section). Writers like Shimizu Morimitsu drew eclectically from Marx, Lenin, Weber, and Wittfogel the argument that village solidarity based on cooperation in water control inhibited formation of class identities, while the concomitant village insularity allowed and demanded the rise of a despotic state. During the war itself, the special "Oriental" character of village *kyōdōtai* took on a new coloration, as Pan-Asianist apologists for Japanese expansion on the mainland sought to identify in village communalism an instinctual pattern of behavior uniting Chinese and Japanese, and distinguishing them from an Occidental society ridden by class conflict. In the postwar years the concept has been rehabilitated, but the revival has sparked new and lively debates. For examples, while Niida Noboru uses evidence of village compacts to argue that modern *kyōdōtai* was a direct legacy of Sung-Ming manorial regimes, others argue that such bonds of local solidarity in fact precluded the division of society into corporate classes and thus made manorialism impossible. Still others who share this view of class and *kyōdōtai* as mutually exclusive find Chinese villages to have been dominated by the former, and Japanese by the latter.[58]

In the work of *kyōdōtai*'s most vigorous proponent among postwar sinologists, Imahori Seiji, an attempt is made to reconcile the two. A Marxist with strong Weberian influences, Imahori has presented a voluminous corpus of documentary and field research in an attempt to demonstrate that *kyōdōtai*-sentiment was deliberately fostered in both rural and urban settings by the "feudal" dominant class. He argues that the Chinese principle of partible inheritance set limits on the size of individual holdings and effectively prevented the emergence of seigneurial domains; as a result landed elites turned to leadership of village "cooperative structures"—irrigation, firefighting, crop-watching societies, and so on—as a means of institutionalizing their hegemony over fellow villagers and their extraction of local surplus product. In arguing to this effect Imahori is at pains to disassociate himself from Western theorists of "Oriental despotism" by insisting that village solidarity served class, not state, interests.[59] Despite considerable criticism in recent years by scholars like Hatada Takashi (who favors a view of kinship, not class or community as the basic structural component of Chinese rural society), the application of kyōdōtai models to China persists in Japan, and is used to explain everything from Skinner's marketing systems to communization under Mao.

The third body of theory relating to village solidarity originates in recent Western social science. Borrowing heavily from Eric R. Wolf's analysis of "closed corporate communities" in Mexico and Indonesia, and from E. P. Thompson's studies of the English crowd, the political scientist James C. Scott created in the 1970s a model of "the moral economy of the peasant" in Southeast Asia.[60] The emphasis of this argument is on the collective provision of subsistence guarantees for all community members and on the maintenance of communal control over local resources. The latter goal may be accomplished through corporate ownership, or less directly through customary legal sanctions against the sale of property to or investment by outsiders, and to some degree against participation in market-oriented activities. Whereas Wolf identified village closure as a distinctly modern reaction to the threat posed by penetration of foreign or urban capital, Scott tends to see the mentality of communal defense as a primordial feature of Asian rural society. Besides Scott himself, the historian Alexander Woodside and the journalist Frances Fitzgerald have made reasonably convincing applications of these general ideas to analysis of the Vietnamese revolution,[61] but most scholars have felt the model not especially applicable to the case of China. The one extended attempt at such an application, by Ralph Thaxton, has received a generally harsh critical reception.[62]

In fact, the chief significance of this third village solidarity theory for Chinese social history may well lie in providing a conceptually sophisticated model of peasant society to which, most scholars would now argue, China stood as an exception. Responding directly to Wolf, G. William Skinner argued that Chinese villages "opened" or "closed" according to their shifting perception of external political or economic conditions.[63] In his own work, Skinner pursues in great detail an alternative view of the communal horizons of the Chinese peasant. Drawing upon ethnographic studies by C. K. Yang and Martin C. Yang, and his own fieldwork in Szechwan during the late 1940s, he offered a broadly revised view of Chinese society and socioeconomic history based on the classical literature of economic geography and central-place theory, particularly the work of August Lösch and Walter Christaller.[64] Skinner proceeds from an assumption of a certain minimal level of marketing activity on the part of all peasant households in the late imperial era, necessitating regular visits by a household member to a nearby periodic market. He then constructs an elaborate hierarchy of marketing centers, each possessing (ideally) hexagonal-shaped commercial hinterlands. Villages cluster around a "standard market," standard markets around an "intermediate market," intermediate markets around a "central market," and so on up the scale of centrality. By introducing this continuum of gradually accruing "urban" functions, Skinner replaces the rigid dichotomy of city and village and the oversimplified assumption of an urban-rural gap with a far more flexible framework of analysis.

Skinner then introduces a second (and very bold) assumption: that marketing areas at least at the lower levels are catchment areas not only of economic activity but of social identity as well; the basic unit of rural community is thus raised one level from the village to the standard marketing area. The significance of this step is very profound, since, in Skinner's scheme, all marketing areas at the intermediate level and above are nondiscrete and overlapping. Instead of the "sheet of loose sand" suggested by an infinitesimal number of self-contained village cells, therefore, we are offered a set of highly integrated building blocks for Chinese society that help explain how generation of organizations for collective action on a wider geographic scale was possible. Several historians have in fact employed Skinnerian principles in highly successful efforts to elucidate just such kinds of action: Philip A. Kuhn to explain the structure of mid-nineteenth century local militarization, and Winston Hsieh to trace the working out of the 1911 revolution in the Canton delta, to cite but two examples.[65]

Skinner's theory has a temporal dimension as well. He analyzes the secular intensification of marketing activities, the proliferation of new markets, and (following reduction of the friction of distance by improvements in transport technology) the atrophy of smaller centers and streamlining of the entire hierarchy. He also works out in considerable detail the implications of his model for the successes and failures of collectivization in the 1950s. A number of scholars have found these elaborations useful and have built upon them in their own research,[66] but it is probably fair to say that to date they have not had the enormous significance of the basic marketing model itself. Overall, Skinner's work constitutes a highly complex and coherent view of Chinese society, yet scholars have found it possible to separate out various strands of his argument to meet the analytical needs of their own data. The simple act of resurrecting central-place theory and demonstrating its utility for historical study has also had a great and growing impact on scholars of other societies.[67] In refocusing our attention on the role of the spatial dimension, Skinner's work undoubtedly constitutes the major methodological contribution of China studies to social history as a whole in the past generation.

State and Society

China's capacity to excite contrary sets of generalizations from intelligent observers is nowhere better illustrated than in regard to the late imperial state. Here traditional thinking left us two opposing characterizations, with almost no middle ground. On the one hand, we have the *wu-wei* (nonintervention) depiction in which the government was seen as exercising little or no real control over the operations of local society. This position may owe its genesis to the influential work of Imperial Customs official-turned-scholar Hosea B. Morse, and his famous dismissal of the state as merely a "taxing and policing agent," with no effective social or economic program.[68] Such a notion was popularized in the writings of Chinese liberal intellectuals of the Republican era such as Hu Shih and Fei Hsiao-t'ung.[69] For Fei, traditional China saw a tyrannical but extremely weak central administration superimposed on a society which, while not exactly democratic, was at least self-regulating according to consensually defined norms. The natural "paternalist" leaders of this society—local gentry, clan and village heads—performed the dual service of enforcing these norms and shielding the population from the arbitrary demands of an irrational state. While this leadership could fairly be termed "exploitative," in contrast to the potential rapacity of a state left unchecked, its exploitation was effected only through popularly approved institutional channels (for example, the land, rent, and kinship systems).

The contrasting view, that of a fully realized "Oriental despotism," has had a broader appeal in China, in Japan, and especially in the West. The European self-conception as a culture founded on the ideal of individual liberty, and the contrasting image of Asian societies as repressive and despotic, seems to have originated in classical Greece, possibly as a propaganda device during the Persian Wars. It was pointedly revived in the thought of Montesquieu and other Enlightenment thinkers, pervaded British liberalism, and gained modern social science legitimacy with Max Weber's characterization of China as a "patrimonial state."[70] Twentieth-century Chinese scholars of a conservative bent, like Liang Ch'i-ch'ao and Tsiang T'ing-fu, coupled acknowledgment of despotism (chu'uan-chih-chu-i) as their national political tradition with prescriptions as to how it might be made more enlightened.[71] But the most complex and persistent theories of despotism as applied to imperial China are those associated with the Kyoto school and with the idea of the "Asiatic mode of production."

Naitō Konan, the progenitor of the Kyoto school, saw the increase of imperial autocracy as characteristic of China's modern era. The institution of an effectively functioning civil service examination system in the Sung period, in Naitō's view, permanently changed the nature of China's social system by completing the destruction of the feudal nobility. Although China had developed a bureaucratic administration centuries earlier, recruitment for governmental posts had been almost completely by aristocratic preferment. The institution of meritocratic selection created the key social group of modern China, the gentry, a nonhereditary "middle class" which both staffed the bureaucracy and managed local society. The shift in the nature of official service from an independent birthright to a conditional appointment by imperial will in effect amounted to a degrading of the bureaucracy itself. Naitō pointed out numerous examples of how the late imperial era was marked by an increasing arrogation of state functions in the emperor's hands and a corresponding elevation of his ritual status. The Ming and Ch'ing saw the culmination of this trend with the loss of officials' rights formally to challenge imperial edicts and the abolition (in the fourteenth century) of the post of prime minister. It should be added that Naitō saw this rise of despotism as on balance a

progressive trend, since it was accompanied by the rise of commoners' rights and their emancipation from the effective slavery of the
aristocratic age.[72]

In the work of Naitō's disciples Miyazaki Ichisada and Saeki Tomi
these views have been provided with an economic foundation and
placed in comparative perspective. Both men characterize the late
imperial era as an age of absolutism (zettaishugi), specifically equated
with that of eighteenth-century France. Given the gradual shift in the
nature of wealth from landholding to more mobile forms of property
and the commercialization of the economy, the central prop for the
throne's increasing arrogation of power was, as in Europe, its alliance
with urban commercial capitalism against the forces of feudal decen-
tralization. Both men note, and Saeki has studied in great detail, the
pivotal role played by the Ming-Ch'ing salt gabelle, an institution
whereby merchants granted imperial franchises for the distribution
of this basic commodity developed into the wealthiest members of
the society. This private wealth was regularly tapped by means of
contributions and subscriptions for application to imperial purposes,
and when the alien Manchus supplanted the native Ming dynasty
they systematically replaced older salt merchants with northern Chinese with whom they had formed preconquest ties. Miyazaki has
suggested that in the "contemporary age" of Sino-Western trade this
key support may have shifted from the salt administration to the
Imperial Maritime Customs.[73]

The second body of theory purporting to explain "Oriental despotism" proceeds from assumptions virtually antithetical to those of the
Kyoto school. As early as 1848, John Stuart Mill in his Principles of
Political Economy noted the existence of a peculiar "Oriental society," a
stage of development immediately beyond pastoralism, characterized
by sedentary agriculture and irrigation works controlled by the state.
Karl Marx pursued this line of thinking in his private and journalistic
writings of the early 1850s, but generally avoided mention of it in his
more systematic theoretical works; the notable exception was his list-
ing, without further comment, of an "Asiatic mode of production"
along with the ancient, feudal, and modern bourgeois modes in the
"Preface" to his 1859 Contribution to the Critique of Political Economy. Like
Mill, Marx clearly felt that the dominant features of China and other
Asiatic societies were their lack of historical development, their low
level of commercialization, the primacy of the village community,
and the overwhelming power of the state based on its role in the

maintenance of waterworks. This increasingly common European conception was echoed also by Max Weber in his *General Economic History* (1927), but was more thoroughly developed in the work of a line of Marxist theoreticians from Karl Kautsky to G. Plekhanov, the early V. I. Lenin, and L. Madyar.[74] By far the most elaborate and celebrated treatment came at the hands of the German Marxist Karl A. Wittfogel, in his monumental *Wirtschaft und Gesellschaft Chinas* (1931), and in subsequent writings in which he sought to expand his sinological studies into a general model of oriental society.[75]

Alone among the exponents of the Asiatic mode of production, Wittfogel was highly expert in the details of Chinese institutional history; alone as well he was cognizant of the realities of historical change within this "stationary" society. Specifically, Wittfogel's recognition that over the course of the imperial period China had developed not only the institution of private property (which earlier Marxist models of the Asiatic mode denied), but also considerable commercialization, monetization, and handicraft industry, led him to characterize it as a "hydraulic society" of the "complex" type. He argued that China's historic practice of sedentary agriculture under semi-arid ecological conditions necessitated large-scale cooperation in irrigation; the construction of massive hydraulic works during the late Chou, Ch'in, and Han periods had occasioned the development of a full-time, professional bureaucracy, a despotic monarchy, and the destruction of the feudal society of earlier times. With the subsequent rise of commerce, the bureaucratic state was able to retain its dominance by virtue of its control over the key avenues of trade, the canals and rivers. Thus, whereas critics like Miyazaki could dismiss earlier "Asiatic mode" theories on the grounds that late imperial China was no longer a simple agrarian state, Wittfogel could respond with his own version of "oriental absolutism," which conceded the alliance of throne and urban merchants but insisted that all commercial privilege was derivative from the state.[76] Because all private wealth existed only at the state's discretion, both property and social class distinctions congingent upon property relations remained "weak"; there could be no "ruling class" in oriental society since the state itself monopolized this role.

His explanation of how it did so led Wittfogel to develop a cyclical model of change within stagnation, which he specifically identified in the Chinese case with the dynastic cycle. When each new dynasty came to power it systematically destroyed the upper class by redistributing land and monopolizing the society's surplus product via confiscatory taxation. Gradually, however, concentration of private wealth inevitably gave rise to a new elite, which competed with the state for control of this surplus through generation of commercial profits and through rent on land. Ultimately the burden on the general population led to peasant rebellion, dynastic change, and a new redistribution of property—"a rejuvenated, though basically unaltered, oriental despotism." By this mechanism the socioeconomic system continued to reproduce itself, rather than developing into a mature capitalism of the Western type.[77]

When Wittfogel and Madyar promulgated these ideas in Moscow and in China during the late 1920s and 1930s they met with a largely cold reception. Chinese intellectuals, apparently offended by the negative picture it offered of their country's developmental potential, either rejected the Asiatic mode of production altogether or (following their reading of Marx's "Preface") located it at some time in China's distant, prefeudal past.[78] A major exception came in the work of the leftist historian Chi Ch'ao-ting, who in 1935 published (in English) his pioneering study of Chinese regional development, *Key Economic Areas in Chinese History.*[79] A disciple of Wittfogel, Chi saw the despotism of the imperial state as contingent upon its ability to extract grain surplus from the society by means of its control of waterways, and the rise and fall of individual ruling houses as determined by the outcome of contests over regional hydraulic systems. At the same time, however, Chi made his peace with Stalinist orthodoxy by describing imperial China as not only despotic but feudal.

The Comintern itself took increasing measures to exclude the Asiatic mode of production from acceptable theory. In 1928 it was declared inapplicable to modern China; in 1931 it was officially rejected as an independent social formation; and in Stalin's 1938 *Dialectical and Historical Materialism* it was pointedly omitted from the orthodox sequence of modes of production, from primitive communism through socialism. Indeed, in Stalin's logic the very concept of oriental society violated two key principles of Marxist theory: (1) It suggested an alternative to the unilinear path of economic development revealed in the European model, and (2) it presented a case which challenged the universality of class struggle as the motive force in history.

With the rejection of his ideas by the Party, Wittfogel began the odyssey to the political right that culminated in his role as star witness for the McCarren committee. In 1957 he published a reworking of his thesis under the title *Oriental Despotism: A Comparative Study of Total Power*.[80] Beyond his extension of the concept of "Asiatic" society to such exotic locations as pre-Columbian Mesoamerica, Wittfogel's revised theory differed from his earlier model in such respects as the insistence on the inapplicability of "feudalism" to *any* period of Chinese history, however, ancient. Most significant was its polemical identification of Soviet-style political systems in China and Russia as merely continuations of those nations' traditions of oriental despotism, and the new application of a totalitarian model (including the primary reliance on state terror) to the depiction of late imperial China. In my view, this anachronistic association of Stalinist tyranny with Ming and Ch'ing governmental policies marred a whole generation of studies produced at the University of Washington (where Wittfogel sojourned for a period in the late 1950s), including such otherwise valuable works as Hsiao Kung-ch'uan's *Rural China: Imperial Control in the Nineteenth Century*.

Probably no other work of scholarship in English ever received as widespread condemnation or as curt a dismissal by historians of China as has *Oriental Despotism*. Early reviews by influential scholars expressed outrage over the work's conceptual fuzziness, its attempt to lump together extremely diverse societies, and its insensitivity to China's historical development. Specifically, Wittfogel was taken to task for misrepresentations of China's customary law, fiscal system, inheritance practices, and institutional constraints on the exercise of imperial will.[81] Probably most telling has been the total rejection of Wittfogel's basic premise: the association of state power with control of hydraulic works; in almost every case where subsequent studies have examined such works in detail, they have been found to have been constructed and maintained largely by local societal initiative, and more often than not in direct opposition to the interests and directives of the state.[82] There has been a noticeable flurry of revived interest in Wittfogel's ideas in the post-Mao People's Republic (Chi Ch'ao-ting's 1935 *Key Economic Areas*, for example, was translated into Chinese for the first time in 1979!), but recent semi-official evaluations, while conceding the Marxist pedigree of the Asiatic mode of production, conclude with a ringing rejection of Wittfogel's "hydraulic society" and the implications this suggested for China's "stagnation" prior to the Western impact.[83]

In recent decades, not only the hydraulic theory but the entire characterization of the late imperial era as one of "despotism" has begun to appear less and less tenable. In the process, the reopened question of the nature of state-society relations has become, at least in the West, probably the most important and exciting issue on the agenda of Chinese social history.

Relations of power within the formal government apparatus no longer seem to support a simple picture of steadily increasing control in imperial hands. Such a process is still usually seen throughout most of the Ming, under the early Manchu rulers, and in the auto-cratic institutional changes (establishment of the Grand Council and the secret memorial system) of the Yung-cheng emperor in the 1720s and 1730s. Yet as early as the K'ang-hsi emperor's famous 1713 deci-sion never to raise the land tax, fiscal power began to slip out of the court's hands into those of lower levels of administration. This pro-cess was accelerated by the epidemic of corruption of the late eigh-teenth century and the financial debilitation that accompanied sup-pression of the White Lotus rebellion (1796–1804); a critical turning point was apparently reached at the time of the mid-century Taiping rebellion, with the advent of provincially controlled commercial tax systems instituted to support regional militarization.[84] The "despo-tism" paradigm has also been shaken by Lloyd Eastman and subse-quent writers on literati politics, who have shown the existence of an increasingly vocal loyal opposition, outside the formal bureaucracy but within the ruling elite (centered in the imperially sponsored Hanlin Academy), which the throne tolerated and at least occasion-ally felt obliged to heed.[85]

Of broader significance than intragovernmental distributions of power, though, are trends now being seen in the overall degree of penetration of society by state authorities at all levels. The existence of cycles of administrative efficacy, roughly corresponding to the rise and fall of dynasties, has of course long been accepted, and has been eloquently reconfirmed by Pierre-Etienne Will in his recent study of flood control in the middle Yangtze region.[86] More surprising has been the growing evidence of a secular decline in the effective level of state presence. Skinner, for example, has pointed out that over the entire imperial period the number of administrative units and local officials remained relatively constant, even as the population increased many times over, and the society became more complex. He concludes that "a unified empire could be maintained ... only by systematically reducing the scope of basic level administrative functions and countenancing a decline of the effectiveness of bureaucratic government within local systems."[87] The Confucian imperative to fiscal restraint, of which the K'ang-hsi decision of 1713 was but one manifestation, certainly played a role in this process. One associated phenomenon was the incremental transference from state to private entrepreneurship in the Ming and Ch'ing of such basic economic activities as grain, tea, and salt circulation, mining of coal and other minerals, and the manufacture of porcelain.[88]

Interest in the nature of the state-society relationship has come to focus (as it did decades ago in the work of Fei Hsiao-t'ung) on the role of the middlemen in this relationship, the gentry. The initial revival of interest in this area of research was sparked by Frederic Wakeman, Jr.'s 1966 *Strangers at the Gate* (a study which virtually single-handedly put local history back in the American modern China curriculum), but the guiding influence since that time has been Philip A. Kuhn, who appears to have made the resolution of this issue his life's work.[89] We have come in recent years to a view of the gradual emergence over the late imperial era of a dramatically greater role for the nonofficial elite in the management of local society than the simple offering of protection from the state. Moreover, there is some agreement on identification of a number of critical moments in this long-term secular process, moments which not surprisingly most often coincided with periods of cyclical decline.

Studies by Shiba Yoshinobu of Ningpo prefecture, Chekiang, and by Mark Elvin of Shanghai county, Kiangsu, over the late imperial period have brought to light changes in the management of firefighting, water control, public security, and other social welfare tasks. The essence of such changes was a permanent shift of responsibility from paid or conscripted agents of the state to members of the local elite. These so-called gentry-managers (*shen-tung*) became increasingly professionalized in the performance of these duties, to be sure, but they remained largely off the state payrolls and only indirectly under state control. The most striking period of their emergence in both localities was the crisis-ridden final decades of Ming rule in the early seventeenth century.[90] Later in the century, but still before the secure and stable consolidation of Ch'ing rule, there began to percolate that school of literati reformism which we know as *feng-chien*, advocating (to no immediate political effect but with major long-term implications) that the entire business of local administration be turned over to enlightened, extrabureaucratic local elites.[91]

A second period of change came at the Ch'ing's own moment of dynastic crisis, the Taiping rebellion. The most remarkable development of this time was the state's abrogation of its formal monopoly on military force, with its acquiescence in the establishment of gentry-led, hierarchically organized local militia networks (t'uan-lien) and mobile personal armies (hsiang-yung). Such developments of course redefined the relationship of the nonofficial elite not only to the state, but also to their neighbors and tenants, who now became their military subordinates or fell under their armed protection.

Probably more significant in the long run, however, was the greatly increased elite role in fiscal extraction, in order to finance first this local militarization and subsequently efforts at post-Taiping reconstruction (shan-hou). Extrabureaucratic elites seem to have dominated from the start the new machinery for collection of revenue from commerce (transit taxes, brokerage license fees) that proliferated at this time. Their level of involvement in collection of the more sacrosanct land tax remains a subject of debate. In some areas of the country proposals were aired, in the feng-chien tradition, for the establishment of elite-staffed collection bureaus which, if implemented, might have given rise to what James Polachek terms "a gentry oligarchy within the framework of superficial bureaucratic control."[92] In those sections of the lower Yangtze where landlord bursaries were then making their appearance, the administration does seem to have struck a bargain offering its offices in enforcing rent collection in exchange for the bursaries' assistance in collection of land tax.[93] One recent Japanese study of these phenomena thus concludes that China was fundamentally transformed in this era from a bureaucratic state into "a gentry-state which conferred on the gentry official authority for local control."[94] But such tendencies toward refeudalization seem to have been more limited than we initially thought. Most scholars would now probably concur in Kuhn's view that the gentry's new involvement in fiscal collection remained largely confined to areas outside the land tax, except insofar as they continued to exercise their customary role in the protection of local communities from the predations of formal state employees.[95]

A third and novel phase in this downward and outward shift of power came with the "local self-government" movement of the Ch'ing's final decade. Through various prescriptions for change, reformers of the day sought to fuse traditional ideals of local elite activism with newly imported Western models of grass roots democracy, ideally thereby mobilizing popular energies in pursuit of national goals. The resulting institutional innovations, local and provincial assemblies, chambers of commerce, and the like, seem to some scholars to have heralded the final breakdown in "the critical balance of power between the bureaucracy and the gentry.... The bureaucracy lost the ability to check gentry exactions from the population at large."[96] A satisfactory understanding of the significance of these years, however, would require also consideration of two simultaneous movements, the court's attempt to reverse suddenly the historic devolution of fiscal authority from the central to the provincial level, and its frenetic efforts to expand radically the role of the state as a whole, through the inauguration of unprecedented and costly reforms in education, national defense, and so on. The results of these coinciding trends included bankruptcy of provincial treasuries, the rapid introduction of new taxes, runaway inflation, and widespread popular resistance. As much as anything else, these factors contributed to the collapse of the Ch'ing and of the imperial system itself—an act in which the new local self-government agencies played a pivotal (if generally supporting) role.

How were these trends played out in the years after 1911? There is probably less solid understanding of this period than of earlier ones, although through the work of Philip A. Kuhn, R. Keith Schoppa, and others, we are beginning to get a sense of certain specific changes.[97] The conventional depiction of the Republican era as a time of sociopolitical "disintegration" is giving way to one of the continued, though uneven, development of a new political infrastructure. Despite regional fragmentation, the state (that is, the formally declared "public sector") continued the unprecedented expansion begun during the late Ch'ing reforms, and culminating in its triumph under the People's Republic. The early Republic saw rapid proliferation of quasi-official associations of emerging professional elites (lawyers, bankers, educators, journalists), and experiments at combining and recombining these at various levels to achieve political ends. With a brief hiatus after 1914, local and provincial self-government organs continued to develop. However in most areas the late 1920s and 1930s saw an attempt toward "rebureaucratization," or the replacement of local voluntarist leadership by paid state appointees. This reflected an increasingly commandist approach to social management on the part of the Nationalist government, based perhaps in equal part on its improved financial capabilities and on its turning away from ambitious social mobilization goals in the face of disappointing performance by indigenous local elites.

The above outline is tentative and leaves unanswered many key questions, several of which have recently been suggested by Philip A. Kuhn and Susan Mann Jones.[98] First, what was the significance during the late imperial period of differentiation within the elite? At least since the pathbreaking work of Chang Chung-li in the 1950s, scholars have tried to distinguish between a "lower gentry" with purely local interests and a tenuous hold on their social status, and a more secure "upper gentry" with national political connections and a "public-minded," *status quo* orientation.[99] Where was the real cleavage between these strata, how self-consciously was it expressed, and just how did the two groups interact to influence the direction of change? Second, what and how significant were spatial variations in the balance of power between the administration and the local elite, either between regions or between more or less urbanized areas within the same region?

Finally, how may we best characterize this entire process of increasingly active elite participation in public affairs? To the extent that such activism was channeled through the establishment of semi-official agencies operating on an ever-finer scale, might we in fact be observing a long-term trend toward state penetration of society, comparable to that in early modern Europe? Or did this process represent rather a withdrawal by the state, very unlike the European pattern, and perhaps dictated simply by the enormous scale of the political unit maintained in the Chinese case? In the latter case, as Kuhn and Jones suggest, we may be seeing the rise of an urbanized "middle class," gradually asserting control over itself and other segments of society, effectively independent of interference by the imperial state —a trend perhaps comparable to much *earlier* periods of European history? These musings await evaluation in the light of new research, which will surely be forthcoming in the near future.

Commerce and Capitalism

At the time of its initial experiments with Western-imitative factory industry in the late nineteenth century, China was one of the most highly commercialized preindustrial societies the world has seen. According to a recent attempt at quantification of the level of commerce, on the eve of the Opium War the annual value of commodities exchanged domestically approached four billion taels (ounces of silver), and the market claimed more than one tenth of all grain, one quarter of all cotton, and one half all raw silk produced by the empire's agriculture.[100] The origins, pace, and effects of this commercialization process have constituted some of the most enduring subjects of study for historians of Chinese society, and for many (especially those in the People's Republic) the extent to which this did or did not occasion a transition to capitalist economic relations and class formations has been and remains the single issue of overriding concern on the social history agenda.

The view that China at any time during the imperial era was made up of wholly self-sufficient villages or kinship groups is no longer accepted. At least since the Han (206 B.C.–220 A.D.) there existed some empirewide trade, not only in luxury goods but also in certain basic commodities such as salt and iron, the distribution of which was claimed as a state monopoly. Still, it seems possible to identify two eras in which the intensification of commercial activity was so pronounced as to justify their designation as "commercial revolutions." The first occurred in the late T'ang and the Sung (ninth to thirteenth centuries A.D.), and was sparked by the increasingly intense settlement of South China by ethnic Chinese. The resulting appearance of distinct economic regions fully within the pale of Chinese civilization, along with the possibility for surplus agricultural production allowed by the more fertile and climatically favored south and the construction of the Grand Canal to facilitate grain supply to the north, created the conditions for commercial capitalism which Kyoto school historians identify with China's transition to "modernity."[101] Characteristics of this first commercial revolution included a greatly expanded level of long-distance trade, including considerable overseas trade with Southeast Asia; significant improvements in transport technology (waterway construction and shipbuilding); the growth of large regional cities such as Hangchow and Soochow which for the first time took commerce as much or more than administration as the basis of their prosperity; the rise of a limited number of very wealthy merchants; new types of economic organizations (partnerships and guilds); and innovations in paper money and credit facilities. Advances made in this era, however, suffered a major setback with the loss of all China to the Mongols in 1279, and under the command economy of the early Ming (1368–1644).[102]

It was what may be called China's second commercial revolution, beginning in the declining years of the Ming and continuing through the height of the Ch'ing in the eighteenth century, which really inaugurated what a growing number of Western scholars consider "modern" China. It now seems safe to assume that although most peasant households continued to remain at least partly self-sufficient into the twentieth century, it was in this era that rural society was first significantly drawn into the market—that peasants in villages throughout the empire began to rely substantially on nonlocally produced goods for consumption and to devote at least a portion of their crop for sale or exchange. This new "circulation economy," first investigated in depth by Japanese scholars in the postwar decade and by Chinese scholars in the mid-1950s,[103] saw a substantial rise in the interregional trade of raw staples and low per-unit cost bulk commodities (grain, beans, vegetable oils), as well as a considerable degree of regional agricultural specialization (Kiangnan cotton, Hunan rice, Kiangsi ramie, Kweichow timber, and so on). Within this circulation economy merchants occupied relatively discrete niches, as financiers, brokers, warehouse owners, wholesale dealers, commission agents, itinerant buyers, and retailers of various types. Diasporas of local-origin-based merchants such as those from Shansi and Hui-chou (Anhwei) fanned out across the empire to manage, and proselytise, cultivation of commercially viable crops.

In part of course this new era represented simply a revival and further elaboration of trends initiated in the Sung, but several specific developments of the time offered incentive to a new level of commercial development. The de facto breakdown of market controls in the late Ming coincided with a government policy of offering special trading rights to merchants who agreed to ship large amounts of grain from south and central China to feed the growing number of troops stationed on China's threatened northern and northwest borders. The spread of cotton cultivation in the Yangtze delta, which accompanied the growing popular preference for cotton textiles over grasscloth and other clothing materials turned the empire's most productive riceland into a grain deficit area. The early Ch'ing exploitation of mines in the southwest likewise created a large regional congregation of nonfood producers whose needs had to be met from surpluses elsewhere. The tremendous influx of New World silver via the Spanish at Manila in the sixteenth century, and again via the British at Canton in the eighteenth, provided extra specie to finance commercial expansion.[104] And, not least, the commutation of agrarian taxes under the "single-whip" reforms considerably monetized the rural economy and stimulated production for the market.

To what extent did this constitute a real qualitative change from the levels of commercialization achieved under the Sung? The initial impression held by many observers was that the Sung inter-regional trade, while of some volume, was essentially still limited to luxury items (silks, porcelain, lacquerware, spices, medicinal herbs) entirely consumed and largely manufactured in the large regional metropolises. Thus the cities remained effectively islands in a noncommercialized agrarian hinterland. Since urban food supplies were acquired primarily via fiscal extraction in kind there was no need for rural markets and small or intermediate cities to develop until the later transformation of the Ming and Ch'ing. More recent research, however, suggests that a graduated marketing hierarchy did exist in the Sung, at least in the most commercially developed portions of the lower Yangtze.[105] Thus the progress from the first to the second commercial revolutions may have been less one of kind than of degree— a spatial diffusion of commercialization and urbanization patterns from more to less advanced regions. Moreover, as Mark Elvin points out, inter-regional trade even in staples had existed in the Sung, if only on an *ad hoc* basis, to make up temporary or accidental shortfalls. What the subsequent revolution introduced, then, was not bulk inter-regional trade itself but rather its routinization.[106] The importance of this step should not, however, be underestimated: It was precisely this routinization which prompted the empirewide diasporas of local-origin merchant groups, the establishment of permanent colonies of such merchants in major commercial cities, the development of such cities into truly cosmopolitan urban centers, and the gradual integration of the national economy.

Certain other spatial features of the intensified commerce after the sixteenth century deserve to be mentioned. First, a strong tradition of regionalism continued, and persists to this day. In a landmark work of 1977, Skinner developed the ramifications of his earlier marketing studies into a model of Chinese economic geography incorporating nine "macroregions," divided by watersheds and each internally unified by drainage systems.[107] He demonstrated, to the satisfaction of most Western scholars (and increasingly to the fascination of Japanese and Chinese as well) that these regions were the proper units of analysis for a great many of the questions of social and economic history that had previously been posed on the basis of administrative divisions, such as the province. He also showed convincingly that economic central places related to one another in hierarchies of function and magnitude which were specific to each region, rather than a single empirewide hierarchy. This suggested theoretically what empirical observation had long shown, that the bulk of commercial exchange was carried on within the parameters of a single regional system. (The related argument that a "national market" could not have existed prior to the advent of steam-powered transport finds less universal support). The inexactitude with which, in Skinner's scheme, the administrative hierarchy of cities overlay the marketing hierarchy, explains the diversity of urban social structures between cities which were preponderantly administrative or commercial in orientation. By conceiving Chinese cities in Skinner's terms, the giant pottery-kiln center of Ching-te-chen or a nonadministrative commercial port such as Hankow no longer seem inexplicable aberrations, but as much a part of the Chinese urban tradition as political centers like Chengtu or Tsinan. Finally, regions as a whole were equivalent but not equal; their levels of population, agricultural productivity, and commercial vitality differed, and shifted according to what Skinner calls "regional cycles." At any given time, various regions were experiencing various phases of their cycles; throughout the modern period, for example, the lower Yangtze remained the dominant economic region in China, until it was joined or eclipsed by industrialized Manchuria in the twentieth century. In all, Skinner has provided a rich and flexible conceptual framework for the analysis of social trends.

Even within regions, of course, some areas were more favored than others. Evelyn S. Rawski had graphically demonstrated that the differential economic, social, and even political development of given local areas under conditions of premodern transport was largely a function of communications access, specifically via waterways. Such areas as the Hsiang River valley of Hunan pioneered in high-yield agriculture and achieved high educational levels, while other equally fertile areas did not, primarily because their physiographic features favored the cost-efficient development of an export staple.[108] Often, as in the Hsiang valley, this export trade was developed primarily by extralocal merchants. What appears to have occurred throughout the empire was a complex pattern of internal colonization, whereby local-origin groups of merchants entered often very distant production areas and developed and managed the export of local commodities. Their continued hold over such trades was often insured by networks of financial dependency (via advance purchases, loans of seeds, and so on), and perhaps even more powerfully by their control over marketing facilities for that commodity at a third, central location such as Hankow or Nanking. What seems to have kept this situation from evolving into the type of systematically exploitative "internal colonialism" described for Britain by Michael Hechter was the fact that such colonizations remained commodity-specific, were undertaken by a large number of different merchant groups, and indeed might even be reciprocal.[109] (For example, Hunan's medicinal herbs exports were overseen by Kiangsi merchants, its rice exports by Hui-chou and other lower Yangtze groups, and its tea by Cantonese and Shansi merchants; yet Hunanese merchants controlled not only their own export timber trade but that of neighboring provinces.)

Before proceeding to ask whether we may find in this era the germ of an indigenous "capitalism," we need to determine what that term means for those who have sought to apply it to China. As descriptive of a socioeconomic system, the term seems to date not from Karl Marx (who according to Fernand Braudel never used it),[110] but rather from the publication around the turn of this century of V. I. Lenin's *The Development of Capitalism in Russia* (1899) and Werner Sombart's *Der moderne Kapitalismus* (1902). The key difference between its usage in these two works hinges on whether capitalism implies merely a system of ownership and investment (Sombart), or the specific application of that system to processes of production (Lenin). In other words, is commercial capitalism truly "capitalism"? According to Werner Sombart and subsequent writers like Max Weber, N. S. B. Gras, and Fernand Braudel, it is. If capitalism means simply the private financing of large-scale shipments of commodities, or more precisely the development of sophisticated capital-accumulation mechanisms to arrange such financing, then it certainly existed in China by at least the Sung. (This is the position taken by Japanese non-Marxist scholars such as Miyazaki Ichisada.) Even within the context of this broad definition of capitalism, however, we may choose to introduce further prerequisites, such as widespread monetization of the economy (à la Weber) or the deliberate effort at control of the open market

(Braudel). With these further stipulations, it seems more justifiable to associate capitalism with China's second commercial revolution than with its first.

Chinese historians themselves first became concerned with this issue during the "social history debate" of the late 1920s and 1930s. Those who at that time saw modern China as essentially capitalist—those who followed the Trotskyite line—argued their case of the basis of the free alienability of land, the contractual and exclusively economic nexus of landlord-tenant relations, the pervasiveness of the money economy, the replacement of rural self-sufficiency by dependency on urban centers, and the dominant role of commercial capital in agriculture.[111] As discussed above, however, the Stalinist line won out, and thus in the canonical work "The Chinese Revolution and the Chinese Communist Party," issued under Mao's signature in 1939, China was described as "semi-colonial" and "semi-feudal," with no mention made of capitalism.

In the decade or so thereafter, Chinese Marxist historians began to revise this view. In part it seems this was based on a new appreciation of Lenin's 1899 model of how capitalism develops (Lenin's work was published in Chinese translation only in 1959, but was well known by reputation before that time). Although he followed Marx in seeing the possibility of simultaneous existence of different economic formations, Lenin drew a clear theoretical distinction between a "commodity economy" (distinguished by a high level of commercialization) and a true "capitalist economy" (which comes into existence only after there has been a transformation in the relationships of production, specifically via the emergence of large handicraft workshops).[112] Through their growing appreciation of Lenin's thought, Chinese Marxists came gradually to the view of capitalism they hold today, succinctly defined by Y. C. Wang as follows: "a production system consisting of the capitalist and free wage earner in which the former hires the latter on a contract basis to produce commodities for sale and to make a profit."[113]

Having thus more rigorously defined "capitalism," however, these same historians now began to search for evidences of it in their own past. The continued rejection of a peculiar, stagnant Asiatic mode of production and the acceptance of Stalinist unilinearism meant that late imperial China needed to be located at some point along the slave society-feudal-capitalist time line. At the same time, the national pride of "New China" suggested (and new historical research confirmed) that preindustrial China must have achieved a stage of development more comparable with Europe than the simple designation "feudal" would allow. Here the Marxist-Leninist idea of the germination of new forms within the old came to the rescue. Thus in the revised edition of "The Chinese Revolution" included in his 1951 *Selected Works* Mao inserted the sentence: "As China's feudal society had developed a commodity economy (*shang-p'in ching-chi*), and so carried within itself the seeds of capitalism (*tzu-pen-chu-i meng-ya*), China would of herself have developed slowly into a capitalist society even without the impact of foreign capitalism."[114]

Throughout the mid-1950s an enormous number of scholarly studies, of varying quality, were produced in the People's Republic identifying cases of these seeds or "sprouts" of Chinese capitalism throughout the late imperial period, but most often in conjunction with the intensification of commerce at the end of the Ming. The debate was quashed (and many of the debaters personally attacked) in the wake of the Anti-Rightist Campaign of 1957, when it was asserted that emphasis on incipient capitalism tended to obscure the evils of feudal landlords and foreign imperialists, and to downplay the necessity of Party-led class struggle. But in the years since Mao's death and the arrest of the Gang of Four the issue has been pointedly revived, and scores of new studies based in many cases on previously untouched archival materials have highlighted once again the deeply transformative character of the period from the late sixteenth through the mid-eighteenth century.[115]

In both of its phases the debate left us with detailed case studies, including ones of pottery kilns in Kiangsi, ironware factories in Foshan (near Canton), distilleries and soy-sauce factories in Shangtung, paper mills in Shansi, salt mines in Szechwan, coal pits near Peking, and, most commonly, the lower Yangtze silk and cotton textile industries and the copper mines of the southwest. In each of these areas, the era of "sprouts" saw a movement beyond the simple commodity economy, dominated by cottage industry and a few larger government enterprises, into a stage of large-scale private entrepreneurship. The new entrepreneurs took advantage of the expanding domestic market, adopting detailed capital accounting procedures in their quest for profits and growth. They were drawn from the ranks of both managerial landlords and the old merchant class, which had heretofore shown little interest in the sphere of production. Where additional capital was required, sophisticated instruments for financing and refinancing were developed, including new types of partnership agreements and the issuance of stock. In both mining and handicraft enterprises capitalist relations of production came into being, with hired labor freely contracted for fixed periods of time, at wage rates determined by levels of skill, difficulty of the task, and ultimately labor supply, and wage payments calculated in terms of either time or output. In the largest workshops and mines hundreds or even thousands of workers might be employed. In certain leading areas such as the Sungkiang cotton workshops a highly refined division of labor began to appear, combining for example spinners, weavers, calendarers, and dyers under a single capitalist.

A number of government policies of the early Ch'ing, suggested by the need for reconstruction of the economy after the late Ming rebellions, facilitated these changes in the relationships of production. The abolition in 1645 of hereditary status distinctions for certain artisan groups and the decreased use after the 1650s of bond-servant labor in imperial silk and pottery factories stimulated the development of free labor. The incremental repeal of the Ming ban on private mining and state encouragement of entrepreneurial efforts sparked a nationwide boom in this area. And the gradual commutation of handicraft, especially textile, taxes in kind redirected energies toward production for the expanding market.[116]

This entire set of late Ming-early Ch'ing changes culminated in the unprecedented level of material prosperity achieved in the mid-eighteenth century, and in what Chinese historians point to as a major social transformation. This is seen as the destruction of the "natural economy" in selected advanced areas of the country, and in an increased "social division of labor" (that is, the rise of nonagrarian classes). There seems to have been a substantial increase in China's free labor force, or "semi-proletariat," remarkably mobile both occupationally and geographically. Large numbers of rootless workers migrated to take advantage of new opportunities, such as the opening of new mines, and congregated to await hire at the large labor markets along major trade routes.[117] In the cities, it is argued, a distinct urban culture and urban population (shih-min) appeared, with merchants, entrepreneurs, urbanized literati, skilled artisans, and casual laborers divided by class interests yet united in their antagonism to the agrarian-based feudal order. The result was a wave of urban collective action in the late Ming (strikes, riots, market disturbances), which was sublimated in the Ch'ing by a combination of economic upturn, social legislation, and more effective government suppression.[118]

Obviously this Chinese historiography follows rather closely the scheme of capitalist development prescribed by Lenin, and indeed it has done so more self-consciously with the passage of time. Some in the West have reacted by castigating the entire project as slavish adherence to a model fundamentally inappropriate to China's historical experience.[119] Yet in its continued diversity of opinion on specifics, its increasing methodological sophistication, and above all its energetic pursuit of new sources, the debate over sprouts of capitalism has contributed incalculably to knowledge of the details of Chinese social history. Indeed, there can be little doubt at this point of the general validity of the conclusions its participants have arrived at regarding the direction of change.

The question then becomes, why did such a promising set of conditions fail to develop into a full-fledged industrial capitalism of the Western type? The remarkable flexibility in ideology and creativity in economic organization which research of the past several decades has revealed as characteristic of the late imperial period make it increasingly difficult to accept the arguments of "traditional society" theorists like Max Weber and Marion J. Levy that China was culturally ill-equipped for the transition to capitalism. Political explanations like the bureaucratic domination seen, for example, by Etienne Balazs and Hatano Yoshihiro, and economic-demographic factors such as those emphasized by Mark Elvin and Gilbert Rozman remain potentially more convincing.[120] In particular, Elvin's notion of a "high-level equilibrium trap"—essentially that the existing human-powered technology had reached such a peak of refinement, and the surplus product derived from such technology so evenly distributed and absorbed by population growth, that the overhead costs of technological revolution proved too heavy to encourage experimentation—has attracted considerable support among Western scholars.

Over the past several decades Chinese historians too have wrestled with this question, but never more strenuously than in the years since 1981, when a concerted historiographic effort has been exerted to explain the prolonged continuation (ch'ang-ch'i yen-hsu) of Chinese feudalism and the corresponding retarded development (fa-chan huanman) of indigenous capitalism.[121] In the voluminous outpouring of literature on this subject two general types of causes have been identified: those inherent in the economic structure and those attributable to the state. Among the former, several scholars have found the continued domination by "feudal" economic organizations like guilds (monopolistic groups which served as instruments of market domination directly for a few centrally placed brokers and indirectly for the state), and lineages (which restricted members' economic activities to within the patriarchically controlled group, and limited contact with the market). Others have questioned the extent to which commercial capital was ever effectively transformed into production of industrial capital, and argued that the great majority of profits from trade and from capitalist-style agriculture were actually turned back into "feudal" investments: rental properties, usury, purchase of gentry ranks, and education in pursuit of bureaucratic careers. Where capitalist agriculture had developed, there was a built-in tendency for "refeudalization," as hired laborers were promoted into tenant status and successful managerial landlords opted to become urbanized rentiers. The exploitative rent system and innovations in the extraction of surplus such as rent deposits discouraged capital improvements by tenants and restricted their capacity to interact with the market. There remains a lively debate over whether the minute scale of Chinese agriculture, resulting not from class contradictions but primarily from fragmenting inheritance practices, in itself constituted an obstacle to development. In any case, the "small producer economy," in which requirements of subsistence had forged an intimate link between peasant agriculture and cottage industry, continued to produce commodities at such low cost as to inhibit the further development of protocapitalist handicraft workshops. In general, it is argued that the "special features" of Chinese feudalism—its greater commercial development and lower degree of social and political rigidity than in Europe—obscured the "contradictions" between itself and bourgeois capitalism, and so forestalled its destruction by the latter.[122]

Ever more prominently, however, it is the imperial state which is assigned the blame for capitalism's retarded development. We are reminded of the state's often enunciated agrarian fundamentalist principles, and such specific antimarket policies as the monopolization of commercial enterprises through the institution of "imperial merchants" (huang-shang). The growing trend toward shifting the state's fiscal burden from agriculture to trade is seen not only as inhibiting in its effect but also as deliberatively punitive in intent. The imposition of state procurement quotas at below market prices is seen as quashing entrepreneurial initiative, especially in the mining sector.[123] Most intriguing is the emphasis accorded to the state's conscientious efforts at maintenance of the "small producer economy." In this view the officially sponsored programs of resettlement in areas devastated by the late Ming rebellions, reclamation of marshland and clearance of highlands, tax remissions in newly settled and famine-stricken areas, and dissemination of new agricultural and handicraft techniques, all pointed in the same, *retrogressive* direction: the maintenance of the individual peasant household as the foundation of the national economy.

There are, it seems to me, a number of important implications in this line of thought. Some of its proponents are remarkably frank about the fact that their view of the "autocratic" state as a major independent actor in socioeconomic developmental processes runs counter to literal Marxist assumptions of politics as superstructure. Moreover, the view of "autocracy" thus advanced is remarkably close to the oriental "despotism" theories formally denounced but obviously of increasing interest to recent Chinese writers (the Chinese *ch'uan-chih-chu-i* is now usually used to translate both terms). It is impossible to miss the convergence with Wittfogel's theory of cyclical crises of the following passage by Hong Huanchun:

> After each peasant uprising, the small peasant economy was rehabilitated [by the state] and the social forces of production were improved while the feudal system remained intact. The changes of dynasties in Chinese history mark the cycle of destruction and rehabilitation. This cyclical crisis of the rural economy kept China's feudal small peasant economy at a low level for ages and precluded steady growth of the forces of production.[124]

Western theorists of Chinese society from Weber to Wittfogel to Elvin, of course, have regularly labeled the imperial (or at least late imperial) era one of stagnation. The specific translation for this term (*t'ing-chih*) appeared in the sprouts of capitalism debate of the 1950s but has been scrupulously avoided in the reopened debate of recent years. The concept nevertheless lurks in the background, so that, for example, Japanese scholars who had sought to expunge it from their own sinological work as an unfortunate remnant of prewar expansionist rhetoric, now find themselves befuddled by its reemergence among Chinese themselves![125]

Initial Chinese researches into the sprouts of capitalism had suggested that as early as the sixteenth century these developments had given birth to an indigenous bourgeoisie, and that such intellectual and political movements as the Tung-lin and the Fu-she of the late Ming were reflections of the aspirations of this class. Current scholarship, both in the West and in China, has come to a fairly universal rejection of this view.[126] For the Chinese it remains an open question whether the Ming-Ch'ing transition did or did not see the rise of an urban class (shih-min), as earlier writers argued, but they harbor no doubt that this was not a true bourgeoisie. The latter is now seen as contingent upon the development of industrial capitalism, and its emergence therefore only in the years around the turn of this century. (Note that the Chinese term for bourgeoisie, tzu-ch'an-chieh-chi, derives not from burg but from property or capital.) Related to this had been a growing discomfort with Mao's 1939 distinction between "national capitalists," whose investments in production were supposedly drawn from profits accrued in the domestic trade, and "compradore capitalists," whose property derived from their treasonous collaboration in imperialist penetration. It is now recognized in China, as in the West, that virtually all modern entrepreneurs must have owed their wealth at least in part to some prior relationship with the foreign trade, and that the degree of nationalism and anti-imperialism displayed by individual Chinese businessmen was often a function of more immediate economic interests than those attributable to their class backgrounds.

One fallout of this revisionist perspective has been that, no matter how ideologically convenient it may have been to portray the events of 1911 as a "bourgeois revolution" preparing the way for the subsequent socialist revolution of 1949, it is simply no longer possible for Chinese historians to make that claim. As Western scholars such as Marie-Claire Bergère have long pointed out, the Chinese bourgeoisie in the early twentieth century was as yet too weak to have been anything more than a passive participant in such a momentous political event. More detailed work in recent years, including that of Bergère and of Parks Coble, has further revealed the untenability of the long-popular Trotskyite view that the Kuomintang era represented the political triumph of the Chinese bourgeoisie; instead, the bureaucratic capitalism of the Kuomintang is now seen as systematic statist repression and exploitation of the emerging entrepreneurial class.[127]

There have been, in other words, some very hopeful trends in recent years. Increased communication between scholars in the People's Republic and the West (and in Japan), and greater ideological flexibility on all sides have begun to yield not only patterns of reciprocal influence,[128] but also an emerging view of China's socioeconomic development that appears more sophisticated, less doctrinaire, and freer from ethnocentric bias than visions held in the past.

Conclusion

What we today would recognize as "social history" of modern China began in the 1920s and 1930s in Japan, where it has continued to develop at a very high level, and in China itself, where its progress has been more uneven. Despite the fact that both these traditions had roots in European social thought, serious study of modern Chinese social history in the West can hardly be dated to any time earlier than the 1950s, and in the United States probably a decade later. The Japanese, Chinese, and Western approaches have evolved with considerable independence from one another. This kind of isolation, of course, has its strengths as well as its weaknesses—it allows the working out of separate problematics which, when eventually compared, can invite useful reexamination of premises and priorities. One such shock of recognition came with the American discovery of Japanese sinology in the late 1960s, a process that is still underway. A second has only just begun, with the renaissance of historical scholarship in the People's Republic and new openings for cross-fertilization with outsiders from Japan and the West. As I have indicated at several points in this essay, the early results have been encouraging. It certainly appears we are entering an era of scholarship that promises unprecedented excitement and productivity.

What specific directions this new scholarship will take cannot be predicted at this time. Let me, however, express a hope that they will include a move away from the attempt to fit China into categories derived from the European historical experience. "Feudalism" and "capitalism" are probably an improvement over "tradition" and "modernity"—the debates over their application have proven quite useful as points of entry into the realities of the Chinese past—but the evidence suggests that, as general constructs, they either do not work or conceal more than they reveal. This is perhaps nowhere better seen than in the predicament of T'ao Hsi-sheng, an intelligent historian with a sophisticated understanding of both Asia and the West, who found himself forced to declare virtually all of China's recorded history a "transitional age" suspended between the two Marxist social formations![129] We have looked above at some attempts to break out of this unilinear, Eurocentric conceptualization of social development—"Oriental despotism" and (in the hands of some) kyōdōtai analysis—but with their implications of stagnation these have proven on the whole even less successful as tools of historical analysis than the more familiar constructs. Very recently we have begun to see analyses in areas such as demography, family history, popular culture, and collective action which, as they have done in Western social history, seem to break free from inherited categories. With luck these trends in the years to come will lead us to develop the new vocabulary and models of social change that modern Chinese history currently needs.

NOTES

1. Chung-li Chang, *The Chinese Gentry: Studies on their Role in Nineteenth-Century Chinese Society* (Seattle: University of Washington Press, 1955); Ping-ti Ho, *The Ladder of Success in Imperial China: Aspects of Social Mobility, 1368–1911* (New York: Columbia University Press, 1962). Gilbert Rozman has recently called for a revival of this sort of quantitative historical analysis, arguing that much of the available data is susceptible to testing for reliability; see his *Population and Marketing Settlements in Ch'ing China* (Cambridge: Cambridge University Press, 1982). A similar revival of empire-wide quantitative analysis has appeared in the work of Chinese historians, drawing data from newly opened sections of the Ming-Ch'ing Archives, Peking; see for example Liu Yung-ch'eng, "Chi'ing-tai ch'ien-ch'i te nung-yeh tsu-tien kuan-hsi" (Tenancy relations in the early Ch'ing), *Ch'ing-shih lun-ts'ung* (Peking), no. 2 (1980): 56–88.

2. Jonathan Spence, *The Death of Woman Wang* (New York: Viking Press, 1978). If we include in this genre oral histories of living individuals, we can add Ida Pruitt's *A Daughter of Han* (New Haven: Yale University Press, 1945), and Margery Wolf's *The House of Lim* (New York: Appleton-Century-Crofts, 1968).

3. Fei-ling Davis, *Primitive Revolutionaries of China* (Honolulu: University of Hawaii Press, 1977); R. Bin Wong, "Food Riots in the Qing Dynasty," *Journal of Asian Studies* 41 (August 1982): 767–88.

4. Paul A. Cohen, *Discovering History in China* (New York: Columbia University Press, 1984). This important historiographic survey came to my attention too late to have substantially influenced the writing of this chapter, but it is obvious that Professor Cohen and I share many views on the development of the field.

5. For representative recent studies in the area of demography, see the works listed in the bibliography by Averill, Barclay, Cartier, Lee, Perdue, and Will. On family history, see Lee and Eng, Wolf and Huang, and Patricia Ebrey, ed., "Symposium on Family Life in Late Traditional China," *Modern China* 10 (October 1984): 379–459. On folk religion, see Wolf (1974), Overmyer, and a forthcoming conference volume on orthodoxy and heterodoxy edited by Kwang-Ching Liu. On popular culture, see Rawski (1979), Link, K. C. Chang, and the conference volume edited by David Johnson, Andrew J. Nathan, and Evelyn S. Rawski, *Popular Culture in Late Imperial China: Diversity and Integration* (Berkeley: University of California Press, 1985). Among numerous recent works on popular movements see those by Naquin, Perry, and David Strand and Richard Wiener, "Social Movements and Political Discourse in 1920s Peking: An Analysis of the Tramway Riot of October 27, 1929," in *Political Leadership and Social Change at the Local Level in China from 1850 to the Present: Select Papers from the Center for Far Eastern Studies*, ed. Susan Mann Jones (Chicago: University of Chicago, 1978–1979), 3:137–80.

6. Max Weber, *The Religion of China* (Glencoe, Ill.: Free Press, 1951).

7. A representative (and brilliant) example of modernization theory as applied to China is Marion J. Levy, Jr., "Contrasting Factors in the Modernization of Japan and China," *Economic Development and Cultural Change* 2 (1953): 161–97.

8. See, for example, John K. Fairbank, *China: The People's Middle Kingdom and the U.S.A.* (Cambridge, Mass.: Harvard University Press, 1967); Ssu-yu Teng and John K. Fairbank, *China's Response to the West* (Cambridge, Mass.: Harvard University Press,

1954). An invaluable source on Fairbank's own perspective and on the origins of the American China curriculum as a whole is his autobiography, *Chinabound* (New York: Harper & Row, 1982).

9. Karl Marx, "Revolution in China and in Europe," in *Marx on China*, ed. Dona Torr (London: Lawrence & Wishart, 1951), 2–3.

10. Frances Moulder, *Japan, China, and the Modern World Economy* (Cambridge: Cambridge University Press, 1977). An important example of Vietnam-era radicalism is Joseph Esherick, "Harvard on China: The Apologetics of Imperialism," *Bulletin of Concerned Asian Scholars* (1973), unpaginated.

11. See Joshua A. Fogel, ed., *Naitō Konan and the Development of the Conception of Modernity in Chinese History*, special issue of *Chinese Studies in History* (Fall 1983); Hisayuki Miyakawa, "An Outline of the Naitō Hypothesis and its Effects on Japanese Studies of China," *Far Eastern Quarterly* 14 (August 1955): 533–53. For the political implications of Naitō's work, see Joshua A. Fogel, *Politics and Sinology: The Case of Naitō Konan (1866–1934)* (Cambridge, Mass.: Harvard University Press, 1984).

12. Naitō's disciple and successor at Kyoto, Miyazaki Ichisada, sought to overcome this difficulty by postulating a most modern age (*saikinsei*), which he saw opening in Europe with the industrial revolution and in China with the Revolution of 1911. See Miyazaki, *Tōyōteki kinsei* (The oriental modern age) (Kyoto: Kyōiku taimususha, 1950).

13. Frederic Wakeman, Jr., "Introduction: The Evolution of Local Control in Late Imperial China," in *Conflict and Control in Late Imperial China*, ed. Frederic Wakeman, Jr., and Carolyn Grant (Berkeley: University of California Press, 1975), 2.

14. The use of this term is proposed, for example, in Paul S. Ropp, *Dissent in Early Modern China: Ju-lin wai-shih and Ch'ing Social Criticism* (Ann Arbor: University of Michigan Press, 1981).

15. Frederic Wakeman, Jr., "Rebellion and Revolution: The Study of Popular Movements in Chinese History," *Journal of Asian Studies* 36 (February 1977): 201–37.

16. See John L. Buck, *Chinese Farm Economy* (Chicago: University of Chicago Press, 1930); idem, *Land Utilization in China* (Chicago: University of Chicago Press, 1937); R. H. Tawney, *Land and Labor in China* (London: G. Allen & Unwin, 1932); Fei Hsiao-t'ung, *Peasant Life in China* (London: Routledge & Kegan Paul, 1939); and Institute of Pacific Relations, ed., *Agrarian China* (Chicago: University of Chicago Press, 1938).

17. Sun Shao-tsun, "Land Ownership and its Concentration in China," in Institute of Pacific Relations, 2.

18. Fei, *Peasant Life in China*, 56–63.

19. See H. Franz Schurmann, "Traditional Property Concepts in China," *Far Eastern Quarterly* 15 (August 1956): 507–16.

20. Recent studies on this subject include Han Heng-yu, "Shih-lun Ch'ing-tai ch'ien-ch'i tien-nung yung-tien-ch'uan te yu-lei chi ch'i hsing-chih" (On the origins and nature of permanent tenancy rights in the early Ch'ing), *Ch'ing-shih lunts'ung* (Peking), no. 1 (1979): 37–53; Lin Hsiang-jui, "Fu-chien yung-tien-ch'uan ch'eng-yin te ch'u-pu k'ao-ch'a" (Preliminary inquiry into the origins of permanent tenancy rights in Fukien), *Chung-kuo-shih yen-chiu* (1982.4): 62–74; and the works of Fujii Hiroshi and Kusano Yasushi summarized in Wada Masahiro (trans. Fogel), "Ming-Ch'ing Studies in Japan, 1980," *Ch'ing-shih wen-t'i* 4 (December 1982): 52–61. The classic discussion in English appears in Fei, *Peasant Life in China*, 178–86.

21. For an overview of this debate, see Kusano Yasushi, "Daitochi shoyu to tenkosei no tenkai" (The development of large landholdings and the tenancy system), in *Sekai rekishi* (World history), comp. Iwanami Koza (Tokyo: Iwanami Koza, 1970), esp. 9:345–50. Briefer summaries in English may be found in Goto Kimpei, "Postwar Japanese Studies on Chinese Social and Economic History," *Monumenta Serica* 17 (1959): 377–78 and 400–3; and in Wakeman, "Rebellion and Revolution," 202, 212.

22. Miyazaki, *Tōyō teki kinsei*, 51–53.

23. See especially Sudō Yoshiyuki, *Chūgoku tochi seido shi kenkyū* (Studies in the history of Chinese land tenure systems) (Tokyo: Tōyō bunko, 1954); Mark Elvin, *The Pattern of the Chinese Past* (Stanford: Stanford University Press, 1973), chap. 6.

24. Fu I-ling, *Ming-Ch'ing nung-ts'un she-hui ching-chi* (Rural society and economy in the Ming and Ch'ing) (Peking: San-lien shu-tien, 1961). See also Elvin, *Pattern*, chap. 15; Mi-chu Wiens, "Lord and Peasant: The Sixteenth to the Eighteenth Centuries," *Modern China* 6 (January 1980): 3–39.

25. Wu Liang-k'ai, "Ch'ing-tai Ch'ien-lung shih-ch'i nung-yeh ching-chi kuan-hsi te yen-pien he fa-chan" (Change and development in agrarian economic relations during the Ch'ien-lung reign of the Ch'ing), *Ch'ing-shih lun-ts'ung* (Peking), no. 1 (1979): 5–36; Liu Yung-ch'eng, "Lun Ch'ing-tai ch'ien-ch'i nung-yeh ku-yung lao-tung te hsing-chih" (The nature of agrarian hired labor during the early Ch'ing), *Ch'ing-shih yen-chiu chi* (Peking: Chung-kuo jen-min ta-hsueh ch'u-pan-she), no. 1 (1980): 91–112.

26. For a different attempt at depiction of zonal variation, see Frederic Wakeman, Jr., *The Fall of Imperial China*, (New York: Free Press, 1975), chap. 1.

27. Land tenure data for areas of North China appear in Martin C. Yang, *A Chinese Village: Taitou, Shantung Province* (New York: Columbia University Press, 1945); Ramon H. Myers, *The Chinese Peasant Economy: Agricultural Development in Hopei and Shantung, 1890–1949* (Cambridge, Mass.: Harvard University Press, 1970); Jing Su and Lo Lun (trans. by Endymion Wilkinson), *Landlord and Labor in China: Case Studies from Shandong* (Cambridge, Mass.: Harvard University Press, 1978); William Hinton, *Fanshen* (New York: Vintage, 1966), chap. 1; Elizabeth Perry, *Rebels and Revolutionaries in North China, 1845–1945* (Stanford: Stanford University Press, 1980), chap. 1; and Susan Naquin, *Shantung Rebellion: The Wang Lun Rebellion of 1774* (New Haven: Yale University Press, 1976), chap. 1. Chinawide statistical analyses drawn upon here and in the following pages are Buck, *Chinese Farm Economy*, which presents survey data from 1921 to 1925, and Liu Yung-ch'eng, "Tsu-tien kuan-hsi," which computes data culled from nearly 900 eighteenth-century legal cases.

28. Perry, *Rebels and Revolutionaries*, 26; Hinton, *Fanshen*, 28.

29. Jing and Lo, *Landlord and Labor*.

30. Tadashi Fukutake, "Village Life in Central China," in his *Asian Rural Society* (Tokyo: University of Tokyo Press, 1967), 82; Buck, *Chinese Farm Economy*, 146.

31. David Faure, "The Rural Economy of Kiangsu Province, 1870–1911" *Journal of the Institute of Chinese Studies* (Hong Kong) 9 (1978): 365–471.

32. Fei, *Peasant Life in China*, 180–81.

33. Fukutake, "Village Life," 83.

34. See especially Liu Yao, "T'ai-p'ing t'ien-kuo shih-pai hou Chiang-nan nung-ts'un ching-chi pien-hua te ts'ai-t'an-t'ao" (A reexamination of changes in the

Kiangnan rural economy in the post-Taiping period), *Li-shih yen-chiu* (1982.3): 105–20.

35. Liu Yung-ch'eng, "Tsu-tien kuan-hsi," 87.

36. Yuji Muramatsu's numerous Japanese-language studies on this subject are summarized in his "A Documentary Study of Chinese Landlordism in Late Ch'ing and Early Republican Kiangnan," *Bulletin of the School of Oriental and African Studies* 29 (1966): 566–99. For a slightly different perspective, see Frank Lojewski, "The Soochow Bursaries: Rent Management during the Late Ch'ing," *Ch-ing-shih wen-t'i* 4 (June 1980): 43–65.

37. Han-seng Ch'en, *Landlord and Peasant in China* [original title: *Agrarian Problems in Southernmost China*] (New York: International Publishers, 1936), viii.

38. Evelyn S. Rawski, *Agricultural Change and the Peasant Economy of South China* (Cambridge, Mass.: Harvard University Press, 1972), 14–27.

39. Han-seng Ch'en, *Landlord and Peasant*, 31–34; Hinton, *Fanshen*, 28. On clan estates in the lower Yangtze, see Denis Twitchett, "The Fan Clan's Charitable Estate, 1050–1760," in *Confucianism in Action*, ed. David Nivison and Arthur F. Wright (Stanford: Stanford University Press, 1959), 97–133; and Jerry Dennerline, "The New Hua Charitable Estate and Local Level Leadership in Wuxi County at the End of the Qing," in *Select Papers from the Center for Far Eastern Studies*, ed. Tang Tsou (Chicago: University of Chicago, 1979–1980), 4:19–70.

40. Han-seng Ch'en, *Landlord and Peasant*, ix, 27–30. For a demonstration of the way one South China lineage extended its hold over members even as far away as London's Chinatown, see James L. Watson, *Emigration and the Chinese Lineage* (Berkeley: University of California Press, 1975).

41. On late-settled lowland areas: Hilary Beattie, *Land and Lineage in China* (Cambridge: Cambridge University Press, 1979); Johanna Meskill, *A Chinese Pioneer Family* (Princeton: Princeton University Press, 1979); Rawski, *Agricultural Change*, chap. 5; and Peter C. Perdue, "Population Growth, Agricultural Development, and Social Conflict in Hunan, 1500–1850," Ph.D. diss., Harvard University, 1981. On highland areas: Rawski, "Agricultural Development in the Han River Highlands," *Ch'ing-shih wen-t'i* 3 (November 1975): 63–81; Steven Averill, "The Shed People and the Opening of the Yangzi Highlands," *Modern China* 9 (January 1983): 84–126; and Fu I-ling, "Capitalism in Chinese Agriculture," *Modern China* 6 (July 1980): 311–16.

42. Fu, "Capitalism," 314.

43. On this institution generally, see Chu Min-chiu, "Rent Deposit and its Tendency to Increase," in Institute of Pacific Relations, 94–96. For its high incidence in later-settled areas, see Rawski, *Agricultural Change*, 122–26; Averill, "Shed People," 117; and Liu Yung-ch'eng, "Tsu-tien kuan-hsi," 67.

44. Elvin, *Pattern*, 69. Wakeman, *Fall*, 6–8, follows this view.

45. Fang Hsing, "Lun Ch'ing-tai ch'ien-ch'i ti-chu ching-chi te fa-chan" (On the development of the early Ch'ing landlord economy) *Chung-kuo-shih yen-chiu* (1983.2): 88.

46. These debates are described in Benjamin Schwartz, "A Marxist Controversy on China," *Far Eastern Quarterly* 13 (February 1954): 143–53; Karl A. Wittfogel, "The Marxist View of China," *China Quarterly*, no. 11 (July–September 1962) and no. 12 (October–December 1962): 1–20, 154–69; and at greater length in Arif Dirlik, *Revolution and History: The Origins of Marxist Historiography in China* (Berkeley: University of

California Press, 1978).

47. Schwartz, "Marxist View," 150.

48. Liu Yung-ch'eng, "Nung-yeh ku-yung lao-tung," 91–112.

49. See for example Ma K'e-yao, "Ying ju-ho li-chieh Hsi-O feng-chien-hua wen-t'i" (How to interpret the feudalization of Western Europe), Li-shih yen-chiu (1982.4): 37–43; and P'ang Cho-heng, "Hsi-O feng-chien she-hui yen-hsu shih-chien chiao-t'uan te ken-pen yuan-yin" (Basic reasons for the relatively brief duration of feudalism in Western Europe), Li-shih yen-chiu 1 (1983): 107–21.

50. Martin Yang, A Chinese Village, 143–44.

51. Arthur H. Smith, Village Life in China, 1898 (reprinted, New York: Haskell House, 1968). For a more recent analysis of village self-defense structures see Perry, Rebels and Revolutionaries, chap. 3.

52. Among Fei's most important works are his village studies Peasant Life in China and (with Chang Chih-i) Earthbound China (Chicago: University of Chicago Press, 1945); his article "Peasantry and Gentry," American Journal of Sociology 52 (July 1946): 1–17; and his popularized but theoretically ambitious Hsiang-t'u Chung-kuo (Rural China), (Shanghai: Kuan-ch'a-she, 1948). An outstanding recent biography is David Arkush, Fei Xiaotong and Sociology in Revolutionary China (Cambridge, Mass.: Harvard University Press, 1981).

53. Fei, Peasant Life in China, 184–85.

54. Fei, Hsiang-t'u Chung-kuo, esp. chaps. 1 and 12.

55. Note that in Japan, unlike the West, Marx and Weber are most often seen as complementary rather than antithetical; see Takeshi Ishida, "A Current Japanese View of Max Weber," The Developing Economies 4 (September 1966): 349–66.

56. See for example Ōtsuka Hisao, "Kyōdōtai no kiso riron" (The basic theory of kyōdōtai), in his Ōtsuka Hisao chōsakushu (Collected works of Otsuka Hisao), (Tokyo: Iwanami shoten, 1970), 7:6–8; and the entry on "Sonraku kyōdōtai" in Ajia rekishi jiten (Encyclopedia of Asian History), comp. Heibonsha (Tokyo: Heibonsha, 1960), 5:413–18. While the same term (read kung-t'ung-t'i) occasionally appears in modern Chinese writing as a translation for "community," it has developed no independent theoretical significance in China.

57. The following discussion is formed by Hatada Takashi, Chūgoku noson to kyōdōtai riron (Chinese villages and the theory of kyōdōtai), (Tokyo: Iwanami shoten, 1973), esp. chap. 2, and by Noriko Kamachi, John K. Fairbank, and Chuzo Ichiko, Japanese Studies of Modern China since 1953 (Cambridge: Harvard University Press, 1975), xxiii–xxv and passim. My understanding of kyōdōtai and its history in Japanese scholarship also owes a great deal to many conversations over the years with Joshua A. Fogel.

58. Niida Noboru, "Chūgoku no dōzoku mata wa sonraku no tochi shoyu mondai" (The problem of landowning by lineages and villages in China), in his Chūgoku hōseishi kenkyū (Studies in Chinese legal history) (Tokyo: University of Tokyo Press, 1962); Hisao Ōtsuka, "Max Weber's View of Asian Society," The Developing Economies 4 (September 1966): 281; Tadashi Fukutake, "The Chinese Village and the Japanese Village," in his Asian Rural Society, esp. 19–25.

59. Imahori Seiji, Chūgoku no shakai kōzō (Chinese social structure), (Tokyo: Yūhi kaku, 1953), esp. chap. 2.

60. Eric R. Wolf, "Closed Corporate Communities in Mesoamerica and Java,"

Southwestern Journal of Anthropology 13 (Spring 1957): 1–18; E. P. Thompson, "The Moral Economy of the English Crowd in the Eighteenth Century," *Past and Present*, no. 50 (February 1971): 76–136; James C. Scott, *The Moral Economy of the Peasant* (New Haven: Yale University Press, 1976). For a contrasting view see Samuel L. Popkin, *The Rational Peasant: The Political Economy of Rural Society in Vietnam* (Berkeley: University of California Press, 1979).

61. Alexander Woodside, *Community and Revolution in Modern Vietnam* (Boston: Houghton Mifflin, 1976); Frances Fitzgerald, *Fire in the Lake: The Vietnamese and the Americans in Vietnam* (Boston: Atlantic-Little Brown, 1972).

62. Ralph Thaxton, *China Turned Rightside Up: Revolutionary Legitimacy in the Peasant World* (New Haven: Yale University Press, 1983). For an implicit refutation of the applicability of these ideas to China, see Perry, *Rebels and Revolutionaries*; for an explicit refutation, see James Polachek, "The Moral Economy of the Kiangsi Soviet (1928–1934)," *Journal of Asian Studies* 42 (August 1983): 805–30.

63. G. William Skinner, "Chinese Peasants and the Closed Community: An Open and Shut Case?" *Comparative Studies in Society and History* 13 (July 1971): 270–81.

64. G. William Skinner, "Marketing and Social Structure in Rural China," *Journal of Asian Studies* 24 (November 1964–May 1965): 3–43, 195–228, 363–99. See also C. K. Yang, *A North China Local Market Economy* (New York: Institute of Pacific Relations, 1944 [mimeo]); Martin Yang, *A Chinese Village*; August Lösch, *The Economics of Location* (New Haven: Yale University Press, 1954).

65. Philip A. Kuhn, *Rebellion and its Enemies in Late Imperial China* (Cambridge, Mass.: Harvard University Press, 1970), 76–92; Winston Hsieh, "Peasant Insurrection and the Marketing Hierarchy in the Canton Delta, 1911–1912," in *The Chinese City Between Two Worlds*, ed. Mark Elvin and G. William Skinner (Stanford: Stanford University Press, 1974), 119–41.

66. See for example H. Franz Schurmann, *Ideology and Organization in Communist China*, 2d ed. (Berkeley: University of California Press, 1968), chap. 7; Lawrence Crissman, "Specific Central Place Models for an Evolving System of Market Towns on the Changhua Plain, Taiwan," in *Regional Analysis* ed. Smith, 1:183–218.

67. Several examples may be found in Smith, ed., *Regional Analysis*.

68. Hosea B. Morse, *The Gilds of China* (London: Longmans, Green, and Company, 1909), 27.

69. Fei, *Hsiang-tu Chung-kuo*, chaps. 10 and 11; Fei, "Peasantry and Gentry," 8. On Hu Shih, see Jerome Grieder, *Intellectuals and the State in Modern China* (New York: Free Press, 1981), 346–48, 377.

70. Christopher Dawson, *The Making of Europe* (Cleveland: Meridian, 1956), 26; Walter Watson, "Interprétation de la Chine: Montesquieu et Voltaire," in *Les rapports entre la Chine et l'Europe au temps des lumières. Actes du IIe colloque international de sinologie* (Paris: Les Belles Lettres, 1980), 16–37; Anne Bailey and Josep Llobera, eds., *The Asiatic Mode of Production* (London: Routledge & Kegan Paul, 1981), 18–21; Ōtsuka, "Max Weber," 283.

71. Grieder, *Intellectuals*, 168, 346–48.

72. Miyakawa, "The Naitō Hypothesis," 537–39; see also Fogel ed., *Naitō Konan and Modernity*.

73. Miyazaki, *Tōyō teki kinsei*, esp. 65–66, 74; Saeki Tomi, various articles reprinted in his *Chūgokushi kenkyū*, vols. 2 and 3 (Kyoto: Tōyōshi kenkyūkai, 1971 and 1978).

The notion that late imperial despotism was founded on an alliance of the throne and urban commercial capital was also entertained by several Chinese scholars during the 1930s; see Dirlik, *Revolution and History*, 209–10.

74. Karl Marx, *Contribution to a Critique of Political Economy*, in *The Marx-Engels Reader*, ed. Robert C. Tucker (New York: W. W. Norton, 1978), 5; Karl A. Wittfogel, "The Marxist View of China," Part I, in *Asiatic Mode*, ed. Bailey and Llobera, 21–22.

75. This summary of Karl A. Wittfogel's views is based on the following of his English-language writings: "The Stages of Development in Chinese Economic and Social History" (1935), in *Asiatic Mode*, ed. Bailey and Llobera, 113–40; "The Theory of Oriental Society," (1938), in *Asiatic Mode*, ed. Bailey and Llobera, 141–57; and "Chinese Society: An Historical Survey," *Journal of Asian Studies* 16 (May 1957): 343–64. For a fascinating but highly uncritical biography, see G. L. Ulmen, *The Science of Society: Toward an Understanding of the Life and Work of Karl August Wittfogel* (The Hague: Mouton, 1978).

76. Miyazaki, *Tōyō teki kinsei*, 65–66; Wittfogel, "Stages of Development," 120–22. Note that Wittfogel's work was translated into Japanese as early as the 1930s.

77. Wittfogel, "Theory of Oriental Society," 16–57. Wittfogel also echoed Weber's view of the nondevelopment of Chinese capitalism due to the failure of autonomous development of cities.

78. Dirlik, *Revolution and History*, 192.

79. Ch'ao-ting Chi, *Key Economic Areas in Chinese History* (Shanghai, 1935; reprinted New York: Paragon, 1963). For Chi's relationship to Wittfogel, see Ulmen, *Science of Society*, 106, 176–79.

80. Karl A. Wittfogel, *Oriental Despotism: A Comparative Study of Total Power* (New Haven: Yale University Press, 1957).

81. See for example Wolfram Eberhard, "Oriental Despotism: Political Weapon or Sociological Concept?" *American Sociological Review* 23 (1958): 446–48; F. W. Mote, "The Growth of Chinese Despotism: A Critique of Wittfogel's Theory of Oriental Despotism as Applied to China," *Oriens Extremus* 8 (August 1961): 1–41.

82. Examples include Imahori Seiji, "Shindai no suiri dantai to seiji kenryoku" (Water control and political power in China), *Aziya kenkyū* 10 (October 1963): 1–22; Meskill, *A Chinese Pioneer Family*, 50–51; Pierre-Etienne Will, "Un cycle hydraulique en Chine," *Bulletin de l'Ecole Française d'Extrême Orient* 68 (1980): 261–87; and most recently Peter C. Perdue, "Official Goals and Local Interests: Water Control in the Dongting Lake Region during the Ming and Qing Periods," *Journal of Asian Studies* 41 (August 1982): 747–56.

83. "Ya-hsi-ya sheng-ch'an fang-shih yu kuo-chia" (The Asiatic mode of production and the state), *Li-shih yen-chiu* (1982.3): 39–52; Wu Ta-k'un, "Ma K'a-erh Wei-t'e-fu te 'Tung-fang ch'uan-chih-chu-i' " (Refuting Karl Wittfogel's *Oriental Despotism*), *Li-shih yen chiu* (1982.4): 27–36.

84. On the financial impact of the White Lotus rebellion see Susan Mann Jones and Philip A. Kuhn, "Dynastic Decline and the Roots of Rebellion," in *The Cambridge History of China*, ed. John K. Fairbank (Cambridge: Cambridge University Press, 1978), esp. 10:144. On fiscal developments of the Taiping years, see P'eng Yü-hsin, "Ch'ing-mo chung-yang yu ko-sheng ts'ai-cheng kuan-hsi" (Center-provincial fiscal relations in the late Ch'ing), *She-hui k'e-hsueh tsa-chih* (1946), and more recently, William T. Rowe, *Hankow: Commerce and Society in a Chinese City, 1796–1889* (Stanford:

Stanford University Press, 1984), esp. chap. 6 and Rowe, "Hu Lin-i's Reform of the Grain Tribute System in Hupeh, 1855–58," Ch'ing-shih wen-t'i 4 (December 1983): 33–86.

85. Lloyd Eastman, "Ch'ing-i and Chinese Policy Formation during the Nineteenth Century," Journal of Asian Studies 24 (August 1965): 595–611; also Mary B. Rankin, "'Public Opinion' and Political Power: Qingyi in Late Nineteenth Century China," Journal of Asian Studies 41 (May 1982): 453–84, and James Polachek, The Inner Opium War (Cambridge, Mass.: Harvard University Press, forthcoming).

86. Will, "Un cycle hydraulique."

87. G. William Skinner, ed., The City in Late Imperial China (Stanford: Stanford University Press, 1977), 21.

88. For concise theoretical treatments of this process see Ramon H. Myers, "Some Issues on Economic Organization during the Ming and Ch'ing Period: A Review Article," Ch'ing-shih wen-t'i 3 (December 1974): 77–97, and Thomas Metzger, "On the Historical Roots of Economic Modernization in China: The Increasing Differentiation of the Economy from the Polity During the Late Ming and Early Ch'ing Times," in Modern Chinese Economic History, ed. Chi-ming Hou and Tzong-shian Yu (Taipei: Institute of Economics, Academia Sinica, 1979), 3–14. For specific examples see Teng T'o, "Tsung Wan-li tao Ch'ien-lung" (From Wan-li to Ch'ien-lung), in Teng, Lun Chung-kuo li-shih chi ke wen-t'i (On several problems in Chinese history), second edition (Peking: San-lien shu-tien, 1979), 189–239; and Lin Yung-k'uang, "Ch'ing-tai te ch'a-ma mao-i" (The tea-for-horses trade during the Ch'ing dynasty), Ch'ing-shih lun-ts'ung (Peking), no. 3 (1982): 100–16.

89. Frederic Wakeman, Jr., Strangers at the Gate: Social Disorder in South China, 1839–61 (Berkeley: University of California Press, 1967); Kuhn, Rebellion and its Enemies in Late Imperial China (see also the important "Preface" to the paperback edition, 1980); Kuhn, "Local Self-Government under the Republic: Problems of Control, Autonomy, and Mobilization," in Conflict and Control, ed. Wakeman and Grant, 257–98; Kuhn, "Local Taxation and Finance in Republican China," in Select Papers, ed. Jones 3:100–36.

90. Yoshinobu Shiba, "Ningpo and its Hinterland," in The City, ed. Skinner, esp. 420–22; Mark Elvin, "Market Towns and Waterways: The County of Shang-hai from 1480 to 1910," in ibid., 441–74. See also Elvin, Pattern, 260–67.

91. Feng-chien (literally feudal, but used here with a more specific referent) ideas were current during the Ming, but became identified for subsequent writers with the thought of the early Ch'ing scholar Ku Yen-wu (1613–82). See Lien-sheng Yang, "Ming Local Administration," in Ming Administration: Seven Studies, ed. Charles O. Hucker (New York: Columbia University Press, 1969), 1–10; Kuhn, "Local Self-Government," esp. 261–68.

92. James Polachek, "Gentry Hegemony: Soochow in the T'ung-chih Restoration," in Conflict and Control, ed. Wakeman and Grant, 246.

93. Muramatsu, "Chinese Landlordism," 596.

94. Hamashita Takeshi (trans. Fogel), "Japanese Studies of Post-Opium War China: 1979," Ch'ing-shih wen-t'i 4 (June 1982): 108.

95. Kuhn, "Local Taxation," esp. 109–17. For an example of local elite protection, see Dennerline, "Hua Charitable Estate."

96. Joseph Esherick, Reform and Revolution in China: The 1911 Revolution in Hunan and

Hubei (Berkeley: University of California Press, 1976), 116. See also the influential article by Chuzo Ichiko, "The Role of the Gentry: An Hypothesis," in *China in Revolution: The First Phase, 1900–1913*, ed. Mary C. Wright (New Haven: Yale University Press, 1968), 297–318.

97. Kuhn, "Local Self-Government"; R. Keith Schoppa, *Chinese Elites and Political Change: Zhejiang Province in the Early Twentieth Century* (Cambridge, Mass.: Harvard University Press, 1982). For related perspectives see Andrew Nathan, *Peking Politics: Factionalism and the Failure of Constitutionalism, 1918–23* (Berkeley: University of California Press, 1976), esp. chaps. 1 and 2; and John Fincher, *Chinese Democracy: The Self-Government Movement in Local, Provincial, and National Polities, 1905–1914* (New York: St. Martin's Press, 1981).

98. Philip A. Kuhn and Susan Mann Jones, "Introduction," in *Select Papers* ed. Jones, 3:v–xix.

99. Chung-li Chang, *The Chinese Gentry*; also Polachek, "Gentry Hegemony," 211–56.

100. Wu Ch'eng-ming, "Lun Ch'ing ch'ien-ch'i wo-kuo kuo-nei shih-ch'ang" (On the domestic market in the early Ch'ing), *Li-shih yen-chiu*, (1983.1): 99.

101. Miyazaki, *Tōyō teki kinsei*, chap. 2

102. See Elvin, *Pattern*, chaps. 10–12; also Shiba Yoshinobu, *Sōdai shōgyōshi kenkyū* (Tokyo: Kazama shobo, 1968), available in an abridged translation by Elvin as *Commerce and Society in Sung China*, (Ann Arbor: Center for Chinese Studies, University of Michigan, 1970).

103. An influential example of this Japanese scholarship is Fujii Hiroshi, "Shin'-an shōnin no kenkyū" (A study of the Hsin-an merchants), *Tōyō gakuhō* 36 (1953–1954): 1–44, 32–60, 65–118, 115–45; among Chinese works the most important is probably Fu I-ling, *Ming-Ch'ing shih-tai shang-jen chi shang-yeh tzu-pen* (Merchants and commercial capital in the Ming and Ch'ing) (Peking: Jen-min ch'u-pan-she, 1956).

104. William Atwell, "International Bullion Flows and the Chinese Economy, c. 1530–1650," *Past and Present*, no. 95 (May 1982): 68–90. Atwell draws upon the pioneering work of the Hong Kong-based scholar Ch'uan Han-sheng. See also Frederic Wakeman, Jr., "The Canton Trade and the Opium War," in *The Cambridge History of China*, ed. John K. Fairbank (Cambridge: Cambridge University Press, 1978), 10:163–212.

105. See for example Shiba Yoshinobu's discussion of marketing around Hui-chou, in his "Urbanization and Development of Markets in the Lower Yangtze," in *Crisis and Prosperity in Sung China* ed. John Winthrop Haeger (Tucson: University of Arizona Press, 1976), 37–41.

106. Elvin, "Chinese Cities Since the Sung Dynasty," in *Towns in Societies*, ed. Philip Abrams and E. A. Wrigley (Cambridge: Cambridge University Press, 1978), 79–89.

107. Skinner, ed., *The City*. One of the influences on Skinner's regional model is Robert Hartwell's seminal article, "A Cycle of Economic Change in Imperial China: Coal and Iron in Northeast China, 750–1350," *Journal of the Economic and Social History of the Orient* 10 (1967): 102–59; Hartwell in turn acknowledges the influence of N. S. B. Gras's studies of the English corn market.

108. Rawski, *Agricultural Change*. See also Skinner's more elaborate conceptualization of "core" and "peripheral" areas within each region, in *The City*. Skinner takes this vocabulary from Edward Shils via Immanuel Wallerstein.

109. Michael Hechter, *International Colonialism: The Celtic Fringe in British National Development, 1536–1966* (Berkeley: University of California Press, 1975).

110. Fernand Braudel, *The Wheels of Commerce* (New York: Harper & Row, 1982), 237.

111. Schwartz, "Marxist Controversy," 146.

112. V. I. Lenin, *The Development of Capitalism in Russia* (Moscow: Progress Publishers, 1956), esp. chaps. 5–7. Lenin speaks of "merchant's capital," but not of "commercial capitalism" as a socioeconomic formation.

113. Yeh-chien Wang, "Notes on the Sprouts of Capitalism," in *Chinese Social and Economic History from the Song to 1900: Report of the American Delegation to a Sino-American Symposium*, ed. Albert Feuerwerker (Ann Arbor: Center for Chinese Studies, University of Michigan, 1982), 51.

114. Mao Tse-tung, *Selected Works* (Peking: Foreign Languages Press, 1951), 1:309.

115. Many of these studies are collected in three large anthologies: *Chung-kuo tzu-pen-chu-i meng-ya wen-t'i t'ao-lun chi* (Collected discussions of the sprouts of capitalism in China) (Peking: San-lien shu-tien, 1957); *Ming-Ch'ing she-hui ching-chi hsing-t'ai te yen-chiu* (Studies of socio-economic formations in the Ming and Ch'ing) (Shanghai: Jen-min ch'u-pan-she, 1957); and *Ming-Ch'ing tzu-pen-chu-i meng-ya yen-chiu lun-wen-shi*, (Collected essays on the sprouts of capitalism in the Ming and Ch'ing) (Shanghai: Jen-min ch'u-pan-she, 1981). An important collection by an individual scholar is Teng T'o, *Lun Chung-kuo li-shih*. Translations of representative studies may be found in *Chinese Studies in History* (Fall–Winter 1981–1982). For historiographic discussions of the first phase of this debate see Albert Feuerwerker, "China's Modern Economic History in Chinese Communist Historiography," in his edited volume, *History in Communist China* (Cambridge, Mass.: MIT Press, 1968), 216–46; and on the second phase, William T. Rowe, "Recent Writing in the People's Republic on Early Ch'ing Economic History," *Ch'ing-shih wen-t'i* 4 (June 1982): 73–90.

116. P'eng Tse-i, "Ch'ing-tai ch'ien-ch'i shou-kung-yeh te fa-ch'an" (The development of handicrafts in the early Ch'ing), *Chung-kuo-shih yen-chiu* (1981.1): 43–60. An English abstract of this important article may be found in Feuerwerker, ed., *Chinese Social and Economic History from the Song to 1900* (Ann Arbor: Center for Chinese Studies, University of Michigan, 1982), 105–6.

117. Liu Yung-ch'eng, "Nung-yeh ku-yung lao-tung," 91–112.

118. See for example, Liu Yen, "Ming-mo ch'eng-shih ching-shi fa-chan hsia te ch'u-ch'i shih-min yun-tung" (On urban popular movements during the economic development of the late Ming), *Li-shih yen-chiu* (1955.6): 29–59. Li Hua, "Shih-lun Ch'ing-tai ch'ien-ch'i te shih-min tou-cheng" (On the struggles of townspeople in the early Ch'ing), *Wen-shih-che* 10 (1957): 54–62. For an English-language treatment, see Tsing Yuan, "Urban Riots and Disturbances," in *From Ming to Ch'ing*, ed. Jonathan Spence and John Wills (New Haven: Yale University Press, 1979), 279–320.

119. For example, Endymion Wilkinson, "Introduction" to Jing and Lo, 1–37; Ramon H. Myers, "Society and Economy in Modern China: Some Historical Interpretations," *Bulletin of the Institute of Modern History, Academia Sinica* (Taiwan) 11 (1982): esp. 217.

120. Etienne Balazs, *Chinese Civilization and Bureaucracy* (New Haven: Yale Univer-

sity Press, 1964); Hatano Yoshihiro, Chūgoku kindai kōgyōshi no kenkyū (Studies in the history of modern Chinese industry) (Kyoto: Tōyōshi kenkyūkai, 1961), esp. part 1; Elvin, Pattern, esp. chap. 17; Rozman, Population and Marketing Settlements.

121. Chinese studies on this subject are far too numerous to list here. Two recent survey articles are T'ien Chu-chien, "Chung-kuo feng-chien she-hui ch'ang-ch'i yen-hsu yuan-yin t'ao-lun ts'o-shu" (Resumé of the debate on why Chinese feudal society lasted so long), Li-shih yen-chiu (1982.1): 103–10, and "Chung-kuo feng-chien she-hui ching-chi chieh-kou hsueh-shu t'ao-lun-hui chi-yao" (Synopsis of the scholarly symposium on the structure of China's feudal society and economy), Chung-kuo-shih yen-chiu (1983.1): 18–31.

122. See especially Wu Liang-k'ai, "Shih-lun ya-p'ien chan-cheng ch'ien Ch'ing-tai nung-yeh tzu-pen-chu-i meng-ya huan-man fa-chan te chu-yao yuan-yin" (A preliminary analysis of the major causes of retarded development of sprouts of capitalism in agriculture in pre-Opium War Ch'ing China), Ch'ing-shih lun-ts'ung (Peking), no. 3 (1982): 75–77.

123. Wei Ch'ing-yuan and Lu Su, "Lun Ch'ing-ch'u shang-pan k'uang-yeh chung tzu-pen-chi-i meng-ya wei-neng cho-chuang ch'eng-ch'ang te yuan-yin" (Why the early Ch'ing sprouts of capitalism in mining were unable to vigorously mature), Chung-kuo-shih yen-shiu (1982.4): 75–86.

124. Hong Huanchun, "The Impact of Feudal Autocracy on Nascent Capitalism in the Ming and Qing Dynasties," Social Sciences in China 1 (1982): 214. See also T'ien Chu-chien, "Chung-kuo feng-chien she-hui," 10, which speaks of the "transcedent stability" of Chinese feudal society, and its ability to survive "cyclical eruptions."

125. Namiki Yorihisa (trans. Fogel), "Japanese Studies of Post-Opium War China: 1980," Ch'ing-shih wen-t'i 4 (June 1983): 67 and 75.

126. For a recent Chinese view see Wang Jingyu, "The Birth of the Chinese Bourgeoisie," Social Sciences in China 1 (1982): 220–40. See also Esherick, Reform and Revolution, 66–69.

127. The leading Western student of this subject is clearly Prof. Bergère; among her studies are "The Role of the Bourgeoisie," in China in Revolution, ed. Wright, 229–96; La bourgeoisie chinoise et la révolution de 1911 (Paris: Mouton, 1968); "The Other China: Shanghai from 1919 to 1949," in Shanghai: Revolution and Development in an Asian Metropolis, ed. Christopher Howe (Cambridge: Cambridge University Press, 1981); and most recently "The Chinese Bourgeoisie, 1911–37," in The Cambridge History of China, ed. John K. Fairbank (Cambridge: Cambridge University Press, 1983), 12:721–825. A detailed exposition of the Trotskyite view is Harold Isaacs, The Tragedy of the Chinese Revolution (Stanford: Stanford University Press, 1961); the convincing refutation is supplied by Parks Coble, Jr., The Shanghai Capitalists and the Nationalist Government, 1927–1937 (Cambridge, Mass.: Harvard University Press, 1980).

128. The Chinese influence on scholars like Bergère and Esherick has long been evident. Influence in the other direction is signaled by such articles as Chang Chung-li, et. al., "Kuo-wai yu-kuan Chung-kuo tzu-ch'an-chieh-chi kai-shu" (Digest of studies by foreign historians of China's bourgeoisie), Li-shih yen-chiu (1983.3): 89–108.

129. Dirlik, Revolution and History, esp. p. 119. I would be happy to see the term

"capitalism" retained as descriptive of a system of entrepreneurial investment and management—perhaps even of a style of economic relations—but feel that as a description of a pervasive social formation it has little applicability to the Chinese case.

BIBLIOGRAPHY

GENERAL

Adams, Richard N. *Energy and Structure: A Theory of Social Power*. Austin: University of Texas Press, 1975.

Aya, Rod. "Theories of Revolution Reconsidered: Contrasting Models of Collective Violence." *Theory and Society* 8 (July 1979): 39–100.

Badie, Bertrand, and Pierre Birnbaum. *Sociologie de l'Etat*. Paris: Bernard Grasset, 1979.

Bailyn, Bernard. "The Challenge of Modern Historiography." *American Historical Review* 87 (February 1982): 1–24.

Barth, Fredrik, ed. *Ethnic Groups and Boundaries: The Social Organization of Culture Difference*. London: G. Allen & Unwin, 1968.

Beard, Charles A., and Mary R. Beard. *The Rise of American Civilization*. New York: Macmillan, 1927.

Berding, Helmut, ed. "Wege der neuen Sozial- und Wirtschaftsgeschichte." Special issue of *Geschichte und Gesellschaft* 6, 1 (1980).

Berg, Maxine, Pat Hudson, and Michael Sonenscher, eds. *Manufacture in Town and Country Before the Factory*. Cambridge: Cambridge University Press, 1983.

Black, Donald. *The Behavior of Law*. New York: Academic Press, 1976.

Bloch, Marc. *Feudal Society*. Chicago: University of Chicago Press, 1961.

Bonnell, Victoria. "The Uses of Theory, Concepts and Comparison in Historical Sociology." *Comparative Studies in Society and History* 22 (April 1980): 156–73.

Bourdieu, Pierre. *Outline of a Theory of Practice*. Cambridge: Cambridge University Press, 1977.

Braudel, Fernand. *Civilization and Capitalism, 15th–18th Century*. Vol. 1, *The Structures of Everyday Life*. Vol. 2, *The Wheels of Commerce*. Vol. 3, *The Perspective of the World*. Translated by Siân Reynolds. New York: Harper & Row, 1981, 1983, 1984.

Bright, Charles, and Susan Harding, eds. *Statemaking and Social Movements: Essays in History and Theory*. Ann Arbor: University of Michigan Press, 1984.

Brown, Peter. *Society and the Holy in Late Antiquity*. Berkeley: University of California Press, 1982.

Burguière, André. "The Fate of the History of Mentalités in the *Annales*." *Comparative Studies in Society and History* 24 (July 1982): 424–37.

Burke, Peter. *Sociology and History*. London: G. Allen & Unwin, 1980.

Calvert, Peter. *The Concept of Class: An Historical Introduction*. London: Hutchinson, 1982.

Chesneaux, Jean. *Du passé faisons table rase? A propos de l'histoire et des historiens*. Paris: Maspéro, 1976.

Chirot, Daniel. *Social Change in the Twentieth Century.* New York: Harcourt Brace Jovanovich, 1977.

Cohen, Abner. *Two Dimensional Man.* London: Routledge & Kegan Paul, 1974.

Cohen, David William, and Jack P. Greene, eds. *Neither Slave Nor Free: The Freedmen of African Descent in the Slave Societies of the New World.* Baltimore: Johns Hopkins University Press, 1972.

Colloque de l'Ecole Normale Supérieure de Saint-Cloud. *L'histoire sociale. Sources et méthodes.* Paris: Presses Universitaires de France, 1967.

Davis, John. "Social Anthropology and the Consumption of History." *Theory and Society* 9 (May 1980): 519–37.

Dupâquier, Jacques. *Pour la démographie historique.* Paris: Presses Universitaires de France, 1984.

Eley, Geoff. "Nationalism and Social History." *Social History* 6 (January 1981): 83–108.

Eley, Geoff, and Keith Nield. "Why Does Social History Ignore Politics?" *Social History* 5 (May 1980): 249–72.

Fogel, Robert William, and G. R. Elton. *Which Road to the Past? Two Views of History.* New Haven: Yale University Press, 1983.

Furet, François. *In the Workshop of History.* Translated by Jonathan Mandelbaum. Chicago: University of Chicago Press, 1984.

Genovese, Eugene D., and Elizabeth Fox-Genovese. *Fruits of Merchant Capital: Slavery and Bourgeois Property in the Rise and Expansion of Capitalism.* New York: Oxford University Press, 1983.

Gilbert, Felix, and Stephen R. Graubard, eds. *Historical Studies Today.* New York: W. W. Norton, 1972.

Ginzburg, Carlo, and Carlo Poni. "La micro-histoire." *Le Débat*, no. 17 (1981): 133–36.

Godelier, Maurice. "Infrastructures, Societies, and History." *Current Anthropology* 19 (December 1978): 763–71.

Gramsci, Antonio. *Selections from the Prison Notebooks.* Edited and translated by Quintin Hoare and Geoffrey Nowell Smith. New York: International Publishers, 1971.

Greene, Jack P. "The New History: From Top to Bottom." *New York Times*, 8 June 1975, 37.

Hexter, Jack H. "Fernand Braudel and the Monde Braudélien." *Journal of Modern History* 44 (December 1972): 480–541.

Higham, John, and Paul K. Conkin, eds. *New Directions in American Intellectual History.* Baltimore: Johns Hopkins University Press, 1979.

Higham, John. *History: Professional Scholarship in America.* Rev. ed. Baltimore: Johns Hopkins University Press, 1983.

Hobsbawm, Eric J. "From Social History to the History of Society." *Daedalus* (Winter 1971): 20–45.

———. "The Revival of Narrative: Some Comments." *Past and Present*, no. 86 (February 1980): 3–8.

Hobsbawm, Eric J., and Terence Ranger, eds. *The Invention of Tradition.* Cambridge: Cambridge University Press, 1983.

Hochstadt, Steve. "Social History and Politics: A Materialist View." *Social History* 7 (January 1982): 75–83.

Kaelble, Hartmut. *Historical Research on Social Mobility.* New York: Columbia University Press, 1981.

Kocka, Jürgen. *Sozialgeschichte. Begriff—Entwicklung—Probleme.* Göttingen: Vandenhoeck & Ruprecht, 1977.

———. "Theory and Social History: Recent Developments in West Germany." *Social Research* 47 (Autumn 1980): 426–57.

Kriedte, Peter, Hans Medick, and Jürgen Schlumbohm. *Industrialisierung vor der Industrialisierung: Gewerbliche Warenproduktion auf dem Land in der Formationsperiode des Kapitalismus.* Göttingen: Vandenhoeck & Ruprecht, 1977.

Laslett, Peter, Karla Oosterveen, and Richard M. Smith, eds. *Bastardy and its Comparative History.* Cambridge: Cambridge University Press, 1980.

Leach, Edmund Ronald. *Rethinking Anthropology.* London: Athlone, 1961.

Le Goff, Jacques, and Pierre Nora, eds. *Faire de l'histoire.* 3 vols. Paris: Gallimard, 1974.

Lee, Ronald Demos. *Econometric Studies of Topics in Demographic History.* New York: Arno, 1978.

Lenin, V. I. *Imperialism: The Highest Stage of Capitalism.* London: Martin Lawrence, 1963.

Le Roy Ladurie, Emmanuel. *The Territory of the Historian.* Translated by Ben and Siân Reynolds. Chicago: University of Chicago Press, 1979.

———. *The Mind and Method of the Historian.* Translated by Ben and Siân Reynolds. Chicago: University of Chicago Press, 1981.

Lévi-Strauss, Claude. "Histoire et ethnologie." *Annales: Economies, sociétés, civilisations* 38 (Novembre–Décembre 1983): 1217–31.

Lorwin, Val, and Jacob M. Price, eds. *The Dimensions of the Past: Materials, Problems, and Opportunities for Quantitative Work in History.* New Haven: Yale University Press, 1972.

Lüdtke, Alf. "The Historiography of Everyday Life: The Personal and the Political." In *Culture, Ideology and Politics,* edited by Raphael Samuel and Gareth Stedman Jones, 38–54. London: Routledge & Kegan Paul, 1982.

McClelland, Peter D. *Causal Explanation and Model Building in History, Economics, and the New Economic History.* Ithaca: Cornell University Press, 1975.

Macfarlane, Alan, Sarah Harrison, and Charles Jardine. *Reconstructing Historical Communities.* Cambridge: Cambridge University Press, 1978.

McKeown, Thomas. *The Modern Rise of Population.* New York: Academic Press, 1976.

McNeill, William H. *Plagues and Peoples.* New York: Anchor Books, 1976.

Marx, Karl, and Frederick Engels. *Selected Works.* New York: International Publishers, 1968.

Moore, Barrington. *Social Origins of Dictatorship and Democracy.* Boston: Beacon Press, 1966.

Moore, Sally Falk. *Law as Process: An Anthropological Perspective.* London: Routledge & Kegan Paul, 1978.

Moulder, Frances. *Japan, China, and the Modern World System.* Cambridge: Cambridge University Press, 1977.

Ortner, Sherry B. "Theory in Anthropology Since the Sixties." *Comparative Studies in Society and History* 26 (January 1984): 126–66.

Palmer, Robert R. *A History of the Modern World.* New York: Alfred A. Knopf, 1950.

Patterson, Orlando. *Slavery and Social Death: A Comparative Study.* Cambridge, Mass.: Harvard University Press, 1982.

Rabb, Theodore K., and Robert Rotberg, eds. *The New History in the 1980s and Beyond. Studies in Interdisciplinary History.* Princeton: Princeton University Press, 1982.

Rothman, David J., and Stanton Wheeler, eds. *Social History and Social Policy.* New York: Academic Press, 1981.

Scott, James C. *The Moral Economy of the Peasant.* New Haven: Yale University Press, 1976.

Shils, Edward. *Center and Periphery: Essays in Macrosociology.* Chicago: University of Chicago Press, 1975.

Skocpol, Theda. *States and Social Revolutions: A Comparative Analysis of France, Russia, and China.* Cambridge: Cambridge University Press, 1979.

———, ed. *Vision and Method in Historical Sociology.* Cambridge: Cambridge University Press, 1984.

Smith, Carol A., ed. *Regional Analysis.* 2 vols. New York: Academic Press, 1976.

Stearns, Peter N. "Toward a Wider Vision: Trends in Social History." In *The Past Before Us: Contemporary Historical Writing in the United States,* edited by Michael Kammen, 205–30. Ithaca: Cornell University Press, 1980.

Stinchcombe, Arthur L. *Theoretical Methods in Social History.* New York: Academic Press, 1978.

Stone, Lawrence. "History and the Social Sciences in the Twentieth Century." In *The Future of History,* edited by Charles F. Delzell, 3–42. Nashville: Vanderbilt University Press, 1977.

Stone, Lawrence. "The Revival of Narrative: Reflections on a New Old History." *Past and Present,* no. 85 (November 1979): 3–24.

Tawney, R. H. *History and Society: Essays.* Edited by J. M. Winter. Boston: Routledge & Kegan Paul, 1978.

Tilly, Charles, ed. *The Formation of National States in Western Europe.* Princeton: Princeton University Press, 1975.

———, ed. *Historical Studies of Changing Fertility.* Princeton: Princeton University Press, 1978.

———. *As Sociology Meets History.* New York: Academic Press, 1981.

Trevelyan, G. M. *English Social History.* London: Longman, 1944.

Vilar, Pierre. *Une histoire en construction. Approche marxiste et problématiques conjoncturelles.* Paris: Gallimard/Le Seuil, 1982.

Vinovskis, Maris A. *Demographic History and the World Population Crisis.* Worcester, Mass.: Clark University Press, 1976.

Wallerstein, Immanuel. *The Modern World System.* 2 vols. to date. Vol. 1, *Capitalist Agriculture and the Origins of the European World Economy in the Sixteenth Century.* Vol. 2, *Mercantilism and the Consolidation of the World-Economy, 1600–1750.* New York: Academic Press, 1974, 1978.

Walters, Ronald E. "Signs of these Times: Clifford Geertz and Historians." *Social Research* 47 (Autumn 1980): 537–56.

Weber, Max. *General Economic History.* Glencoe, Ill.: Free Press, 1950.
Werbner, R. P., ed. *Regional Cults.* New York: Academic Press, 1977.
Wheatley, Paul. *The Pivot of the Four Quarters: A Preliminary Enquiry into the Origins and Character of the Ancient Chinese City.* Chicago: Aldine, 1971.
Williams, Raymond. *Culture and Society, 1780–1950.* New York: Columbia University Press, 1958.
Wittfogel, Karl A. *Oriental Despotism.* New Haven: Yale University Press, 1957.
Wolf, Eric R. *Europe and the People Without History.* Berkeley: University of California Press, 1972.
Wrigley, E. A., ed. *Identifying People in the Past.* London: Edward Arnold, 1973.

EUROPE

Agulhon, Maurice. *The Republic in the Village. The People of the Var from the French Revolution to the Second Republic.* 2d ed. Cambridge: Cambridge University Press, 1982.
Åkerman, Sune, Hans Christian Johansen, and David Gaunt, eds. *Chance and Change: Social and Economic Studies in Historical Demography in the Baltic Area.* Odense: Scandinavian Universities Press, 1978.
Aminzade, Ronald. *Class, Politics and Early Industrial Capitalism: A Study of Mid-Nineteenth Century Toulouse.* Albany: SUNY Press, 1981.
Anderson, Michael. *Family Structure in Nineteenth-Century Lancashire.* Cambridge: Cambridge University Press, 1971.
Ariès, Philippe. *Histoire des populations françaises et de leurs attitudes devant la vie depuis le XVIIIe siècle.* Paris: Seuil, 1971.
Armstrong, Alan. *Stability and Change in an English Country Town: A Social Study of York, 1801–1851.* Cambridge: Cambridge University Press, 1974.
Bardet, Jean-Pierre. *Rouen aux XVIIe et XVIIIe siècles. Les mutations d'un espace urbain.* 2 vols. Paris: SEDES, 1983.
Biraben, Jean-Noël. *Les hommes et la peste en France et dans les pays européens et méditerranéens.* 2 vols. Paris: Mouton, 1975.
Blasius, Dirk. *Kriminalität und Alltag. Zur Konfliktgeschichte des Alltagslebens im 19. Jahrhundert.* Göttingen: Vandenhoeck & Ruprecht, 1978.
Blok, Anton. *The Mafia of a Sicilian Village, 1860–1960.* Oxford: Basil Blackwell.
Bohstedt, John. *Riots and Community Politics in England and Wales, 1790–1810.* Cambridge, Mass.: Harvard University Press, 1983.
Boll, Friedhelm. *Massenbewegungen in Niedersachsen 1906–1920.* Bonn: Verlag Neue Gesellschaft, 1981.
Bonnell, Victoria. *Roots of Rebellion. Workers' Politics and Organizations in St. Petersburg and Moscow, 1900–1914.* Berkeley: University of California Press, 1983.
Borscheid, Peter. *Textilarbeiterschaft in der Industrialisierung: Soziale Lage und Mobilität in Württemberg (19. Jahrhundert).* Stuttgart: Klett-Cotta, 1978.
Botz, Gerhard, and Josef Weidenholzer, eds. *Mündliche Geschichte und Arbeiterbewegung.* Vienna: Bödhlhaus, 1984.
Burke, Peter. *Popular Culture in Early Modern Europe.* London: Temple Smith, 1978.
Cannadine, David. "The Past and the Present in the English Industrial Revolution, 1880–1980." *Past and Present,* no. 103 (May 1984): 131–72.

302 Bibliography

Cattaruzza, Marina. *La formazione del proletariato urbano. Immigrati, operai di mestiere, donne a Trieste dalla metà del secolo XIX alla prima guerra mondiale*. Turin: Musolini, 1979.

Cella, Gian Primo, ed. *Il movimento degli scioperi nel XX secolo*. Bologna: Il Mulino, 1979.

Charlesworth, Andrew, ed. *An Atlas of Rural Protest in Britain, 1548–1900*. London: Croom Helm, 1983.

Châtelain, Abel. *Les migrants temporaires en France de 1800 à 1914*. 2 vols. Villeneuve-d'Ascq: Publications de l'Université de Lille III, 1976.

Chesnais, Jean-Claude. *Histoire de la violence en Occident de 1800 à nos jours*. Paris: Laffont, 1981.

Christian, William A., Jr. *Local Religion in Sixteenth-Century Spain*. Princeton: Princeton University Press, 1981.

Cipolla, Carlo M. *Faith, Reason, and the Plague in Seventeenth-Century Tuscany*. Ithaca: Cornell University Press.

Clark, Samuel. *Social Origins of the Irish Land War*. Princeton: Princeton University Press.

Coale, Ansley, Barbara Anderson, and Enna Harm. *Human Fertility in Russia since the Nineteenth Century*. Princeton: Princeton University Press, 1979.

Cobb, Richard. *Les armées révolutionnaires, instrument de la Terreur dans les départments*. 2 vols. Paris: Mouton, 1961–1963.

———. *Reactions to the French Revolution*. London: Oxford University Press, 1972.

Cohn, Samuel Kline, Jr. *The Laboring Classes in Renaissance Florence*. New York: Academic Press, 1980.

Conze, Werner, ed. *Sozialgeschichte der Familie in der Neuzeit Europas*. Stuttgart: Ernst Klett, 1976.

Corbin, Alain. *Archaisme et modernité en Limousin au XIXe siècle*. Paris: Marcel Rivière, 1975.

Cronin, James. *Industrial Conflict in Modern Britain*. London: Croom Helm, 1979.

Daumard, Adeline, et al. *Les fortunes françaises au XIXe siècle*. Paris: Mouton, 1973.

Davis, Natalie Zemon. *Society and Culture in Early Modern France: Eight Essays*. Stanford: Stanford University Press, 1975.

Dupâquier, Jacques. *La population rurale du Bassin Parisien à l'époque de Louis XIV*. Paris: Editions de l'Ecole des Hautes Etudes en Sciences Sociales, 1979.

Flinn, Michael W. *The European Demographic System, 1500–1820*. Baltimore: Johns Hopkins University Press, 1981.

Foster, John. *Class Struggle and the Industrial Revolution: Early Industrial Capitalism in Three Towns*. London: Weidenfeld & Nicolson, 1974.

Furet, François, and Jacques Ozouf. *Lire et écrire: L'alphabétisation des français de Calvin à Jules Ferry*. 2 vols. Paris: Editions de Minuit, 1977.

Gillis, John R. *Youth and History: Tradition and Change in European Age Relations*. Rev. ed. New York: Academic Press, 1981.

Glen, Robert. *Urban Workers in the Early Industrial Revolution*. London: Croom Helm, 1984.

Goody, Jack, Joan Thirsk, and E. P. Thompson, eds. *Family and Inheritance: Rural Society in Western Europe, 1200–1800*. Cambridge: Cambridge University Press, 1976.

Goubert, Pierre, and Daniel Roche. *Les Français et l'Ancien Régime.* Vol.1, *La société et l'Etat.* Vol. 2, *Culture et société.* Paris: Armand Colin, 1984.

Grillo, R. D. "Nation" and "State" in Europe. *Anthropological Perspectives.* New York: Academic Press: 1980.

Gschwind, Franz. *Bevölkerungsentwicklung und Wirtschaftsstruktur der Landschaft Basel im 18. Jahrhundert.* Liestal: Kantonale Drucksachen- und Materialzentrale, 1977.

Gustafson, Uno. *Industrialismens Storstad. Studier Rörande Stockholms Sociala, Ekonomiska och Demografiska Struktur 1860–1910.* Stockholm: Kommunalforvaltning, 1976.

Gutmann, Myron P. *War and Rural Life in the Early Modern Low Countries.* Princeton: Princeton University Press, 1980.

Haines, Michael. *Fertility and Occupation: Population Patterns in Industrialization.* New York: Academic Press, 1977.

Hanagan, Michael P. *The Logic of Solidarity: Artisans and Industrial Workers in Three French Towns, 1871–1914.* Urbana: University of Illinois Press, 1980.

Hay, Douglas, et al. *Albion's Fatal Tree: Crime and Society in Eighteenth-Century England.* New York: Pantheon, 1975.

Hechter, Michael. *Internal Colonialism. The Celtic Fringe in British National Development, 1536–1966.* Berkeley: University of California Press, 1975.

Hobsbawm, Eric J. *The Age of Capital, 1848–1875.* London: Weidenfeld & Nicolson, 1975.

Hobsbawm, Eric J., and George Rudé. *Captain Swing.* London: Lawrence & Wishart, 1969.

Hunt, Lynn Avery. *Politics, Culture and Class in the French Revolution.* Berkeley: University of California Press, 1984.

Imhof, Arthur E. *Die Gewonnenen Jahre: Von der Zunahme unserer Lebensspanne seit dreihundert Jahren oder von der Notwendigkeit einer neuen Einstellung zu Leben un Sterben. Ein historischer Essay.* Munich: Beck, 1981.

Jasper, Karlbernhard. *Der Urbanizierungsprozess dargestellt am Beispiel der Stadt Köln.* Cologne: Rheinisch-Westfälisches Wirtschaftsarchiv zu Köln, 1977.

Johansen, Hans Christian. *Vevolkningsudvikling og familie Struktur: det 18. arhunderede.* Odense: Odense University Press, 1975.

Johnson, Robert Eugene. *Peasant and Proletarian: The Working Class of Moscow in the Late Nineteenth Century.* New Brunswick, N.J.: Rutgers University Press, 1979.

Kaplan, Temma. *Anarchists of Andalusia, 1868–1903.* Princeton: Princeton University Press, 1977.

Kellenbenz, Hermann, ed. *Agrarische Nebengewerbe und Formen der Reagrarisierung im Spätmittelalter und 19./20. Jahrhundert.* Stuttgart: Gustav Fischer, 1975.

Kussmaul, Ann. *Servants in Husbandry in Early Modern England.* Cambridge: Cambridge University Press, 1981.

Lebrun, François. *Les hommes et la mort en Anjou aux XVIIe et XVIIIe siècles. Essai de démographie et de psychologie historiques.* Paris: Mouton, 1971.

Lees, Lynn Hollen. *Exiles of Erin. Irish Migrants in Victorian London.* Ithaca: Cornell University Press, 1979.

Lefebvre, Georges. *Les paysans du Nord pendant la Révolution française.* First published in 1924. Bari: Laterza, 1959.

Léon, Pierre, François Crouzet, and Raymond Gascon, eds. *L'industrialisation en eu-*

rope au XIXe siècle. Cartographie et typologie. Paris: Editions du Centre National de la Recherche Scientifique, 1972.

Léon, Pierre. Géographie de la fortune et structures sociales à Lyon au XIXe siècle (1815–1914). Lyon: Centre d'Histoire Economique et Sociale de la Région Lyonnaise, 1974.

Lequin, Yves. Les ouvriers de la région lyonnaise (1848–1914). 2 vols. Lyon: Presses Universitaires de Lyon, 1977.

Le Roy Ladurie, Emmanuel. Montaillou, village occitan de 1292 à 1324. Paris: Gallimard, 1975.

_____. Le Carnaval de Romans: De la Chandeleur au mercredi des Cendres 1579–1580. Paris: Gallimard, 1979.

Lesthaeghe, Ron J. The Decline of Belgian Fertility, 1800–1970. Princeton: Princeton University Press, 1977.

Levine, David. Family Formation in an Age of Nascent Capitalism. New York: Academic Press, 1977.

Lis, Catarina, and Hugo Soly. Poverty and Capitalism in Pre-Industrial Europe. Atlantic Highlands, N.J.: Humanities Press, 1979.

Lottes, Gunther. Politische Aufklärung und plebejisches Publikum: Zur Theorie und Praxis des englischen Radikalismus im späten 18. Jahrhundert. Munich: Oldenbourg, 1979.

Lottin, Alain. Vie et mentalité d'un lillois sous Louis XIV. Lille: E. Raoust, 1968.

Lucassen, Jan. Naar de Kusten van de Noordzee. Trekarbeid in Europees Perspektief, 1600–1900. Gouda: privately published, 1984.

Margadant, Ted. French Peasants in Revolt: The Insurrection of 1851. Princeton: Princeton University Press, 1979.

Martinius, Sture. Peasant Destinies: The History of 552 Swedes Born 1810–12. Stockholm: Almqvist & Wiksell, 1975.

Medick, Hans. "Plebeian Culture in the Transition to Capitalism." In Culture, Ideology and Politics, edited by Raphael Samuel and Gareth Stedman Jones, 84–112. London: Routledge & Kegan Paul, 1982.

Medick, Hans, and David W. Sabean, eds. Interest and Emotion: Essays on the Study of Family and Kinship. Cambridge: Cambridge University Press, 1984.

Mendels, Franklin. "Aux origines de la proto-industrialisation." Bulletin du Centre d'Histoire Economique et Sociale de la Région Lyonnaise no. 2 (1978): 1–27.

Merriman, John M., ed. Consciousness and Class Experience in Nineteenth Century Europe. New York: Holmes & Meier, 1979.

Mikkelsen, Flemming. Arbejderkultur. Skitse til en hverdagslivets socialhistorie. Aarhus: Universitetsforlaget, 1981.

Moch, Leslie Page. Paths to the City. Regional Migration in Nineteenth-Century France. Beverly Hills: Sage, 1983.

Mokyr, Joel. Industrialization in the Low Countries, 1850–1975. New Haven: Yale University Press, 1976.

Musso, Stefano. Gli Operai di Torino, 1900–1920. Milan: Feltrinelli, 1980.

Niethammer, Lutz, ed. Wohnen im Wandel. Beiträge zur Geschichte des Alltags in der bürgerlichen Gesellschaft. Wuppertal: Hammer, 1979.

Öhngren, Bo. Folk i rörelse: Samhallsutveckling, Flyttnningsmonster och folkrörelseer i Eskilstuna, 1870–1900. Uppsala: Almqvist & Wiksell, 1974.

Outhwaite, R. B., ed. *Marriage and Society. Studies in the Social History of Marriage.* London: Europa, 1981.

Parker, William N., and Eric L. Jones, eds. *European Peasants and their Markets: Essays in Agrarian Economic History.* Princeton: Princeton University Press, 1975.

Passerini, Luisa. *Torino operaia e Fascismo.* Bari: Laterza, 1984.

Perrenoud, Alfred. *La population de Genève du XVIe au début du XIXe siècle.* 2 vols. Geneva: Jullien, 1979.

Perrot, Jean-Claude. *Genèse d'une ville moderne: Caen au XVIIIe siècle.* 2 vols. Paris: Mouton, 1974.

Perrot, Michelle. *Les ouvriers en grève: France, 1871–1890.* 2 vols. Paris: Mouton, 1975.

Pohl, Hans. *Forschungen zur Lage der Arbeiter im Industrialisierungsprozess.* Stuttgart: Klett-Cotta, 1978.

Poitrineau, Abel. *Remues d'hommes. Les migrations montagnardes en France, XVIIe–XVIIIe siècles.* Paris: Aubier, 1983.

Pullat, Raimo, ed. *Problemy istoricheskoĭ demografii SSSR.* Tallinn: Institute of History, Academy of Sciences, Estonian SSR, 1977.

Ramella, Franco. *Terra e Telai. Sistemi di parentela e manufattura nel Biellese dell'Ottocento.* Turin: Einaudi, 1984.

Rebel, Hermann. *Peasant Classes: The Bureaucratization of Property and Family Relations Under Early Habsburg Absolutism, 1511–1636.* Princeton: Princeton University Press, 1983.

Roche, Daniel. *Le siècle des Lumières en province: Académies et académiciens provinciaux, 1680–1789.* 2 vols. Paris: Mouton, 1978.

Rokkan, Stein and Derek W. Urwin, eds. *The Politics of Territorial Identity. Studies in European Regionalism.* Beverly Hills: Sage, 1982.

Rudé, George. *Protest and Punishment: The Story of the Social and Political Protesters Transported to Australia, 1788–1868.* Oxford: Clarendon Press, 1978.

Runblom, Harald, and Hans Norman, eds. *From Sweden to America. A History of the Migration.* Minneapolis: University of Minnesota Press, 1976.

Schneider, Jane, and Peter Schneider. *Culture and Political Economy in Western Sicily.* New York: Academic Press, 1976.

Schofer, Lawrence. *The Formation of a Modern Labor Force: Upper Silesia 1865–1914.* Berkeley: University of California Press, 1975.

Sewell, William H., Jr. *Work and Revolution: The Language of Labor from the Old Regime to 1848.* Cambridge: Cambridge University Press, 1980.

Shorter, Edward. *The Making of the Modern Family.* New York: Basic Books, 1975.

Smith, Richard. "Fertility, Economy and Household Formation in England over Three Centuries." *Population and Development Review* 7 (December 1981): 595–622.

Soboul, Albert. *Les sans-culottes parisiens en l'An II. Mouvement populaire et gouvernement révolutionnaire 2 juin 1793—9 thermidor An II.* Paris: Clavreuil, 1958.

Spufford, Margaret. *Contrasting Communities. English Villagers in the Sixteenth and Seventeenth Centuries.* Cambridge: Cambridge University Press, 1974.

Stearns, Peter N. *Lives of Labor: Work in a Maturing Industrial Society.* New York: Holmes & Meier, 1975.

Stone, Lawrence. *The Crisis of the Aristocracy, 1558–1641.* Oxford: Clarendon Press, 1965.

_____. *The Family, Sex and Marriage in England, 1500–1800.* New York: Harper & Row, 1977.

Storch, Robert D., ed. *Popular Culture and Custom in Nineteenth-Century England.* London: Croom Helm, 1982.

Tanner, Albert. *Spulen—Weben—Sticken. Die Industrialisierung in Appenzell Ausserrhoden.* Zurich: Juris Druck, 1982.

Tawney, R. H. *The Agrarian Problem in the Sixteenth Century.* London: Longman, 1912.

Tenfelde, Klaus. *Sozialgeschichte der Bergarbeiterschaft an der Ruhr im 19. Jahrhundert.* Bonn: Neue Gesellschaft, 1977.

Thompson, E. P. *The Making of the English Working Class.* London: Gollancz, 1963.

_____. *Whigs and Hunters: The Origins of the Black Act.* New York: Pantheon, 1975.

_____. "Eighteenth-Century English Society: Class Struggle Without Class?" *Social History* 3 (May 1978): 133–66.

Tilly, Louise A., and Joan W. Scott. *Women, Work, and Family.* New York: Holt, Rinehart & Winston, 1978.

Tilly, Richard. *Kapital, Staat und sozialer Protest in der deutschen Industrialisierung.* Göttingen: Vandenhoeck & Ruprecht, 1980.

Tønnesson, Kare. *La défaite des sans-culottes. Mouvement populaire et réaction bourgeoise en l'an III.* Paris: Presses Universitaires de France, 1959.

Trexler, Richard. *Public Life in Renaissance Florence.* New York: Academic Press, 1980.

Trumbach, Randolph. *The Rise of the Egalitarian Family. Aristocratic Kinship and Domestic Relations in Eighteenth-Century England.* New York: Academic Press, 1978.

Van der Wee, Herman, and Eddy van Cauwenberghe, eds. *Productivity of Land and Agricultural Innovation in the Low Countries (1250–1800).* Louvain: Leuven University Press, 1978.

Verdery, Katherine. *Transylvanian Villagers. Three Centuries of Political, Economic and Ethnic Change.* Berkeley: University of California Press, 1983.

Vovelle, Michel. *Ville et campagne au XVIIe siècle (Chartres et la Beauce).* Paris: Editions Sociales, 1980.

Vries, Jan de. *The Dutch Rural Economy in the Golden Age, 1500–1700.* New Haven: Yale University Press, 1974.

_____. *European Urbanization: 1500–1800.* Cambridge, Mass.: Harvard University Press, 1984.

Weber, Eugen. *Peasants into Frenchmen: The Modernization of Rural France, 1870–1914.* Stanford: Stanford University Press, 1976.

Wrightson, Keith, and David Levine. *Poverty and Piety in an English Village: Terling, 1525–1700.* New York: Academic Press, 1979.

Wrightson, Keith. *English Society, 1580–1680.* London: Hutchinson, 1982.

Wrigley, E. A., and R. S. Schofield. *The Population History of England, 1541–1871: A Reconstruction.* London: Arnold, 1981.

UNITED STATES

Achenbaum, W. Andrew. *Old Age in the New Land: The American Experience since 1790.* Baltimore: Johns Hopkins University Press, 1978.

Barron, Harold. *Those Who Stayed Behind: Rural Society in Nineteenth Century New England.* Cambridge: Cambridge University Press, 1984.

Barton, Josef J. *Peasants and Strangers: Italians, Rumanians, and Slovaks in an American City, 1890–1950.* Cambridge, Mass.: Harvard University Press, 1975.

Bender, Thomas. *Toward an Urban Vision: Ideas and Institutions in Nineteenth-Century America.* Lexington: University of Kentucky Press, 1975.

———. *Community and Social Change.* New Brunswick, N.J.: Rutgers University Press, 1978.

Benson, Lee. *The Concept of Jacksonian Democracy: New York as a Test Case.* Princeton: Princeton University Press, 1961.

Berlin, Ira. *Slaves Without Masters: The Free Negro In the Antebellum South.* New York: Vintage Books, 1974.

Blassingame, John W. *Black New Orleans, 1860–1880.* Chicago: University of Chicago Press, 1973.

Bledstein, Burton J. *The Culture of Professionalism: The Middle Class and the Development of Higher Education in America.* New York: W. W. Norton, 1976.

Blumin, Stuart M. *The Urban Threshold: Growth and Change in a Nineteenth-Century American Community.* Chicago: University of Chicago Press, 1976.

Bodnar, John, Roger Simon, and Michel P. Weber. *Lives of Their Own: Blacks, Italians, and Poles in Pittsburgh, 1900–1960.* Urbana: University of Illinois Press, 1982.

Bogue, Allan, G. *Clio and the Bitch Goddess: Quantification in American Political History.* Beverly Hills: Sage, 1983.

Borchert, James. *Alley Life in Washington: Family, Community, Religion, and Folklife in the City, 1850–1970.* Urbana: University of Illinois Press, 1980.

Boyer, Paul S. *Urban Masses and Moral Order in America, 1820–1920.* Cambridge, Mass.: Harvard University Press, 1978.

Brock, William R. *Investigation and Responsibility: Public Responsibility in the United States, 1865–1900.* Cambridge: Cambridge University Press, 1984.

Bruchey, Stuart W. *Small Business in American Life.* New York: Columbia University Press, 1980.

Chandler, Alfred D., Jr. *The Visible Hand: The Managerial Revolution in American Business.* Cambridge, Mass.: Harvard University Press, 1977.

Chudacoff, Howard P. *Mobile Americans: Residential and Social Mobility in Omaha, 1880–1920.* New York: Oxford University Press, 1972.

Cinel, Dino. *From Italy to San Francisco. The Immigrant Experience.* Stanford: Stanford University Press, 1982.

Cohen, Patricia Cline. *A Calculating People: The Spread of Numeracy in Early America.* Chicago: University of Chicago Press, 1982.

Commons, John R. et al. *History of Labour in the United States.* 4 vols. New York: Macmillan, 1918–1935.

Conzen, Kathleen Neils. *Immigrant Milwaukee, 1836–1860: Accommodation and Community in a Frontier City.* Cambridge, Mass.: Harvard University Press, 1976.

———. "Community Studies, Urban History, and American Local History." In *The Past Before Us: Contemporary Historical Writing in the United States,* edited by Michael Kammen, 270–91. Ithaca: Cornell University Press, 1980.

———. "Historical Approaches to the Study of Rural Ethnic Communities." In

Ethnicity on the Great Plains, edited by Frederick C. Luebke, 1–18. Lincoln: University of Nebraska Press, 1980.

Conzen, Michael P. "The American Urban System in the Nineteenth Century." In *Geography and the Urban Environment: Progress in Research and Applications*, edited by D. T. Herbert and R. J. Johnston, vol. IV, 295–347. New York: John Wiley, 1981.

Curti, Merle Eugene. *The Making of an American Community: A Case Study of Democracy in a Frontier Country.* Stanford: Stanford University Press, 1959.

Davis, David Brion. *Slavery and Human Progress.* New York: Oxford University Press, 1984.

Dawley, Alan. *Class and Community: The Industrial Revolution in Lynn.* Cambridge, Mass.: Harvard University Press, 1976.

Decker, Peter R. *Fortunes and Failures: White-Collar Mobility in Nineteenth Century San Francisco.* Cambridge, Mass.: Harvard University Press, 1978.

Demos, John. *Entertaining Satan: Witchcraft and the Culture of Early New England.* New York: Oxford University Press, 1984.

Dublin, Thomas. *Women at Work: The Transformation of Work and Community in Lowell, Massachusetts, 1826–1860.* New York: Columbia University Press, 1981.

Fogel, Robert William, and Stanley L. Engerman. *Time on the Cross.* Vol. 1, *The Economics of American Negro Slavery.* Vol. 2, *Evidence and Methods.* Boston: Little, Brown, 1974.

Formisano, Robert P. *The Birth of Mass Political Parties, Michigan, 1827–1861.* Princeton: Princeton University Press, 1971.

Fox, Richard Wightman, and T. J. Jackson Lears, eds. *The Culture of Consumption: Critical Essays in American History, 1880–1980.* New York: Pantheon, 1983.

Franklin, John Hope. *Racial Equality in America.* Chicago: University of Chicago Press, 1976.

Frisch, Michael H. *Town into City: Springfield, Massachusetts and the Meaning of Community, 1840–1880.* Cambridge, Mass.: Harvard University Press, 1972.

Frisch, Michael H., and Daniel J. Walkowitz, eds. *Working-Class America: Essays on Labor, Community, and American Society.* Urbana: University of Illinois Press, 1983.

Gaston, Paul M. *The Women of Fair Hope.* Athens: University of Georgia Press, 1984.

Geison, Gerald L., ed. *Professions and Professional Ideologies in America.* Chapel Hill: University of North Carolina Press, 1983.

Genovese, Eugene D. *Roll, Jordan, Roll: The World the Slaves Made.* New York: Pantheon, 1974.

Gordon, David, Richard Edwards, and Michael Reich. *Segmented Work, Divided Workers: The Historical Transformation of Labor in the United States.* Cambridge: Cambridge University Press, 1982.

Greene, Jack P. "The Social Origins of the American Revolution." *Political Science Quarterly* 88 (March 1973): 1–22.

Greven, Philip. *The Protestant Temperament: Patterns of Childrearing, Religious Experience, and the Self in Early America.* New York: Alfred A. Knopf, 1977.

Griffen, Clyde, and Sally Griffen. *Natives and Newcomers: The Ordering of Opportunity in Mid-Nineteenth-Century Poughkeepsie.* Cambridge, Mass.: Harvard University Press, 1978.

Gross, Robert A. *The Minutemen and their World.* New York: Hill & Wang, 1976.

Gutman, Herbert G. *The Black Family in Slavery and Freedom, 1750–1925*. New York: Pantheon, 1976.

———. *Work, Culture and Society in Industrializing America: Essays in American Working-Class and Social History*. New York: Alfred A. Knopf, 1976.

Hahn, Steven. *The Roots of Southern Populism: Yeoman Farmers and the Transformation of the Georgia Upcountry, 1850–1890*. New York: Oxford University Press, 1983.

Hahn, Steven, and Jonathan Prude. *The Countryside in the Age of Capitalist Transformation*. Chapel Hill: University of North Carolina Press, 1985.

Handlin, Oscar. *Boston's Immigrants, 1790–1865: A Study in Acculturation*. Cambridge, Mass.: Harvard University Press, 1941.

Hareven, Tamara K. *Family Time and Industrial Time: The Relationship Between Family and Work in a New England Industrial Community*. Cambridge: Cambridge University Press, 1982.

Hays, Samuel P. *American Political History as Social Analysis*. Knoxville: University of Tennessee Press, 1980.

Hershberg, Theodore, ed. *Philadelphia: Work, Space, Family, and Group Experience in the Nineteenth Century*. New York: Oxford University Press, 1981.

Higham, John. "Current Trends in the Study of Ethnicity in the United States." *Journal of American Ethnic History* 2 (Fall 1982): 5–15.

———. *Send These to Me: Jews and Other Immigrants in Urban America*. Rev. ed. Baltimore: Johns Hopkins University Press, 1984.

Hirsch, Arnold R. *Making the Second Ghetto: Race and Housing in Chicago, 1940–1960*. Cambridge: Cambridge University Press, 1983.

Holt, Thomas. *Black over White: Negro Political Leadership in South Carolina during Reconstruction*. Urbana: University of Illinois Press, 1977.

Hvidt, Kristian. *Flight to America: The Social Background of 300,000 Danish Emigrants*. New York: Academic Press, 1975.

Innes, Stephen. *Labor in a New Land: Economy and Society in Seventeenth-Century Springfield*. Princeton: Princeton University Press, 1983.

Isaac, Rhys. *The Transformation of Virginia, 1740–1790*. Chapel Hill: University of North Carolina Press, 1981.

Johnson, Paul E. *A Shopkeeper's Millennium: Society and Revivals in Rochester, New York, 1815–1837*. New York: Hill & Wang, 1978.

Jones, Alice Hanson. *Wealth of a Nation To Be: The American Colonies on the Eve of the Revolution*. New York: Columbia University Press, 1980.

Katz, Michael B. *The People of Hamilton, Canada West*. Cambridge, Mass.: Harvard University Press, 1975.

Katzman, David M. *Seven Days a Week: Women and Domestic Service in Industrializing America*. New York: Oxford University Press, 1978.

Katznelson, Ira. *City Trenches: Urban Politics and the Patterning of Class in the United States*. New York: Pantheon, 1981.

Keller, Morton. *Affairs of State: Public Life in Late Nineteenth-Century America*. Cambridge, Mass.: Harvard University Press, 1977.

Kessler-Harris, Alice. *Out to Work: A History of Wage Earning Women in the United States*. Oxford: Oxford University Press, 1982.

Kessner, Thomas. *The Golden Door: Italian and Jewish Immigrant Mobility in New York City,*

1880–1915. New York: Oxford University Press, 1977.

Kett, Joseph F. *Rites of Passage: Adolescence in America 1790 to the Present*. New York: Basic Books, 1977.

Kleppner, Paul. *The Third Electoral System, 1853–1892: Parties, Voters, and Political Cultures*. Chapel Hill: University of North Carolina Press, 1979.

Knights, Peter R. *The Plain People of Boston, 1830–1860: A Study in City Growth*. New York: Oxford University Press, 1971.

Kocka, Jürgen. *White Collar Workers in America, 1890–1940*. Translated by Maura Kealey. Beverly Hills: Sage, 1980.

Kolko, Gabriel. *Main Currents in Modern American History*. New York: Harper & Row, 1976.

Kusmer, Kenneth L. *A Ghetto Takes Shape: Black Cleveland, 1870–1930*. Urbana: University of Illinois Press, 1976.

Licht, Walter. *Working for the Railroad: The Organization of Work in the Nineteenth Century*. Princeton: Princeton University Press, 1983.

Lockridge, Kenneth A. *A New England Town: The First Hundred Years*. Dedham, Massachusetts, 1636–1736. New York: W. W. Norton, 1970.

Main, Gloria L. *Tobacco Colony: Life in Early Maryland, 1650–1720*. Princeton: Princeton University Press, 1982.

May, Elaine Tyler. *Great Expectations: Marriage and Divorce in Post-Victorian America*. Chicago: University of Chicago Press, 1980.

Monkkonen, Eric H. *Police in Urban America, 1860–1920*. Cambridge: Cambridge University Press, 1981.

Montgomery, David. *Workers' Control in America: Studies in the History of Work, Technology, and Labor Struggles*. Cambridge: Cambridge University Press, 1979.

Murrin, John M. "Review Essay." *History & Theory: Studies in the Philosophy of History* 11 (1972): 226–75

Nash, Gary B. *The Urban Crucible: Social Change, Political Consciousness and the Origins of the American Revolution*. Cambridge, Mass.: Harvard University Press, 1979.

Nelson, William E. *The Roots of American Bureaucracy, 1830–1900*. Cambridge, Mass.: Harvard University Press, 1982.

Nugent, Walter T. K. *Structures of American Social History*. Bloomington: Indiana University Press, 1981.

Owsley, Frank Lawrence. *Plain Folk of the Old South*. Baton Rouge: Louisiana State University Press, 1949.

Patterson, James. *America's Struggle Against Poverty*. Cambridge, Mass.: Harvard University Press, 1981.

Pessen, Edward, ed. *Three Centuries of Social Mobility in America*. Lexington, Mass.: Heath, 1974.

Potter, David M. *People of Plenty: Economic Abundance and the American Character*. Chicago: University of Chicago Press, 1954.

Pred, Allan. *Urban Growth and City Systems in the United States, 1840–1860*. Cambridge, Mass.: Harvard University Press, 1980.

Prude, Jonathan. *The Coming of the Industrial Order: Town and Factory Life in Rural Massachusetts, 1810–1860*. Cambridge: Cambridge University Press, 1983.

Robinson, Armstead L. "Beyond the Realm of Social Consensus: New Meanings of Reconstruction for American History." *Journal of American History* 68 (September 1981): 276–97.

Rodgers, Daniel T. *The Work Ethic in Industrial America, 1850–1920.* Chicago: University of Chicago Press, 1978.

Rosner, David. *A Once Charitable Enterprise: Hospitals and Health Care in Brooklyn and New York, 1885–1915.* Cambridge: Cambridge University Press, 1982.

Ryan, Mary P. *Cradle of the Middle Class: The Family in Oneida County, New York.* Cambridge: Cambridge University Press, 1981.

Schlesinger, Arthur Maier. *The Rise of the City, 1878–1898.* New York: Macmillan, 1933.

Sklar, Kathryn Kish. *Catharine Beecher: A Study in American Domesticity.* New Haven: Yale University Press, 1973.

Skowronek, Stephen. *Building a New American State: The Expansion of National Administrative Capacities, 1877–1920.* Cambridge: Cambridge University Press, 1982.

Tentler, Leslie Woodcock. *Wage Earning Women: Industrial Work and Family Life in the United States, 1900–1930.* New York: Oxford University Press, 1979.

Thernstrom, Stephan. *The Other Bostonians: Poverty and Progress in the American Metropolis, 1880–1970.* Cambridge, Mass.: Harvard University Press, 1973.

————, ed. *Harvard Encyclopedia of American Ethnic Groups.* Cambridge, Mass.: Harvard University Press, 1980.

Vinovskis, Maris A. *Fertility in Massachusetts from the Revolution to the Civil War.* New York: Academic Press, 1981.

Wade, Richard C. *Slavery in the Cities: The South, 1820–1860.* New York: Oxford University Press, 1964.

Wallace, Anthony F. C. *Rockdale: The Growth of an American Village in the Early Industrial Revolution.* New York: Alfred A. Knopf, 1978.

Warner, Sam Bass, Jr. *The Private City: Philadelphia in Three Periods of its Growth.* Philadelphia: University of Pennsylvania Press, 1968.

Wiebe, Robert H. *The Search for Order, 1877–1920.* New York: Hill & Wang, 1967.

Wilentz, Sean. *Chants Democratic: New York City and the Rise of the American Working Class, 1789–1850.* New York: Oxford University Press, 1984.

Woodman, Harold. "Sequel to Slavery: The New History Views the Postbellum South." *Journal of Southern History* 43 (November 1977): 523–54.

Woodward, C. Vann. *The Burden of Southern History.* Rev. ed. Baton Rouge: Louisiana State University Press, 1968.

Zunz, Olivier. *The Changing Face of Inequality. Urbanization, Industrial Development and Immigrants in Detroit, 1880–1920.* Chicago: University of Chicago Press, 1982.

LATIN AMERICA

Assadourian, Carlos Sempat. *El sistema de la economía colonial. Mercado interno, regiones, y espacio económico.* Lima: Instituto de Estudios Peruanos, 1982.

Bakewell, Peter J. *Silver Mining and Society in Colonial Mexico, Zacatecas, 1546–1700.* Cambridge: Cambridge University Press, 1971.

Balmori, Diana, Stuart F. Voss, and Miles Wortman. *Notable Family Networks in Latin*

America. Chicago: University of Chicago Press, 1984.

Bauer, Arnold J. *Chilean Rural Society from the Spanish Conquest to 1930.* Cambridge: Cambridge University Press, 1975.

Bergquist, Charles W. "Recent United States Studies in Latin American History: Trends Since 1965." *Latin American Research Review* 9 (Spring 1974): 3–37.

_____. *Coffee and Conflict in Colombia, 1886–1910.* Durham, N.C.: Duke University Press, 1978.

_____. "Latin America: A Dissenting View of 'Latin American History in World Perspective.'" In *International Handbook of Historical Studies,* edited by Georg Iggers and Harold T. Parker, 371–86. Westport, Conn.: Greenwood Press, 1979.

Borah, Woodrow. *Justice by Insurance: The General Indian Court of Colonial Mexico and the Legal Aides of the Half-Real.* Berkeley: University of California Press, 1983.

Bowser, Frederick P. *The African Slave in Colonial Peru, 1524–1650.* Stanford: Stanford University Press, 1974.

Brading, David A. *Miners and Merchants in Bourbon Mexico, 1763–1810.* Cambridge: Cambridge University Press, 1971.

_____. *Haciendas and Ranchos in the Mexican Bajío: Leon, 1700–1860.* Cambridge: Cambridge University Press, 1978.

Cardoso, Ciro F. S., ed. *Formación y desarrollo de la burguesía en México, siglo XIX.* Mexico: Siglo Veintiuno Editores, 1978.

_____, ed. *México en el siglo XIX (1821–1910): Historia económica y de la estructura social.* Mexico: Editorial Nueva Imagen, 1980.

Cardoso, Fernando H., and Enzo Faletto. *Dependency and Development in Latin America.* First Spanish language edition in 1969, expanded and emended edition. Berkeley: University of California Press, 1979.

Carmagnani, Marcello. *Formación y crisis de un sistema feudal: América Latina del siglo XVI a nuestros días.* Mexico: Siglo XXI, 1976.

Chilcote, Ronald, ed., *Dependency and Marxism: Toward a Resolution of the Debate.* Boulder: Westview Press, 1982.

Clendinnen, Inga. "Landscape and World View: The Survival of Yucatec Maya Culture Under Spanish Conquest." *Comparative Studies in Society and History* 22 (July 1980): 374–93.

Coatsworth, John H. *Growth Against Development: The Economic Impact of Railroads in Porfirian Mexico.* DeKalb: Northern Illinois University Press, 1981.

_____. "The Limits of Colonial Absolutism: The State in Eighteenth-Century Mexico." In *Essays in the Political, Economic, and Social History of Colonial Latin America,* edited by Karen Spalding, 25–52. Newark: University of Delaware Latin American Studies Program, 1982.

Collier, George, Renato I. Rosaldo, and John D. Wirth, eds., *The Inca and Aztec States, 1400–1800: Anthropology and History.* New York: Academic Press, 1982.

De la Peña, Guillermo. *A Legacy of Promises: Agriculture, Politics and Ritual in the Morelos Highlands of Mexico.* Manchester: Manchester University Press, 1982.

Delumeau, Jean. *Catholicism Between Luther and Voltaire.* Philadelphia: Westminster Press, 1977.

Duncan, Kenneth, and Ian Rutledge, eds., *Land and Labour in Latin America: Essays on the Development of Agrarian Capitalism in the Nineteenth and Twentieth Centuries.* Cambridge: Cambridge University Press, 1977.

Farriss, Nancy. *Maya Society under Colonial Rule: The Collective Enterprise of Survival*. Princeton: Princeton University Press, 1984.

Frank, André Gunder. *Capitalism and Underdevelopment in Latin America: Historical Studies in Chile and Brazil*. New York: Monthly Review Press, 1967.

Garavaglia, Juan Carlos. *Mercado interno y economía colonial*. Mexico: Editorial Grijalbo, 1983.

Gibson, Charles. *The Aztecs Under Spanish Rule: A History of the Indians of the Valley of Mexico, 1519–1810*. Stanford: Stanford University Press, 1964.

Gilbert, Joseph. *Revolution from Without: Yucatan, Mexico, and the United States, 1880–1924*. Cambridge: Cambridge University Press, 1982.

González y González, Luis. *Pueblo en vilo: Microhistoria de San José de Gracia*. Mexico: El Colegio de México, 1968.

Grieshaber, Erwin P. "Survival of Indian Communities in Nineteenth-Century Bolivia: A Regional Comparison." *Journal of Latin American Studies* 12 (November 1980): 223–69.

Halperín Donghi, Tulio. *Historia contemporánea de América Latina*. 3d ed. Madrid: Alianza Editorial, 1972.

Haring, Clarence. *The Spanish Empire in America*. New York: Oxford University Press, 1947.

Hoberman, Louisa. "Merchants in Seventeenth-Century Mexico City: A Preliminary Portrait." *Hispanic American Historical Review* 57 (August 1977): 479–503.

Hunefeldt, Christine. "Comunidad, curas, y comuneros hacia fines del período colonial." *HISLA: Revista Latinoamericana de Historia Económica y Social* 2 (1983): 3–32.

Lafaye, Jacques. *Quetzalcoatl and Guadalupe: The Formation of Mexican National Consciousness, 1531–1813*. Chicago: University of Chicago Press, 1976.

LeGrand, Catherine C. "Perspectives for the Historical Study of Rural Politics and the Colombian Case: An Overview." *Latin American Research Review* 12 (1977): 7–36.

———. "Labor Acquisition and Social Conflict on the Colombian Frontier." *Journal of Latin American Studies* 16 (May 1984): 27–49.

Lira, Andrés. *Comunidades indígenas frente a la ciudad de México: Tenochtitlán y Tlatelolco, sus pueblos y barrios, 1812–1919*. Mexico: El Colegio de México/El Colegio de Michoacán, 1983.

Lockhart, James. *Spanish Peru, 1532–1560*. Madison: University of Wisconsin Press, 1968.

———. "The Social History of Colonial Spanish America." *Latin American Research Review* 7 (Spring 1972): 6–46.

Lockhart, James, and Stuart B. Schwartz. *Early Latin America: A History of Colonial Spanish America and Brazil*. Cambridge: Cambridge University Press, 1983.

MacLeod, Murdo. *Spanish Central America: A Socioeconomic History, 1520–1720*. Berkeley: University of California Press, 1973.

Mallon, Florencia E. *The Defense of Community in Peru's Central Highlands: Peasant Struggle and Capitalist Transition, 1860–1940*. Princeton: Princeton University Press, 1983.

Martínez Alier, Verena. *Marriage, Class and Colour in Nineteenth-Century Cuba: A Study of Racial Attitudes and Sexual Values in a Slave Society*. Cambridge: Cambridge University Press, 1974.

Mintz, Sidney W. "Time, Sugar and Sweetness." *Marxist Perspectives* 2 (Winter 1979–1980): 56–73.

Mintz, Sidney W., and Richard Price. *An Anthropological Approach to the Afro-American Past: A Caribbean Perspective*. Philadelphia: Institute for the Study of Human Issues, 1976.

Moreno Fraginals, Manuel. *La historia como arma y otros estudios sobre esclavos, ingenios y plantaciones*. Barcelona: Editorial Crítica, 1983.

Morin, Claude. *Michoacán en la Nueva España del siglo XVIII: Crecimiento y desigualdad en una economía colonial*. Mexico: Fondo de Cultura Económica, 1979.

Mörner, Magnus. *Historia social latinoamericana (nuevos enfoques)*. Caracas: Universidad Católica Andrés Bello, 1979.

————. *La corona española y los foráneos en los pueblos de indios de América*. Stockholm: Almqvist & Wiksell, 1970.

————. "Economic Factors and Stratification in Colonial Spanish America with Special Regard to Elites." *Hispanic American Historical Review* 63 (May 1983): 335–70.

Pastor. Rodolfo. "La comunidad agraria y el Estado en México: Una historia cíclica." *Diálogos*, no. 108 (November–December 1982): 16–26.

Platt, Tristan. *Estado boliviano y ayllu andino. Tierra y tributo en el norte de Potosí*. Lima: Instituto de Estudios Peruanos, 1982.

Preston, James J., ed. *Mother Worship: Theme and Variations*. Chapel Hill: University of North Carolina Press, 1982.

Schwartz, Stuart B. *Sovereignty and Society in Colonial Brazil: The High Court of Bahia and Its Judges, 1609–1751*. Berkeley: University of California Press, 1973.

Scott, Rebecca. "Gradual Abolition and the Dynamics of Slave Emancipation in Cuba, 1868–1886." *Hispanic American Historical Review* 63 (February 1983): 449–77.

Smith, Carol A. "Local History in Global Context: Social and Economic Transitions in Western Guatemala." *Comparative Studies in Society and History* 26 (April 1984): 193–228.

Socolow, Susan M. *The Merchants of Buenos Aires, 1778–1810: Family and Commerce*. Cambridge: Cambridge University Press, 1978.

Spalding, Karen. *Huarochirí: An Andean Society Under Inca and Spanish Rule*. Stanford: Stanford University Press, 1984.

Stein, Stanley, and Barbara Stein. *The Colonial Heritage of Latin America: Essays on Economic Dependence in Perspective*. New York: Oxford University Press, 1970.

Stern, Steve J. *Peru's Indian Peoples and the Challenge of Spanish Conquest: Huamanga to 1640*. Madison: University of Wisconsin Press, 1982.

Taussig, Michael T. *The Devil and Commodity Fetishism in South America*. Chapel Hill: University of North Carolina Press, 1980.

Taylor, William B. *Drinking, Homicide, and Rebellion in Colonial Mexican Villages*. Stanford: Stanford University Press, 1979.

Turner, Victor. *The Forest of Symbols*. Ithaca: Cornell University Press, 1967.

Turner, Victor, and Edith Turner. *Image and Pilgrimage in Christian Culture*. New York: Columbia University Press, 1978.

Warman, Arturo. *"We Come to Object": The Peasants of Morelos and the National State*. Baltimore: Johns Hopkins University Press, 1980.

Wolf, Eric R. "Types of Latin American Peasantry: A Preliminary Discussion." *American Anthropologist* 57 (June 1955): 452–71.

————. "Closed Corporate Communities in Mesoamerica and Java." *Southwestern Journal of Anthropology* 13 (Spring 1957): 1–18.

———. "The Virgin of Guadalupe: Mexican National Symbol." *Journal of American Folklore* 71 (January–March 1958): 34–39.
Womack, John. *Zapata and the Mexican Revolution.* New York: Alfred A. Knopf, 1969.
Wortman, Miles. *Government and Society in Central America, 1680–1840.* New York: Columbia University Press, 1982.

AFRICA

Adas, Michael. *Prophets of Rebellion: Millenarian Protest Movements Against the European Colonial Order.* Chapel Hill: University of North Carolina Press, 1979.
Ajayi, Jacob F. A. "The Continuity of African Institutions Under Colonialism." In *Emerging Themes in African History,* edited by Terence O. Ranger, 189–200. Nairobi: East African Publishing House, 1968.
Allen, James de V. "Swahili Culture and the Nature of East Coast Settlement." *International Journal of African Historical Studies* 14 (1981): 306–34.
Alpers, Edward A. *Ivory and Slaves in East Central Africa: Changing Patterns of Trade in East Central Africa.* London: Heinemann, 1975.
Armah, Ayi Kwei. *The Beautyful Ones Are Not Yet Born.* London: Heinemann, 1969.
Atieno-Odhiambo, E. S. "The Movement of Ideas: A Case Study of Intellectual Responses to Colonialism Among the Liganua Peasants." In *History and Social Change in East Africa,* edited by Bethwell A. Ogot, 165–85. Nairobi: East African Publishing House, 1976.
Beinart, William. "Joyini Inkomo: Cattle Advances and the Origins of Migrancy from Pondoland." *Journal of Southern African Studies* 5 (April 1979): 199–219.
Berger, Iris. *Religion and Resistance: East African Kingdoms in the Precolonial Period.* Tervuren, Belg.: Musée Royal de l'Afrique Centrale, 1981.
Berque, Jacques. *Ulémas, fondateurs, insurgés du Maghreb. XVIIe siècle.* Paris: Sindbad, 1982.
Berry, Sara S. "The Food Crisis and Agrarian Change in Africa: A Review Essay." *African Studies Review* 27 (June 1984): 59–112.
Blount, Ben G. "Agreeing to Agree on Genealogy: A Luo Sociology of Knowledge." In *Sociocultural Dimensions of Language Use,* edited by Mary Sanches and Ben G. Blount, 117–35. New York: Academic Press, 1975.
Botte, Roger "Burundi: de quoi vivait l'Etat." *Cahiers d'Etudes Africaines* 87–8 (1982): 277–324.
Buchanan, Carole. "Perceptions of Ethnic Interaction in the East African Interior: The Kitara Complex." *International Journal of African Historical Studies* 11 (1978): 410–28.
Clarence-Smith, W. Gervais. "Slaves, Commoners and Landlords in Bulozi, c. 1875 to 1906." *Journal of African History* 20 (1979): 219–34.
Cohen, Abner *Custom and Politics in Urban Africa: A Study of Hausa Migrants in Yoruba Towns.* Berkeley: University of California Press, 1969.
Cohen, David William. *Womunafu's Bunafu: A Study of Authority in a Nineteenth Century African Community.* Princeton: Princeton University Press, 1977.
———. "The Face of Contact: A Model of a Cultural and Linguistic Frontier in Early Eastern Uganda." In *Nilotic Studies. Proceedings of the International Symposium on*

Languages and History of the Nilotic Peoples, Cologne, January 4–6, 1982, edited by Rainer Vössen and Marianne Bechhaus-Gerst, 339–55. Berlin: Dietrich Reimer, 1983.

Cohen, Robin, and Jean Copans, eds. *African Labor History*. Beverly Hills: Sage, 1978.

Cooper, Frederick. "The Problem of Slavery in African Culture." *Journal of African History* 20 (1979): 103–25.

————. *From Slaves to Squatters: Plantation Labor and Agriculture in Zanzibar and Coastal Kenya, 1890–1925*. New Haven: Yale University Press, 1980.

————. "Africa and the World Economy." *African Studies Review* 24 (April 1981): 1–86.

————, ed. *Struggle for the City*. Beverly Hills: Sage, 1983.

Copans, Jean. *Les marabouts de l'arachide*. Paris: Sycamore, 1980.

Curtin, Philip D. *The Image of Africa: British Ideas and Action, 1780–1850*. Madison: University of Wisconsin Press, 1964.

————. *The Atlantic Slave Trade: A Census*. Madison: University of Wisconsin Press, 1969.

————. *Economic Change in Precolonial Africa: Senegambia in the Era of the Slave Trade*. Madison: University of Wisconsin Press, 1975.

Fage, John D. "Slaves and Society in Western Africa, c. 1445–c. 1700." *Journal of African History* 21 (1980): 289–310.

Fox, Lorene Kimball, ed. *East African Childhood: Three Versions*. Nairobi: Oxford University Press, 1967.

Freund, Bill. "Labor and Labor History in Africa: A Review of the Literature." *African Studies Review* 27 (June 1984): 1–58.

Furedi, Fred. "The Kikuyu Squatters in the Rift Valley: 1918–1929." In *Hadith 5: Economic and Social History of East Africa*, edited by Bethwell A. Ogot, 177–94. Nairobi: East African Literature Bureau, 1975.

Fyfe, Christopher, ed. *African Studies Since 1945: A Tribute to Basil Davidson*. New York: Holmes & Meier, 1976.

Goody, Esther N. *Parenthood and Social Reproduction: Fostering and Occupational Roles in West Africa*. Cambridge: Cambridge University Press, 1982.

Goody, Jack. *Production and Reproduction: A Comparative Study of the Domestic Domain*. Cambridge: Cambridge University Press, 1976.

Guyer, Jane. "Household and Community in African Studies." *African Studies Review* 24 (April 1981): 87–137.

Gwassa, G. C. K. "Kinjikitile and the ideology of Maji Maji." In *The Historical Study of African Religion*, edited by Terence O. Ranger and I. Kimambo, 202–17. Berkeley: University of California Press, 1972.

Haliburton, Gordon M. *The Prophet Harris: A Study of an African Prophet and His Mass-Movement in the Ivory Coast and the Gold Coast, 1913–1915*. New York: Oxford University Press, 1971.

Harms, Robert. *River of Wealth, River of Sorrow: The Central Zaire Basin in the Era of the Slave and Ivory Trade, 1500–1891*. New Haven: Yale University Press, 1981.

Hopkins, Elizabeth. "The Nyabingi Cult of Southwestern Uganda." In *Protest and Power in Black Africa*, edited by Robert I. Rotberg and Ali Mazrui, 258–336. New York: Oxford University Press, 1970.

Horton, Robin. "From Fishing Village to City State: A Social History of New

Calabar." In *Man in Africa*, edited by Mary Douglas and Phyllis M. Kaberry, 38–60. London: Tavistock, 1969.

Howard, Allen. "The Relevance of Spatial Analysis for African Economic History: The Sierra Leone-Guinea System." *Journal of African History* 17 (1976) 365–88.

Iliffe, John. "Poverty in Nineteenth-Century Yorubaland." *Journal of African History* 25 (1984): 43–57.

Jensen, Jurgen. "Die Erweiterung des Lungenfisch-Clans in Buganda durch den Anschluss von Bavuma-Gruppen." *Sociologus* 19 (1969): 153–66.

Kabwegyere, Tarsis B. "Land and the Growth of Social Stratification in Uganda: A Sociological Interpretation." In *History and Social Change in East Africa*, edited by Bethwell A. Ogot, 111–33. Nairobi: East African Publishing House, 1976.

Kea, Ray A. *Settlements, Trade, and Polities in the Seventeenth-Century Gold Coast*. Baltimore: Johns Hopkins University Press, 1982.

Kitching, Gavin. *Class and Economic Change in Kenya: The Making of an African Petite Bourgeoisie, 1905–1970*. New Haven: Yale University Press, 1980.

Kottak, Conrad. "Ecological Variables in the Origin and Evolution of African States: The Buganda Example." *Comparative Studies in Society and History* 14 (September 1972): 351–80.

Law, Robin. "In search of a Marxist Perspective on Pre-Colonial Tropical Africa." *Journal of African History* 19 (1978): 441–52.

Linden, Ian. *Church and Revolution in Rwanda*. Manchester: Manchester University Press, 1977.

Lonsdale, John, and Bruce Berman. "Coping with the Contradictions: The Development of the Colonial State in Kenya." *Journal of African History* 20 (1979): 487–506.

Lovejoy, Paul. "The Volume of the Slave Trade: A Synthesis." *Journal of African History* 23 (1982): 473–501.

Low, D. Anthony. *Religion and Society in Buganda: 1875–1900*. Kampala: East African Institute of Social Research, c. 1957.

McCaskie, Thomas C. "State and Society, Marriage and Adultery: Some Considerations Towards a Social History of Pre-Colonial Asante." *Journal of African History* 22 (1981): 477–94.

Manning, Patrick. "The Enslavement of Africans: A Demographic Model." *Canadian Journal of African Studies* 15 (1981): 499–526.

Mapunda, O. B., and G. R. Mpangara. 1969. *The Maji Maji War in Ungoni*. Nairobi: East African Publishing House, 1972.

Marks, Shula, and Anthony Atmore, eds. *Economy and Society in Pre-Industrial South Africa*. London: Longman, 1980.

Marks, Shula, and Richard Rathbone, eds. *Industrialisation and Social Change in South Africa. African Class Formation, Culture and Consciousness, 1870–1930*. London: Longman, 1982.

Meillassoux, C. *L'esclavage en Afrique pré-coloniale*. Paris: Maspéro, 1975.

Miller, Joseph C. *Kings and Kinsmen: Early Mbundu States in Angola*. Oxford: Clarendon Press, 1976.

Murray, Colin. *Families Divided. The Impact of Migrant Labour in Lesotho*. Cambridge: Cambridge University Press, 1981.

Newbury, David S. "Clan Alterations and Political Centralization on Ijwi Island, Zaire, ca. 1780–ca. 1840." *Cahiers d'Etudes Africaines* 22 (1982): 441–54.

Ogot, Bethwell A., and Frederick B. Welbourn. *A Place to Feel at Home: A Study of Two Independent Churches in Western Kenya*. London: Oxford University Press, 1968.

Ogot, Bethwell A., and W. R. Ochieng'. "Mumboism—An Anti-Colonial Movement." In *War and Society in Africa*, edited by Bethwell A. Ogot, 149–77. London: Frank Cass, 1972.

Olusanya, G. O. "The Freed Slaves' Homes: An Unknown Aspect of Northern Nigerian Social History." *Journal of the Historical Society of Nigeria* 3 (1966): 523–38.

Oppong, Christine, ed. *Female and Male in West Africa*. London: G. Allen & Unwin, 1983.

Packard, Randall. "Social Change and the History of Misfortune Among the Bashu of Eastern Zaire." In *Explorations in African Systems of Thought*, edited by Ivan Karp and Charles S. Bird, 237–67. Bloomington: Indiana University Press, 1980.

Palmer, Robin, and Neil Parsons, eds. *The Roots of Rural Poverty in Central and Southern Africa*. Berkeley: University of California Press, 1977.

Peel, John D. Y. *Aladura: A Religious Movement Among the Yoruba*. London: Oxford University Press for the International African Institute, 1968.

Peukert, Wilhelm. *Der atlantische Sklavenhandel von Dahomey (1740–1797)*. Wiesbaden: Steiner, 1978.

Prins, Gwyn. *The Hidden Hippopotamous. Reappraisal in African History: The Early Colonial Experience in Western Zambia*. Cambridge: Cambridge University Press, 1980.

Ranger, Terence O. *Dance and Society in Eastern Africa, 1890–1970: The Beni Ngoma*. Berkeley: University of California Press, 1975.

Ranger, Terence O., and I. Kimambo, eds. *The Historical Study of African Religion*. Berkeley: University of California Press, 1972.

Raum, Otto F. *Chaga Childhood: A Description of Indigenous Education in an East African Tribe*. London: Oxford University Press for the International African Institute, 1940.

Roberts, Andrew D. *A History of the Bemba: Political Growth and Change in Northeastern Zambia Before 1900*. London: Longman, 1973.

Roberts, Richard. "Long Distance Trade and Production: Sinsani in the Nineteenth Century." *Journal of African History* 21 (1980): 169–88.

Roberts, Richard, and Martin Klein. "The Banamba Slave Exodus of 1905 and the Decline of Slavery in the Western Sudan." *Journal of African History* 21 (1980): 375–94.

Rodney, Walter. *A History of the Upper Guinea Coast, 1545–1800*. Oxford: Clarendon Press, 1970.

———. *How Europe Underdeveloped Africa*. London: Bogle-L'Ouverture, 1972.

Salim, Ahmed I. "'Native or Non-Native?' The Problem of Identity and the Social Stratification of the Arab-Swahili of Kenya." In *History and Social Change in East Africa*, edited by Bethwell A. Ogot, 65–85. Nairobi: East African Literature Bureau, 1976.

Sandbrook, Richard, and Robin Cohen, eds. *The Development of an African Working Class*. Toronto: Toronto University Press, 1975.

Schildkrout, Enid. *People of the Zongo: The Transformation of Ethnic Identities in Ghana*. Cambridge: Cambridge University Press, 1978.

Spittler, Gerd. "Administration in a Peasant State." Sociologia Ruralis 23 (1983): 130–44.

Sundkler, Bengt G. M. Bantu Prophets in South Africa. London: Oxford University Press for the International African Institute, 1961.

Tamrat, Tadesse. Church and State in Ethiopia, 1270–1527. Oxford: Clarendon Press, 1975.

Temu, Arnold, and B. Swai. Historians and Africanist History: A Critique. London: Zed Press, 1981.

Terray, Emmanuel. "Long Distance Exchange and the Formation of the State." Economy and Society 3 (August 1974): 315–45.

Thornton, John K. "The Kingdom of Kongo, ca. 1390–1678: The Development of an African Social Formation." Cahiers d'Etudes Africaines 22 (1982): 325–42.

Tosh, John. "Lango Agriculture During the Early Colonial Period: Land and Labour in a Cash-Crop Economy." Journal of African History 19 (1978): 415–39.

———. "The Cash Crop Revolution in Tropical Africa: An Agricultural Reappraisal." African Affairs 79 (1980): 79–94.

Valensi, Lucette. Fellahs tunisiens. L'économie rurale et la vie des campagnes aux XVIIIe et XIXe siècles. Paris: Mouton, 1977.

van Onselen, Charles. Chibaro: African Mine Labour in Southern Rhodesia, 1900–1933. London: Pluto Press, 1976.

———. Studies in the Social and Economic History of the Witwatersrand, 1890–1914. 2 vols. London: Longman, 1982.

Vansina, Jan. The Tio Kingdom of the Middle Congo, 1880–1892. London: Oxford University Press for the International African Institute, 1973.

Vaughan, Megan. "Which Family?: Problems in the Reconstruction of the History of the Family as an Economic and Cultural Unit." Journal of African History 24 (1983): 275–83.

Vincent, Joan. Teso in Transformation: The Political Economy of Peasant and Class in Eastern Africa. Berkeley: University of California Press, 1982.

Webster, James Bertin, ed. Chronology, Migration, and Drought in Interlacustrine Africa. Halifax: Dalhousie University Press, 1979.

Wilks, Ivor. Asante in the Nineteenth Century: The Structure and Evolution of a Political Order. Cambridge: Cambridge University Press, 1975.

———. "Land, Labour, Capital and the Forest Kingdom of Asante." In The Evolution of Social Systems, edited by J. Friedman and M. J. Rowlands, 487–534. Pittsburgh: University of Pittsburgh Press, 1977.

Willis, Roy. A State in the Making: Myth, History and Social Transformation in Pre-colonial Ufipa. Bloomington: Indiana University Press, 1981.

CHINA

Atwell, William. "International Bullion Flows and the Chinese Economy, circa 1530–1650." Past and Present, no. 95 (May 1982): 68–90.

Averill, Steven. "The Shed People and the Settlement of the Yangzi Highlands." Modern China 9 (January 1983): 84–126.

Barclay, George, Ansley J. Coale, Michael A. Stoto, and T. James Trussell. "A

Reassessment of the Demography of Traditional Rural China." *Population Index* 42 (1976): 606–35.

Bastid-Bruguière, Marianne. "Currents of Social Change." In *The Cambridge History of China*, edited by John K. Fairbank and Kwang-Ching Liu, vol. 11, 536–602. Cambridge: Cambridge University Press, 1980.

Beattie, Hilary. *Land and Lineage in China: A Study of T'ung-Ch'eng County, Anhwei, in the Ming and Ch'ing Dynasties.* Cambridge: Cambridge University Press, 1979.

Bergère, Marie-Claire. *La bourgeoisie chinoise et la révolution de 1911.* Paris: Mouton, 1968.

――――. "The Other China: Shanghai from 1919 to 1949." In *Shanghai: Revolution and Development in an Asian Metropolis*, edited by Christopher Howe. Cambridge: Cambridge University Press, 1981.

――――. "The Chinese Bourgeoisie, 1911–37." In *The Cambridge History of China*, edited by John K. Fairbank, vol. 12, 721–825. Cambridge: Cambridge University Press, 1983.

Cartier, Michel. "La Croissance démographique chinoise du XVIIIe siècle et l'enregistrement des pao-chia." *Annales de démographie historique* (1979): 9–28.

Chang, Chung-li. *The Chinese Gentry: Studies on their Role in Nineteenth-Century Chinese Society.* Seattle: University of Washington Press, 1955.

Chang, Kwang-chih, ed. *Food in Chinese Culture: Anthropological and Historical Perspectives.* New Haven: Yale University Press, 1977.

Chen, Fu-mei Chang, and Ramon H. Myers. "Customary Law and the Economic Development of China during the Ch'ing Period." *Ch'ing-shih wen-t'i* 3 (November 1976): 1–32 and 3 (November 1978): 4–27.

Chesneaux, Jean. *The Chinese Labor Movement, 1919–1927.* Stanford: Stanford University Press, 1968.

――――, ed. *Popular Movements and Secret Societies in China, 1840–1950.* Stanford: Stanford University Press, 1972.

Ch'u, T'ung-tsu. *Local Government in China under the Ch'ing.* Cambridge, Mass.: Harvard University Press, 1962.

Ch'uan, Han-sheng, and Richard Kraus. *Mid-Ch'ing Rice Markets and Trade: A Study in Price History.* Cambridge, Mass.: Harvard University Press, 1975.

Cohen, Paul A. *China and Christianity.* Cambridge, Mass.: Harvard University Press, 1963.

Crissman, Lawrence. "The Segmentary Structure of Urban Overseas Chinese Communities." *Man* 2 (June 1967): 185–209.

Dennerline, Jerry. *The Chia-ting Loyalists.* New Haven: Yale University Press, 1981.

Elvin, Mark. *The Pattern of the Chinese Past.* Stanford: Stanford University Press, 1973.

Elvin, Mark, and G. William Skinner, eds. *The Chinese City Between Two Worlds.* Stanford: Stanford University Press, 1974.

Esherick, Joseph. *Reform and Revolution in China: The 1911 Revolution in Hunan and Hubei.* Berkeley: University of California Press, 1976.

Faure, David. "The Rural Economy of Kiangsu Province, 1870–1911." *Journal of the Institute of Chinese Studies* (Hong Kong) 9 (1978): 365–471.

Freedman, Maurice. *Lineage Organization in Southeastern China.* London: Athlone Press, 1958.

Hinton, William. *Fanshen: A Documentary of Revolution in a Chinese Village*. New York: Alfred A. Knopf, 1966.

Ho, Ping-ti. "The Salt Merchants of Yang-chou: A Study of Commercial Capitalism in Eighteenth Century China." *Harvard Journal of Asiatic Studies* 17 (June 1954): 130–68.

———. *Studies on the Population of China, 1368–1953*. Cambridge, Mass.: Harvard University Press, 1959.

———. *The Ladder of Success in Imperial China: Aspects of Social Mobility, 1368–1911*. New York: Columbia University Press, 1962.

———. "The Geographic Distribution of Hui-kuan (*Landsmannschaften*) in Central and Upper Yangtze Provinces." *Tsinghua Journal of Chinese Studies*, New Series 5 (December 1966): 120–52.

Hsiao, Kung-ch'uan. *Rural China: Imperial Control in the Nineteenth Century*. Seattle: University of Washington Press, 1960.

Jing, Su, and Lo Lun. *Landlord and Labor in Late Imperial China: Case Studies from Shandong*. Edited by Endymion Wilkinson. Cambridge, Mass.: Harvard University Press, 1978.

Johnson, Kay Ann. *Women, the Family, and Peasant Revolution in China*. Chicago: University of Chicago Press, 1983.

Jones, Susan Mann, ed. *Political Leadership and Social Change at the Local Level in China from 1850 to the Present: Select Papers from the Center for Far Eastern Studies*. No. 3. Chicago: University of Chicago, 1978–79.

Jones, Susan Mann, and Philip A. Kuhn. "Dynastic Decline and the Roots of Rebellion." In *The Cambridge History of China*, edited by John K. Fairbank, vol. 10, 107–62. Cambridge: Cambridge University Press, 1978.

Kuhn, Philip A. *Rebellion and its Enemies in Late Imperial China: Militarization and Social Structure*. Cambridge, Mass.: Harvard University Press, 1970.

Lamley, Harry J. "Hsieh-tou: The Pathology of Violence in Southeastern China." *Ch'ing-shih wen-t'i* 3 (November 1977): 1–39.

Lee, James, and Robert Eng. "Population and Family History in Eighteenth-Century Manchuria." *Ch'ing-shih wen-t'i* 5 (June 1984): 1–35.

Lee, James. "Food Supply and Population Growth in Southwest China, 1250–1050." *Journal of Asian Studies* 41 (August 1982): 711–46.

Levy, Marion J. *The Family Revolution in Modern China*. Cambridge, Mass.: Harvard University Press, 1949.

Li, Lillian. *China's Silk Trade: Traditional Industry in the Modern World, 1842–1937*. Cambridge, Mass.: Harvard University Press, 1981.

Lieberthal, Kenneth. *Revolution and Tradition in Tientsin, 1949–52*. Stanford: Stanford University Press, 1980.

Link, E. Perry. *Mandarin Ducks and Butterflies: Popular Fiction in Early Twentieth-Century Chinese Cities*. Berkeley: University of California Press, 1981.

Liu, Yung-ch'eng. "The Handicraft Guilds of Soochow During the Ch'ing Dynasty." *Chinese Studies in History* (Fall–Winter 1981–1982): 113–67.

McDonald, Angus, Jr. *The Urban Origins of Rural Revolution*. Berkeley: University of California Press, 1978.

Marks, Robert B. *Rural Revolution in South China: Peasants and the Making of History in*

322 Bibliography

Haifeng County, 1570–1930. Madison: University of Wisconsin Press, 1984.
Meskill, Johanna. A Chinese Pioneer Family: The Lins of Wu-feng, Taiwan. Princeton: Princeton University Press, 1979.
Miyazaki, Ichisada. China's Examination Hell. New Haven: Yale University Press, 1981.
Muramatsu, Yuji. "A Documentary Study of Chinese Landlordism in Late Ch'ing and Early Republican Kiangnan." Bulletin of the School of Oriental and African Studies 29 (1966): 566–99.
Myers, Ramon H. "Some Issues on Economic Organization during the Ming and Ch'ing Periods." Ch'ing-shih wen-t'i 3 (November 1974): 77–97.
Naquin, Susan. Millenarian Rebellion in China: The Eight Trigrams Rebellion of 1813. New Haven: Yale University Press, 1976.
———. Shantung Rebellion: The Wang Lun Rebellion of 1774. New Haven: Yale University Press, 1981.
Nivison, David, and Arthur Wright, eds. Confucianism in Action. Stanford: Stanford University Press, 1959.
Overmyer, Daniel L. Folk Buddhist Religion: Dissenting Sects in Late Traditional China. Cambridge, Mass.: Harvard University Press, 1976.
Perdue, Peter C. "Official Goals and Local Interests: Water Control in the Dongting Lake Region during the Ming and Qing Periods." Journal of Asian Studies 41 (August 1982): 747–66.
Perry, Elizabeth. Rebels and Revolutionaries in North China, 1845–1945. Stanford: Stanford University Press, 1980.
Prazniak, Roxann. "Tax Protest at Laiyang, Shandong, 1910: Commoner Organization Versus the County Political Elite." Modern China 6 (January 1980): 41–72.
Rawski, Evelyn S. Agricultural Change and the Peasant Economy of South China. Cambridge, Mass.: Harvard University Press, 1972.
———. "Agricultural Development in the Han River Highlands." Ch'ing-shih wen-t'i 3 (November 1975): 63–81.
———. Education and Popular Literacy in Ch'ing China. Ann Arbor: University of Michigan Press, 1979.
Ropp, Paul S. Dissent in Early Modern China: Ju-lin wai-shih and Ch'ing Social Criticism. Ann Arbor: University of Michigan Press, 1981.
Rowe, William T. Hankow: Commerce and Society in a Chinese City, 1796–1889. Stanford: Stanford University Press, 1984.
Rozman, Gilbert. Population and Marketing Settlements in Ch'ing China. Cambridge: Cambridge University Press, 1982.
Schoppa, R. Keith. Chinese Elites and Political Change: Zhejiang Province in the Early Twentieth Century. Cambridge, Mass.: Harvard University Press, 1982.
Skinner, G. William. "Marketing and Social Structure in Rural China." Three parts, Journal of Asian Studies 24 (November 1964–May 1965): 3–43, 195–228, 363–99.
———, ed. The City in Late Imperial China. Stanford: Stanford University Press, 1976.
Spence, Jonathan. The Death of Woman Wang. New York: Viking, 1978.
Teng, T'o. "En Chine, du XVIe au XVIIIe siècle: les mines de charbon de Men-t'ou-kou." Translated by Michel Cartier. Annales: Economies, sociétés, civilisations 22 (Janvier–Février 1967): 50–87.
Tsou, Tang, ed. Political Leadership and Social Change at the Local Level in China from 1850

to the Present: Select Papers from the Center for Far Eastern Studies. No. 4. Chicago: University of Chicago, 1979–1980.

Wakeman, Frederic, Jr. Strangers at the Gate: Social Disorder in South China, 1839–1861. Berkeley: University of California Press, 1966.

———. The Fall of Imperial China. New York: Free Press, 1975.

Wakeman, Frederic, Jr., and Carolyn Grant, eds. Conflict and Control in Late Imperial China. Berkeley: University of California Press, 1975.

Wang, Yeh-chien. "The Secular Trend of Prices during the Ch'ing Period (1644–1911)." Journal of the Institute of Chinese Studies (Hong Kong) 5 (1973): 347–71.

Wiens, Mi-chu. "Cotton Textile Production and Rural Social Transformation in Early Modern China." Journal of the Institute of Chinese Studies (Hong Kong) 7 (1974): 515–34.

———. "Lord and Peasant in China: The Sixteenth to the Eighteenth Centuries." Modern China 6 (January 1980): 3–39.

Will, Pierre-Etienne. Bureaucratie et famine en Chine au XVIIIe siècle. Paris: Mouton, 1980.

———. "Un cycle hydraulique en Chine: La province du Hubei du XVIe au XIXe siècles." Bulletin de l'Ecole Française d'Extrême Orient 68 (1980): 261–87.

Willmott, W. E., ed. Economic Organization in Chinese Society. Stanford: Stanford University Press, 1972.

Wolf, Arthur P., ed. Religion and Ritual in Chinese Society. Stanford: Stanford University Press, 1974.

Wolf, Arthur P., and Chieh-shan Huang. Marriage and Adoption in China, 1845–1945. Stanford: Stanford University Press, 1980.

Wolf, Margery, and Roxane Witke, eds. Women in Chinese Society. Stanford: Stanford University Press, 1975.

Wong, R. Bin. "Food Riots in the Qing Dynasty." Journal of Asian Studies 41 (August 1982): 767–88.

Wou, Odoric. "The Political Kin Unit and the Family Origin of Ch'ing Local Officials." In Perspectives on a Changing China: Essays in Honor of Professor C. Martin Wilbur, edited by Joshua A. Fogel and William T. Rowe, 69–88. Boulder: Westview Press, 1979.

Wright, Mary C., ed. China in Revolution: The First Phase, 1900–1913. New Haven: Yale University Press, 1968.

Yang, Lien-sheng. "Government Control of Urban Merchants in Traditional China." Tsinghua Journal of Chinese Studies, New Series 8 (August 1970): 186–206.

Yuan, Tsing. "Urban Riots and Disturbances." In From Ming to Ch'ing, edited by Jonathan Spence and John Wills, 279–320. New Haven: Yale University Press, 1979.

CONTRIBUTORS

David William Cohen, born in 1943, received his Ph.D. from the University of London. His principal research interest is the historical anthropology of the pre-colonial Lakes Plateau region of eastern and central Africa. He has done field-work in Uganda and in Kenya. He is the author of *The Historical Tradition of Busoga: Mukama and Kintu* (Oxford: Clarendon Press, 1972) and *Womunafu's Bunafu: A Study of Authority in a Nineteenth Century African Community* (Princeton: Princeton University Press, 1977) and co-editor (with Jack P. Greene) of *Neither Slave Nor Free: The Freedmen of African Descent in the Slave Societies of the New World* (Baltimore: Johns Hopkins University Press, 1972). He is Professor of History and Anthropology at the Johns Hopkins University where he directs the Program in Atlantic History, Culture and Society.

William T. Rowe, born in 1947, holds a Ph.D. from Columbia University, and is Assistant Professor of History at the Johns Hopkins University. He is the author of numerous articles on modern Chinese social and economic history, and of *Hankow: Commerce and Society in a Chinese City, 1796–1889* (Stanford: Stanford University Press, 1984), and co-editor (with Joshua A. Fogel) of *Perspectives on a Changing China* (Boulder, Col.: Westview Press, 1979). His current research focuses on violence and working-class organization in the Ch'ing dynasty, and on the politics of water control in rural China.

William B. Taylor's current research centers on parish priests in central and western Mexico and New Mexico in the eighteenth and nineteenth centuries. Born in 1943, he received his Ph.D. from the University of Michigan and is Professor of History at the University of Virginia. His regional studies of rural Mexico include *Landlord and Peasant in Colonial Oaxaca* (Stanford: Stanford University Press, 1972), *Drinking, Homicide, and Rebellion in Colonial Mexican Villages* (Stanford: Stanford University Press, 1979), and the forthcoming collection of essays on rural history *Pueblos de la Virgen: ensayos sobre el medio rural de Jalisco a fines de la colonia*.

Charles Tilly is Distinguished Professor of Sociology and History at the New School for Social Research and Director of its Center for Studies of Social Change. Born in 1929, he received his Ph.D. from Harvard University and taught for fifteen years at the University of Michigan before joining the New School. His current research and writing include a study of the impact of statemaking and the development of capitalism on popular collective action in France since the seventeenth century, studies of contention and social change in Great Britain in the eighteenth and nineteenth centuries, and an examination of the proletarianization of the European population. His most recent books are *As Sociology Meets*

325

History (New York: Academic Press, 1981), Big Structures, Large Processes, Huge Comparisons (New York: Russell Sage Foundation, 1985), and the forthcoming The Contentious French (Cambridge, Mass.: Harvard University Press).

Olivier Zunz, born in 1946, was raised and educated in France and holds a Doctorat ès lettres from the Sorbonne. His studies of American urban society include The Changing Face of Inequality: Urbanization, Industrial Development, and Immigrants in Detroit, 1880–1920 (Chicago: University of Chicago Press, 1982) and numerous articles on American social history. His current research centers on the social change fostered by the expansion of corporate capitalism in the late nineteenth and early twentieth centuries, especially the rise of the white-collar work force and its consequence for the American class structure. He is Associate Professor of History at the University of Virginia and visiting professor at the Ecole des Hautes Etudes en Sciences Sociales.

INDEX

Abolitionists, 77, 200
Abundance, 54, 56
Acculturation: in Africa, 221; in Latin
    America, 172
Adams, Henry, 55
Adams, Richard N., 182n, 186n
Alger, Horatio, 83
Allen, James de V., 219
American exceptionalism, 9, 54–56
American Historical Review, 87
Andorka, Rudolf, 34
Annales de Démographie Historique, 19
Annales: Economies, sociétés, civilisations, 13,
    19, 58, 79
Anthropology: in Africa, 205; in China,
    256; and history, 122, 177n, 181–82n,
    186n
Antiquarianism, 60
Artisans: and household income in Af-
    rica, 213
Assimilation, 60, 81–83; cultural and
    structural, 88–89. *See also* Accultura-
    tion
Autonomy: in American society, 83,
    93; in Latin American villages, 152,
    160, 162; workers' control as a form
    of, 84

Bagú, Sergio, 129
Bailyn, Bernard, 103n, 110n, 119, 121
Bakewell, Peter J., 170
Balazs, Etienne, 279
Baran, Paul, 129
Bardet, Jean-Pierre, 23
Barron, Harold, 67
Barton, Josef J., 85
Bellamy, Edward, 55
Bender, Thomas, 75

Bergad, Laird W., 134, 136–37
Bergère, Marie-Claire, 282
Bergquist, Charles W., 130
Black, Donald, 163
Black legend/White legend, 116, 169
Bloch, Marc, 13, 60, 253
Blount, Ben G., 193–94
Blumin, Stuart, 68
Bodnar, John, 85
Bohstedt, John, 24
Borah, Woodrow, 163–64
Bourgeoisie: Chinese, 282. *See also* Mid-
    dle class
Bradby, Rev. Robert L., 72
Bradford, William, 55
Braudel, Fernand, 6, 131, 275–76
Breakdown theories, 17–19, 84–85
Brewer, John, 21, 26
Buck, John L., 241, 248–49
Bureaucracy: in China, 253, 261, 263–
    64, 268–69; in Europe, 44, 46; in the
    United States, 60, 96–97. *See also* State
Burke, Peter, 12
Byington, Margaret F., 70, 72

Capitalism: commercial, 125, 262, 270–
    71, 274; corporate, 81; debate on
    "sprouts" of, in China, 277, 279, 281–
    82; industrial, 125, 279; local version
    of, 28; and ordinary lives, 16, 43, 196;
    political economy of, 78; as system
    of production, 8, 11, 40, 177–79n,
    274, 296n; and underdevelopment,
    170; as world system, 124, 136, 140,
    175–76n, 196–97, 224, 239, 253
Cardoso, Ciro F. S., 130, 132
Cardoso, Fernando H., 128–29
Center and periphery, 153, 183n. *See*